Sport in the Global Society
General Editors: J.A. Mangan and Boria Majumdar

As Robert Hands in *The Times* recently observed the growth of sports studies in recent years has been considerable. This unique series with over one hundred volumes in the last decade has played its part. Politically, culturally, emotionally and aesthetically, sport is a major force in the modern world. Its impact will grow as the world embraces ever more tightly the contemporary secular trinity: the English language, technology and sport. *Sport in the Global Society* will continue to record sport's phenomenal progress across the world stage.

Other Titles in the Series

Africa, Football and FIFA
Politics, Colonialism and Resistance
Paul Darby

Amateurism in British Sport
'It Matters Not Who Won or Lost'
Edited by Dilwyn Porter and Stephen Wagg

Amateurism in Sport
An Analysis and Defence
Lincoln Allison

America's Game(s)
A Critical Anthropology of Sport
Edited by Benjamin Eastman, Sean Brown and Michael Ralph

A Social History of Indian Cricket
22 Yards to Freedom
Boria Majumdar

A Social History of Indian Football
Striving to Score
Kausik Bandyopadhya and Boria Majumdar

A Social History of Swimming in England, 1800 – 1918
Splashing in the Serpentine
Christopher Love

A Sport-Loving Society
Victorian and Edwardian Middle-Class England at Play
Edited by J.A. Mangan

Athleticism in the Victorian and Edwardian Public School
The Emergence and Consolidation of an Educational Ideology
J.A. Mangan

Australian Beach Cultures
The History of Sun, Sand and Surf
Douglas Booth

Australian Sport
Antipodean waves of change
Edited by Kristine Toohey and Tracy Taylor

Barbarians, Gentlemen and Players
A Sociological Study of the Development of Rugby Football, Second Edition
Eric Dunning and Kenneth Sheard

Baseball and Moral Authority in Contemporary Cuba
Edited by Benjamin Eastman

Beijing 2008: Preparing for Glory
Building for the Beijing Olympics
Edited by J.A. Mangan and Dong Jinxia

Football Fans Around the World

This volume seeks to shed light on the way in which football supporters around the world express themselves as followers of teams, whether they be professional, amateur or national. The diverse geographical and cultural array of contributions to this volume highlights not only the different ways groups of fans express themselves, but their commonalities as well. The collection brings together scholars from North and South America, Europe, Asia and Africa to present a global picture of fan culture.

The collection will show that while every group of fans around the world has its own characteristics, there are also commonalities across all regions and cultures.

This book was previously published as special issue of *Soccer and Society*.

Sean Brown works on fan culture in sport at Northeastern University, Boston.

Sport in the Global Society

General Editors: J. A. Mangan and Boria Majumdar

Football Fans Around the World
From Supporters to Fanatics

Football Fans Around the World

From Supporters to Fanatics

Edited by Sean Brown

LONDON AND NEW YORK

First published 2007 by Routledge
2 Park Square, Milton Park, Abingdon, Oxon, OX14 4RN

Simultaneously published in the USA and Canada
by Routledge
270 Madison Avenue, New York, NY 10016

Routledge is an imprint of the Taylor & Francis Group, an informa business

Transferred to Digital Printing 2009

© 2007 Sean Brown

Typeset in Minion by Genesis Typesetting Ltd, Rochester, Kent

British Library Cataloguing in Publication Data
A catalogue record for this book is available from the British Library

ISBN 10: 0-415-39505-4 (hbk)
ISBN 10: 0-415-49564-4 (pbk)

ISBN 13: 978-0-415-39505-2 (hbk)
ISBN 13: 978-0-415-49564-6 (pbk)

CONTENTS

Series Editors' Foreword

SPORT IN THE GLOBAL SOCIETY was launched in the late nineties. It now has over one hundred volumes. Until recently an odd myopia characterised academia with regard to sport. The global *groves of academe* remained essentially Cartesian in inclination. They favoured a mind/body dichotomy: thus the study of ideas was acceptable; the study of sport was not. All that has now changed. Sport is now incorporated, intelligently, within debate about *inter alia* ideologies, power, stratification, mobility and inequality. The reason is simple. In the modern world sport is everywhere: it is as ubiquitous as war. E.J. Hobsbawm , the Marxist historian, once called it the one of the most significant of the new manifestations of late nineteenth century Europe. Today it is one of the most significant manifestations of the twenty-first century world. Such is its power, politically, culturally, economically, spiritually and aesthetically, that sport beckons the academic more persuasively than ever- to borrow ,and refocus, an expression of the radical historian Peter Gay- ' to explore its familiar terrain and to wrest new interpretations from its inexhaustible materials'. As a subject for inquiry, it is replete , as he remarked of history, with profound ' questions unanswered and for that matter questions unasked'.

Sport seduces the teeming 'global village'; it is the new opiate of the masses; it is one of the great modern experiences; its attraction astonishes only the recluse; its appeal spans the globe. Without exaggeration, sport is a mirror in which nations, communities, men and women now see themselves. That reflection is sometimes bright, sometimes dark, sometimes distorted, sometimes magnified. This metaphorical mirror is a source of mass exhilaration and depression, security and insecurity, pride and humiliation, bonding and alienation. Sport , for many, has replaced religion as a source of emotional catharsis and spiritual passion, and for many, since it is among the earliest of memorable childhood experiences, it infiltrates memory, shapes enthusiasms, serves fantasies. To co-opt Gay again: it blends memory and desire.

Sport, in addition, can be a lens through which to scrutinise major themes in the political and social sciences: democracy and despotism and the great associated movements of socialism, fascism, communism and capitalism as well as political cohesion and confrontation, social reform and social stability.

The story of modern sport is the story of the modern world-in microcosm; a modern global tapestry permanently being woven. Furthermore, nationalist and imperialist, philosopher and politician, radical and conservative have all sought in sport a manifestation of national identity, status and superiority.

Finally, for countless millions sport is the personal pursuit of ambition, assertion, well-being and enjoyment.

For all the above reasons, sport demands the attention of the academic. *Sport in the Global Society* is a response.

J.A.Mangan
Boria Majumdar

Series Editors
Sport in the Global Society

Introduction: Commonality Amongst Diversity: Modernization and Soccer Fans

Sean Brown

It is perhaps beyond cliché to speak of modernization anymore. As with any concept that achieves significant reach throughout the academic world, modernity has been sliced, diced, reconstructed, refuted and, finally, all but emptied of any meaning. Any mention of modernization now must be accompanied by a clarification, a qualification, or perhaps an apology. It is a word and a concept void of any inherent meaning anymore, so when one uses it, it seems as though one is copping out, as if they had nothing precise to say, but felt the need to label a phenomenon anyway.

It is with this understanding in mind that this collection is presented for consumption bearing a theme of modernization, and it is done so for several reasons. The papers within this volume represent a wide array of work, not only in terms of geographic reach, but also in terms of interdisciplinary endeavour. They are in turn historical, anthropological, sociological and occasionally political. What better way then to capture such a wide and diverse collection than with a nearly completely empty concept such as modernization?

As mentioned above, the invocation of modernization requires that the user establish the parameters of the discussion, in order that critiques can be focused on specific areas covered … or neglected. Further, modernization must be broken out into specific sub-fields, owing to the fact that political modernity was not established at the same time as scientific or economic modernity, nor in the same places, nor with the same general principles. The attempt here will be to briefly outline modernization as it relates chiefly to sport, and to provide a place for the pieces contained within.

Within classical modernization, the tendency is towards oversimplification through an evolutionary lens. That is, the process of modernization is very explicitly tied up in evolutionary thought, much as it remains in classical biology.[1] Of course, the critique of this line of thought is extensive. In its place lies a softened version of much the same principle. 'Self-consciously modern societies could distinguish themselves from the traditional societies they were replacing by applying human reason to the "problems" of personal and social development.'[2] Humankind's saviour became science, objectivity, reason. Gruneau goes on to argue that the modernization of sport occurred on many of the same principles. Guttman lists seven characteristics that distinguish modern sport from more traditional forms of physical activity: secularism, equality of opportunity, specialization of roles, rationalization, bureaucratic organization, quantification, the quest for records.[3] If one replaces the word 'sport' with 'business' or 'politics', many of the same characteristics remain. We can then gather a general, if inexact, understanding of modernization as it relates to this volume. Indeed, soccer as we currently know it could not exist without these processes, as they are the principles on which the organized game is founded. That is, this is not a claim that organized soccer developed before modernization processes commenced … quite the opposite. However, as modernization is a process and not an event, as long as the same processes are operating, it will continue to have an effect on sport fans.

Within Guttman's conceptions are included the tension between the amateur and the professional. Guttman sees the distinction between the two as an anachronism, rooted mainly in class distinctions and social hierarchies.[4] Surely a more contemporary version of modernization in sport would have to include increasing professionalization, and the increasing prevalence of rational capitalism. Modern sport has never been particularly understood as an end unto itself. It has always been steeped in the ulterior motives of its benefactors.[5] However, often these ulterior motives were other-directed. De Coubertin saw the revival of the Olympic Games as a way to combat some of the very problems created by modernity.[6] Rational capitalism is anything but other-directed. As such, those who stand to profit economically from modern sport are not particularly concerned with those who stand to profit from it emotionally or even spiritually – the fans. Modern capitalism inevitably creates a tension between those tied to a team financially and those tied to it emotionally. Both are operating under the same modern ideas, that is, success. However, tension arises because success is defined in competing terms for the entities. How this tension develops and plays itself is the key theme running through this collection.

This view of modernization suffers from specific shortcomings if left as it is. As it pertains to this collection, it leaves out the possibility for the fan to act on their own behalf. To this point, it suffers from the same issues as Gruneau points out in previous work, in that it views modern sport as 'a symbolic representation and physical embodiment of capitalism's insatiable demand for "performance" in the service of profit'.[7] The final works in this collection go a long way towards addressing the ways in which soccer fans have become active in reclaiming the game for their own edification, using the very tools of modernization such as satellite television and the internet. Thus, a specific sub-theme running through much of this volume is the constant tension between the liberation of the fan versus his or her oppression at the hands of those financially tied to teams, the insatiable.

Embedded then in the concept of modernity are the opposing discourses of liberation and disciplinization, or the opposing concepts of increasing and decreasing liberty as a result of modernization.[8] The liberation discourse centres around Enlightenment philosophy conceiving of the autonomous individual striving for the realization of inalienable rights. In opposition to this conception was the discourse of disciplinization, within which it was maintained that this freedom was an illusion, as apparatuses inherently opposed to self-actualization and unfettered liberty were always present to keep the individual in check.

The papers in this volume in many ways play out these competing discourses; while some accentuate the growth of soccer as a mass pastime, others emphasize the ways in which professionalization and rationalization robbed the sport of its spontaneity and its natural affinities. In any event, the fans documented here are interacting with both the processes and the products of modernization, whether within a traditional mindset, that is, actively reacting against the processes of modernization, or within a more progressive mindset, that is, actively incorporating the processes or products of modernization into the fan experience.

The volume opens with perhaps the most explicit expression of the role of modernization in football fandom. Chris Stone traces the development of the mundane in our lives as contrasted with the extraordinary realms such as politics. In doing so, he is able to trace the development and the distinction of soccer fandom from merely a match-day occurrence (the extraordinary) to being bound up with the daily identity of the supporter (the mundane).

The following two pieces are distinctly historical in nature. Graham Curry details the development of organized soccer and fan culture in Sheffield in the nineteenth century. In this piece, he shows one of the first areas of resistance to industrialization and rational capitalism in the practice of Saint Monday, where the first day of the working week was spent in leisure activity, usually with the tacit consent of the factory owners, but against the prevailing thought in Victorian England. Interestingly, Curry also details some of the earliest hooligan activity in Sheffield, which was rare but occasionally serious. This behaviour seems to be linked to early efforts at professionalization.

In the second exclusively historical work, Andrew McFarland describes the development of soccer in Spain from a middle-class activity into a mass one, a commentary on the discourse of liberation as described above. As new stadiums were constructed, they were specifically built to allow for the attendance of many different social classes, opening up the world of spectatorship to people who previously had no access. Additional leisure time and increased financial security ensured the participation of the working classes, which then ensured the survival of soccer in the Spanish sporting culture.

Udo Merkel, in his study of German fans, first delves into the history of soccer in Germany, particularly the resistance of many traditional German sportsmen to the intrusion of English sport into the German *Turner* activities. Many of their criticisms revolved around the distinctly modern concepts in soccer such as commercialization and professionalization. In the second half of the paper, Merkel illustrates the power of soccer as a unifying national element in a country with a fractious political history.

The next work is interesting as a work of historiography. Russell Hargrave, in a dual book review, examines the conflict between official histories and the actual events that they purport to describe. In this work are descriptions of the attempts of gatekeepers such as soccer clubs to control the flow of information, thus attempting to control the impressions that fans of the club have. The books reviewed are seen as an attempt to counteract the official histories of the club, and reverse the idea that club supporters are nothing but passive consumers of official club doctrine.

From there, the emphasis shifts from the development of fan cultures within the process of modernization and into the interactions fan cultures have with modernity as a particular condition. The political and cultural expressions of Italian fans are the foci of Matthew Guschwan's work. Guschwan treats the behaviour of the Italian fans as cultural performances that are bound up 'to the long history of Italian culture as well as the immediate conditions of contemporary life'. In his look at the organization of fan activity, the Weberian rationalization is seen to be operating, even if the content of the performances themselves cannot be expressed or understood without knowledge of Italian history.

Marcos Natali examines Brazilian fans from a similar standpoint. The tepid celebration in Brazil in honour of the 1994 World Cup winning team was a stunning rebuke of hyper-rationalization and modernization taking root in other realms of the country. By revelling in teams that played with typical Brazilian flair but lost rather than in the organized defensive-oriented scheme that the 1994 team utilized, the Brazilian fan base yearned for a time not when winning was not important, but for a time when *how* one went about success was as important as the success itself.

The next two pieces deal with Australia, where soccer is not the national football code. Roy Hay and Christopher Hallinan *et al.* detail the efforts to successfully launch a stable and profitable professional league in Australia. Both pieces deal with the efforts of league organizers to create fan bases based on geography rather than ethnicity. Additionally, both pieces detail the corporate and rational structure on which the league is based. While Hallinan, Hughson and Burke take a macro-level look at the A-League, Roy Hay's work is a specific look at Melbourne, and the specific attempts at a successful launch and unification of divergent soccer interests there.

As with Australia, the Netherlands pieces are also coupled. Ramon Spaaij details the development and contemporary forms of hooliganism in the Netherlands. Of specific interest are the contemporary trends of coordination and organization as well as the diversity within the hooligan groups. Spaaij shows that hooligan activity is not always a white phenomenon. Müller, van Zoonen and de Roode examine racism in particular, attempting to show that racist behaviour does not necessarily correspond to racist feelings amongst the participants, who often seem to not pay particular attention to the words they are chanting, singing, et cetera. Often those that do know what they say trivialize the words in favour of their own personal knowledge of being non-racists. What is dangerous about this type of behaviour is what it means to the victims of racist behaviour by fans, as victims are often left to take the abuse or be labelled as overly sensitive. As racism becomes less and less acceptable, it seems that many fans, rather than address their own racist behaviour, attempt to rationalize it as being no more than a 'joke'.

The final four works develop from various resistances and reactions to modernization into pieces that examine ways in which fans utilize the tools of modernity, be it public opinion, as with Rodríguez Díaz's work on *ultras* in Andalusia; or the technological tools such as satellite television or the internet that have transformed fandom, and perhaps finally given the final word to liberation of the fan from the throes of the oppression of modernity.

My own work in this volume deals with the problem of soccer as foreign in the United States. Much as Hallinan described soccer as having 'failed the test of "Australian-ness"', soccer has suffered a similar fate in the United States. However, the American situation is distinct from the Australian. American professional clubs never had the ethnic identification that plagued the earlier Australian clubs. Instead, this process continues to play itself out at the national level, where the United States Soccer Federation cannot schedule national team matches in certain parts of the country against Confederation of North, Central American, and Caribbean Associated Football (CONCACAF) opponents without virtually guaranteeing a hostile crowd for the home side. The second part of the paper seeks to understand how the most ardent supporters of American soccer view themselves, and use electronic media to project a certain image of themselves to the rest of the American sporting culture.

Wayne Wilson makes even more explicit the use of the Internet by American soccer fans. The Internet has become a major empowering tool for American soccer fans as a way to make connections and build 'virtual communities' in the face of continuing mainstream media apathy to the game. His study of the use of the message board Bigsoccer.com is extremely important for anyone wanting to understand the ways in which soccer is supported in the United States.

The volume closes with perhaps the most extreme manifestation of the transformation of fandom that modernization has allowed. Mike Weed has examined ethnographically the fan culture that has grown up around watching matches in pubs rather than in stadiums. He details those fans' understandings of the advantages of watching soccer in pubs rather than in the stadiums. In their view, the pubs represent the new terraces, places where they are allowed to stand packed as sardines, and chant their chants and sing their songs without regard for the people surrounding. It is a fitting way to close the volume, as it encompasses a technological turn: the use of ultra-modern technology for the chance to capture a glimpse of a lost tradition.

Notes

[1]   Harrison, *Sociology of Modernization*, 2.
[2]   Gruneau, 'The Critique of Sport in Modernity', 87.
[3]   Guttman, *From Ritual to Record*, 16.
[4]   Ibid., 32.
[5]   Gruneau, 'The Critique of Sport in Modernity'.
[6]   Ibid.
[7]   Gruneau, quoted in Dunning, Maguire and Pearton, 'Perspectives on the Making of Modern Sports', 15.
[8]   Wagner, *A Sociology of Modernity*, 5–7.

References

Dunning, Eric, Joseph Maguire and Robert Pearton. 'Perspectives on the Making of Modern Sports.' In *The Sports Process: A Comparative and Developmental Approach,* edited by Eric Dunning, Joseph Maguire and Robert Pearton. Champaign, IL: Human Kinetics Publishers, 1993.

Gruneau, Richard. 'The Critique of Sport in Modernity: Theorising Power, Culture, and the Politics of the Body.' In *The Sports Process: A Comparative and Developmental Approach,* edited by Eric Dunning, Joseph Maguire and Robert Pearton. Champaign, IL: Human Kinetics Publishers, 1993.

Guttmann, Allen. *From Ritual to Record: The Nature of Modern Sports.* New York: Columbia University Press, 1978.

Harrison, David. *The Sociology of Modernization and Development.* London and Boston: Unwin Hyman, 1988.

Wagner, Peter. *A Sociology of Modernity: liberty and discipline.* London and New York: Routledge, 1994.

The Role of Football in Everyday Life

Chris Stone

Introduction

In his study of sports consumption Crawford suggests that a crucial element is missing in the research on the relationship between sports audiences and the subject of their fandom beyond that of regular attendance at sporting contests. He observes that, 'research on sport audiences has focused almost exclusively on those who regularly attend "live" sporting events, leaving largely ignored how sport is experienced and consumed in people's everyday lives away from the "live" venues, and in particular overlooks those who do not regularly attend "live" sport.'[1]

Research on football in particular supports this notion, tending as it has done to focus on 'exceptional' forms of support through the mass of literature based around hooliganism in and around football grounds and interpretations based upon the perceived responses to increased commodification in football by the most 'dedicated' types of supporters that contribute to the 'resistance' movement as fanzine writers or members and organizers of independent supporters groups.

In this sense it has reflected the study of other fields within sociology by concentrating on the spectacular, deviant subcultures in society as opposed to the 'everyday' features of life. What is missing is an extensive study of the mundane behaviours and more subtle expressions of football identity as it is experienced by less specific groups within their day to day lives.

It is in everyday life that football culture is primarily perpetuated, expressed and experienced. That is not to say that the spectacle of match-days and the actuality of football teams' performances and results do not play an important part for many supporters, but it is not the primary aspect of football culture that affects individuals' notions of self-identity, belonging and interpersonal relations; all of which are initi-ated, reinforced and challenged through the enactment, internalization, embodiment and contestation of structural influences within the daily practices of life.

What follows is an examination of football's position as a part of the fabric of every-day life and forms the basis of a doctoral thesis carried out in the city of Sheffield during the past three years. Unlike Armstrong's Sheffield-based ethnography which is partic-ularly focused on certain supporters of one of the clubs from the city, Sheffield United, this study engages with football at a much broader level.[2] This reflects the pervasive nature of football culture beyond localized connections but is rooted in understandings and meanings of more global influences at the local level within individuals' daily lives.

One of the difficulties with such a project is conceptualizing 'everyday life' to be theoretically consistent, sociologically informative and of practical use. The solution has been to find an interpretive middle ground between a highly focused biography and the overwhelming amount of detail which could be obtained through a project like that of Mass Observation.[3] This paper attempts to offer a reading of football in line with the experience of contemporary life using Robson's[4] (2000) study of embodied foot-ball identity as a foil for a more fluid exploration drawing upon the work of Bauman,[5] Butler[6] and Maffesoli.[7]

Meanings of 'Everyday Life': An Exposition

What 'everyday life' actually represents is open to debate. It implies familiarity and repe-tition; quite literally, that which happens every day. Though as Gardiner summarily acknowledges, 'everyday life is not a fixed or eternal feature of social life … it has a discernable history'.[8] In fact, it is with the onset of modernity and the specialization and rationalization of the social world that the experience of day to day living has seen to become segregated from, and subordinate to, more 'superior' activities in such fields as politics, science and the arts. In pre-modern societies these different activities and knowledges were more fully integrated within the daily lives of all.[9] So 'everyday life' becomes an arena overlooked in favour of a concentration on the structural implications and management of people's day to day behaviours rather than the accommodations and refutations of imposed structural procedures upon the agency of individuals' every-day lives. Thus, it is merely the backdrop of mundane happenings that allows the more important aspects of life to take place and resultantly more consequential research topics to be studied. The overarching view seems to have been that, 'If everyday life is equivalent to normality then it might seem that one runs the risk of either labouring the obvious or of imbuing the mundane with inappropriate complexity and/or significance'.[10]

It is the work of feminist writers such as Dorothy Smith, Agnes Heller and Judith Butler amongst others that highlight the significance of conflating everyday under-standings of the world with normality and unchallenged acceptance. The feminist gaze problematizes the everyday world, showing how it is the most mundane, taken-for-granted activities that serve to reinforce gender hierarchies and patriarchal norms.[11] Likewise, it is at an everyday level that football's cultural influences are most pervasive - through conversation, the media, clothing, bodily comportment, self-concept and interpersonal relations; at work, at home, in the pub or on the bus. These everyday understandings of football work dialectically to help maintain as well as challenge discursive notions of authenticity, masculinity and communal belonging, feeding into individuals' subjectivities and modes of being in the world.

The critical analysis of everyday life is, furthermore, upheld by theorists within the field of popular culture. Originally, these debates were either class-ridden formulations of the damage popular cultural forms were having on the appreciation of high-culture,[12] or framed within Marxist theories concerning the nature of consumption and the commodification of daily life through the hegemony of the 'culture industries'.[13] Either way, popular culture was vilified because of its homogenizing, pacifying and thoroughly degenerative effects. More recent analyses, both theoretical and empirical, have sought to explore a less one dimensional power balance between consumers of popular cultural forms and the influences they have on individuals' everyday lives.[14]

This provides two dimensions upon which to focus the study of football as a part of everyday life. One is the subtle ways in which football is entwined with the multitude of miniscule happenings that take place during the course of each and every day. Secondly, is the relationship between different interpretations of football that both challenge and perpetuate the dominant discourses within contemporary (football) culture as they are understood and made meaningful within the practices of everyday life. The connection between these dimensions lies in the different ways that football is constructed and consumed on a daily basis in order to assert a sense of selfhood, belonging and authority within the patterns of people's everyday lives.

The Expression of Football Identities in Everyday Life

In Robson's ethnographically-based examination of football, its role within the lives of the male working class, at least those supporting Millwall around which his study is based, is the embodiment of cultural practices the roots of which lie in the historical social fabric of South East London where the club is located.[15] The expressive nature of being a fan of Millwall is defined through a process of commemorative ritualization which is described as, 'not a discrete or isolable socio-cultural "event", but rather an extension of the everyday'.[16] The match 'event' itself is just a physical manifestation of certain regularity that fuels an ongoing process of identity formation within the day to day lives of those involved.

Robson's work explores the 'experiential symbolisation' that occurs when a certain level of commitment allows the self and cultural symbol to merge and the symbolic aspects of the cognitive self are transformed and internalized at the level of experience so that, for some supporters, the club becomes a constituent part of themselves. He notes how individuals, 'tend to use their participation in Millwallism as a means of metaphorically/symbolically expressing, encapsulating and dramatizing characteristic varieties of social identity and consciousness', which are used to 'exemplify and amplify salient themes in local, everyday experience'.[17] In other words, 'being Millwall' becomes an essential element for the negotiation of everyday life.

He adopts Bourdieu's concept of 'bodily hexis' which 'is an attempt to account for the ways in which the habitus inscribes social consciousness, meaning and identity in the body itself'.[18] He argues that Millwallism is an embodied extension of the routine use of the body for working-class males to experience and express mastery over the social and material environment which is embedded in the ritualized movements and expressions as conveyed and understood within English football culture.[19]

Armstrong similarly locates football identity in relation to the contingencies of masculine identity, offering an analysis of the position of football in daily life through his ethnography of the hooligan phenomenon in Sheffield.[20] For a specific group of men regularly involved in violent disturbances both in and around match-day scenarios as well as other incidents related to their being 'Blades' in pubs and clubs, parks and the streets of Sheffield, the affirmation of personal identity through football, and Sheffield United in particular, is seen as a constant within their daily lives.

He notes however that, 'Blades play to various audiences'[21] and, in an invocation of Goffman's analysis of social interaction, their performances are contextual, negotiated and improvised with regard to notions of 'correct' masculinity and comportment.[22] Individuals within these collective gatherings are schooled to know how and when to exhibit certain behaviour, to act on and react to certain signals, and to play to different audiences, be they other Blades, other hooligan 'crews', onlooking public or the police. Armstrong offers highly detailed examinations of these performances that involve a combination of 'clothes, posture, gait, conversational topics and opinions, and the threat of, or actual execution of, physical violence',[23] which in Goffman's terms, are reliant for their success on the correct use of 'stage props', the adoption of appropriate 'role attitudes' and movement between 'front' and 'back stage', and conviction, by both cast and audience, in what is being enacted.

Performance and Performativity: Goffman v Butler

Identity, for Goffman, is self-consciously contingent on the desired image one wants to portray in any given situation and implicitly suggests that there is a 'true self' behind the façades that monitors and manipulates the acting selves. Football identities are thus performed so as to be appropriate to being, for example, in the pub after a game, before being altered in accordance with what are known expectations of how to behave back at the family home and then further manipulated on going to work the following day. There are, however, contradictions in this interpretation as football also at times constitutes a disruption to the expected behaviour normally ascribed to a situation as competing identities battle for supremacy. For some it may be the dominant discourse of football masculinity at odds with performing the role of caring spouse, whilst for others the reverse may be true as middle-class sensibilities are displaced by alternative value systems. The degree to which different performances are available is connected to interpersonal power relationships and subjective positions within the matrix of institutionalized forms of power. In Bourdieu's schema this is a result of collisions between cultural capital within different fields upon which the *habitus* acts.[24]

Whilst Goffman's work acknowledges the contingencies of contemporary life and the tactics adopted to cope with its fluidity, it is rooted within modernist conceptions of 'truth', 'reality' and the solid foundations of a fixed self. Butler's critique suggests that the 'I' (Goffman's underlying 'true self') does not precede the performative identity but is in fact constituted and created through the repetition of its performative elements.[25] In an extension of de Beauvoir's insight that, 'one is not born, but rather becomes, a woman', she suggests that identity is not something we 'are' but is something we 'do'. It is therefore a process, without origin or completion; it is a negotiation in discourse.[26]

Her work concentrates on gender, which as a concept is particularly rooted in notions of a fixed and natural identity, connected as it is with biological determinism and the scientific discourse of knowledge. What Butler believes is that, 'Gender is the repeated stylization of the body, a set of repeated acts within a highly rigid regulatory frame that congeal over time to produce the appearance of substance, of a natural sort of being'.[27] Her work attempts to desolidify this coagulation by enquiring how 'woman' came to be so widely accepted as an ontological given. Through a Foucauldian-based 'genealogy of gender ontology' she investigates 'the political stakes in designating as an *origin* and *cause* those identity categories that are in fact the *effects* of institutions, practices, discourses, with multiple points of origin'.[28]

Identities are thus discursively constructed. The subject, rather than pre-existing the deed is performatively constituted through the acts that are purported to be the result of its being. And as Nietzsche makes clear, 'there is no "being" behind doing, acting, becoming; "the doer" is merely a fiction imposed on the doing – the doing itself is everything'.[29] The choice of which identity to 'do' then becomes contingent on those discursively available/proposed. A very small choice, in Butler's terms, within the heterocentric culture that governs gender.

What this means for Robson's embodied football identities is that the various discourses (historical, geographical, physical) that combine to form the unique Millwall *habitus*, which in turn, 'inscribes social consciousness, meaning and identity in the body itself',[30] are 'corporeally stylised',[31] or to use Foucault's terminology, 'inscribed on the body', in order to performatively constitute the Millwall identity.

Bourdieu's concept of the habitus offers a useful explanation for the particular dispositions that comprise a Millwall identity but is perhaps too rigid and self deterministic. Through her discussion of transvestisism, Butler's understanding of identity allows for deep-rooted performative affects, such as those constitutive of Millwallism, to be challenged and undermined. Furthermore, it is important not to dismiss Goffman's ideas completely as he offers astute observations of interaction within everyday life but it should be remembered that the performance is just the 'front end' of performativity.[32] There may not be an all-knowing self upon which to centre the establishment and control of identity formations and expressions but subjects knowingly perform certain roles at different times to different audiences even if they are not fully aware of the discourses to which the roles are unconsciously tied. In fact for Butler (following Foucault), the concept of agency is reliant on the release of performative subjects from the constraints of an individual, fixed self through acts that are both constitutive of and constituted by discourse.[33]

The types of habitus upon which Millwallism is founded are certainly present in the discursive construction of football identities beyond South East London, but in an increasingly self-conscious daily struggle for certainty, the performativity of football provides both reflexive and unreflexive modes of being for different types of supporters in different situations.

Patterns of Everyday Life: Repetition and the Mundane

Explicit examinations of 'the everyday' as a field of study focus on the routine, taken-for-granted aspects of life that are proposed as fundamental to the success and failure of our daily interactions.[34] For Garfinkel, such routine activities are always subject to a reflexive understanding, but it is only in situations that breach a certain level of expectancy that this reflexivity is apparent. In general, everyday interaction is based upon repetitively gained knowledges of mutual understanding reproduced in familiar situations to the extent that they can be seen as unreflective responses. These responses, which Bourdieu would suggest are a product of the *habitus* as applied to a particular field in which one finds oneself, are iteratively based upon previously unreflexive notions of class, gender, race and any number of other modernist classifications to which our subjectivities have been perpetually confined.[35] As a result, Marxist inspired theorists such as Lefebvre, point to the alienating affects inherent within modern everyday life and the solipsistic attitude, 'that is centred on an individual's particular occupational specialization, family life, and class determined forms of commodity consumption',which prevents the realization of autonomous self-expression.[36]

In contrast, however, feminist standpoint theory celebrates everyday life as a resource for exposing the values of dominant gender hierarchies and realigning the prevailing orthodoxy. Rather than denigrating the habitual nature and stasis of everyday life, it is argued that through a grounding in the mundanities of daily living a more realistic and pragmatic understanding of the world offers a greater freedom.[37] This work, of course, tends to focus on female repression and is heavily informed by, and dichotomously opposed to, the predominant (male) view of everyday life as something to be transcended.

It is a view highlighted by Lefebvre and informs much of the writing not just on football but sport and leisure in general. The perspective adopted in this paper however is that although football may at times transcend everyday life it is also very much embedded within the daily routines and spatial practices of people's lives. For some it is a way of overcoming the monotony of the daily routine, for others it offers the only routine around which their lives can be structured. For the majority, football provides both transcendence and routine at different times. Moreover, football culture itself has its own alienating characteristics to be negotiated.

In trying to unravel what everyday life has meant in modernity, Felski has provided a useful summary and conceptualization drawing on the works of Lefebvre, Heller and Schutz. She writes: 'The temporality of the everyday, I suggest, is that of repetition, the spatial ordering of the everyday is anchored in a sense of home and the characteristic way of experiencing the everyday is that of habit.'[38] There are clear parallels to be drawn between such notions of the everyday and the structuring of football in many people's lives: the regularity of the match, the topophilic affinity of supporters for their team's 'home' ground and the habitual behaviours that make up football culture. Beyond the match-day experience however it might be suggested that on a daily basis football is an important element in the structuring of many people's lives: to some, offering a coherent sense of self, feelings of belonging and unreflexive modes of being; to others, an intrusion into more meaningful domestic affairs, the perpetuation of unacceptable attitudes or an unnecessary test of cultural competence. Moreover, it may be that other key organizing processes of everyday life are becoming ever more invalid leaving people clinging to football as a way of giving meaning to their increasingly frag-mented lives. In fact, leaving them clinging to a discursively defined cultural product itself continuously under great strain from progressive social forces.

Meanings of Football: Continuity and Change

Football culture has never been a static affair. Modes of support and the structural and informal organization thereof have constantly been subject to changes in accordance with other socio-historical influences.[39] However, as Crawford criticizes, academic debates surrounding fan culture tend to be dominated by a search for 'authenticity' whereby patterns of support are located in relation to some notion of 'traditional' behaviour resistant to bourgeois intervention and corporate ideals.[40]

To avoid the dichotomies constructed around authenticity, Nash[41] suggests that fan cultures should be conceptualized as 'imagined communities'[42] that by their nature are not subject to considerations of truth validity. Acknowledging King and Redhead,[43] he reinforces the point that at no time has football fandom remained static in such a way that recourse to a 'traditional' mode of support can be made, insisting rather that all fan cultures are 'an amalgam of historical episodes, myths, "traditions" and plain inaccuracies'.[44] King's work[45] in particular shows how important these 'invented traditions' are to the identities of certain types of supporter.[46] He explores the paradoxes of compliance and resistance to the new consumption of football within a group of Manchester United supporters (the 'lads') who view themselves as members of a more authentic working-class support base whose masculine solidarity is being threatened by the more affluent customers being attracted to Old Trafford.

He challenges the very essence of the lads' self-belief in their argument that as work-ing-class men they are the natural inheritors of the working-class game and thus true benefactors of football culture. By questioning the certitude of appeals to class formation within the current social climate as nothing more than an attempt to legitimize their own masculine forms of support, any argument of authenticity is undermined. However, he does admit that, 'although the lads' claims of traditionalism cannot be sustained, their imaginings of this traditionalism serves to reaffirm their notions of themselves and the distinctiveness of their style of support'.[47]

Similarly, Crabbe and Brown [48] challenge the seemingly universal acceptance as social fact that football fandom has undergone some massive cultural revolution in the last decade, as suggested in the work of Redhead and Giulianotti.[49] There has undoubtedly been a shift in the structural organization of professional football in the wake of the Taylor Report, the inauguration of the Premier League and the regular broadcasting of live matches on satellite television. But although this has inevitably affected football audience demographics and spectator behaviour at the grounds and led to the discourses of change described in their paper, they highlight the tendency to overlook the continuities extant within football culture. Any interest in the processes involved in, and reasons for, maintaining such continuity within the fluidity of football supporter cultures has been supplanted by a concentration on 'new ways of being a fan'.[50] A focus on the meanings of football in people's everyday lives is of course subject to the discourses that pervade football culture and must acknowledge these claims and counterclaims to authenticity. The aim here though is to contextualize this within contemporary understandings of how individuals negotiate their way through daily life and the role that football plays in this process.

Meanings of Football: Discourses of Support

Giulianotti has attempted to map the identities of different types of football supporter in light of observed changes to football consumption.[51] Updating the work of Taylor and Critcher he provides a taxonomy of four idealized spectator types: supporters, followers, fans and *flaneurs*.[52] These definitions are based upon the motivations for watching football and spatial relationships with the material environment of the sport. Divided by two axes, spectators can be placed in one of four quadrants equating to one of the four 'ideal' types, based on their position between the poles of 'traditional-consumer' levels of material investment and 'hot-cool' levels of self-formation through identification with football clubs. 'Traditional spectators will have a longer, more local and popular cultural identification with the club, whereas consumer fans will have a more market-centred relationship to the club as reflected in the centrality of consuming club products … Hot forms of loyalty emphasize intense kinds of identification and solidarity with the club; cool forms denote the reverse.'[53]

The diametric opposition of supporters and *flaneurs* manifests itself within the popular discourse as a reinforcement of supporters' 'authenticity' as they challenge the emotional commitment and genuine worth of more market-centred relationships to the game. According to Giulianotti, the *flaneur* is the most detached form of spectator, strolling from one football experience to the next, enjoying the multiplicity of mediated forms available to the contemporary consumer. At its most extreme, no single club will be completely valued above another as the continuously changing cultural gaze shifts from one aesthetic moment to the next. As noted above, however, it is important to observe the continuities and the dialectic exchange that feed into varying forms of identification amongst football audiences.

Whether as a follower, fan, supporter or *flaneur,* expression of these identities does not take place in a vacuum. Neither is it restricted solely to the football stadium or football-specific environments. In fact, football is such a part of the current Zeitgeist that it pervades institutions, cultural practices and personal interactions across many different domains. It has become part of the battle of identity politics. Appeals to these varying football identities are part of a negotiated realm of authenticity, performativity, hegemony and reflexivity. They are (per)formed on a daily basis in all manner of locales and both constitute, and are constituted by, the specific norms associated with different spaces.

Everyday Life in Liquid Modernity

In 'liquid modernity', as discussed by Bauman, the human condition has slipped from certainty to uncertainty, conformity to self-expression, from unmoving, assuredly solid referents to ever-shifting, consciously acknowledged, liquid moments.[54] By definition, it is not by any means a project or phase that is completely finalized, or possibly ever will be. What Bauman highlights is how the processes of modernity that once dissolved pre-modern patterns of dependency and interaction and replaced them with progressively similar yet distinctly new and equally solid structures have reached a point whereby they themselves are being liquefied to the extent that such patterns become far less restrictive but also far less tangible.

> It does not mean that our contemporaries are guided solely by their imagination and resolve and are free to construct their mode of life from scratch and at will ... But it does mean that we are presently moving from an era of pre-allocated 'reference groups' into the epoch of 'universal comparison', in which the destination of individual self-constructing labours ... is not given in advance, and tends to undergo numerous and profound changes.[55]

Bauman is to some extent undermining the fixedness of Bourdieu's notion of habitus by suggesting that the fluidity of individuals, both physically and via increasingly diverse forms of communication technologies, increases everyone's self-consciousness and individualizes responsibility for well-being and self-attainment, encouraging less static modes of being. However, it should not be overstated that individuals are completely free to act however they choose as choice itself is subject to the circulation of discursive ideas, some of which remain rooted within the structures of modernity. There is perhaps a greater variety of discourses being more widely circulated and for Bauman what is most compelling about our current situation is the connection between freedom, responsibility and the individual. If it is possible to grasp one overriding discourse that impacts on each and everyone's liquid lives it is one of choice: more than ever before we have the freedom to choose our way in the world but what we do not have a choice about is whether we want to make those decisions. Whether we are actually free to achieve whatever we want or be whoever we want is irrelevant because in the consumerist world of liquid modernity we are constantly required to present ourselves anew. In contrast to solid modernity's aspirational but ultimately unreachable transcendence of the repetitivity of everyday life, liquid moderns are in a position where they must take responsibility for the creation of their own lives on a daily basis, whether they like it or not. With such responsibility comes less certainty; with more 'freedom', less 'security'.

Where Lefebvre defines the quotidian as what is 'humble and solid' in comparison with the greater project of modernity as 'daring and transitory', Bauman claims that solid is no longer a consideration, and even the quotidian is infused with possibility and uncertainty.[56] The previously unreflexive acts of day to day living that unquestionably routinized and reinforced our life worlds are much more open to disruptions through the increased flows of stimuli from different sources. In a similar way that the breaches forced by Garfinkel's experiments caused those involved to question their taken-for-granted understandings of mundane features of daily life, aspects such as greater physical and social mobility, instantaneous access to global information networks, hyper-commodification of resources and the normalization of such expectations within people's everyday worlds have forced far more reflexive attitudes towards daily life.

This is contra to Robson's study which demonstrates that for some their sense of self is singularly embodied in their relationship with football and pervades their whole sense of being.[57] For him, this is a result of the specific cultural *habitus* to which the members of his study are continually exposed though he does acknowledge the growing numbers of fans that do not perhaps have the depth of personal involvement with Millwall and all that the club symbolizes. For these fans the embodiment of traditionally local, masculine forms of working-class life are not necessarily primary to the expression of their self identity. He suggests that at Millwall these fans are still very much a minority and that, 'This is likely to be most true … of small and medium-sized clubs with little or no appeal beyond their own historical and social-ecological limits'.[58] This may be so, but in liquid modernity these limits dissolve so that the appeal of small and medium-sized clubs becomes a performative expression of something lost; the 'collective imaginary' becomes an imagined collective in search of authenticity, community and identity on each and everyone's own terms.

Where Robson explores how the everyday culture of a specific locale becomes embodied in the expression of support for a football club, there is a need to examine how these identities are in turn expressed as a part of the fabric of everyday life in liquid modernity. Furthermore, the ubiquity of football in any number of mediated forms offers almost unlimited levels of engagement which can be utilized in different ways, at different times, for different reasons. This is recognized by Giulianotti's taxonomy and his description of 'football *flaneurs*' but as we slip further into a liquid modern world it is necessary to go beyond this to both those who recognize themselves as having 'hotter' relationships with football and those with more indirect relationships, whose everyday experience of it is through the identifications of others: friends, relatives, colleagues, partners.[59]

Football, both as the experience of a collective allegiance and as the symbolic representation of individuality, forms part of the expression of a 'liquid' self as its presence emerges in some situations and diminishes at other times. It is, however, just one element of an array of characteristics which people may draw upon to express themselves. Wherever placed in Giulianotti's typology the part that football plays in the expression of an individual's identity will be contingent upon the specific conditions of any interaction.[60] Furthermore, as Crawford's career path model for sports fans' level of engagement shows, these identities can be seen as temporal and fluid, undergoing different manifestations throughout each and every day.[61]

It is assumed here that individual identity is a work in progress which reflects the dialectic relationship between self-reflexive understandings and externally enforced subjectivities. A project which is worked upon within the ordinariness of everyday life through a combination of moments of self-contemplation, familiar interactions with family, friends and colleagues, subconscious reactions to strangers and the discursive nature of structural influences. It is also assumed that personal identities are multiple, fluid and contingent. For in 'liquid modernity' our lives are fragmented into a 'succession of ill-connected episodes', the narrative for which is no longer some notion of Cartesian transcendence nor the negotiation of conformity within the structured identities of modernity, but a desire and a need to communicate some sense of who we are at each juncture.

Furthermore, in 'liquid modernity' the loss of the social anchors that made identity seem 'natural', predetermined and non-negotiable leads the individual on a desperate search for a 'we' through which, and in relation to, a sense of the self can be negotiated. The enduring link between football identities and the traditional affiliations of social class, gender and place mean that current discussions surrounding the dissolution of such affiliations have an impact on the role of football in the construction and expression of individual and communal identities as they are performatively embedded within everyday life.

The notion of 'community' represents, for Bauman, a utopia that, despite being the basis for a communitarianism that presupposes the existence of community, is inevitably unachievable. He argues that 'community' promises security but delivers only nostalgia and illusion and the re-emergence of the term in recent social and political discourse is unsurprising given the concerns of contemporary living: the insecurity of short-term employment, the uncertainty of individual futures, the hazardous nature of urban life. In short, 'community' is being resurrected in order to deal with the incongruencies of a world seeking ever more freedom whilst lamenting the loss of a secure and recognizable way of life.

Delaney suggests that sport offers a sense of belonging and security increasingly absent in other aspects of contemporary life.[62] He highlights the role of face-to-face communication in the creation of mutual identification and togetherness such as that found at live sporting venues. Crawford furthers this argument by noting the opportunity that the attendance of 'live' sport offers to connect with more geographically dispersed communities in the face of increasingly fragmented 'localised' communities.[63]

The sports venue offers a topophilic focus for the sense of belonging that may have arisen historically as an organic part of an identification with the neighbourhood community but, as King notes in his study of Manchester United fans, any sense of locality is now 'reinvented' or 'reimagined' through consumptive patterns of contemporary football support. Patterns that may exist beyond the venue itself and beyond the match-day experience to become embodied in the practices of everyday life.[64]

The necessity to move away from the idea of totalizing communities is prevalent within current literature on the subject. Delanty feels the need to rescue the term from communitarian discourse which has come to 'perpetuate the myth of community' and override any alternative possibilities for its definition.[65] His contention is that the associations of community with totality, proximity and place that have dominated throughout the twentieth century are less appropriate to any contemporary conception of community. He suggests that a more successful way of seeing community is, 'in expressing the emotional demands and needs of solidarity, trust and autonomy'.[66] Without wishing to overstate Delanty's defining characteristics of community, they do offer more appropriate terms of reference for the relationships that form around football and the expression of such connections within everyday life. As already suggested, proximity and place still have a part to play, as does the liminality involved with the 'football occasion', but these are as much 'imagined' conditions of community as they are actual.

The emotional depth of such 'imagined communities' is for Maffesoli the key to understanding the role of 'community' in contemporary society.[67] He uses the notion of emotional communities to describe in his terms the heterogeneity and aesthetic sensibility of small social groupings that are formed and sustained through forms of consumption and in informal friendship networks. Characterized by the fluidity of occasional gatherings and sudden dispersal he highlights the temporary character of such communities, invoking the liminal qualities of life in postmodernity that is unbounded by traditional notions of time and space.

He explores this through the metaphor of tribalism, based upon immanence, proximity, ritual and affective relations. 'This metaphor ... allows us to bring out ... the search for a more hedonistic everyday life, that is, less finalized, less determined by the "ought" and by work.'[68] His thesis is that the instrumental reason that dominated modernity and promised a better life through the discovery of universal truth has sought to mould society through a discourse of politics. Neo-tribes operate in such a way that the social exists now in a celebration of the present rather than devotion to a future project (projected future). They are thus destined to constant metamorphosis and not subject to exclusivity as members move from one to another, sometimes being present in different groups simultaneously. According to Maffesoli, this is made possible because proximity is not based on linear notions of spatiality but what Berque calls 'areolar space'. This proximity is defined by an area expanding from the self and so is always relatively local even though the network may be extensive in terms of physical space. The recognition, by their members, of being a part of such communities as he is describing is by iconoclastic reference points 'imbedded in the daily fabric'.[69] He qualifies his use of the term icon to be representative of 'a whole range of local emblems'. Most notably he suggests that the significance of the emblematic image is increased by technological innovations:

> the television or advertising image ... takes its inspiration from several archetypal
> figures ... [and] as a result, addresses 'target' audiences, what I am calling tribes,

which give rise to and recognize, through various modes of representation and imagination, the products, goods, services and ways of being that constitute them as
groups.[70]

Finally, individuals are connected in almost infinitesimal ways by forms of communication, both verbal and non-verbal. The prevalence of a rationalist perspective used to
mean that social connections predicated on verbalization were accorded status. Which
for Maffesoli is, 'completely foreign to the popular way of life, the festive and daily
customs and the *habitus* which lie at the deepest heart of everyday life, without necessarily ever being verbalised'.[71] Framed within an 'aesthetic paradigm', this unrecognized form which he labels 'sociality' is, unlike say Turner's theory of communitas in
which liminal moments provide passionate refreshment of collective identities, the
very essence of solidarity within neo-tribes.[72]

Spaces of Everyday Life

Everyday life in liquid modernity is then more uncertain and transient. However, for
many, it must also be recognized that life still comprises familiar routines. People still
live in structures they call homes, travel to their places of work and subject themselves
to regular patterns over the course of the day, the week and the year. Football provides
the illusion of persistence within these patterns but is also accommodating to the slide
into liquid modernity.

Through a combination of theoretical outlooks about everyday life and preliminary
empirical findings from time-diaries distributed to a number of supporters, four
primary sites within everyday life were identified: home, work, the pub and other transitional spaces within the city. Each location has ideological and metaphorical attachments and is in no way isolated from aspects and phenomena that cut across boundaries.
Whether conceptualized as activity spaces,[73] areola space[74] or *milieux*,[75] the
spatial ordering of daily life has proved to be the most practical and mundane way of
exploring the embedded nature of football in people's everyday lives as it defines, crosses
and dissolves discursive boundaries and cultural fields. Massey explains that, 'The activity space of something is the spatial network of links and activities, of spatial connections
and of locations, within which a particular agent operates'.[76] Thus, individuals have
daily activity spaces which tend to be focused around, and as much as possible
consciously segregated between, their domicile, their places of work, the pathways,
modes of transport and venues that connect the two and sites defined by their leisure
pursuits. Furthermore, the activity space of football extends into people's homes, work-
places and many spaces in between, connecting supporters within and across spatial
boundaries to one another, to the products, images and discursive renderings of football
culture and to collective memories of embodied experiences across space and time.
Consequently, football identities can be carried between sites via different mechanisms
but they can also disappear as the liquid self is encouraged to discard one cloak in favour
of another. Or more accurately, performative elements of which identities are composed
will be present in greater or lesser degrees from location to location and situation to
situation as defined by competing discourses at any given moment.

Notes

[1]   Crawford, *Consuming Sport*, 105

[2]   Armstrong, *Football Hooligans*.

[3]   Mass-Observation, *Mass Observation*.

[4]   Robson, *No One Likes Us, We Don't Care*.

[5]   Bauman, *Liquid Modernity*.

[6]   Butler, *Gender Trouble*.

[7]   Maffesoli, *The Time of the Tribes*.

[8]   Gardiner, *Critiques of Everyday Life*, 10.

[9]   Bauman, 'Desert Spectacular'.

[10]   Chaney, *Cultural Change and Everyday Life*, 35.

[11]   Smith, *The Everyday World as Problematic*.

[12]   For example, Leavis, *Mass Civilisation and Minority Culture*; Hoggart, *The Uses of Literacy*.

[13]   For example, Adorno & Horkheimer, *Dialectic of Enlightenment*; Marcuse, *One Dimensional Man*.

[14]   For example, Hall, 'Encoding/Decoding'; de Certeau, *The Practice of Everyday Life*; Fiske, *Understanding Popular Culture*; Silverstone, *Television and Everyday Life*.

[15]   Robson, *No One Likes Us, We Don't Care*.

[16]   Ibid., 9.

[17]   Ibid., 159.

[18]   Bourdieu, *Outline of a Theory of Practice*, 72.

[19]   Robson, *No One Likes Us, We Don't Care*, 74–9.

[20]   Armstrong, *Football Hooligans*.

[21]   Ibid., 233.

[22]   Goffman, *The Presentation of Self in Everyday Life*.

[23]   Armstrong, *Football Hooligans*, 141

[24]   Bourdieu, *Outline of a Theory of Practice*.

[25]   Butler, *Gender Trouble*.

[26]   De Beauvoir, *The Second Sex*, 295.

[27]   Butler, *Gender Trouble*, 33.

[28]   Ibid., viii–ix, original emphasis.

[29]   Nietzsche, *On the Genealogy of Morals*, 29.

[30]   Robson, *No One Likes Us, We Don't Care*, 72.

[31]   Butler, *Gender Trouble*.

[32]   Blackshaw and Crabbe, *New Perspectives on Sport and 'Deviance'*.

[33]   Butler, *Gender Trouble*, 13.

[34]   Schutz, *The Phenomenology of the Social World*; Goffman, *The Presentation of Self*; Garfinkel, *Studies in Ethnomethodology*.

[35]   Bourdieu, *Outline of a Theory of Practice*.

[36]   Lefebvre, *Everyday Life in the Modern World*; Gardiner, *Critiques of Everyday Life*, 83.

[37]   Felski, 'The Invention of Everyday Life'.

[38]   Ibid., 18.

[39]   Critcher, 'Football Since the War'; Fishwick, *English Football and Society 1910–1950*; Holt, *Sport and the British*; Mason, *Association Football and English Society*.

[40]   Crawford, *Consuming Sport*, 33.

[41]   Nash, 'Contestation in Modern English Professional Football'.

[42]   Anderson, *Imagined Communities*.

[43]   King, *The End of the Terraces* and Redhead, *The Passion and the Fashion*.

[44]   Nash, 'Contestation in Modern English Professional Football', 468

[45]   King, *The End of the Terraces*.

[46]   Hobsbawm and Ranger, *The Invention of Tradition.*
[47]   King, *The End of the Terraces*, 166.
[48]   Crabbe and Brown, '"You're not welcome any more"'.
[49]   Redhead, *Post-Fandom and the Millenial Blues* and Giulianotti, 'Supporters, Followers, Fans and *Flaneurs*' and *Football: a sociology of the global game.*
[50]   Taylor, "It's a Whole New Ball Game'; cited in Crabbe and Brown, '"You're not welcome any more"', 3.
[51]   Giulianotti, 'Supporters, Followers, Fans and *Flaneurs*'.
[52]   Taylor, 'Football Mad' and Critcher, 'Football Since the War'.
[53]   Giulianotti, 'Supporters, Followers, Fans and *Flaneurs*', 31.
[54]   Bauman, *Liquid Modernity.*
[55]   Ibid., 7.
[56]   Lefebvre, *Everyday Life in the Modern World*, 24.
[57]   Robson, *No One Likes Us, We Don't Care.*
[58]   Ibid., 6.
[59]   Giulianotti, 'Supporters, Followers, Fans and *Flaneurs*'.
[60]   Ibid.
[61]   Crawford, *Consuming Sport.*
[62]   Delaney, *Community, Sport and Leisure.*
[63]   Crawford, *Consuming Sport.*
[64]   King, 'Football Fandom and Post-National Identity in the New Europe'.
[65]   Delanty, *Community.*
[66]   Ibid., 118.
[67]   Maffesoli, *The Time of the Tribes.*
[68]   Ibid., 143.
[69]   Ibid., 137.
[70]   Ibid., 138.
[71]   Ibid., 80.
[72]   Turner, *The Ritual Process.*
[73]   Massey, 'A Place Called Home?'
[74]   Maffesoli, *The Time of the Tribes.*
[75]   Deleuze and Guattari, *A Thousand Plateaus.*
[76]   Massey, 'A Place Called Home?', 54.

References

Adorno, T. and M. Horkheimer. *Dialectic of Enlightenment.* London: Verso, 1979.
Anderson, B. *Imagined Communities.* London: Verso, 1983.
Armstrong, G. *Football Hooligans: Knowing the Score.* Oxford: Berg, 1998.
Bauman, Z. 'Desert Spectacular'. In *The Flaneur,* edited by K. Tester. London: Routledge, 1994.
Bauman, Z. *Liquid Modernity.* Cambridge: Blackwell, 2000.
Blackshaw, T. and T. Crabbe. *New Perspectives on Sport and 'Deviance': Consumption, Performativity and Social Control.* Cambridge: Routledge, 2004.
Bourdieu, P. *Outline of a Theory of Practice.* Cambridge: Cambridge University Press, 1977.
Butler, J. *Gender Trouble: Feminism and the Subversion of Identity.* London: Routledge, 1990.
Chaney, D. *Cultural Change and Everyday Life.* Basingstoke: Palgrave, 2002.
Crabbe, T. and A. Brown. '"You're not welcome any more": The Football Crowd, Class and Social Exclusion.' In *Soccer and Social Exclusion,* edited by S. Wagg. London: Frank Cass, 2004.
Crawford, G. *Consuming Sport: Fans, Sport and Culture.* London: Routledge, 2004.
Critcher, C. 'Football Since the War.' In *Working Class Culture: Studies in History and Theory,* edited by J. Clarke, C. Critcher and R. Johnson. London: Hutchinson, 1979.

De Beauvoir, S. *The Second Sex* [Translated by H.M. Parshley, 1972]. London: Penguin, 1949.

De Certeau, M. *The Practice of Everyday Life.* Berkeley: University of California Press, 1984.

Delaney, T. *Community, Sport and Leisure.* New York: Legend Books, 2001.

Delanty, G. *Community.* London: Routledge, 2003.

Deleuze, G. and F. Guattari. *A Thousand Plateaus: Capitalism and Schizophrenia.* Minneapolis: University of Minnesota Press, 1987.

Felski, R. 'The Invention of Everyday Life.' *Foundations 39,* Winter (1999–2000): 15–31.

Fishwick, N. *English Football and Society 1910–1950.* Manchester: University Press, 1989.

Fiske, J. *Understanding Popular Culture.* London: Unwin Hyman, 1989.

Foucault, M. *Power/Knowledge: Selected Interviews and Other Writings 1972–1977.* London: Harvester Press, 1980.

Gardiner, M.E. *Critiques of Everyday Life.* London: Routledge, 2000.

Garfinkel, H. *Studies in Ethnomethodology.* Englewood Cliffs: Prentice Hall, 1967.

Giulianotti, R. 'Supporters, Followers, Fans and *Flaneurs*'. *Journal of Sport and Social Issues 26,* no.1 (2002): 25–46.

Giulianotti, R. *Football: a sociology of the global game,* Cambridge: Polity Press, 1999.

Goffman, E. *The Presentation of Self in Everyday Life.* Middlesex: Penguin, 1959.

Hall, S. 'Encoding/Decoding'. In *Culture, Media, Language,* edited by Stuart Hall, Dorothy Hobsbawm, E. and T. Ranger. *The Invention of tradition.* Cambridge: Cambridge University Press, 1983.

Hobson, Andrew Lowe and Paul Willis. London: Hutchinson, 1980: 128–38.

Hoggart, R. *The Uses of Literacy.* London: Penguin, 1958.

Holt, R. *Sport and the British.* Oxford: Oxford University Press, 1989.

King, A. 'Football Fandom and Post-National Identity in the New Europe.' *British Journal of Sociology 51,* 3(4): 419–442.

King, A. *The End of the Terraces.* London: Leicester University, 1998.

Leavis, F.R. *Mass Civilisation and Minority Culture.* Folcroft: Folcroft Library, 1974.

Lefebvre, H. *Everyday Life in the Modern World.* London: Continuum, 1984.

Maffesoli, M. *The Time of the Tribes.* London: Sage, 1996.

Marcuse, H. *One Dimensional Man.* London: Sphere, 1968.

Mason, T. *Association Football and English Society: 1863–1915.* Brighton: Harvester Press, 1981.

Mass-Observation. *Mass Observation.* London: Frederick Miller, 1937.

Massey, D. 'A Place Called Home?' *New Formations, 17* (1992): 3–15.

Nash, R. 'Contestation in Modern English Professional Football: The Independent Supporters Association Movement.' *International Review for the Sociology of Sport 35,* no.4 (2000): 465–86.

Nietzsche, F. *On the Genealogy of Morals.* Indianapolis: Hackett Publishing, [1887] 1998.

Redhead, S. *Post-Fandom and the Millenial Blues.* London: Routledge, 1997.

Redhead, S. *The Passion and the Fashion.* Aldershot: Averbury, 1993.

Robson, G. *No One Likes Us, We Don't Care: The Myth and Reality of Millwall Fandom.* Oxford: Berg, 2000.

Schutz, A. *The Phenomenology of the Social World.* London: Heinemann, 1967.

Silverstone, R. *Television and Everyday Life.* London: Routledge, 1994.

Smith, D. *The Everyday World as Problematic: A Feminist Sociology.* Milton Keynes: Open University Press, 1987.

Taylor, I. "It's a Whole New Ball Game': Sports Television the Cultural Industries and the Condition of Football in England', *Salford Papers in Sociology,* no. 17 Salford: University of Salford, 1995.

Taylor, I. 'Football Mad: A Speculative Sociology of Football Hooliganism.' In *The Sociology of Sport: A Selection of Readings,* edited by E. Dunning. London: Frank Cass, 1971.

Turner, V. *The Ritual Process: Structure and Anti-Structure.* London: Routledge & Kegan Paul, 1969.

Football Spectatorship in mid-to-late Victorian Sheffield

Graham Curry

By the mid-nineteenth century the game of football had barely developed beyond its mob or folk form. It remained relatively violent and was only just being organized in wider English society. Though a degree of organization was taking place in and around London, a vibrant and successful sub-culture was beginning in the South Yorkshire city of Sheffield. Why this particular locality was ripe for such development is at present unclear. However, it is certainly true that the footballers of the area were some of the first to establish a coordinated programme of fixtures between a network of thriving clubs. It should be noted that there has been some work completed on the history and social impact of football on the city community, though there remains a multitude of areas yet to be researched. For instance, the growth in attendance figures, the type of people who attended matches and the behaviour of football crowds have all yet to be analysed in any great detail. It is with this in mind that this article tackles two issues of importance regarding fan culture in the mid-to-late Victorian Sheffield football community. Initially the paper will seek to uncover the extent to which the game of football was being played and watched during midweek. In doing so it will note through the medium of football not only the amount played on each day but also the continuance of the tradition of Saint Monday. Secondly, there will be an attempt to analyse the types of spectator disorder linked to Sheffield football around this time by providing examples of such misbehaviour and examining these through existing theories.

The Importance of the Sheffield Footballing Sub-culture

During the early development of the modern Association form of football, the players and administrators of the game in Sheffield can be credited with being in the vanguard of the game's growth and rise. Nathaniel Creswick and William Prest are generally credited with the formation in 1857 of the first club outside a school or university setting founded with the sole intention of playing the game, Sheffield Football Club. Indeed, as early as 1860, organized fixtures were being played in the area as Sheffield had a local rival in the form of Hallam FC. Between this point and 1877, when the Sheffield Football Association accepted the hegemony of the national body, Sheffield was at particular points in time one of the most important footballing sub-cultures in the whole country. Before 1877, the officers of the association had continued to promote and play by their own sets of rules and the influence of Sheffield in footballing terms stretched at different times to such diverse places as Middlesbrough, Nottingham, Chesterfield and Derby. Given the level of development reached by the footballing sub-culture in Sheffield, it is significant that there is clear evidence of early professionalism in the city.[1] The city produced such great players and characters as John (Jack) Hunter and William (Billy) Mosforth and administrators such as the brothers John Charles Clegg and William Edwin Clegg who were influential on a national as well as a local stage. There exist three interesting histories of the game in Sheffield by Richard Sparling, Percy Young and Keith Farnsworth. However, none of the three is devoted entirely to the initial history of football in Sheffield, that is before 1890, with each author dedicating less than a third of his book to deal with this period. Recently Adrian Harvey has produced an informative chapter on Sheffield football in his book *Football: The First Hundred Years. The Untold Story*.[2]

Sheffield, as a football city, has failed to retain the importance and influence of its early days. Sheffield Wednesday is by some way the senior professional club in the city, being formed as early as 1867. Sheffield United was founded over 20 years later, in 1889. Wednesday have been English champions four times, though not since 1929–30, whilst United have one solitary top division title to their credit gained in 1897–98. The FA Cup has been a little kinder to the city's clubs with United triumphing on four occasions to Wednesday's three, though neither has been victorious since 1934–35. Wednesday have triumphed once in the Football League Cup and competed in European competition on three occasions. Indeed, there have been calls from time to time for Wednesday and United to merge and form one club with the prestige and material wherewithal to be capable of competing consistently on both national and European stages. Because of the intensity of English football rivalry, and Sheffield is as good an example of these enmities as anywhere, there appears little chance of such a merger taking place. United's present ground and premier Victorian sports venue in the city, Bramall Lane, was used for an international between England and Scotland as early as 1883 and one between England and Ireland four years later. The semi-final of the FA Cup between Preston North End and West Bromwich Albion was also played there in the 1888–89 season. A replay of the FA Cup Final was held there when Barnsley defeated West Bromwich Albion in 1911–12. Originally a three-sided ground and a venue for cricket, Bramall Lane held its final Yorkshire county fixture in 1973 and during the following winter Sheffield United Football Club enclosed the open side with a large stand holding over 7,000 spectators. Wednesday's excellent ground at Hillsborough has been accorded many FA Cup semi-finals and also four World Cup matches during the 1966 Finals in England.

It seems rather sad, therefore, that a city which has provided so many positive aspects for the game – the first football club, the first floodlit match, support for the FA in time of need, to name but three – should be connected with a great spectator tragedy. The 1989 FA Cup semi-final between Liverpool and Nottingham Forest, at the time the thirty-first held at the ground, is regarded by many as a watershed in the way the game is watched in England. On 15 April 1989, 96 football fans died in the overcrowding at the Leppings Lane end of the ground in the early moments of the match. It seems sufficient to say that the tragedy led to new thinking in terms of the construction of English football grounds and ushered in a safer, though for some perhaps sanitised, era in football spectatorship in England.

Saint Monday

The importance of the Sheffield football sub-culture provides for fruitful research. A detailed study of local newspapers and a scanning of the sports pages between the months of October and March in mid-to-late Victorian times throw up some interesting patterns. One such trend worthy of further analysis is the amount of football games played during midweek. The first part of this paper will make an in depth study of this trend, providing original data for the period 1876 to 1886.

Robert Malcolmson has stated that 'Work and recreation were commonly polarised' in early Victorian England, going on to note that 'Recreation was commonly seen as an impediment, a threat of substantial proportions to steady and productive labour'.[3] It may, then, have been possible to forecast with some confidence that most if not all of the popular customs of the lower class at that time would have been eroded or even extinguished by the latter half of the nineteenth century. One practice which might have been expected to suffer was Saint Monday, whereby employees often treated the day as leisure and subsequently absented themselves from work. This appears not to have been the case. E.P. Thompson claims that in 1874, 'In Sheffield, where the cutlers had for centuries tenaciously honoured the Saint [Monday], it had become "a settled habit and custom" which the steel mills themselves honoured'.[4] Thompson also interestingly observes:

> Saint Monday, indeed, appears to have been honoured almost universally wherever small-scale domestic, and outwork industries existed; was generally found in the pits; and sometimes continued in manufacturing and heavy industry. It was perpetuated, in England, into the nineteenth – and, indeed, into the twentieth – centuries for complex economic and social reasons.[5]

Douglas A. Reid, in his article 'The Decline of Saint Monday: 1766–1876' makes additional points with regard to the impromptu holiday. Importantly, he suggests that Saint Monday lasted a good deal longer in Sheffield as a workshop-based observance than elsewhere. Furthermore he notes that the main reason for the erosion of the practice was the introduction of the Saturday half-holiday, which, he says, first appeared in Sheffield in the 1840s. As a consequence, the leisure emphasis swiftly shifted from Monday to Saturday, at least in the eyes of the majority of employers.[6] Also noteworthy in terms of the situation in Sheffield around 1874 is Thompson's comment that Monday was so frequently taken as a holiday that the large factory owners were eventually forced to treat it as a repair day.[7]

Might it be possible to postulate as to the extent that leisure was, at times, taking precedence over work in Sheffield during late Victorian times? This paper seeks to study the way in which participants and spectators alike used the sport of football to influence this process in that specific South Yorkshire city. The evidence and arguments in this section of the paper attempt to show that, in Sheffield and its surrounding districts at least, local football enthusiasts were, indeed, playing and watching the game in large numbers on midweek days, certainly between the surveyed seasons of 1876–77 and 1885–86. Together with the importance of the Sheffield footballing sub-culture and the fact that the sub-culture was undergoing significant changes in terms of emerging professionalization, these particular seasons have been chosen primarily because newspaper match reports were considerable and provide an indication of football activity around this time. For instance, there appeared just one report on the opening day of the season in 1871–72, whilst for the 1876–77 campaign there were ten and in 1885–86 as many as 24.[8] These events were taking place not simply on Monday but also on other days of the supposed working week. Consequently, although the main focus remains Saint Monday, the data for the rest of the week remain important and are worth recording. The study also hopes to advance present knowledge in this area through detailed investigation of the football matches played in the Sheffield region during midweek, presenting new and substantial information on the social and sporting habits of football enthusiasts in that locality.

The Data

The *Sheffield and Rotherham Independent* was primarily used to gather data from match reports appearing in that newspaper. The *Sheffield Daily Telegraph* was occasionally employed as an additional source. Although the former has been extensively trawled, more games may well have been played which went unreported. Matches have only been included which specifically mention the day of the match in the newspaper report. The trawl includes data from 1 September to 31 March for each football season, this being the recognized length of a season in late Victorian times. This was certainly the case in Sheffield and it may have been closely connected to the popularity of cricket in the city and in the county of Yorkshire as a whole. Indeed, there was little or no football activity before the beginning of October and a mere six midweek games reported in the month of April for the ten surveyed seasons.

Fixtures played on Boxing Day (26 December), New Year's Day (1 January) or Shrove Tuesday (Dates varied) have not been included. This information appears to inflate figures for midweek football, as these were recognized holiday dates when attendances would have increased and both players and spectators would have been more likely to be in possession of agreed free time. However, although these holiday encounters may distort the impact of a thriving midweek football culture, they are surely of interest to those seeking a continuation of a mob/folk football custom at these traditional festival times. Although it is not the intention of this article to shed light on this particular area, it is worthy of note that there was substantial football activity in and around Sheffield on Shrove Tuesday especially and this may well be deserving of further study. For instance for 5 March 1878, Shrove Tuesday of that year, there were no less than thirteen matches recorded in the *Sheffield and Rotherham Independent.*

Several patterns have emerged from the above data. Although the main thrust of this paper is concerned with spectators, it seems foolhardy not to briefly analyse some of the clubs involved. For instance, many midweek fixtures appear to have involved what might be described as 'senior' clubs – in other words, clubs capable of attracting a reasonable number of interested spectators. Certainly, Wednesday and Heeley were the two most successful sides in Sheffield around this time. Wednesday were a thriving cup team both locally and nationally, growing from an already existing cricket club, and were soon considered the pre-eminent football organization in the city. The Heeley club, which began playing matches as early as 1863, had also enjoyed a good deal of success and represented an area in the south of the city. However, they were unfortunate in mirroring the rise of the Wednesday and invariably finished runners-up to their illustrious opponents. Heeley possessed some excellent players, none more so than the aforementioned Jack Hunter together with Peter Andrews, a Scottish international whose job had necessitated a move, first to Leeds and then to Sheffield.

The practice of high profile clubs being involved in midweek encounters might lead us to speculate whether there existed any kind of financial inducement to be gained from playing in midweek. If a charge was levied at the gate – there are few indications in newspaper reports whether this actually took place – there would be a steady stream of income from these high profile fixtures. This stream was eventually tapped by the Sheffield Zulu players who played exhibitions and seemingly split the profits among themselves. The Zulus were an interesting phenomenon. Between the years 1879 and 1882, a group of Sheffield footballers began playing matches dressed as members of the Southern African Zulu tribe. The initial game was for the benefit of dependants of men killed during the Anglo-Zulu war but, as the novelty became more popular, the players began to charge entrance fees from which they seemingly rewarded themselves. The

Table 1   Football matches played in Sheffield and surrounding districts in midweek for the seasons 1876–77 to 1885–86 inclusive

Season	Mon	Tues	Wed	Thurs	Fri	Total
1876–77	42	9	11	10	0	72
1877–78	41	2	5	7	1	56
1878–79	22	0	2	6	2	32
1879–80	28	5	2	5	0	40
1880–81	23	1	3	3	0	30
1881–82	22	5	5	3	0	35
1882–83	16	5	4	1	0	26
1883–84	25	2	3	3	0	33
1884–85	45	2	7	3	0	57
1885–86	30	2	0	0	0	32

practice was cut short by the local association and a number of players were banned, though they were quickly reinstated following appropriate apologies. It is therefore not impossible that this may have constituted an early form of soccer professionalism. However, it should be stated that during extensive trawls of the *Sheffield and Rotherham Independent* no mention has been unearthed which has suggested payment to players involved in midweek games, other than those involved with the Zulus.

Not only did so-called 'senior' clubs compete in midweek, some of the clubs playing on weekdays were from the second rank of clubs in the Sheffield area. They often represented specific areas of the city and occasionally challenged the established footballing order, but never made a lasting impact in terms of winning trophies on a regular basis. These included Providence who became Park Grange at the beginning of the 1882–83 season, Walkley, Pyebank, Millhouses and Attercliffe. Others, such as Surrey, Norfolk, Clinton and Oxford were all named after streets in the city, whilst Burton Star appears to have been a club side though its exact origins are at present unknown. Worksop represented a town in North Nottinghamshire, some twenty miles east of Sheffield. It is improbable that these players were remunerated for their footballing services and

Table 2   Clubs playing ten or more midweek games during the seasons 1876–77 and 1885–86 inclusive

Heeley	45	Thursday Wanderers	18
Wednesday	34	Surrey	15
Lockwood Brothers	29	Clinton	14
Chesterfield	25	Norfolk	14
Providence/Park Grange	22	Millhouses	12
Staveley	22	Burton Star	11
Pyebank	20	Oxford	11
Sheffield	20	Attercliffe	10
Walkley	20	Worksop	10

strengthens the view that, although the likes of the Wednesday and Heeley teams may have received money from gate receipts, these individuals were simply taking advantage of the practice of Saint Monday and pursuing their favourite leisure activity. It is significant that none of these second rank teams appear in the games involving the largest attendances of the period (see Table 3 below).

Other important patterns have emerged which help to explain why certain teams played matches in midweek. Firstly, several of the clubs involved were school sides, with the majority of fixtures taking place on Wednesday afternoons. The teams included Sheffield Collegiate School, Spinkhill College, St Matthias, Broom Park, Montgomery College, Wesley College and Sheffield Royal Grammar. The practice of educational establishments utilizing Wednesday afternoon for sport is still relatively commonplace in the early part of the twenty-first century, with schools and universities electing to play many of their fixtures at this time. Another similar club active in midweek was Sheffield Medical Students. At this point, it should be stated that not all clubs playing on Wednesday were school sides as combinations such as Surrey, Broombank Rovers and White Cross often challenged the educational establishments in midweek. Furthermore, the Retford club, based some 25 miles east of Sheffield though

Table 3   Attendances of 1000 spectators and above at football matches in midweek involving Sheffield clubs for the seasons 1876–77 to 1885–86 inclusive. All are newspaper approximations. At Bramall Lane unless stated

Day Played	Date	Teams	Attendance
Monday	15.02.1886	Pantomimists v Garrick	20,000
Monday	06.03.1882	Wednesday v Blackburn Rovers*	12,500
Wednesday	15.03.1882	Wednesday v Blackburn Rovers**	10,000
Monday	23.02.1885	Pantomimists v Garrick	5,500
Tuesday	07.02.1882	Wednesday v Upton Park	4,500
Monday	09.11.1885	Heeley v Lockwood Brothers	3,500
Tuesday	27.03.1883	Wednesday v Lockwood Brothers	3,500
Monday	05.02.1887	Sheffield Association Trial***	3,000
Tuesday	09.03.1886	Wednesday v Preston North End	3,000
Monday	12.02.1883	Wednesday v Notts. County	3,000
Monday	22.10.1883	Heeley v Pyebank	2,000
Monday	10.11.1879	Sheffield XI v Sheffield Zulus	2,000
Monday	30.10.1876	Sheffield Association Trial	1,500
Monday	05.11.1883	Wednesday v Heeley	1,200
Monday	10.03.1884	Mexborough v Heeley ****	1,000
Monday	17.10.1881	Heeley v Lockwood Brothers	1,000
Thursday	21.10.1880	Wednesday v Queen's Park	1,000
Monday	06.11.1876	Sheffield Association Trial	1,000

* At Huddersfield
** At Whalley Range Ground, Manchester
*** At Walkley
**** At the Recreation Ground, Mexborough

coming under its footballing aegis, arranged all six of their midweek encounters for the 1884–85 season on Wednesdays.

There is also clear evidence that certain factory owners in Sheffield were not averse to seeing some of their employees representing the firm on the football field in midweek. Lockwood Brothers was described in the 1852 Sheffield Directory as 'merchants, tableknife, sheep shear [and] file edge tool manufacturers' of 74 Arundel Street and Spital Hill in Sheffield. The midweek games that Lockwood Brothers were engaged in would probably have been with the blessing of the management and would have been viewed as being of benefit to the firm in terms of worker morale. Certainly, Lockwood Brothers would have been viewed as by far the busiest of the factory sides, playing their games on Ecclesall Road, just outside the city centre. A number of their encounters were against Joseph Rodgers and Sons FC, another local firm whose business was barely half a mile distant. This was not the last time that the name of Lockwood Brothers would come to the fore in Sheffield footballing circles. Indeed, in the 1886–87 season, with the Wednesday club's administrators still dithering about whether to sanction professionalism and submitting their FA Cup entry form too late, several of their players decided to throw in their lot with the factory team. They enjoyed an exhilarating cup run, reaching the fifth round, but, more importantly, pressured the Wednesday committee into finally recognizing that, in order to continue to attract better players, they would have to turn professional. The business of Joseph Rodgers and Sons was based on Norfolk Street in Sheffield and has a plaque commemorating its existence in Esperanto Place in the city, bizarrely placed on the wall of the Roxy Bingo Club. At one point, the firm employed over 1,700 skilled craftsmen on the site. Other factory sides included Holmes and Bessemer and Exchange Brewery.

Another club busy in midweek was Chesterfield. A footballing connection between Sheffield and Chesterfield players certainly existed, as the latter town lies only 15 miles south of Sheffield and played under Sheffield rules. Regular fixtures took place between clubs from both areas and there was a good deal of interchanging of personnel. Indeed, both the Chesterfield club – founded in 1866 and recognized as the fourth oldest English league club – and their local rivals, Spital, were actively involved in the Sheffield district's footballing sub-culture. Nearby Staveley, the small town which lies five miles east of Chesterfield, were also involved in the Sheffield football sub-culture and enjoyed several midweek encounters. Winners of the inaugural Derbyshire Senior Cup in 1884, the club also reached the last 16 of the FA Cup in seasons 1883–84 and 1885–86, but were beaten easily by eventual winners Blackburn Rovers on each occasion. The team earned a reputation for uncompromising play and were expelled from the Sheffield FA in 1888.

During the 1876–77, 1877–78 and 1878–79 seasons in particular, the Thursday Wanderers club provides an interesting example of midweek footballing activities around this time. In these three seasons alone they were involved in no less than 17 games taking place on Thursday afternoon. The club attempted a revival, which was noted in the *Sheffield and Rotherham Independent* during the 1882–83 season. However, this only appears to have amounted to one fixture against an invitation eleven and the attendance for the match was recorded as being quite small. It is interesting to study the make up of the Thursday Wanderers club in terms of the social class of its members. The vast majority of its players were drawn from middle-class professionals in and around Sheffield. In 1876 the team comprised a strong contingent from the Sheffield Football Club, well known for its antipathy towards professionalism and championing of the amateur ethos.[9] Most of Sheffield's members were well-connected people in the city with well-paid, secure employment, often connected to the steel industry. For instance, three players involved in a Thursday Wanderers fixture in 1876 were from the Sorby family who were all successful businessmen in Sheffield. For the isolated game at Bramall Lane in December 1882 the Wanderers imported two distinctly middle-class gentlemen from Nottingham, Henry (H.A.) and Arthur (A.W.) Cursham. Both had already been capped by England, whilst Henry (Harry) would go on to represent the Corinthians, a famous combination of ex-public school and university men who propounded amateur values such as fair play and participation rather than winning at all costs. By February 1879, however, the club was being criticized in the local press for these persistent importations. The connection with the Sheffield club remained strong with the newspaper reporter referring to Thursday Wanderers as 'Sheffield' when noting that they won the toss before the start of the game.[10]

Not only were *players* involved on weekdays, but also the more important matches attracted large numbers of *spectators*. The majority of newspaper reports make no mention of attendance figures, though some allude to the number of spectators without ever being precise in terms of figures. Phrases such as 'a numerous and respectable company' (Sheffield FC v Notts., Thursday 20 December 1877), 'a large concourse of spectators' (Staveley v Heeley, Monday 20 January 1880) and 'a fair muster' (Heeley v Derby Midland, Monday 30 November 1885) were commonly used in press reports. Other correspondents were more accurate. For instance, at the local derby between Heeley and Hallam on Monday 2 December 1878, 'nearly 1,000 spectators' were in attendance. Furthermore, the specially arranged encounter between a Sheffield XI and the Sheffield Zulus on Monday 10 November 1879 saw a crowd of between '1,500 or 2,000'. Other games drew large crowds. For instance, on Monday 30 October 1876, it was reported that there were '1,500 spectators' present at a Sheffield Association trial match, whilst FA Cup ties such as the one involving Wednesday and Upton Park on Tuesday 7 February 1882 attracted much interest and consequently a large crowd of 4,500 at Bramall Lane. The inclusion in Table 3 of the FA Cup semi-final at Huddersfield and the replay in Manchester could be challenged, but the games did involve a Sheffield team, and a newspaper reporter noted the fact that several special trains ran from Sheffield specifically to see both matches. What is clear is that a good deal of football was taking place in midweek in the Sheffield area in this period with substantial numbers of players and, more particularly, spectators, involved.

The presence of the 'Pantomimists' at the top of the attendance list deserves a more complete explanation. Actors performing at two local theatres rather appropriately played against members of the Garrick club named after the famous Shakespearean actor of the late eighteenth century, David Garrick, at Bramall Lane. The proceeds were donated to three local charities. The reporter commented interestingly on the social background of some of the spectators. He noted that 'a host of "horny-handed sons of toil" (many of whom were perhaps devotees of St. Monday) had gathered'.[11] This represents a direct reference to the practice of Saint Monday in the Sheffield press of the time and appears to be a strong indication that the local populace was aware of such behaviour and may even signal a degree of acceptance.

Finally it is interesting to note that even by 1890 little had changed in terms of Saint Monday in Sheffield. The first Sheffield derby between Wednesday and United was played on Monday 15 December of that year at the beginning of what was known locally as 'bull week'. These days before Christmas were used by workers to register as many hours as possible in order to increase their wages and ensure a bumper pay packet to carry them through the Christmas and New Year break. In this sense it appears a strange decision to hold the match on a Monday, as most people would be busy augmenting their wages. However, despite this, more than 10,000 supporters still turned out to watch this important game, thus maintaining a Saint Monday tradition in Sheffield. The newspaper columnist, who by his turn of phrase may have been the same reporter who penned the 'Pantomimist' article five years earlier, noted that 'Though the horny-handed sons of toil predominated in the throng, there were representatives of other classes', identifying the presence of manufacturers, commercial travellers, clerks, publicans and publicans' wives in the crowd.[12] Even as late as 1890, the practice of Saint Monday was being observed in Sheffield despite the motivation of 'bull week'.

Spectator Disorder

This section of the paper began with the intention of researching football fan culture in Victorian Sheffield by highlighting and analysing such areas as crowd composition, attendances and general spectator behaviour. However, it metamorphosed into one concentrating on crowd disorder. Using local newspapers as one's primary sources means that the researcher mostly discovers bad behaviour rather than good when looking at press reports of football matches, the reporting being influenced by what the reading public seemingly thought was newsworthy. This section, therefore, seeks to examine only one element of the spectator sub-culture that existed within the Sheffield football community towards the end of the nineteenth century through a close examination of four particular examples of crowd misbehaviour. The motivation behind this study is to note the types of misconduct taking place in what, in Sheffield terms, were fairly notorious spectator incidents. Other examples of theories and hypotheses concerning crowd disorder before 1892 are also discussed. The article, therefore, hopes to provide additional insight into football spectator behaviour in a regional and local context that has hitherto been relatively neglected.

The Data

Following an exhaustive trawl through Sheffield newspapers between the years 1881 and 1892 it is difficult to argue that football spectator misbehaviour was a major problem in the city during the period studied. However, this is not to say that it did not exist. Indeed, there were four major incidents which indicate that such misbehaviour was occasionally present and worrying enough for elements of the sporting press to draw attention to it and pass opinion on proceedings. Interestingly, three of them occurred between October 1890 and January 1892, that is in the space of sixteen months, at Sheffield Wednesday home fixtures on their Olive Grove ground, a site just south of the city centre. Whilst mention will be made of the first incident, the three linked with the Wednesday club will be analysed in greater depth as they indicate a pattern of misbehaviour which might be of interest.

The Pierce Dix Incident – Local Enmities Surface during Crowd Misbehaviour – 24 January 1881

Tales of professionalism surfaced in Sheffield between the years 1879 and 1881 when, as previously mentioned in this paper, a set of enterprising individuals formed a team by the name of the Sheffield Zulus and began playing matches dressed as members of the Southern African tribe. The practice was cut short by the local association and a number of players were banned, though they were quickly reinstated following appropriate apologies. Then, in January 1881, another Zulu game was found to have taken place and 11 players were suspended

A lengthy correspondence began in Sheffield newspapers concerning the affair. Many contributors expressed surprise at the omission of Jack Hunter, the local noteworthy player previously mentioned in this paper, from the team selected to represent the North v South at Bramall Lane. In his reply, the Honorary Secretary of the Sheffield FA, Mr William Pierce Dix, stated that Hunter's Zulu activities were the reason for his non-selection. Pierce Dix was an important character in English football around this time. As well as holding the position of Honorary Secretary of the Sheffield FA, he was an important referee and respected both nationally and locally as a football administrator.

The banning of players implicated in Zulu encounters had further ramifications. It deprived local clubs Heeley and Wednesday of important members of their teams for a semi-final in a local competition, the Wharncliffe Cup. Interestingly Pierce Dix was chosen to referee this sensitive fixture. Wednesday emerged comfortable victors by seven goals to two, though the Wharncliffe Cup competition for the season 1880–81 was ultimately abandoned. The reporter of the *Sheffield and Rotherham Independent* commented:

> At the Wharncliffe Charity Cup match between Heeley and Wednesday on Monday last, there was quite a scene and remarks, of a character not calculated to enhance football in the minds of the gentler sex, were loud and frequent, Mr Dix being the object of the wrath of the multitude. After the match he was grossly assaulted by those who should certainly have set a better example to the lower order and the whole affair had such an effect on the official named that he almost immediately tendered his resignation.[13]

The controversy gave rise to a plethora of letters in the press, one of which was penned by Charles Clegg, in defence of his brother-in-law, Pierce Dix. Clegg has already been noted in this article as an influential figure in English football and, more particularly, he was a vociferous critic of professionalism. At a meeting of the Sheffield FA delegates had expressed 'their disgust at the personal attack upon Mr Dix' and voiced support for his subsequent actions. The Zulu players apologised and were reinstated in February 1881.

The furore was seemingly at an end when on 12 February Hunter represented Sheffield against Glasgow and was even named as captain for the occasion. Hunter's Zulu activities would certainly have forced him to miss the North versus South international trial scheduled for Saturday 22 January in Sheffield. Fortunately for him the trial was postponed due to bad weather and, following his apology, he was reinstated and played in the re-arranged fixture on Saturday 19 February. He was subsequently picked to play in two of England's internationals later that season against Scotland and Wales, even being appointed as captain for the latter encounter.

A Tale of Defeat – Disturbances involving Spectators at three Sheffield Wednesday Home Games

Three further major spectator incidents all involved the Sheffield Wednesday club. Having turned professional in time for the 1887–88 season, they were disappointed to be rejected for entry into the first Football League competition of the following campaign. However, Wednesday and a further 11 of the unsuccessful applicants swiftly came together to form the Football Alliance for the 1889–90 season, a competition won by the Sheffield team. Wednesday failed miserably to defend their crown, finishing bottom of the table in the following season. Interestingly, two of the disturbances described below took place during the club's lean spell and this may have been a contributory factor in the crowd's frustration at, and refusal to accept, unpopular refereeing decisions.

Sheffield Wednesday v Crewe Alexandra – Saturday 18 October 1890

The initial incident must be understood in terms of football officiating at the time. In 1890 the referee was a neutral official, but each competing club provided the two umpires, whom, in 2005, are referred to as assistant referees (formerly linesmen). These umpires were expected to appeal to the judgement of the referee if they believed a dispute had occurred and, if both umpires appealed concerning the same dispute, the referee was called upon to make a decision. This marked a transition from a situation of player self-management to external officiating. So it was that Wednesday, lacking an umpire at the start of their match against Crewe Alexandra in the Alliance league, made a call for a volunteer from the crowd. Up stepped William Robert Wake, who took his place as the Wednesday umpire despite objections from the Sheffield players. During the game he seemingly failed to make certain expected appeals for Wednesday and was felt to be responsible for a Crewe goal which spectators and players alike thought to be offside. At the conclusion of the game, which Wednesday lost, 'a number of spectators, probably some 700 or 800, excitedly swarmed round the officials as they left the ground uttering cries of anger and disappointment'.[14] In total there were reported to have been around 7,000 present at the ground and it might be suggested that 700–800 is quite a high percentage to be involved in a crowd disturbance. Indeed, it is hard to argue that this represented a small percentage of those present. Subsequently, as he stood in front of the committee room under the main stand, Wake entered into an argument with 'a tall and respectably dressed individual',[15] both being eventually ushered inside by policemen. Incredibly Wake re-emerged and began arguing with some of the remaining crowd – there were still hundreds in front of the committee rooms – but was eventually persuaded to leave the ground by policemen. It is interesting that one of the crowd with whom Wake argued was described as being 'respectably dressed' and the individual concerned appears to have been from the same relatively high social class as Pierce Dix's assailants in 1881.

It later emerged that Wake, a local solicitor, ex-player for the Thursday Wanderers club and former Yorkshire cricketer, had been involved in a disagreement with certain Wednesday players in the previous season and it may have been that he wished to exact a certain amount of revenge. Nevertheless, the disturbance was worthy of a good deal of adverse press coverage and might be seen as a precursor of things to come on the Sheffield football scene. It was certainly an example of threatening behaviour by a crowd towards an official and, though a strange representation because of a probable history of bad blood between Wake and the Wednesday club, certainly shocked elements of the press into effusive comment.

Sheffield Wednesday v Newton Heath – Saturday 24 January 1891

For the second time in the same season at Wednesday's Olive Grove ground 'a very unseemly display of hostility was made towards the referee by a portion of the spectators'.[16] The game was yet another in a string of defeats suffered by the Sheffield team, one which the crowd deemed had been directly caused by a specific decision against the home side by the referee. The official, Mr L.G. Wright of Derby, had to be ushered off the field by members of the Wednesday committee, the whole group being pelted with mud as they made their escape. Interestingly, a newspaper reporter describes certain of the miscreants saying about them: 'Some scores of excited and vengeance-threatening individuals of a somewhat rough appearance … remained in front of the stand waiting for the reappearance of the referee'.[17] More importantly, a reporter in the Tuesday edition of a local newspaper noted the following:

> It has long been the proud boast of Sheffield footballers that spectators in the cutlery metropolis know how to behave themselves. They were not like those unmanerly [sic] Lancashire crowds at Darwen or Newton Heath, not they![18]

This is an extremely interesting statement and seems to indicate two things. Firstly it would appear that Sheffield crowd behaviour was perceived by reporters of Sheffield newspapers to be generally good, and secondly, that, compared to Lancashire football spectators they were especially well behaved. However, the local reporter may have been exhibiting considerable bias in regards to behaviour within the city's footballing community and we might be wary of his comments regarding this aspect of Sheffield life. There is evidence to suggest that there may have been ill feeling between the Sheffield Wednesday and Newton Heath clubs. Wednesday had concluded their programme of the previous season, 1889–90 – a season in which they won the Football Alliance title and reached the FA Cup Final, only to be heavily defeated by Blackburn Rovers – at Newton Heath. The home team, in front of a crowd of around 4,000, had a man sent off and Wednesday players were attacked by home supporters at half and full time. Two players were injured. Billy Ingram was pushed over an advertising board whilst Teddy Brayshaw was assaulted with a stick. Furthermore, Harry Winterbottom, their injured captain who was acting as umpire, had his cap stolen and, we are told, felt fortunate to escape a chasing mob.[19]

Sheffield Wednesday v Small Heath – Saturday 30 January 1892

The final example of spectator misbehaviour in a Wednesday home encounter was an incident at a second round FA Cup tie at Olive Grove. The game against Small Heath from Birmingham, which Wednesday won 2-0, was a particularly physical affair with two Sheffield players, Richardson and Duncan Gemmell, being sent off. At the final whistle, in scenes reminiscent of the two previous incidents, a portion of the crowd rushed on to the pitch and headed for the referee. Again mud was thrown and the official had to be surrounded and shepherded from the field by Wednesday officials and police. In a later edition of a local newspaper the reporter attempted to play down the misbehaviour, being keen to point out that the crowd's actions were similar to those frequently seen at 'political and electioneering meetings', though the people involved in the incident are described as appearing 'not too refined'.[20]

The happenings at Olive Grove drew several responses in the correspondence columns of newspapers, none more interesting than that penned by 'An Old Foot-baller'. As a former spectator at Wednesday's games he felt unable to attend at that present time due to 'the filthy language used on almost every occasion'.[21] It seems clear that this type of crowd misbehaviour had continued for some time, though one cannot prove with any certainty the identities of the people responsible for the 'filthy language'.

The Analysis

There have been a number of attempts to explain the 'football hooliganism' phenom-enon. From an essentially Marxist perspective Ian Taylor sought to place the problem in its social context, suggesting an explanation based on post-Second World War changes in British football and how those changes impacted on the working class. Taylor suggested that prior to 1939 football fans believed that there existed a close rela-tionship between themselves and the local club, even to the extent that these supporters exerted influence on policies and players. He termed this 'participatory democracy', which in turn was part of a deeply imbued 'soccer consciousness'. After 1945, as leisure patterns changed and football's administrators courted a classless audience, the controllers of the game jettisoned some of its previous characteristics and loyalties. 'Bourgeoisification', the implementation of clearly defined measures to attract middle-class spectators, together with 'internationalisation', the embracing of a European or even world perspective, combined to alienate working-class support. The latter's reaction was an attempt to re-assert a 'participatory democracy' through violent acts of football hooliganism. Peter Marsh, Elizabeth Rosser and Rom Harré spent three years in the mid-1970s analysing the nature, behaviour and composition of the youthful followers of Oxford United. They contended that football hooligan encounters can be orderly meetings lacking real violence and term such confrontations as often being little more than ritual aggression, largely symbolic and closely controlled by a set of unwritten rules. They strongly believed that the submission of opponents rather than injury is the prime objective. Gary Armstrong and Rosemary Harris approached the subject from an anthropological standpoint basing their conclusions on in-depth evidence gained from participant observation of fans in Sheffield. They principally used this data to cast doubt on the degree of organization of such hooligan groups.[22]

Before 1988 only John Hutchinson, Tony Mason and Wray Vamplew had examined the problem in historical terms.[23] Despite a lack of historical analysis of this area there appeared, in 1988, a study which seemed to break new ground by extensively and deliberately basing much of its research in an historical context. This was *The Roots of Football Hooliganism: An Historical and Sociological Study* by Eric Dunning, Patrick Murphy and John Williams.[24] In 2000 Eric Dunning published further thoughts on the subject offering 'a sociological diagnosis of football hooliganism as a world phenomenon'.[25] As the authors state in *The Roots of Football Hooliganism*, one of the principal reasons why they approached the problem from an historical standpoint was because they were, and in all except one case still are, adherents to figurational sociology advanced principally by Norbert Elias. They placed great stress on the study of long-term processes, which enabled them to provide empirically sound historical judgements and added understanding to aspects of their study through detailed processual analysis. Dunning, Murphy and Williams provided a large amount of data to indicate that spectator misbehaviour existed before 1900, thereby exploding any myth that might have suggested the phenomenon only began in the 1960s. Some critics have maintained that the actual amount of data was relatively small, and this may be true when compared to evidence presented for the decade of the 1970s. Indeed, to be additionally critical, their sole use of the *Leicester Mercury* to note spectator misconduct on a local and national scale between 1894 and 1914 may not have revealed as much as we might have expected from a nationwide survey.[26] It is also slightly disappointing that the study did not begin earlier for, as this paper shows with the examination of the Pierce Dix incident, spectator disorderliness, at least in Sheffield, existed prior to that date. The authors do make it clear, however, that their study both locally and nationally begins when Football Association records on crowd misbehaviour first appeared. More positively, in terms of this article, *The Roots of Football Hooliganism* provides an extremely useful framework for study, suggesting that spectator misbehaviour at the time might be divided into seven different areas. In Chapter 3 the authors list these as: inappropriate language, pitch invasions, attacks on match officials, attacks on players, vandalism, fighting between fan groups and incidents away from football grounds. They observe that the most frequent type of crowd indiscipline reported during this period was attacks directed against players or match officials.[27] Fighting between opposing fan groups, something which, after 1960, we might readily associate with football hooliganism – an imprecise phrase and 'a construct of politicians and the media'[28] – was found to be less prevalent in mid-to-late Victorian times. Incidents also tended to occur at or very near football grounds, only rarely spreading beyond the vicinity of the grounds themselves.[29]

R.W. Lewis (1996) has provided the most noteworthy critique of the *Roots* hypothesis,[30] to which Murphy, Dunning and Maguire (1998) responded eighteen months later with a counter-critique.[31] Lewis, using data gathered from football encounters in Lancashire, plays down the actual seriousness of the violence in incidents involving clubs from that geographical area – he quotes 73 separate cases noted in the newspaper *Football Field* from 1884 to 1914 – offering the opinion that the episodes 'were relatively few and untypical'.[32] However, the comments of the reporter from the *Sheffield and Rotherham Independent* that Sheffield crowds were far better behaved than their Lancashire counterparts when noting crowd disturbances at the Wednesday versus Newton Heath clash of 1891, appears to contradict this view. Furthermore, evidence from this encounter might lead us to believe that at times a large minority of the crowd became involved in disorder and not the 'small clique connected with betting' which Lewis has suggested.[33] Moreover, we must be prepared to consider local bias when quoting from such sources. In a more recent article, Martin Johnes also casts doubt on the actual level of violence that took place in Victorian crowd disturbances.[34] He finds himself in agreement with Lewis, maintaining that 'disorder was small-scale and infrequent'.[35] However, Dunning *et al.* feel that not only did this disorderliness occur on a fairly regular basis, but that events were more serious than has often been portrayed.

Evidence earlier in this paper suggests that, in a Sheffield context at least, disorderly events were, in fact, rather serious but only at one particular time, fairly frequent. Indeed, it is hard to feel empathy with Johnes' case when, in discussing the throwing of missiles by angry spectators, he rather naively notes that 'few hit home'.[36] This type of explanation reminds one of the theories of Peter Marsh and his colleagues when describing much of the behaviour of a soccer crowd as being 'ritualistic'. Marsh *et al.* suggest that football spectators engage in 'a mode of fighting which seems almost guaranteed to inflict the least possible amount of death and injury' on their opponents.[37] It is hard to understand how this particular form of violent behaviour, the throwing of missiles, can possibly be controlled or be anything other than extremely dangerous with potentially fatal consequences. Presumably a missile already thrown cannot be aborted. Consequently Marsh and his colleagues presumably discount the fact that ritualised aggression can ultimately be extremely violent. Harmless ritual has a tendency to escalate.

As regards the Sheffield evidence, the data are indisputably qualitative. It should again be stated that there appears to have been very little spectator misbehaviour linked to Sheffield football towards the end of the nineteenth century. However, the proximity in terms of the timing of the incidents involving Sheffield Wednesday followers should be carefully noted. They might be described as classic late-Victorian football disorder in that the disgruntled crowd aimed their wrath and disappointment directly at officials or players. Vamplew categorizes these incidents as frustration disorders, 'when fans believe that an incompetent or biased official has cost their team victory'[38] and not, as is the case in more modern times, when fighting between opposing supporters has been more the norm. It is true, however, that because transport links were in those days in their infancy, opposing supporter individuals or groups were rarely present at away fixtures where extensive travelling was required. If, however, opposing fan groups or individuals were present – something which would have taken place at neutral venues employed for matches in the later stages of cup competitions – any instances of fighting, when compared to the number of attacks on officials or players, were relatively rare. Dunning *et al.*, Lewis, Mason and Vamplew quote over 60 examples of different types of spectator disorder between 1884 and 1892. Their data show that over 50 per cent of those quoted were attacks on players or match officials.[39]

It is surely additionally significant that the Sheffield incidents reported here happened during a period when the Wednesday club, despite initial success in winning the Football Alliance league at their first attempt in the 1889–90 season, were experiencing a lean spell of results in the second season of that same competition. For the officials threatened it must have been a harrowing experience and to argue otherwise is to take a dangerously detached, dispassionate and unsympathetic stance. It appears rather blasé to dismiss such incidents as 'small-scale' and 'seldom serious' when personal safety was being directly threatened.[40] The numbers involved, certainly in the 'Wake' incident, were considerable and being pursued by over 700 angry and disgruntled football spectators could only be described as traumatic. In his seminal study of mid-to-late Victorian football, *Association Football and English Society 1863–1915*, Tony Mason also appears to 'miss the point' when excusing some cases of crowd disorder because 'some referees were a trifle irritating'.[41] Should threatening behaviour be excused because the official has, in the view of some partisan spectators, allowed more time at the end of the game than he might have? Might intimidation be overlooked because of the awarding of what, in some quarters, might be deemed to have been a dubious goal? Mason, concurring with Lewis and Johnes, plays down the seriousness of the incidents, saying, 'they were relatively easily contained'.[42] Yet, significantly, in the very next sentence, Mason also notes that the referees were so concerned by rising levels of violence towards them that, in 1908–09, they formed themselves into a union, presumably for their own protection. Do Lewis, Johnes and Mason believe that this type of behaviour is socially acceptable in *any* context or simply those which can be excused by 'irritating referees'? Are all three guilty of maintaining and promoting a romantic vision of working-class culture which seemingly allows them to excuse such excesses of partisanship? Let us be in no doubt that stones which hit the target generally cause injury. In short, the structure of a game of football generally permits acceptable degrees of tension between players and among spectators. However, in the cases described above the human beings involved appear to have allowed passions to rise to *unacceptable* levels, causing injury and trauma to individuals deemed to have been responsible for undesirable sporting outcomes.

Finally, the trawl of local newspapers carried out for the years 1882 to 1892 provides little indication of widespread disruption of football matches by spectators at this time.

This does not mean, of course, that disruption did not take place. Under-reporting may have been taking place as correspondents would have been few and may well have relied on second-hand evidence. In a word the rudimentary methods employed at the time would lead us to believe that some disorders went unheeded and the wider public would have remained unaware of their occurrence.

Conclusion and Suggestions for Further Research

The strength of this paper is that it offers more information on one of the most important early footballing sub-cultures in mid-to-late Victorian England. Not only has detailed analysis of initial Sheffield football itself been sadly lacking, but local football studies in particular have been sorely neglected. Add to this the fact that any study of an early historical period, perhaps because it requires painstaking research, has rarely been tackled, the paper appears to add substantially to existing knowledge and, hopefully, motivate others to undertake more regional studies of this kind. Specifically the first section establishes the fact that Saint Monday, and midweek football generally, was relatively common in Sheffield in the decade from 1876 to 1886. Secondly, the qualitative assessment of crowd disorder in the city suggests that players and officials rather than opposing supporters were the main targets. The disorder appears to have been rather more threatening than other academics have previously proposed. As regards further research, Martin Johnes' excellent study of soccer in South Wales would seem to present a way forward in regional analysis, though one still waits patiently for someone to extend Molyneux's work on recreation in Birmingham.[43] The fact that this fine investigation was completed as long ago as 1957 appears to suggest that its application to subsequent investigation is long overdue.

Acknowledgements

Yet again I am indebted to Professor Eric Dunning for reading and correcting an early draft of this paper and to Douglas A. Reid for his help and suggestions with 'Saint Monday'. I am also thankful for the help of the Sheffield Library Local Studies section and particularly Alison Darby, who checked a section of the paper.

Notes

[1]   See Curry, 'Playing for Money'.
[2]   See Sparling, *The Romance of the Wednesday*: 1867–1926; Young, *Football in Sheffield*; Farnsworth, *Sheffield Football: A History*; Harvey, *Football: The First Hundred Years*.
[3]   Malcolmson, *Popular Recreations and English Society*, 94.
[4]   Thompson, 'Time, Work-Discipline and Industrial Capitalism', 74.
[5]   Ibid.
[6]   Douglas A. Reid, 'The Decline of Saint Monday 1766–1876'. See also Reid, 'Weddings, Weekdays, Work and Leisure in Urban England 1791–1911'. Also worthy of note are Lowerson's articles on Sheffield angling during midweek, 'Brothers of the Angle' and 'Angling'.

[7]   Thompson, 'Time, Work-Discipline and Industrial Capitalism', p.74.

[8]   *Sheffield and Rotherham Independent*, 10 October 1871, 10 October 1876 and 5 October 1885.

[9]   Young, *Football in Sheffield*, 17.

[10] *Sheffield and Rotherham Independent*, 13 and 15 February 1879.

[11] Ibid., 24 February 1885.

[12] Ibid., 16 December 1890. In *Association Football and English Society*, 143, Tony Mason notes that the Sheffield derby at Bramall Lane on a Monday afternoon in October 1891 saw a crowd of 23,000.

[13] *Sheffield and Rotherham Independent*, 29 January 1881.

[14] Ibid., 20 October 1890.

[15] Ibid.

[16] Ibid., 26 January 1891.

[17] Ibid.

[18] Ibid., 27 January 1891.

[19] *Sheffield Daily Telegraph*, 28 April 1890.

[20] *Sheffield and Rotherham Independent*, 2 February 1892.

[21] Ibid., 6 February 1892.

[22] Taylor, 'Football Mad'; Marsh, Rosser and Harré, *The Rules of Disorder*; Armstrong and Harris, 'Football Hooligans: Theory and Evidence.'

[23] Hutchinson, 'Some Aspects of Football Crowds before 1914'; Mason, *Association Football*; Vamplew, 'Sports Crowd Disorder in Britain 1870–1914' and 'Ungentlemanly Conduct'.

[24] Dunning, Murphy and Williams, *The Roots of Football Hooliganism*.

[25] Dunning, 'Towards a Sociological Understanding of Football Hooliganism as a World Phenomenon'.

[26] Dunning *et al.*, *The Roots of Football Hooliganism*, 48.

[27] Ibid., 59.

[28] Dunning, 'Towards a Sociological Understanding of Football Hooliganism as a World Phenomenon', 142.

[29] Dunning *et al.*, *The Roots of Football Hooliganism*, 69.

[30] R.W. Lewis, 'Football Hooliganism in England before 1914'.

[31] Murphy, Dunning and Maguire, 'Football Spectator Violence and Disorder before the First World War'.

[32] Lewis, 'Football Hooliganism', 332.

[33] Ibid., 320.

[34] Johnes, 'Hooligans and Barrackers'.

[35] Ibid., 24.

[36] Ibid., 23.

[37] Marsh *et al.*, *Rules of Disorder*, 126.

[38] Vamplew, 'Sports Crowd Disorder', 141.

[39] Dunning *et al.*, *The Roots of Football Hooliganism*; Lewis, 'Football Hooliganism'; Mason, *Association Football*; Vamplew, 'Sports Crowd Disorder'.

[40] Lewis, 'Football Hooliganism', 335; Johnes, 'Hooligans and Barrackers', 23.

[41] Mason, *Association Football*, 161.

[42] Ibid., 162.

[43] Johnes, *Soccer and Society*; Molyneux, 'The Development of Physical Recreation in the Birmingham District from 1871–1892'.

References

Armstrong, Gary and Rosemary Harris. 'Football Hooligans: Theory and Evidence.' *Sociological Review 39*, no.3 (1991): 427–58.

Curry, Graham. 'Playing for Money: James J. Lang and Emergent Soccer Professionalism in Sheffield.' *Soccer and Society 5,* no.3 (2004): 336–55.

Dunning, Eric, Patrick Murphy and John Williams. *The Roots of Football Hooliganism: An Historical and Sociological Study.* London: Routledge and Kegan Paul, 1988.

Dunning, Eric. 'Towards a Sociological Understanding of Football Hooliganism as a World Phenomenon.' *European Journal on Criminal Policy and Research 8,* no. 2 (2000): 141–62.

Farnsworth, Keith. *Sheffield Football: A History. 2 vols.* Sheffield: Hallamshire Press, 1995.

Harvey, Adrian. *Football: The First Hundred Years. The Untold Story.* Cambridge: Routledge, 2005.

Hutchinson, John. 'Some Aspects of Football Crowds before 1914.' In *The Working Class and Leisure.* University of Sussex conference report, 1975.

Johnes, Martin. 'Hooligans and Barrackers: Crowd Disorder and Soccer in South Wales.' *Soccer and Society 1,* no.2 (2000): 19–35.

Johnes, Martin. *Soccer and Society: South Wales, 1900–1939.* Cardiff: University of Wales Press, 2002.

Lewis, R.W. 'Football Hooliganism in England before 1914: A Critique of the Dunning Thesis.' *International Journal of the History of Sport 15,* no.1 (1996): 310–39.

Lowerson, John. 'Angling.' In *Sport in Britain: A Social History,* edited by Tony Mason. Cambridge: Cambridge University Press, 1989.

Lowerson, John. 'Brothers of the Angle: Coarse Fishing and English Working-Class Culture, 1850–1914.' In *Pleasure, Profit, Proselytism: British Culture and Sport at Home and Abroad 1700–1914,* edited by J.A. Mangan. London: Frank Cass, 1988.

Malcolmson, Robert W. *Popular Recreations and English Society: 1700–1850.* Cambridge: Cambridge University Press, 1973.

Marsh, Peter, Elizabeth Rosser, and Rom Harré. *The Rules of Disorder.* London: Routledge and Kegan Paul, 1978.

Mason, Tony. *Association Football and English Society, 1863–1915.* Brighton: Harvester, 1980.

Molyneux, D. D. 'The Development of Physical Recreation in the Birmingham District from 1871–1892.' University of Birmingham, MA thesis, 1957.

Murphy, Patrick, Eric Dunning and Joseph Maguire. 'Football Spectator Violence and Disorder before the First World War: A Reply to R.W. Lewis.' *International Journal of the History of Sport 15,* no.1 (1998): 141–62.

Reid, Douglas A. 'The Decline of Saint Monday 1766–1876.' *Past and Present,* no.71 (May 1976): 76–101.

Reid, Douglas A. 'Weddings, Weekdays, Work and Leisure in Urban England 1791–1911: The Decline of Saint Monday Revisited.' *Past and Present,* 153 (November 1996): 135–63.

Sparling, Richard A. *The Romance of the Wednesday: 1867–1926,* Sheffield: Leng & Co., 1926.

Taylor, Ian. 'Football Mad: A Speculative Sociology of Football Hooliganism.' In *The Sociology of Sport: A Selection of Readings,* edited by Eric Dunning. London: Frank Cass, 1971.

Thompson, E.P. 'Time, Work-Discipline and Industrial Capitalism.' *Past and Present,* no. 38 (1967): 56–97.

Vamplew, Wray. 'Sports Crowd Disorder in Britain 1870–1914: Causes and Controls.' *Journal of Sport History 7,* no.1 (1980): 5–20.

Vamplew, Wray. 'Ungentlemanly Conduct: The Control of Soccer Crowd Behaviour in England, 1888–1914.' In *The Search for Wealth and Stability,* edited by T.C. Smout. London: Macmillan, 1979.

Young, Percy M. *Football in Sheffield.* London: Stanley Paul, 1962.

Building a Mass Activity: Fandom, Class and Business in Early Spanish Football

Andrew McFarland

Introduction

International soccer has a widespread reputation as a predominantly working-class sport, and in general this identity is well earned and deserved. However, in most countries football was introduced in the early 1900s to the local elite, who aspired to British power and prestige and emulated the educators and merchants of Great Britain. From there, the sport went through a transition period as it spread gradually into the general population, spurring professionalization and turning football into a mass activity within that nation. Almost every country in the world went through some form of this transition, usually establishing local styles in the *barrios* of Buenos Aires, the colonial battlegrounds of southwest Africa, and hundreds of other locations. Many writers have discussed this transition through the lens of professionalization itself or with a focus on working-class identity, but what is often lost in such discussions is that a transformation into a mass activity fundamentally requires the creation of fans. For the first time people must be drawn to the field and be willing to hand over money to watch with no possibility of participating themselves – instead they come to enjoy a spectacle. This essay focuses on some of the ways that Spanish football began to make the transition from a middle-class activity to a mass sport over the course of the 1910s. It was not until the 1920s that football truly gained a mass audience in Spain, but the 1910s were in many ways an even more critical period when clubs and organizational bodies established the institutions and identities that later allowed for rapid growth.

Football was introduced to Spain during the last decade of the nineteenth century by various foreigners visiting Spain on business and Spaniards who travelled to Britain for their education and brought back the new sport and the ideals of muscular Christianity. Once introduced to the nation's already vibrant and growing athletic communities, football rapidly became a popular activity among the Spanish urban middle classes of Barcelona, the Basque Country, Madrid, and even within the depths of Extremadura. Clubs were established, tournaments were organized, and youths began dreaming of impressing their friends with exploits on the pitch. However in these early days every member expected to play personally and paid for his own equipment and travel expenses and by 1910 this began to limit the sport's expansion as the country's small professional middle classes became saturated.

During the 1910s, Spain's industries and economy expanded rapidly because the nation's neutrality during the First World War allowed Spanish merchants to trade war commodities with both sides. In this positive economic climate, football became a regular part of Spanish culture as the nation's urban population expanded rapidly and workers developed their first significant disposable incomes. As a result, more and more working-class people developed an interest in football over the course of the 1910s and early 1920s, weakening the older, middle-class pedagogical arguments for sport and the amateur ideal. To make this possible the clubs themselves had to undergo change, partially to turn an essentially intramural activity into a regulated spectacle and partially because clubs increasingly needed money to compete and that meant drawing a fan base willing to regularly pay for tickets. The first section of the essay tracks the general expansion of football as a popular activity in Spain's largest cities, Madrid, Barcelona and Bilbao, which can be measured to some extent through increasing membership rolls, rising attendance figures and growing numbers of clubs. The rest of the paper will focus on several developing institutions that strove to create a regulated spectacle for a popular audience in one form or another. It was during the 1910s that the first stadiums were built to accommodate paying fans, complete with differentiated seating that separated the classes, but allowed everyone to attend. Less physical institutions also developed that simultaneously promoted and relied on growing fan interest. Most prominently, sports journalism rose as an accredited profession with its own publications as well as important footholds in the mainstream media. Lastly, clubs built up strong identities that connected them to specific sections of local society through regional, national and class bonds. These identities bolstered fan interest beyond the sport alone, drew in greater numbers of people, and improved the incomes of often struggling clubs. These changes provided the Spanish football world with an organizational foundation that made gradual growth possible in the 1910s, set the stage for exponential expansion in 1920s, and created the first generation of Spanish soccer fans.

Increasing Participation and Economic Development

The most important change Spanish football experienced during the 1910s was the sheer increase in the number of people participating. Over the course of the decade, more teams were founded, more members joined each club, and more youths played the sport in the streets and fields across the country that ever before. This growth can be measured in a variety of ways and brought numerous changes to Spanish popular culture, such as larger attendance figures and profits, but this increase only happened gradually. The rising attendance numbers marked the increasing participation of the members of the working classes, especially after the eight hour work day was established in 1919 and workers had more time to devote to entertainment.[1] In comparison, prior to 1910 the sport had stagnated as both economic recession and the limited size of the Spanish urban middle class placed a brake on its expansion. Some clubs folded and many more merged together to survive. At the beginning of the decade, clubs and players still had to search for money to pay for equipment and travel and their participation frequently lost them money. For example, in the early 1910s Athletic de Bilbao made a trip to Bordeaux for a match and, after paying for train fares and accommodation, ended up losing 273 pesetas during the trip, despite its share of gate receipts.[2] Similarly, in 1908 F.C. Barcelona fell to 38 members, almost folded, and was only saved by its foreign, originally-Protestant, founder Hans Gamper, while other early Barcelonan clubs like FC Catalá disbanded and liquidated their assets.[3] Football at the time, therefore, depended almost entirely on participant funding and was subject to the rising and falling fortunes of the educated middle-class people who played the sport.

Over the course of the decade, however, this fiscal situation gradually improved for clubs across the country. As early as 1915–16, Athletic de Bilbao was bringing in 30,661 pesetas from the monthly fees of *socios* and 20,303 pesetas from matches, even making 6,877 pesetas in one day from a championship match against their Basque rival from San Sebastián, Real Sociedad.[4] Matches that profitable were few and far between, but such profits were a far cry from the losses of five years earlier. While Athletic began with only 24 members (*socios*) in 1900, the number grew to 87 in 1914, and 112 by 1915–16.[5] Even more impressively, membership numbers at FC Barcelona increased by more than 100 a year for the entire decade with Barça claiming a massive 3,574 *socios* paying membership dues by 1920.[6] These membership numbers are somewhat suspect because the club tended to inflate its member rolls, but any downward adjustment still remains impressive compared to the 38 *socios* of 1908. Madrid FC also saw similar growth that turned the club into an economically viable business. Over the 1912–13 season, Madrid averaged 252 paying spectators per match, which brought in a total income of 3,881.20 pesetas over the season.[7] Seven years later, the club's average attendance was 1,389 and their total income from ticket sales rose to 21,303.26 pesetas. Although the increase in net income varied significantly from year to year, depending on the number of matches played and foreign clubs attracted for friendlies, after 1916 Madrid FC never again averaged less than 1,000 spectators a match and a year later the club reached the milestone of 500 dues-paying *socios*. In Spain's three largest cities, therefore, the interest and income of the most important football clubs increased dramatically over the decade reaching significant numbers as a mass attraction.

Not only did attendance and finances improve over the decade, but the number of clubs rose dramatically, as a brief illustration dealing with Vizcaya and Catalonia alone makes clear. In 1909 in the Basque Country, Athletic de Bilbao, Arenas de Gaucho, Club Ciclista de San Sebastián (soon to be Real Sociedad), and Racing de Irún were the only important clubs and the whole area was administered by the Federación Norte. In comparison, when the Norte divided into the Vizcayan Federation and the Guipuzcoana Federation in 1917 the clubs involved were: Arenas, Deportivo Portugalete, Deportivo Cantabria, Racing Club, Rolando Club, Barreda Sport, Erandio, Santander FC, Elexalde, Esperanza de Santander, Siempre Adelante de Santander, Irrintzi, Fortuna, Duesto, Ariñ Sport, Athletic, Acero F.C., Baracaldo FC, Vizcaya Union, Arrapazenbazaitut, Real Sociedad, Real Unión de Irún, Esperanza, Club Deportivo Irunés, Racing de San Sebastián, Luchana, Ariñ de Eiber, Old Boy's, and Español (de Bilbao).[8] These clubs were divided into two divisions that held separate championships, and all of them were represented and considered when changes were made to the regional federation. Significantly, many of these clubs like Duesto, Acero FC and Baracaldo FC represented industrial areas, where football was becoming popular among the industrial working classes. Similarly, the number of teams participating in Catalonia also grew rapidly and had established two divisions by 1920 when the main clubs included FC Barcelona, Español, Jupiter, Sans, Badalona, Athletic de Sabadell, Sabadell FC, Club Gimnástica de Tarragona, Catalá (a different version from the 1900 Catalá), l'Avenç, Gimnástica A.E.P., Palamós, Catalònia, Europa Esportiu, Manresa, Mataró, Vilassar, Catalunya, Sarrià, T.B.H., and Esparta and many more in lesser divisions. Just as in Vizcaya, this list includes representatives from most of the industrial towns around Catalonia and several of Barcelona's larger neighbourhoods as well, such as Sabadell, Manresa, Tarragona, Badalona and Sans. Football was gradually becoming an activity of the working class, not the middle class alone. Quite simply, times were changing and the sport was bigger than it had ever been before, a transition that would have serious consequences for the sport's organization and created a greater demand for supporters for each club and victory on the pitch.

By mid-decade, football matches drew enough fans to be deemed a risk to public order on numerous occasions due to both the increasing numbers of fans and the class they came from. At a match between Athletic and Arenas de Gaucho in 1916, the crowd rushed the field in protest over a referee's decision and play had to be suspended, while at the replay only the physical intervention of the Guardia Civil prevented a second invasion of the pitch.[9] That same year a regional cup final between Athletic and Real Sociedad at the neutral site of Irún's Amate field was called off by the civil governor because of 'the climate of passion that had been promoted by the press' before the match.[10] In 1918, similar problems developed in Barcelona where heated rivalries within the city stoked fans' passions for one of the first times when FC Barcelona and Español met in the finals of the Catalan championship. As a prominent journalist, José Lasplazas, described it: 'it is – like all the matches in those times between the eternal rivals – a hard fight, so many arguments and invasions of the public onto the field of play … It is the time of the passionate "fan clubs", of "supporters" who search for deserted streets in which to fight'.[11] Despite the early date, this description calls to mind images of hooligans mobbing the streets and fights breaking out, but also the more typical images of Barcelona in the 1910s and 1920s, a time when anarchist *pistoleros* and undercover government policemen fought regular battles throughout the city and made it one of the most violent in Europe. The passion of fans and political dissidence, therefore, came to be expressed through similar street fights and mass demonstrations focused on certain squares and prone to violent outbursts, a tradition that continues today in Madrid where the fans of Real Madrid FC and Atlético de Madrid flock to the Plaza de Cebeles and Plaza de Neptuno, respectively, for mass celebrations whenever their club achieves something significant.

Nor did this level of interest only exist in the three largest cities. In Galicia, the early rivalry between Deportivo de la Coruña, Celta de Vigo and Fortuna de Vigo also became a threat to the public order. As early as 1916, several matches between the first two clubs led their fans to become dangerously violent and 'the repercussion of the incidents in La Coruña was such that the civil governor of the province decided to suspend the matches of regional rivalry'.[12] The ban did not last very long and the teams simply played an unofficial match to avoid government interference (almost like two gangs taking their fight underground to avoid the authorities). Similarly, the 1919 Galician championship was marred by the absence of Fortuna de Vigo, which was banned from official participation for several months due to constant public disturbances surrounding their matches. These problems with fans and the intervention of the civil authorities to maintain order marked a critical mass that football was reaching even in the country's smaller cities. In both good and bad ways, the sport was forcing itself into mainstream culture and building core groups of supporters who were willing to defend their club financially, vocally and physically.

Stadiums

A natural corollary to football's rising interest and fan support was the need for larger structures to house fans and control attendance. This essentially made the 1910s the first age of stadium building in Spain. The idea of building large outdoor arenas, of course, was not particularly novel in a country where every significant city already had a permanent bullring, and football quickly followed bullfighting's example.[13] On the most basic level stadiums provided closed-off areas in which the club could control attendance and charge a fee, but they also allowed for different sections within the stadium, including better accommodation generally called the *tribuna* and/or *preferencia* for which teams could charge higher prices. The *tribuna* usually consisted of a grandstand with raised, shaded seats and a genteel audience, while the *preferencia* were seats along the sideline around the *tribuna* and open to the sun. Lastly, there were general entrance tickets for simple standing room at the ends of the field or the side opposite the *tribuna* and *preferencia*. These divisions were a logical extension of established bullfighting practices, where seats were divided between *sol y sombra* (sun and shaded seats) that divided the classes based on comfort. These multiple sections produced more expensive seating that increased a team's income per match and also separated the increasingly working-class fans from middle and upper-class club members and attendees in the *tribuna*. This allowed some of the social distinction of football as a form of conspicuous consumption that had drawn people to it in the first decade of the century to continue in the 1910s and 1920s by segregating the working-class fans from the middle-class organizers, members and players who could afford the more expensive sections. Certainly, some social mixing did occur, but sectioned seating limited it as much as possible in the increasingly consumer sport.

As in other areas, Athletic de Bilbao, and the Basque Country in general, pioneered many of these developments and built two football stadiums in the first half of the 1910s to host its rapidly increasing fan base. The club built the first, Jolaseta, for the 1911 national cup championship and used it to host most of the nation's largest clubs for the tournament. For the project Athletic de Bilbao hired the substantial construction firm Sociedad Terrenos de Neguri and the stadium included provisions for complex ticket prices that were also connected with railway travel in package deals.[14] Seats in the *tribuna* with a first class train ticket cost 3.50 pesetas, while *tribuna* seats with a second class ticket were 3 pesetas.[15] The next step down were *billetes de preferencia* with first-class train tickets for 2.90 pesetas and second-class ones for 2.50, and seats in the general section ran 2 and 1.60 pesetas with their respective train tickets. Finally, entries without train tickets cost 2.30 for the *tribuna*, 1.75 for *preferencia*, and 0.86 for entry into general seating. Admittedly, Athletic de Bilbao was a leader in this area, but other clubs and cities followed their model. This system of differentiated prices marked the varied elite, middle-class, and working-class social levels attending matches. Similarly, the packaging of rail and entrance tickets emphasizes how routine the marketing tactic of collaboration between football and railroad companies had become as early as 1911. Bilbao was an expanding city and the organization of transportation to matches reflected the changes urbanization was bringing to both Bilbao and other cities across Spain. Cities were no longer small enough for people to easily walk to their destinations and these larger numbers necessitated public transportation systems for the first time. Football clubs helped to spur those developments and established connections with rail companies that provided sure markets for entrepreneurs who invested in transportation industries.

Jolaseta, however, almost immediately became too small to hold Athletic's burgeoning supporter base and on December 1912 the mostly middle-class members agreed to build a new stadium. The club called upon the leading bankers and industrialists in Bilbao for money both as a financial venture and to ensure luxury accommodations away from the growing masses of plebeian fans. Soon, they established a fund-raising goal of 50,000 pesetas for the project, raised the money, and purchased land at the end of the Gran Vía in Bilbao next to the Asilo de San Mamés.[16] The location itself was significant because it placed the new stadium far enough outside Bilbao to remove it from working-class neighbourhoods, but near a railroad line so that the masses could be easily (and temporarily) transported in.

The club reaffirmed its regional identity by hiring a local architect, Manuel María Smith, to plan the stadium and work began with a public ceremony on 20 January 1913,

Figure 1   'San Mamés', José Arrúe, 1915.

attended by numerous players, such as the club's star Pichichi, and a local priest, Manuel Ortúzar, who consecrated the field.[17] Bringing in Ortúzar and the club's best known players for a public consecration affirmed Athletic de Bilbao's Catholicism and placed it within the traditions of the region. In the end, the stadium cost 89,061 pesetas, a huge sum for the period that marked the young football club's affluence and sports writers across the country lauded the new field's features and compared it favourably to British football stadiums, the ultimate compliment at the time.[18] The mayor of Bilbao sent a congratulatory telegram to mark the field's completion and King Alfonso XIII himself even attended the inaugural match. This prestige produced the nickname that the stadium's current incarnation still holds today – the 'catedral de fútbol' – and marked an important step in football's rising role as a form of mass culture.

Although Bilbao led the way with San Mamés, clubs in other regions also built their first substantial football fields in the 1910s, although few were really modern stadiums until the 1920s. In Barcelona, the profusion of smaller clubs delayed large-scale stadium building mostly until the 1920s with Español de Barcelona and FC Barcelona spending most of the decade at the relatively small fields of calle Muntaner[19] and Las Corts, respectively, until they each built stadiums in 1923. However, there were ongoing attempts to build a large stadium atop Montjuic. A group named Stadium Club was established in 1919 to build an Olympic-level stadium atop the mountain, led by the influential Baron Joan Antoni de Güell (son of Eusebi Güell, the patron of the architect Antoni Gaudi) and with the approval of Fransesc Cambó (the leader of the powerful *Catalanista* political party the Lliga Regionalista).[20] They continued their campaign in the 1920s and eventually succeeded in building one of the first world-class stadiums in Spain on the slopes of Montjuic near where the Olympic stadium sits today.

In Madrid, clubs also built new fields with the most important naturally being that of Madrid FC, which played at the Campo de O'Donnell between 1910 and 1923 in the solid middle-class neighbourhood east of the Retiro Park. Even by the standards of the day, it was a small field that only covered a 300m square, but its gradual expansion can be followed clearly over the decade. In the fall of 1912, Madrid FC added the first grandstand,[21] including 495 seats in the *preferencia* and 1,200 general entrance tickets.[22] The original entrance price for general entrance was an affordable 20 céntimos that even at this early point made occasional attendance possible for the working classes. The stadium subsequently received facelifts in 1914, 1916 and the early 1920s[23] by which point O'Donnell had a capacity of 3,500 spectators. Madrid FC consciously developed its two price distinctions, *preferencia* and general, to promote popular participation and kept general entrance prices within a range that the working class could afford throughout the decade. Between 1912 and 1920, the prices for tickets to the *preferencia* rose from 77 céntimos to 1.69 pesetas while the general entrance started as only 33 céntimos and rose to 87 céntimos.[24] Although prices increased slightly more for general admission than for *preferencia*, Madrid kept the price of general entrance roughly equivalent to one hour of work for a skilled worker so that the general public could afford their matches.

On a smaller scale, clubs in other cities also built fields and established many of the names that became legendary in Spanish football. In La Coruña, Club Deportivo de la Sala Calvet (which received a royal title on 5 February 1909 and changed its name to Real Club Deportivo de la Coruña) opened its first stadium on 9 May 1909.[25] Like Athletic de Bilbao, the club built on the outskirts of the city where there was both open space and easy transportation, naming their new field Riazor after a nearby beach and a stadium has stood there ever since. In San Sebastián, the 1909 national champion from the city, Club Ciclista, obtained and fitted out the field of Ondaretta, although it was closed four years later after a merger of the city's largest clubs in favour of the older fields at Atocha.[26] The now united Real Sociedad turned Atocha into a true stadium over the decade, just as Madrid FC gradually expanded O'Donnell. By the 1920s, Atocha held significant seating, hosted numerous international matches, and became one of the most important stadiums in the country. In other areas, Real Unión de Irún built the field of Amute and in the city of Gijón grounds named El Molinón were established.[27] In the south, Seville FC acquired rights to a section of the Prado de San Sebastián next to the Circulo Mercantil in 1908 and established their first pitch, the Campo de Mercantil. As in Barcelona, Seville's stadium was built on grounds used for expositions, allowing the city to make use of the land when no expositions were being held, and the club only charged fifteen céntimos per chair. By 1910, stands had been added with a 'tribuna and a terrace with chairs [that] saw itself full with a distinguished assembly, and among them the most beautiful señoras and señoritas of good society, who contributed to the greater attraction of that square that only the paintbrush of the nature can form'.[28] This emphasized that the *tribuna* and terrace helped bring in the middle-class or better audience that increasingly became part of the club's identity. Seville's local rival, Sevilla Balompíe (later Real Betis) established a second field in the city at Huerta de la Mariana in 1907, then it built its own stadium, Patronato Obrero, near the middle-class neighbourhood of Porvenir in 1918.[29] Despite its location, the name of this new field also emphasized that Betis was taking up a working-class identity in comparison to Seville FC. Finally, Valencia joined in when several smaller groups established a large club under the name Valencia Foot-Ball Club in early 1919. The new organization opened the field of Algirós on 7 December 1919, in the neighbourhood of the same name located in a somewhat isolated region of the city that was nonetheless both close to downtown and connected by rail for easy fan travel. The choice of location for Algirós, therefore, directly reflected the city's urbanization and the logistics of attendance for the masses, an approach that worked so well that Valencia built its next stadium, Mestalla, right next door. Algirós opened with the low ticket cost of 60 céntimos for the *preferencia* and 35 for general entrance that reflected the more popular focus that football had reached by the end of the decade as well as the club's junior status and need for supporters.[30] Lower ticket prices meant more of the working class could afford them, attend the matches, and participate in the identities being forged. Throughout the country, then, football clubs built stadiums that could cater to various classes of people and that were located in regions that made them accessible to the masses as the cities they were located in expanded. They successfully catered to larger and larger collections of fans across the country and allowed both the middle and the working classes to participate.

Media

Around the increasing numbers of football fans, clubs and stadiums during the 1910s, a journalistic community dedicated to sports also developed. All over the country and particularly in Bilbao, Madrid and Barcelona, athletics became a regular topic for news coverage and built up a following that sustained several publications and turned sports columns into regular sections of mainstream broadsheets. Many of these sports publications were short lived, but as the decade progressed they became more economically successful and a few established themselves as permanent features of the journalistic landscape until the outbreak of the Spanish Civil War, developments that resulted both from football's increasing popularity and rising literacy rates across Spain.

During the decade, sports journalism not only expanded, but the genre itself changed as well. At the start of the decade, sports publications focused entirely on a middle and upper-class readership, but as time progressed and the social classes involved broadened, a different emphasis developed within the sporting press that reflected the influx of working-class spectators. Magazines catering to higher social levels separated themselves by emphasizing motor sports, shooting and fencing, while football, cycling and boxing became increasingly important in newspapers. Nonetheless, this difference was a matter of emphasis and even the most aristocratic publications covered football throughout the 1910s.

In Madrid, there were various short-lived publications going back into the 1900s including *Gran Mundo y Sport* (1906–07), *Sport Universal* (1906) and *Los Sports* (1910). The first two lasting sports publications in the city were *Gran Vida* (1903–36) and *España Sportiva* (1912–33). *Gran Vida* was the more important of the two and openly embraced the older, middle-class tradition that emphasized the pedagogical benefits of physical education as a way to physically regenerate the country.[31] However, the directors of *Gran Vida* also worked with Carlos Padrós, a founder of Real Madrid, and the publication became the first voice of Madrid's football community. By 1920, however, the most important athletic publication in Madrid was *Heraldo Deportivo*, which began on 25 May 1915 and continued until 1936.[32] The long-running magazine printed three issues a month, cost 15 pesetas for an annual subscription in 1916 and 50 céntimos per issue in 1919, and was filled with pictures and other expensive production techniques. These elements mark *Heraldo* as a classic elite publication that emphasized automobiles, airplanes and other expensive activities and its pages were filled with advertisements from Chevrolet, Peugeot, Harley-Davidson, Goodyear and Renault. Nonetheless, it was still very involved with football and its director, Ricardo Ruiz Ferry, was one of the most influential sportswriters prior to 1936 and also the first president of the reunited Federación Española de Fútbol in 1913.[33] Sports also became a regular feature of mainstream newspapers in Madrid with Ricardo Ruiz Ferry alone writing articles for *Heraldo de Madrid*, *El Imparcial* and *El Sol*, all of which published regular match reports.

In Barcelona, an even more vibrant and better organized journalistic community developed. *El Mundo Deportivo* started publication in 1906 and gradually increased its frequency until it produced Monday, Wednesday and Friday editions, used a broadsheet format, and cost only 10 céntimos per issue or 15 pesetas for a year's subscription in 1920. This format and pricing marked it as a publication with a mass audience that reflected Barcelona's more consumer-oriented athletic community. Other newspapers also appeared in Barcelona, such as *Sports* in 1906 and *Stadium* in 1910, which became increasingly important within the city. *Stadium* reached out to a similar audience as *Heraldo Deportivo* in Madrid with less frequent issues, a magazine format, and pages filled with expensive glossy photographs.[34] It also took a special interest in expensive sports and was the official organ of the Real Automóvil Club de Cataluña, the Asociación de Lawn-Tennis de Cataluña, the Moto Club Deportivo de Barcelona, the Real Polo Jockey Club, and the Federación de Sociedades Deportivas. Nonetheless, its pricing was 20 céntimos per issue and 10 pesetas a year per subscription making individual issues occasionally affordable for the masses, even if its main target were the middle classes and above. As in Madrid, by 1910 sports were regularly covered in the mainline broadsheets including the Catalan language *La Veu de Catalunya*, *Diario de Barcelona* and *La Publicidad* and the Castilian language *La Vanguardia*, *Las Noticias* and *El Diluvio*.[35] By the 1910s, therefore, people of different classes, regional identities and political groups in Barcelona were interested in sport, not just one section of the city.

Other areas also developed traditions of sports journalism in the 1910s, although they were usually confined to sections of mainstream newspapers. In Bilbao, a sports newspaper creatively named *Hércules* published issues in 1914 and others developed in competition with it such as *Los Deportes de Bilbao*. The most important sports columns, however, were printed in *Gaceta del Norte* with its large circulation and mass audience. There was also a short-lived publication named *Sport Sevillano* that appeared in 1913 and revealed the interest in that region as well. Not only did newspapers report scores and describe events, they also served as communication centres for sporting communities and locations for stores to advertise in and use football to sell their product to fans. The media also helped publicize events and stirred up interest in general, helping to build rivalries and passions over specific matches around which club identities were formed.

Club Identities

One of the driving forces behind football's growing popularity was each club's development of an identity that drew in supporters. Interest soared when fans came to view a club as 'theirs', so clubs did everything they could to create a bond between fans and players. Teams consciously created identities and introduced colours, flags and other symbols so that they stood for something within their local community. They cast themselves as the representatives of regions, cities, neighbourhoods and social classes and made choices to use words in Spanish, English and Catalan to validate those identities. To promote unity, clubs organized celebrations for victories, group travel to matches, sponsorships from prominent city figures, products that enhanced their images and, most importantly, rivalries with other clubs. Essentially, football teams embraced anything that built interest in matches and raised the paid attendance and *socio* numbers as they transitioned from friendly associations into businesses.

One area where identity became particularly controversial was the issue of language because football was an inherently British activity that came with a whole vocabulary of English words that were often adopted directly until Castilian equivalents gradually replaced them. In the 1910s, this was a sensitive topic that many clubs and journalists addressed directly. In *Heraldo Deportivo*, Ricardo Ruiz Ferry (under the pseudonym of Chipli-Chapla) discussed the problem in relation to a proposition made to the Academia Española de la Lengua to invent a Castilian vocabulary for football. Ruíz Ferry noted that with good or bad pronunciations most Spaniards used 'offside' or 'corner' instead of their equivalents 'fuera de juego' and 'saque de esquina' and also asked 'Who today says or writes *balompié*? Nobody; and the same will happen with the rest of the words.'[36] In the end, he concluded that translating everything was simply impractical and that a mixed adaptation of terms as suggested by the contemporary president of Madrid FC was the only solution.

More practically, some clubs emphasized their Spanish identity by directly incorporating a Spanish word and syntax into their names. Madrid FC, for example eventually changed their name to Real Madrid CF to emphasize the Castilian phrase 'club de fútbol' over the English 'football club'. Similarly, the journalist Mariano de Cavia organized a newspaper campaign against the use and abuse of English football terms in 1907. De Cavia was a famous journalist who spent most of his career writing for *El Liberal* in Madrid and had a long history of fighting to reform customs and promote the precise use of language. In response, one of the most important teams in Seville adopted the Spanish translation 'balompié' instead of the English 'football club' in its name, a choice that usually identified the team with the working classes who usually preferred a more 'Spanish' identity.[37] This played out in Seville with Seville FC and

Real Betis Balompíe developing distinctly different class identities, despite both being basically middle class and originating from a club established by students of the local Escuela Politécnica. In 1909, one of this early club's leaders wanted to add an excellent player who worked at the school – even though he was from the working class.[38] The directors refused and the club split between those willing to accept working-class players (who in 1914 became Real Betis) and those who would not (who became Seville FC). As their rivalry developed between 1910 and 1915, Betis became the team of the working class and promoted this through their inclusion of 'balompíe' in their name, while Seville FC developed an elite identity.[39] This was especially important with working-class supporters who were more parochial in their self-perceptions than the Europeanizing members of the middle classes. The world *balompíe*, therefore, became a way for clubs to assert a working-class identity in the growing consumer sport. Such an overt attempt to mould perceptions reflected, in a popular setting, the divisions among the educated elite between liberals, who wanted to Europeanize Spain, and conservatives, who strove to centralize the country and assert the dominance of traditional values. As a result, the use of English words remained common and acceptable for clubs in Catalonia, Barcelona and other areas with more regional and pro-international identities, while clubs in regions more closely connected to the Spanish national identity like Andalucía and Castile were far more likely to adopt 'balompíe' and other hispanizations because it was more important to the local fans – or at least because the elites chose to foster that self-perception on the working class.

Other clubs created an identity by developing their society into an organization that did more than just play football, or as FC Barcelona later put it, they became 'more than a club'. Besides football, many teams organized a plethora of activities that gave them a larger identity in the city and allowed some of them to become community centres for their supporters and neighbourhoods. They also took up public roles in their cities by organizing benefit matches for victims of natural disasters and general events that emphasized their positive role in the community. The best examples of this approach were the two branches of Athletic, de Bilbao and de Madrid, which both regularly contributed to the communities that supported and cheered them. Athletic de Bilbao promoted Basque national identity in general, the city's professional middle class in particular, and strove to have a positive influence on the city. For example, in 1918 the Spanish flu ravaged Bilbao and to support the stricken community, Athletic de Bilbao organized a benefit match and handed over all the proceeds to a fund for the victims and their families, increasing the club's respect and social importance and showing that it could directly help people in troubled times.[40]

Athletic de Madrid played an even more important role for Basques living in Madrid. As a minority in the capital, they gravitated together and the club provided them with a community centre that organized numerous activities. Run by the influential Julian Ruete, Athletic de Madrid developed into one of the most important football clubs and the largest tennis club in Madrid. During the 1913–14 season, it absorbed Madrid Hockey Club and by 1917 had added sections dedicated to football and track and field.[41] Also, in 1914 Ruete opened the club to women and within a year they had three hundred female members, bringing wives and daughters into the society and making it a family organization for everyone in the local Basque community. Athletic de Madrid, therefore, became an organization that ran numerous sports that the whole family could participate in. The family emphasis was particularly important in the Basque urban, immigrant community because it kept everyone involved from a variety of social classes and provided them facilities to share as well.

Two more examples of drawing fan support through identity creation came from Barcelona where politics and sport quickly intertwined. When Hans Gamper reclaimed the presidency of FC Barcelona in December 1908, the club was on the verge of disintegration. He saved it through an aggressive search for financial support that led him to promote it as a 'Catalan' club, gaining the sympathy and support of Barcelona's professional bourgeoisie, who supported the Catalan autonomy movement. This led FC Barcelona to a conservative, middle-class identity and to the conservative, Catalan political party, the Lliga Regionalista.[42] As early as 1908, he established a relationship with Francesc Cambó i Batlle, a city councillor, leader of the Lliga Regionalista (after the death of Prat de la Riba in 1917), and later minister of Fomento and Hacienda in the national government. Also brought into the fold was Joan Ventosa i Calvell, another important member of the Lliga Regionalista, the original director of the Catalanista newspaper *El Poble Català* and a conservative nationalist who was a board member of several important companies. This approach became particularly attractive after March 1914 when the Catalan movement succeeded in creating the Mancomunitat de Catalunya, a special regional government that provided a rallying point for the Catalan autonomy movement and drew wide ranging support in the city that reached beyond the Lliga alone. The Mancomunitat and FC Barcelona worked together to further their common cause and communication between the leaders of the two organizations naturally grew. As a result of these connections, FC Barcelona became an active, athletic symbol of Catalanismo, especially in the 1920s when Catalanismo became less conservative and more popular. This shift allowed FC Barcelona's Catalan identity to attract a mass following at the same time as football was becoming a working-class attraction, led to direct conflict between the club and the civil authorities, and confirmed the importance of FC Barcelona as the team of ALL of Catalonia and not just the conservative, middle-class Catalonia of the Lliga Regionalista. The result was the creation of a huge fan base for FC Barcelona by the 1920s because fans were not only attracted to the entertainment on the field, but the club's identity as well.

The counterpoise to FC Barcelona was Real Club Deportivo de Español, which established a Spanish and working-class identity within the Catalan city. Español already had the tradition of being anti-foreigner or anti-Protestant by 1910 after a series of controversies between the two clubs between 1899 and 1901. By 1910, they club had connection to the Radical Republican political party led by Alejandro Lerroux's that drew its support from the immigrant working classes of Barcelona.[43] For decades, Lerrouxism stood in opposition to Catalan nationalism within the region and Lerroux clashed directly with Francesc Cambó in 1907 when he was accused of subverting the regional movement in an election. With these connections, the club naturally emphasized their Spanish identity by choosing the name 'Español' and obtaining the royal title in 1912 to assert their connection to the whole country. By the end of the decade, clashes between the fans of Barcelona and Espanola became regular occurrences and the two clubs openly disrespected one another. A critical point came in 1919, which was the highpoint of the political movement for Catalan autonomy. The Catalan football federation organized a match to honour FC Barcelona and every first-division club in Catalonia attended in a show unity – every club except Español which distanced itself from the event, presumably to demonstrate its political differences. Here again, therefore, a club was establishing a clear political identity that drew out fans and developed supporters for reasons beyond the sport alone. This process of creating an identity was critical to developing a fan base and the regular financial support it brought.

The Institutions for an Industry

The story of Spanish football was only just beginning with the arrival of the year 1920. In fact, most histories from within the sport start there because it was then that the first Spanish national side stunned the world, and themselves, with a second place finish in the Antwerp Olympic Games. The 1910s, however, were a critical period of transition when the sport attracted its first working-class fans and established the institutions that allowed football to develop from a middle-class activity into one that included mass participation. The core of this transition was football's simple rise in popularity measured by more clubs in existence, larger attendance numbers, and the first serious concerns with profitability. Connected to this growing interest were institutions that strove to draw out and organize these growing numbers effectively. The first stadiums were built to hold and control a mass audience in almost every large city across Spain. Similarly, a sporting press developed with its own publications and sections within broadsheets that catered directly to the fans and stoked their interest to greater heights. Clubs also drew people into the sport by identifying themselves with larger social and political groups, such as different classes, neighbourhoods and cities; thus creating imagined communities based around football with a larger social identity that support-ers could join for the price of a ticket. This sort of vicarious identity drew in thousands and helped football penetrate beyond the Spanish middle-classes. Essentially, it was during the 1910s that Spanish football satisfied the preconditions to allow it to become a true mass entertainment industry in the next decade and exploit the national spot-light brought on by their Antwerp success. It made the new sport fan friendly and broke through the class barriers that could have limited expansion so that matches became an activity for those who never expected to play and instead paid for entertainment and inclusion.

Notes

[1]   Fusi, *Unsiglo de España*, 56–7.
[2]   Mateos, *Los cincuenta años de Atlético de Bilbao 1898–1948*, 17–18.
[3]   Some sources list Barcelona as having 68 *socios* (members) in 1908. That number is their total at the end of the year, but 38 was the low point in membership at the meeting.

[4]   Mateos, *Los cincuenta años*, 34.

[5]   Ibid.

[6]   Lasplazas and Pardo, *El Barcelona C.F. hacia su medio siglo de historia*, 92–3.

[7]   Bahamonde, *El Real Madrid: en la historia de España*, 53–4. On page 53, Bahamonde has put together a wonderfully complete table listing number of matches, season attendance, per match attendance, annual income, per match income and price per spectator. The table ranges from the 1912–13 season to the 1925–26 season and his sources are the archived accounting records of Real Madrid.

[8]   'Fútbol', *Heraldo Deportivo 4*, no.117 (15 August 1918), 262.

[9]   *San Mamés, la catedral*, 86–7.

[10] Ibérico Europa de Ediciones (IEE), *Historia de la Copa*, 57.

[11] Lasplazas and Pardo, *El Barcelona*, 49–50.

[12] Fernández Santander, *Historia del Real Club Deportivo de La Coruña*, 19–21.

[13] The authoritative work on bullfighting in Spain and its commercial development, such as the building of bullrings, is Adrian Shubert's *Death and Money in the Afternoon: A History of the Spanish Bullfight*.

[14] Mateos, *Los cincuenta años*, 21–22.

[15] Ibid., 21.

[16] Ibid., 28–9.

[17] *San Mamés*, 62.

[18] Ibid., 67–80.

[19] Lasplazas and Pardo, *Historial del Real Club Deportivo Española*, 23, 33.

[20] *Heraldo Deportivo 5*, no.160 (25 October 1919), 416.

[21] Prados de la Plaza, *Real Madrid: Centenario*, 62–5.

[22] Bahamonde Magro, *El Real Madrid*, 56.

[23] Ibid.

[24] Ibid., 58.

[25] Fernández Santander, *Historia del Real Club Deportivo de La Coruña*, 12.

[26] Aranjuelo, *Historial de la Real Sociedad de San Sebastián*, 26, 33, 43.

[27] De Caso, *Fútbol*, 23.

[28] Otero, *Historial del Sevilla Club de Futbol*, 11–15.

[29] Rodríguez López *et al.*, *Historia del Real Betis Balompié (de 1900 a 1936)*, 19, 75.

[30] Hernández Perpiñá, *Historia del Valencia F.C.*, 15–16.

[31] Bahamonde Magro, *El Real Madrid*, 47.

[32] Information taken from a survey of *Heraldo Deportivo* available at the Hemeroteca de Madrid (HM).

[33] IEE, *Historia de la Copa*, 21.

[34] Information taken from the banners of *Stadium* between 1916 and 1920 (HM).

[35] Artells, *Barça, Barça, Barça*, 80.

[36] Ricardo Ruíz Ferry, 'Fútbol: Un proposición el foot-ball á la academia.' *Heraldo Deportivo 2*, no.28 (25 February 1916), 52–3.

[37] Rodríguez López *et al.*, *Historia del Real Betis Balompié*, 46.

[38] Ibid., 35, 41.

[39] How much these identities really represented the makeup of the each club is highly debatable. This is driven home by the fact that it was Betis, not Seville, that obtained the royal title through one of their presidents Pedro Rodríguez de la Borbolla, the son of a minister to the crown, but then that differentiation between reality and image itself is significant.

[40] *San Mamés*, 94–5.

[41] 'Sociedades Deportivas.' *Heraldo Deportivo 3*, no.86 (5 October 1917), 346–9.

[42] Artells, *Barça, Barça, Barça*, 86–8.

[43] Alvarez Junco, *El emperador del paralelo*.

References

Alvarez Junco, José. *El emperador del paralelo: Lerroux y la demagogia populista*. Madrid: Alianza Editorial, 1990.

Aranjuelo, José J. [pseud. Erostarbe]. *Historial de la Real Sociedad de San Sebastián*. Madrid/Burgos: Ediciones Alonso: Publicaciones Deportivas, no.12, 1941.

Artells, Joan Joseph. *Barça, Barça, Barça: F.C. Barcelona, esport i ciutadania*. Barcelona: Editorial Laia, 1972.

Bahamonde Magro, Angel. *El Real Madrid: en la historia de España*. Madrid: Taurus, 2002.

De Caso, Alonso. *Fútbol: asociación y rugby*. Madrid: Biblioteca de Deportes- Calpe, 1924.

Fernández Santander, Carlos. *Historia del Real Club Deportivo de La Coruña (1906–1999)*. La Coruña: Librería Arenas, 1999.

Fusi, Juan Pablo. *Un siglo de España: la cultural*. Madrid: Marcial Pons, 1999.

Hernández Perpiñá, Jaime. *Historia del Valencia F.C.*. Barcelona: C.G. Creaciones Gráficas, S.A, 1974.

Ibérico Europa de Ediciones (IEE). *Historia de la Copa*. Madrid: Ibérico Europa de Ediciones, 1973.

Lasplazas, José L. *Historial del Real Club Deportivo Española*. Madrid/Burgos: Ediciones Alonso: Publicaciones Deportivas, no.11, 1941.

Lasplazas, José L. and Pardo, Carlos, *El Barcelona C.F. hacia su medio siglo de historia*. Madrid: Ediciones Alonso: Publicaciones Deportivas, no.9, May 1941.

Mateos, José Maria. *Los cincuenta años de Atlético de Bilbao 1898–1948*. Bilbao: Tall. Escuelas T. de P. de Menores, 1948.

Otero, Arturo. *Historial del Sevilla Club de Futbol: 35 años de vida deportiva*. Madrid/Burgos: Ediciones Alonso: Publicaciones Deportivas, no.8, 1941.

Prados de la Plaza, Luis. *Real Madrid: Centenario*. Madrid: Sílex, 2001.

San Mamés, la catedral. Bilbao: Internacional Book Creation, 1982.

Rodríguez López, Manuel, Tomas Furest Rivero, José Manual García González and Manolo Ruesga Bono. *Historia del Real Betis Balompié (de 1900 a 1936)*. Sevilla: Biblioteca de Ediciones Andaluzas, 1981.

Shubert, Adrian. *Death and Money in the Afternoon: A History of the Spanish Bullfight*. Oxford, Oxford University Press, 1999.

Milestones in the Development of Football Fandom in Germany: Global Impacts on Local Contests

Udo Merkel

Introduction

The 2002 Soccer World Cup in Japan/Korea was full of surprises on and off the pitch. The expectations of the German fans were rather humble and modest due to their team's poor performances in the qualifying stages. The most startling of these had been the dramatic 5-1 home defeat to England in September 2001. Reaching the final of the 2002 World Cup with a team of unknowns was, therefore, a major achievement and celebrated at home as if the German squad had in fact won this prestigious competition.

For many commentators the poor performance of the German national side over the last years is largely due to the post-Bosman influx of foreign players which has made the German *Bundesliga* a very global affair and inhibits the development of local talents. Germany's first division currently hosts more than 100 foreign players, not only from 'traditional' football nations, such as Brazil and Argentina, but also from countries such as the United States or even Iran. The running radio commentary at any top *Bundesliga* match not only requires some specialist linguistic skills (to pronounce names like Hassan Salihamidiz, Bajramovic, Diego Klimovic, Andres d'Allesandro, Oude Kamphuis, Youssef Mokhtari or Emile Mpenza) but also a detailed understanding of world geography, to explain the origins of these players.[1] Many of these foreign players have been elevated to the status of local heroes. Such players include Sergej Barbarez (Hamburg), Ivan Klasnic (Bremen), Marcelinho (Berlin) and Roy Makaay (Munich). Although some of the German players like Michael Ballack and Oliver Kahn are well known to the international football community, none of them has been able to achieve the popularity, celebrity status and global recognition of the stars of the 1970s, such as Franz Beckenbauer.

For the critical observer of German culture and society the symbols accompanying the 2002 World Cup fever and celebrations in Germany came as even more of a surprise. Never before in the sporting and political history of this country had so many black-red-golden flags been waved, fixed to cars, been displayed in windows, used to decorate the streets and sewn onto clothes. Many young people looked like contemporary warriors, having painted their faces black-red-gold or even dyed their hair before going into action. In a development that had been unimaginable for a long period of time, this flag became during the 2002 Soccer World Cup an emblem that embraced class, creed and colour. This was the same flag that, since its reinstatement, had been flying mostly over old, stuffy, official state and governmental buildings, to highlight their importance or to honour the dead: it became an unlikely partner in the short-lived creation of a sense of Germanness. The fact that so many people from so many different backgrounds could wrap themselves in this abstract emblem demonstrated again the significance of international sporting success in the creation of national identities.

For the Germans this is particularly important as they live in one of the youngest European nation states that has gone through several major changes in a relatively short period of time. Since the foundation of the German Empire in 1871, there have been at least six different states called Germany, each with its own rationale, borders, economy, population, society and political order.[2] The period between 1949 and 1990 even saw the parallel existence of two German states with two opposing political orders: the Federal Republic of Germany and the German Democratic Republic. For both, sport was an important means to demonstrate the superiority of their political system, to establish a positive image and reputation in the world, and to create a unique and distinctively different national identity.

Less cosmopolitan and united but equally colourful is the fan culture of German football grounds on which this chapter will focus, in particular young supporters, their cultural practices and their relationship with the game. Whilst doing this and using a developmental approach, at least two significant themes will be explored in more depth: firstly, the construction, reconstruction and celebration of personal, social, regional and national identities; and secondly, those cultural and social conflicts manifest within the world of football, which are both mirroring as well as shaping wider social developments.

The essay will concentrate on several milestones in the history of football fandom in Germany. These are the working-class origins of German fan culture, the wide ranging impact of winning the first World Cup title in 1954, the changing and increasingly complex relationship between football clubs, players and supporters in the aftermath of the relatively late professionalization and commercialization of German football, and the impact of other European fan cultures, particularly English and Italian, on the cultural practices of German football supporters.

Due to the limited scope of this essay several themes have to be ignored or can only be touched upon, for example, the regular display of racism, xenophobia and jingoism in German football grounds, gender issues, the development of hooliganism over the last two decades, the role of the media in the production and consumption of football, and the activities of right-wing fan groups and neo-Nazis in the context of international matches.

The Beginnings of Football (Fandom)

When the first German nation state was founded in 1871, the modern concept of sport had just arrived as a kind of by-product of the engineering, mining and textile know-how of the British, who helped to industrialize the German Empire. By that time the Germans had already developed and consolidated their own, distinctive form of physical culture, *Turnen* (gymnastics). The large number of *Turner* (gymnasts) were part of a national movement that had actively promoted the political unification of the German people and democratization of society. The conservative *Turner* reacted to the arrival of English sport(s) initially with indifference which quickly turned into open hostility and led to a controversial public debate between *Turner* and the supporters of the new concept of sport.[3]

The key argument of the *Turner* in this debate was sport's lack of an ideological basis. They saw games like football as a set of mechanical activities, which had no deeper meaning and lacked a distinctive spiritual underpinning. Furthermore, sport was ridiculed as an unhealthy and decadent leisure activity without positive virtues fostering only specialization, exaggerated selfishness, competitiveness and the principle of individual achievement. The narrow and focused training of athletes and the emerging commercialization and professionalization in English football grounds and boxing rings were also criticized. This thinking reflects an emerging Anglophobia and must be seen against the background of intense political and economic competition between the two major industrial powers in Europe, namely Britain and Germany during the Wilhelmine Empire.[4]

These conservative forces of German society were, however, unable to stop the triumphal march of modern sport and the final quarter of the nineteenth century witnessed a number of changes, particularly a revolution in popular habits. The first to take up and play soccer on a fairly regular basis as a part of the extra-curricular activities in their schools were the sons of the German middle class. Subsequently, male adult members of the middle class started to found the first clubs. However, 'football's break-through in Germany was, by and large, less a result of private middle class initiative'[5] but rather of the emergence of workers' sports clubs and associations. From the 1920s onwards it became the sport of the German industrial working class, particularly in the

Ruhr area, a heavily industrialized region dominated by coal mining and the steel production in North Rhine Westphalia, which is still a dominant geographical stronghold of the game. 'The peak of (working class) club foundations then was in the 1920s, immediately after the successful fight for the 8-hour-working-day'[6] in 1919. These clubs put a lot of effort into generating a distinctive identity. This is reflected, for example, in the careful selection of the name of the club, in the choice of a distinctive colour combination and the club banners. A very common type of name from the beginning contained the aim, the place and the year of foundation of the club. Clubs intending to express their close link to a certain area or region usually added names such as 'Bayern' (Bavaria), 'Westfalia' (Westphalia), 'Preussen' or 'Borussia' (both Prussia). Particularly popular were names which included a specific attitude or character quality such as 'Vorwärts' (forwards), 'Wacker' (brave), 'Viktoria' and 'Fortuna' (referring to the goddesses of victory and fate, respectively) or a term which stressed the principle of comradeship and cohesion of the group such as 'Sportfreunde' (sport friends), 'Eintracht' or 'Concordia' (both harmony).[7]

In some cases the chosen colours became synonyms for, and interchangeable with, the club name like 'the Royal Blue' (SV Schalke 04) or 'the Red Devils' (Kaiserslautern), 'the Zebras' (MSV Duisburg) or the 'Black-Yellows' (Dortmund). Flags and pennants also played an important role. They were often made by the local female supporters themselves and, thus, were very likely to have a characteristic shape. All these props were supposed to symbolize the cultural tradition of a club which in fact was achieved by a variety of common activities, 'such as playing together, participating in excursions and celebrating together'.[8]

This widespread enthusiasm for football clubs in working-class areas can only be explained with reference to the socio-historical context and development of these regions. The history of the Ruhr area, for example, is a history of continuous migration. At the turn of this century due to the emergence and expansion of industrial production in this region there was an enormous demand for additional workers who came from all over central Europe, particularly from areas which had once been Prussia. 'While in 1861 there were altogether 16 (!) Polish living in the counties of Rhineland and Westphalia, this number increased to more than 30,000' in 1910. In 1907, in many mines the proportion of workers from the old German eastern areas and from Poland was higher than 50%.'[9] By 1914, more than three million people lived in this region, with almost half a million working in the mining industry. These people faced two related dilemmas: the rapidity of social change and the lack of a common cultural tradition. Against this context football clubs provided the potential to develop communal relationships and a sense of belonging. In addition, they provided a framework to perform cultural practices which were often borrowed from their traditional rural communities they had left.

However, the popularity of this new sport was not restricted to the industrial North-Rhine Westphalia. In the South of Germany, Nuremberg emerged as an early power house which attracted large crowds. In 1920, the match between Nuremberg and their local rivals Fürth in Frankfurt drew a crowd of 35,000 people. It was also one of the first matches for which extra trains were provided. Already in the early 1920s Nuremberg supporters, mostly industrial workers, were well known for causing trouble on the terraces.[10]

The Suppression of Working-Class Football (Supporters)

The above mentioned rivalry between *Turnen* and sport was also an integral part of the conflicts between German middle and working classes. Working-class organizations suffered from severe suppression by the state between 1878 and 1890 due to the Anti-Socialist Laws that prohibited the activities of Socialist, Communist and working-class organizations, including sport and gymnastic clubs. This changed with the new constitution of the Weimar Republic (1918–33) which provided a liberal legal framework and opportunities for self-organization. Consequently, the interest of the German working class in establishing their own football clubs rose dramatically during this period. This was widely and systematically supported by Weimar state institutions which allied themselves with the working-class demand for exciting leisure activities against the remaining protagonists of rigorous state control and suppression – an alliance which allowed the proletariat in the first instance to gain greater access to physically active forms of leisure and in a later stage to dominate some sports, such as football.[11]

The German Football Association (DFB), however, remained rather sceptical concerning the far-reaching democratic reforms of the Weimar Republic.[12] Since its inauguration the DFB's policies had been decided by a small group of conservative and elitist middle-class men. Consequently, the rise of working-class football during the 1920s was perceived to be a threat to the established order and leading members desperately attempted to consolidate their privileged positions. The subsequent policies and measures of the DFB affected both working-class players and supporters. The latter's behaviour was frequently used as a pretext for some drastic measures.[13]

When it became obvious in the early 1920s that the new working-class clubs, such as Schalke 04 based in Gelsenkirchen in the Ruhr area, were going to dominate the football scene, the West German Football Association, a regional subdivision of the DFB, decided in 1923 to introduce a policy entitled 'The New Way'. This policy suspended any promotion and relegation for two years. Officially, the rationale behind this measure was to counteract the increasingly unfair and violent behaviour on and off the pitch resulting from the growing competitiveness among the teams. The aim was to improve the standards of behaviour of both players and spectators. Although newspaper articles frequently reported violent outbreaks during football matches, for many 'The New Way' was a policy taken to secure the dominant position of bourgeois clubs whilst stopping the proletarian clubs on their way to success and fame.[14]

Furthermore, the concept of amateurism played an important role in the escalating battle between DFB and working-class organizations. Only football clubs whose players were amateurs could become a member of the DFB. Professionals were defined as those players who received money or goods as rewards, broken time payments, who taught football in order to earn a living or who accepted reimbursements for travel expenses which were beyond the actual costs incurred. Although already at the beginning of the twentieth century a few clubs had started to charge admission fees, the question of amateurism and professionalism became a pressing issue only in the 1920s when spectator sports, such as football, experienced an enormous boom. In 1922, 35,000 spectators witnessed the goalless football match between Hungary and Germany in Bochum and two years later 40,000 people had gathered in Duisburg to see Italy beating Germany 1-0. After Schalke 04 had opened their own football ground in Gelsenkirchen in 1928 the team regularly drew more than 30,000 spectators.[15]

The increasing popularity of football as a spectator sport clearly undermined the amateur ethos as players started to demand their share of the gate money. Although it was no secret that many received illegal payments, the DFB was not prepared to move away from the rigid amateurism clause. As a consequence, rules, regulations and punishments became more extensive, detailed and draconian.[16] On the other hand, this attitude did not prevent the DFB from charging admission fees for international games.

In 1930, Schalke 04 became a prominent victim of the DFB's crusade against professionalism as an inquiry found evidence of illegal payments, gifts and loans to many of its first team's players and declared them to be professionals. This meant that they were excluded from participating in any DFB competitions and, as almost all of them had working-class origins, were driven into unemployment. In addition, they had to pay large fines and Schalke's board of directors was urged to retire. Subsequently, Schalke's treasurer committed suicide. However, the public uproar of a whole region and the threat of a breakaway league forced the DFB to ease the draconian punishment so that one year later most of the players were rehabilitated and allowed to play again.[17] The first match of the reinstated first team of Schalke 04 took then place on 1 June 1931 in front of 70,000 spectators and was a friendly against Fortuna Düsseldorf.

A Nation (of Football Fans) is Re-born – The Miracle of Berne

The 1954 World Cup took place in Switzerland and ended with one of the biggest surprises of modern football history. In the final the underdog, Germany, won against the runaway favourite, Hungary, one of the outstanding teams of this tournament showing everything that good soccer is about: superb technical skills, perfect cooperation, physical toughness, speed and endurance, imagination and determination.[18]

This success comes even more as a surprise considering that Germany's players were still amateurs and that the country did not even have a national league. Since the Allies had allowed Germans to play football again, it was played in five *Oberligen* (regional leagues). From September 1947 there had been four of these regional leagues (Berlin, North, West and South). One year later the French authorities agreed to a fifth Oberliga (South-West). Clubs in the east of Germany, which was occupied and administered by the Russian armed forces, played in the Berlin league but were withdrawn from there after the end of the 1949–50 season. In May 1949 a new democratic constitution for the Federal Republic of Germany had been finalized and five months later, in October, the German Democratic Republic came into existence, which started its own *Oberliga*.[19]

For the national coach, Sepp Herberger, these fragmented organizational structures were a real problem as the regional leagues were usually dominated by one or two outstanding clubs whose best players remained fairly unchallenged during most of the season. For the stars of these teams, real competitive matches began only in April when the nationwide finals started. Football's popularity, however, did not suffer from this set-up. The 1951 final between Kaiserslautern and Münster attracted a record audience of 85,000 people and a year later 84,000 spectators watched Stuttgart beating Saarbrücken.

However, the lack of a national league in the 1950s meant that local and regional rivalries were much stronger developed than national rivalries. Supporters were primarily local patriots displaying an explicit parochialism and an enthusiastic involvement in local and regional football affairs.[20] However, up to the early 1950s they were fairly unaware of, and often uninterested in, international football. This changed dramatically with the 1954 World Cup in Switzerland.

Although there were a few thousand German spectators in the Wankdorf Stadium in the Swiss capital and despite record sales of television sets in Germany (a considerable rise from about 11,500 to more than 84,000) the vast majority of football supporters experienced this match on the radio, listening to the journalist Herbert Zimmermann. His words during the 90 minute match were full of self-doubt, guilt-ridden undertones, modesty and resignation, respect for and admiration of the Hungarian team, hope and eventually uninhibited emotional outbreaks of joy – very much a reflection of, and in tune with, the emotional state of the millions of his listeners. His description and commentary of the third and decisive German goal makes compelling listening:

> Schäfer nach innen geflankt …
> Kopfball … abgewehrt
> Aus dem Hintergrund müsste Rahn schiessen! … Rahn schiesst!
> Tor! Tor! Tor! Tor!
> (Schäfer delivers a cross into the penalty box …
> header … cleared
> Rahn should shoot from deep! … Rahn shoots.
> Goal! Goal! Goal! Goal!)

And eight seconds later:

> Tor für Deutschland! Linksschuss von Rahn. Drei zu zwei führt Deutschland fünf Minuten vor dem Spielende. Halten Sie mich für verrückt, halten Sie mich für übergeschnappt!
>
> (Goal for Germany. Left footed shot by Rahn. Germany leads three to two five minutes before the end of the match. Call me crazy, call me insane!)

It is not his resemblance to some contemporary South-American TV and radio journalists who tend to repeat the term 'GOL' endlessly which makes his coverage so interesting. It is much more the combination of total emotional involvement with the politically correct detachment to the new nation state. According to Zimmermann's description it was Germany who were leading the Hungarians but not 'we' or 'us', although he later used the phrase 'our team' several times. Zimmerman became a legend in his own right as he did not only describe what he saw on the pitch but also what he felt. Due to its historical significance the broadcast was later printed on vinyl and sold very well. Most older Germans can actually recite most of these lines as if they were a poem.

Shortly after the end of the match as part of the presentation ceremony the German anthem was played. Large parts of the crowds joined in and sang the deeply nationalistic and now taboo first verse instead of the inoffensive third verse which had officially replaced it in the new Germany. However, as this decision had only been taken in 1952 the lyrics of the third verse were still largely unknown. East German and Swiss radio stations, however, immediately interrupted their coverage and the incident gave the World Cup winners a bad press in some European countries.[21]

Only a few days after winning the World Cup the head of the DFB caused the next stir with a victory speech which was full of nationalistic metaphors, chauvinistic language, revisionist propaganda and Nazi rhetoric. His speech awoke such a lot of unpleasant memories that Munich's radio station stopped its transmission in horror. Later he was reprimanded by the West German president.

Much more pleasant and full of uninhibited joy was the return journey of the players. The route of their train was lined with thousands of fans who wanted to gain a glimpse of their heroes. Most train stations and platforms on their way were overcrowded with celebrating people. When the players returned to their home towns the reception was sensational: in Munich half a million of people turned up, in Kaiserslautern more than 100,000 and in Düsseldorf almost 200,000.[22] For the first time since the end of the Second World War Germans felt a sense of genuine pride as well as belonging and, most of all, were not concerned about displaying it.

There is no doubt that Germany's first World Cup title in 1954 is of enormous social, cultural and national significance as this success contributed significantly to the promotion of a national identity.[23] For many commentators the new Federal Republic of Germany was in fact born on 4 July 1954, five years after the democratic constitution marked the official foundation of another German state.

The New Football (Fan) Order

Eventually, the German Football Association had to relinquish its resistance towards professionalism and commercialization in the 1960s due to the emigration of top players (primarily to Italy), the introduction of the European Champions Cup in 1956 and the lack of success in European club competitions. In 1963 a national league, the *Bundesliga*, comprising 16 clubs with professional players was introduced. It took another five years before the maximum transfer fees were abolished, and from 1972 onwards, players were also allowed to earn whatever their employers were prepared to pay them. These fundamental changes were caused and accompanied by the increasing internationalization and televisation of football, which led to a gradual disintegration of the social and cultural roots of the game. Consequently, in each big town or city one major representative club emerged.[24] The majority of the traditional small suburban clubs perished, that is, they were downgraded to be providers of home-grown talents. So, most of the local clubs that dominated German soccer in the first half of this century ceased to be symbolic extensions of the local community.

The opponents of this modernization had always argued that the professionalization and commercialization of the game would have disastrous consequences. In the summer of 1971 their worst fears became reality when evidence emerged that several matches of the previous season (1970–71) had been fixed and that large sums of cash had changed hands. The subsequent investigation revealed that more than one million Deutschmark had changed hands in order to manipulate the outcome of 18 matches. Two clubs, two managers, five administrators and 52 players from seven clubs were punished. Offenbach and Bielefeld lost their licences, whilst Berlin, Braunschweig and Schalke suffered severely through their top players being banned. A small number of players were no longer eligible for the national squad and missed out on the 1974 World Cup.[25] But most importantly, the reputation of German football and the comparatively young *Bundesliga* had been tarnished severely. In the following season the fans voted with their feet and attendance figures of the 1972–73 season reached a historic low. On average only 16,000 people went to see *Bundesliga* matches.[26]

Despite the public's outrage about the greediness of several individual players, the organizational structures of professional football were largely to blame for this scandal. The greatest weakness of the relatively new *Bundesliga* was that relegated teams moved straight into one of the (mostly semi-professional) regional divisions. This usually resulted in considerable financial losses from which clubs struggled to recover. Furthermore, outdated stipulations of maximum wages also contributed to the financial temptation of many players. The German Football Association drew similar conclusions and abolished maximum wages (1,200 Deutschmarks per month, including bonuses) in 1972.[27] Two years later the 'Second Bundesliga' was introduced, comprising one northern and one southern division.

Hosting and winning the 1974 World Cup also helped to reconcile German fans. In addition, it provided the young modernization process with an extraordinary boost as this tournament showed openly that 'big business' had entered and become an essential part of the football world. Never before had so many players been involved in advertising and marketing campaigns, publicly praising the benefits of certain petrol brands, toys, sweets and many other products. Top earners in this area were Franz Beckenbauer, Gerd Müller and Günther Netzer.

All these developments had a major impact on the social and cultural position of football in German society, particularly on its supporter base. The working-class roots of the game slowly disintegrated and the game gradually started to adjust to middle-class culture. The players, once local heroes, became national (a few even international) stars; the supporters turned into fans; the clubs changed into businesses. This gradual loss of economic and social closeness between clubs and supporters changed their relationship dramatically. While the early players and supporters knew each other, lived in the same area and had the same social background, from the late 1960s onwards it was increasingly anonymity and distant admiration that characterized the relationship between star and fan.[28] Thus, their commitment to the club changed fundamentally. While in the past the bond had been emotional and personal, and club life an integral part of the local community celebrating coherence and solidarity, the modern era increasingly needed synthetic symbols, such as flags, kits, badges or scarves to display support and closeness and to bridge the growing distance between team and fans. However, the artificial nature of these props lacked the intensity of the traditional relationship between local community and team. Consequently, an important opportunity for individuals to locate themselves socially and culturally gradually disappeared.

These dramatic and far-reaching changes that football was undergoing in the late 1960s and early 1970s must be seen against the context of changing consumption patterns, and the (re-) emergence of the leisure and entertainment industry in Germany at the same time. Reduction in working hours and increased affluence during the period of reconstruction after the Second World War meant that leisure time became time for consumption. Particularly, the Germany of the 1960s and 1970s experienced the emergence and growth of a new consumer culture. Consequently, the leisure industry with all its different branches boomed.

Although professional football is economically and legally not a branch of the entertainment industry this sport started to compete with traditional forms of entertainment for new customers. Taylor observed with reference to the English game that this 'process involved a transformation of the stereotype of the football supporter. Where once the stereotypical supporter was a working-class man, living for Saturday and inextricably involved – in his own perception – with the fortunes of the club, now he was of undefined class membership'.[29] This description is equally applicable to the German context. Subsequently, the social composition of the spectators in the football grounds became more complex and less homogenous.

Raymond Williams showed that there are three possible cultural relationships between an individual and a social group or institution.[30] Applying this system to the realm of football, it is possible to differentiate between consumers, customers and members. According to Charles Critcher, a member,

> however illusorily, thinks of himself as a member, and may recognise an informal set of reciprocal duties and obligations between himself and the institution. The customer, more detached, is seeking satisfaction for specific wants: if they are not met over a certain period of time, he may, somewhat reluctantly, take his patronage elsewhere. But the consumer has no loyalty or habit. He is informed of the choices open to him, and when he wants something will make a rational decision about where he will get the best bargain.[31]

While the majority of traditional supporters certainly belonged to the group of 'members' the successful efforts of football clubs to win new target groups meant that 'numerically, the fans gradually step back behind the consumers'.[32] The Association of Active Football Fans (BAFF) estimates that since the early 1990s only about 15 per cent of the football audiences in German stadia are traditional (young) fans.[33]

This process caused a number of contradictions and tensions which are most obvious and clearly visible on match days. Whilst many football stadiums are very modern and high-tech architectural temples (for example, the new state-of-the-art venues in Munich and Gelsenkirchen, the latter even having a retractable roof, or the enlarged and modernized Westfalienstadion in Dortmund), in 16 out 18 stadiums fans are still allowed to stand. On match day the Westfalienstadion in Dortmund with a total capacity of over 80,000 looks like something from the 1970s as it is usually packed with nearly

25,000 standing fans. Behind the terraces there is a huge pile of plastic seats that can be temporarily fitted for European and international matches that have to be all-seater.

In comparison to many other European countries, ticket prices are still very reasonable across Germany, that is, they are set at a level ordinary people can afford with reductions of up to 50 per cent available for pensioners, students and the unemployed. Consequently, the whole age spectrum is usually represented at a match. In many cities the ticket price includes free public transport to and from the stadium. On the other hand the name of many stadia no longer reflects their geographical location but displays the name of one of the club's sponsors, for example, the Veltins (beer) Arena in Gelsenkirchen, the AOL Arena in Hamburg, the RheinEnergie Stadium in Cologne and the Allianz (insurance) Arena in Munich.

Although professional football in Germany is highly commercialized with a few clubs even quoted on the stock market, most stadia are still owned by the local councils which regard them (and their team) as prestige objects. Despite the ailing German economy and the financial crisis of many local authorities, to let the local football ground decay is unthinkable. Consequently, Germany never had an Ibrox (1971), Bradford (1985) or Hillsborough (1989) disaster.[34]

European Role Models and Influences

From the 1980s to the mid 1990s the subcultural style of young German football fans was largely a mirror image of their English counterparts.[35] Many of their first chants were translations of English songs and the first mass-produced scarves that were sold in Germany were manufactured in Britain.[36] For German fans, visiting a football match in the English 'First Division' was the climax in their fan career. Subsequently, from the mid 1990s onwards, however, German fans increasingly incorporated subcultural practices of the Italian Ultras in their behaviour. This is closely linked to a major generational shift on German football terraces,[37] the far-ranging changes English football went through in the early 1990s, in particular the gradual introduction of all-seater stadia from 1992 onwards, and the increased media coverage of Italian football through private television stations.

Traditionally, the outfit of young German fans comprises football shirts, kits, jumpers, coats, scarves, wristbands, (baseball) caps and/or hats in their team's colours. Very often, the club emblem is attached as a badge or small flag. More recently, it has become popular to temporarily colour hair and face in the club's colours; fairly rare but growing in popularity are tattoos. Mostly as an act of provocation many fans very wear Che Guevara stickers or badges of the Red Army Faction, a well-known post Second World War left-wing terrorist organization, next to fascist symbols, such as the swastika.[38] A large number of fans wear personalized football shirts with the name and number of a specific player on the back. These polyester symbols of admiration and identification have seen the most dramatic growth in popularity in the early 1990s.

The fairly uniform outward appearance not only demonstrates their allegiance to a certain team, which is at the heart of football fandom, but also contributes to a sense of belonging among fans on the terraces. The 'increased longing for group, for like-minded peers, for community'[39] must be seen against the context of the increasing individualization in modern societies and the relatively unstructured transitional phase of life these young people have to cope with. This illusionary membership of a large group of like-minded individuals helps young people to cope with the challenges of their transitional life stage. The public demonstration of partisanship requires, in turn, a high degree of loyalty towards other fans with the same reference object. So the voluntary uniformity of these fans contributes significantly to their solidarity and creates strong peer pressures which provide the basis for their collective behaviour.

The way many fans orchestrate their appearance clearly shows that physical strength and aggressive masculinity are core elements of their body perception.[40] Considering the technological changes that have undermined the centrality of muscular strength to industrial production and also the increasing interest of the middle class in body building, particularly in 'body shaping' and 'body styling', this celebration of physical strength and power appears to be rather conservative and outdated.

The most striking feature of modern football grounds usually is the constant level of noise consisting of regularly occurring chants and songs, whistling and rhythmic clapping. This ritualistic singing and chanting usually starts hours before the kick off and only ends when the last groups have split up long after the end of the match. These songs and chants comprise a mixture of witty comments, insults and defamations of the opponents, encouragement and praise for their own team, disappointment and despair, provocations and ridicule, as well as optimism and dreams. On a superficial level, all these songs and chants express the fans' affiliation and commitment to a specific team. However, on a deeper level, the underlying themes of these verbal expressions are dominance, superiority, courage and invincibility. They demonstrate not only an (imaginary) symbiotic relationship between supporters and team but also show an omnipotent self-perception. Since opponents are a potential threat to this identity and the fragile illusion of closeness, their marginal status as well as inferiority are recurring themes.[41]

The growing popularity of the subcultural practices of the Italian Ultras among German football fans can be seen in various respects. Since the mid 1990s, flags have become larger and more imaginative. Very often they look like colourful political banners and contain short messages. Due to their size and weight they are supported by two poles (one on each side) and carried by two fans. Whilst traditionally many fans carried small copies of the official, industrially produced club's flag with them, nowadays they are often hand-made patch work. The dominant feature is obviously the colour combination of one's team and its official emblem and/or the club's name. Many fans, however, have added other culturally important visual symbols. Particularly popular are the official flags of the native countries of the foreign players. Other supporters have sewn the name of their group onto the fabric whilst some banners highlight the club's achievements. These impressive visual symbols have gained the regular attention of television crews, who are keen to include pictures from colourful terraces in their reports. In some stadia an official parade of the most imaginative and largest flags shortly before kick-off has become an integral part of the proceedings. Given the marginal status of fans in the world of football, this exposure is very likely to produce a significant sense of power or, at least, a feeling of success as visibility is a key theme and aim of Ultra groups. This desire to be visible and noticed also explains the regular employment of colourful fireworks, smoke grenades and large banners. Although most Ultras claim that their behaviour is fun and action-oriented, spontaneous and creative, some groups even rehearse their short performances for weeks before they display it in the football ground. This applies for example to the clapping of specific rhythms and the choreography of movements of large groups on the terraces. A few of these fans spend most of the 90 minutes with their back to the pitch in order to initiate, direct and coordinate certain activities. Whilst some of them communicate their instructions through megaphones, in Frankfurt the Ultras even use a PR system to organize their activities. Comparing and judging the choreographic performances and visual installations of the opposing Ultra groups is for this new breed of fans as important as the actual football match. Almost all Ultra groups have their own web pages which document their activities on photos and video clips, and provide a forum for self-presentation, discussion and the exchange of information.[42] There are several other striking differences between the Ultras and the previous generation of fans: Whilst their predecessors employed a variety of politically provocative symbols, the Ultras draw on more contemporary cultural icons and themes, for example, the 'Simpsons' and 'South Park', and employ a much more left-wing, liberal rhetoric. There is also a considerably larger number of young women involved in the Ultra groups. Furthermore, the consumption of alcohol does not play an important role. Instead marijuana and hashish appear to be more popular.

There is no doubt that these new patterns of fan behaviour represent a massive generational shift on the terraces. It also demonstrates that the admiration, attractiveness and role model function of English fans have decreased considerably. 'So far, the German Ultras perceive themselves as politically independent fans and stay clear of the rightwing shift among their Italian role models. They are primarily concerned with an improvement and revitalization of the fan culture.'[43] In contrast to the previous fan generation the Ultras appear to be more interested in the politics of club management, are often very critical, do not hesitate publicly to voice their concerns, question decisions and take action. The near bankruptcy of one of Germany's top clubs, Borussia Dortmund, in early 2005 caused the home-grown Ultras to regularly organize rallies and demonstrations in the city centre and outside the football ground. At one point, a blockade of all the stadium exits forced players and management into dialogue with the fans concerning business policies, attitudes as well as salaries of those centrally involved in and responsible for this crisis. This combination of devotion and critical detachment, creative improvisation and rehearsed performances is a promising mixture and exciting base for the future development of a versatile and varied fan culture in Germany.

Nation, Nationality and Nationalism

However, less promising and entertaining but rather disturbing is the behaviour of some German fans in the context of international football matches. Their display of nationalist, chauvinist and racist attitudes is often combined with hooligan behaviour, particularly in foreign countries. Although this development had already commenced in the mid 1980s, German hooliganism became most visible to the world at the 1988 European Championships on home soil. A few years later the right-wing and neo-Nazi elements of German hooliganism received a considerable boost through German 're-unification' and the subsequent uncritical, public celebration of *Volk und Vaterland* (people and fatherland) by politicians of all major parties.

In the early 1990s, violent incidents at international level involving German hooligans occurred in the context of matches against France, the Netherlands, Belgium and Poland. This new style of international football violence, which combines aggressive and often violent expressions of masculinity with the exaggerated celebration of the national community, led to two matches being cancelled: the first against a selection of East-German players in December 1990 to celebrate the 're-unification' of German football, and the other against England in 1994, originally scheduled for 20 April, Adolf Hitler's birthday. Although the German Football Association initiated and contributed to a few anti-racist and anti-xenophobic PR campaigns, for example, 'Mein Freund ist Ausländer' (My friend is a foreigner), to plan a friendly against England on that date clearly displays a high degree of political naivety and a lack of historical sensitivity. However, such ineptness is an integral part of the 100 year history of German Football Association. During the 1978 World Cup in Argentina, the then president of the DFB, Herrman Neuberger, invited the former Nazi fighter pilot Hans Ulrich Rudel, although exiled in South America still an icon of German neo-Nazis, to visit the German team's camp, while not allowing Günter Netzer, a former top-class player who worked as a journalist, access.[44] Equally embarrassing are statements of the current DFB president, Gerhard Mayer-Vorfelder, a well known right-wing member of Germany's conservative party (CDU), in which he regrets the loss of German colonies as otherwise Southwest-Africans would be eligible to play for the national team.[45]

In 1998, more than 600 German hooligans, among them 80 neo-Nazis, were in Lens for the crucial match between Germany and Yugoslavia at the World Cup in France. One of their favourite chants 'Wir sind wieder einmarschiert' (We have invaded France again) left no doubt about their ideological orientation. When French police officers attempted to restrain the hooligans, one small group slipped into a side street where David Nivel, a 44-year-old French Gendarme, and a colleague were posted. The hooligans surrounded Nivel and beat him with a metal rod. The beating lasted only a minute but left Nivel blind in one eye, speech-impaired and with difficulties concentrating. The hooligans involved in this incident, one of them a well-know neo-Nazi, were later convicted and given sentences ranging from three-and-a-half to ten years in prison.

In 2000 at the European Championships in the Netherlands and Belgium, it was the turn of the Belgian town of Charleroi to count the cost of German hooliganism. Despite moving the potentially volatile clash between England and Germany to a stadium better equipped to cope with partisan fans, the authorities did not foresee the anarchy that would reduce the town centre to a war-zone when the two rival 'firms' met in the alcohol-drenched hours before the game.

Most recently, in March 2005 when Germany played Slovenia in a friendly match in preparation for the World Cup 2006 over 40 German hooligans were arrested in the wake of rioting involving over 200 fans before, during and after the match in Celje. The violence raised fears of a resurgent hooligan element preparing to disrupt the global soccer festival in Germany in 2006. However, complex ticket regulations, stadium bans for trouble-makers, fast track court proceedings and undercover officers are intended to prevent such events from happening.

What these violent events at international football matches have in common is that they are initiated and driven by a group of German hooligans with an explicit right-wing agenda and fascist ideological underpinning. The matches of the national side have been viewed by these right wingers as the symbolically most appropriate forum for the expression of their nationalistic excesses. In 1996, 57 years after the invasion of Poland, a friendly took place between the German and the Polish national side in Zabrze, only about 30km away from one of the largest concentration camp of the Fascist era, Auschwitz. During the German occupation of Poland the local football stadium was called 'Adolf Hitler Arena'. German hooligans welcomed and celebrated this opportunity with the public demonstration of the Hitler salute whilst singing the first verse of the national anthem, the singing of the Horst Wessel Lied (a once poplar fascist song) and the visual and verbal display of anti-Semitic slogans such as 'Schindler Juden – Wir grüssen euch' (Schindler Jews – We greet you), 'Wir fahren nach Polen, um Juden zu versohlen' (We come to Poland to beat up Jews), or 'Heute gehört uns Deutschland, morgen die ganze Welt' (Today we own Germany, tomorrow the whole world).[46]

This is in stark contrast to *Bundesliga* matches where organized extreme right-wing organizations hardly play a role. Academic research and police intelligence agree that only a very small number of *Bundesliga* clubs are supported by fan groups with an explicit right-wing or fascist ideological underpinning, and the repeated recruitment activities of several right-wing political organizations and parties in German football grounds have always remained unsuccessful. This does not mean that German fans are immune from racist, xenophobic, anti-Semitic, nationalist and fascist ideas; quite the opposite: ideologies like these that provide simple answers to often very complex questions are undeniably popular among German football fans. This is clearly reflected in the frequent racist and xenophobic abuse of (opposing) players which draws on traditional conventions of 'race',[47] the systematic and subtle use of fascist symbols and the often homophobic songs and chants.

Conclusion

There are not many activities that have a more central place in the national culture of Germany than football. Played by hundreds of thousands, watched by millions, the game enriches people's daily conversation with a fascinating topic, vivid descriptions and enthusiastic involvement. Soccer features prominently on the title pages of the print media and the broadcasting programmes of the mass media. Despite the very recent corruption scandal in German football watching soccer matches is more popular than ever before. For the 2005–06 season the 18 *Bundesliga* clubs sold 376,045 season tickets. Twelve years ago, only about 150,000 people purchased season tickets. Compared to the first match day of previous seasons, the 391,527 people who turned up to support their team on the first August weekend in 2005 created a new record, as never before had so many spectators attended the nine matches on the first day of the season. Towards the end of the last season the *Bundesliga* in fact celebrated its highest attendance figure ever when 416,730 people went through the turnstiles.

Football fandom in Germany has undergone a number of significant changes during the last 100 years. The first part of this essay tried to capture some of these more historical aspects whilst the second part focused on the post-war developments, in particular the emergence of a new, more differentiated spectator culture whose most colourful and conspicuous sections are made up of young people. Their distinctive and often very colourful subcultural style, their cultural practices and activities in the context of football matches integrate some interesting historical as well as cross-cultural influences.

Despite the obvious tensions and contradictions in the world of commercial and professional German football, fans and spectators have always been treated differently in order to avoid their total alienation through pay-TV, absurdly inflated ticket prices and kick-off times tailored to suit media interests. Football in Germany has been largely inclusive rather than exclusive. And yet, there is an ugly side to football fandom in Germany which is dominated by hooligans and right-wing groups who – in the context of international matches – regularly remind people of the darkest chapters of German history.

Notes

[1]   In addition, there are a small number of foreign managers: the Italian Giovanni Trappatoni is, for example, in charge at Stuttgart, whilst the Dutch Bert Van Merwijk manages Dortmund.
[2]   For more details on the complex German history and the search for a national identity see, Dann, *Nation und Nationalismus in Deutschland 1770–1990*.
[3]   A thoroughly researched and extremely detailed analysis can be found in Eisenberg, '*English Sports' und Deutsche Bürger. Eine Gesellschaftsgeschichte 1800–1939*.
[4]   Merkel, 'The Politics of Physical Culture and German Nationalism: *Turnen* versus English Sports and French Olympism'.
[5]   Eisenberg, 'The Middle Class and Competition', 265.
[6]   Lindner and Breuer, *Sind doch nicht alles Beckenbauers*, 9.
[7]   For a detailed analysis of the construction of the names of German football clubs see Hesse-Lichtenberger, *Tor! – The Story of German Football*, 28–32.
[8]   Hickethier, 'Der synthetische Fan', 94.
[9]   Lindner and Breuer, *Sind doch nicht alles Beckenbauers*, 35–7.
[10] Hesse-Lichtenberger, *Tor! – The Story of German Football*, 45–6.
[11] Merkel, 'Sport, Power and the State in Weimar Germany'.
[12] Heinrich, *Der Deutsche Fußballbund – Eine politische Geschichte*.
[13] Merkel, 'The Hidden History of the German Football Association (DFB): 1900–1950'.
[14] Gehrmann, *Fußball-Vereine-Politik. Zur Sportgeschichte des Reviers*, 95–6.
[15] For a detailed analysis of football in the Weimar Republic see Eggers, *Fussball in der Weimarer Republik*.

[16]   Schulze-Marmeling, *Der gezähmte Fußball – Zur Geschichte einer subversiven Sportart*, 53.

[17]   Gehrmann, *Fußball-Vereine-Politik. Zur Sportgeschichte des Reviers*, 99–101.

[18]   Huba, *Die Geschichte der Fussball-Weltmeisterschaft*.

[19]   Hesse-Lichtenberger, *Tor! – The Story of German Football*, 108–12.

[20]   Ibid., 116.

[21]   Schulze-Marmeling, *Die Geschichte der Fußball Nationalmannschaft*, 143.

[22]   Ibid., 144.

[23]   Heinrich, *Tooor! Toor! Tor! 40 Jahre 3:2*.

[24]   Merkel, 'Soccer Made in Germany: Solid, Reliable and Undramatic but Successful'.

[25]   Beck, 'Wir haben den Sumpf trocken gelegt', 433–5.

[26]   This dramatic decline in attendance figures might have also been influenced by the first reports about hooligan activities during the previous season, although they were fairly restricted to local derbys, most notably to matches between Dortmund and Schalke.

[27]   Heinrich, *Tooor! Toor! Tor! 40 Jahre 3:2*, 189.

[28]   Merkel, *Soccer Made in Germany: Solid, Reliable and Undramatic but Successful*, 99–103.

[29]   Taylor, 'Soccer Consciousness and Soccer Hooliganism', 163.

[30]   Williams, *The Long Revolution*.

[31]   Critcher, 'Football since the War', 227.

[32]   Hopf, *Fußball – Soziologie und Sozialgeschichte einer populären Sportart*.

[33]   Dembowski, 'Spieler kommen, Trainer gehen - Fans bleiben; Kleine Standortbestimmung des Fußballfans', 17.

[34]   Having said this, the history of German football fandom had its tragic events too. One of them happened on 24 March 1979 when more than 70 football fans were injured in Hamburg due to overcrowding on the terraces of the stadium. For a detailed account of the tragedy see Hesse-Lichtenberger, *Tor! – The Story of German Football*, 203.

[35]   Redhead, 'An Era of the End, or the End of an Era: Football and Youth Culture', 160–86.

[36]   Gabriel, 'Ultra Bewegungen in Deutschland', 180.

[37]   Scheidle (Ultratrecht)s in Italien, 92) claims that the vast majority of contemporary football fans are aged between 16 and 24 years.

[38]   For more information on the use of fascist symbols, activities of right-wing political groups, ethnic divisions in German sport, the marginal position of the large Turkish Community, etc. See Merkel, 'Sport in Divided Societies-The Case of the Old, the New and the 'Re-United' Germany'.

[39]   Pramann, *Fußballfans – Betrachtungen einer Subkultur*, 47.

[40]   Becker, 'Haut'se, Haut'se in'ne Schnauze – Das Fußballstadium als Ort der Reproduktion sozialer Strukturen', 80.

[41]   Ibid., 72–84.

[42]   Gabriel, 'Ultra Bewegungen in Deutschland', 189–91.

[43]   Scheidle, 'Ultra(recht)s in Italien', 98.

[44]   Hesse-Lichtenberger, *Tor! – The Story of German Football*, 198.

[45]   Schulze-Marmeling and Dahlkamp, 'Deutsche Tugenden', 462.

[46]   Buderus, 'Bild dir deine Meinung – Medien, Rassismus und Fussball', 46. Dembowski and Noack, 'Am Tatort Stadion – Neonazistische Beschleuniger in Deutschlands Fußballszenen', 110–13.

[47]   Merkel, Sombert and Tokarski, 'Football, Racism and Xenophobia in Germany : 50 Years Later – Here We Go Again?'

References

Beck, O. 'Wir haben den Sumpf trocken gelegt'. In *100 Jahre DFB – Die Geschichte des Deutschen Fußball-Bundes*, edited by Deutscher Fußball Bund. Berlin: Sportverlag Berlin, 1999.

Becker, P. 'Haut'se, Haut'se in'ne Schnauze – Das Fußballstadium als Ort der Reproduktion sozialer Strukturen.' In *Sport und Körperliche Gewalt,* edited by G.A. Pilz. Reinbek: Rowohlt Verlag, 1982.

Buderus, A. 'Bild dir deine Meinung – Medien, Rassismus und Fussball – Die vierte Gewalt als Katalysator einer rassistischen Grundströmung.' In *Tatort Stadion – Rassismus, Antisemitismus und Sexismus im Fußball,* edited by G. Dembowski and J. Scheidle. Köln: PapyRossa Verlag, 2002.

Critcher, C. 'Football since the War.' In *Popular Culture: Past and Present,* edited by B. Waites, T. Bennett and G. Martin. London: Croom Helm, 1982.

Dann, O. *Nation und Nationalismus in Deutschland 1770–1990.* Munich: Verlag C.H. Beck, 1996.

Dembowski, G. 'Spieler kommen, Trainer gehen – Fans bleiben; Kleine Standortbestimmung des Fußballfans.' In *Ballbesitz ist Diebstahl – Fans zwischen Kultur und Kommerz,* edited by Bündnis Aktiver Fussballfans. Göttingen: Verlag Die Werkstatt, 2004.

Dembowski, G. and R. Noack. 'Am Tatort Stadion – Neonazistische Beschleuniger in Deutschlands Fußballszenen.' In *Ballbesitz ist Diebstahl – Fans zwischen Kultur und Kommerz,* edited by Bündnis Aktiver Fussballfans. Göttingen: Verlag Die Werkstatt, 2004.

Eggers, E. *Fussball in der Weimarer Republik.* Kassel: Agon Sportverlag, 2001.

Eisenberg, C. 'The Middle Class and Competition: Some Considerations of the beginnings of Modern Sport in England and Germany.' *The International Journal of the History of Sport 7,* no.2 (1990): 265–82.

Eisenberg, C. *'English Sports' und Deutsche Bürger – Eine Gesellschaftsgeschichte 1800 – 1939.* Paderborn: Schöningh, 1999.

Gabriel, M. 'Ultra Bewegungen in Deutschland; Von Doppelhaltern und Choreografien – die Antwort der Kurve auf den Fußball als Event' In *Ballbesitz ist Diebstahl – Fans zwischen Kultur und Kommerz,* edited by Bündnis Aktiver Fussballfans. Göttingen: Verlag Die Werkstatt, 2004.

Gehrmann, S. *Fußball-Vereine-Politik. Zur Sportgeschichte des Reviers.* Essen: Reimar Hobbing Verlag, 1988.

Heinrich, A. *Tooor! Toor! Tor! 40 Jahre 3:2.* Nördlingen: Rotbuch Verlag, 1994.

Heinrich, A. *Der Deutsche Fußballbund – Eine politische Geschichte.* Köln: PapyRossa, 2000.

Hesse-Lichtenberger, U. *Tor! – The Story of German Football.* London: WSC Books, 2003.

Hickethier, K. 'Der synthetische Fan.' In *Der Fußballfan – Ansichten vom Zuschauer,* edited by R. Lindner. Frankfurt: Syndicat, 1980.

Hopf, W., ed. *Fussball – Soziologie und Sozialgeschichte einer populären Sportart.* Bensheim: Päd Extra, 1979.

Huba, K.-H., ed. *Die Geschichte der Fussball-Weltmeisterschaft – Stories, Daten Hintergründe.* Munich: Copress Verlag, 1990.

James, H. *A German Identity.* London: Weidenfeld and Nicolson, 1990.

Lindner, R. and H. Th. Breuer. *Sind doch nicht alles Beckenbauers.* Frankfurt: Syndicat Verlag, 1982.

Merkel, U. 'Soccer Made in Germany: Solid, Reliable and Undramatic but Successful.' In *Hosts and Champions – Soccer Cultures, National Identities and the World Cup in the USA,* edited by J. Sugden and A. Tomlinson. Avebury: Gower Press, 1994.

Merkel, U. 'Sport in Divided Nations – The Case of the old, new and "re-united" Germany.' In *Sport in Divided Societies,* edited by A. Bairner and J. Sugden. Aachen: Meyer and Meyer, 1998.

Merkel, U. 'The Hidden History of the German Football Association (DFB): 1900–1950.' *Soccer and Society 1,* no.2 (2000): 167–86.

Merkel, U. 'Sport, Power and the State in Weimar Germany.' In *Power Games – Theory and Method for a Critical Sociology of Sport,* edited by J. Sugden and A. Tomlinson. London: Routledge, 2002.

Merkel, U. 'The Politics of Physical Culture and German Nationalism: *Turnen* versus English Sports and French Olympism.' *German Politics and Society 21,* no.2 (2003): 69–96.

Merkel, U., K. Sombert and W. Tokarski. 'Football, Racism and Xenophobia in Germany: 50 Years Later – Here We Go Again?' In *Racism and Xenophobia in European Football,* edited by U. Merkel and W. Tokarski. Aachen: Meyer and Meyer, 1996.

Pramann, U. *Fußballfans – Betrachtungen einer Subkultur.* Hamburg: Stern-Bücher, 1983.

Redhead, S. 'An Era of the End, or the End of an Era: Football and Youth Culture.' In *British Football and Social Change – Getting into Europe,* edited by J. Williams and S. Wagg. Leicester: Leicester University Press, 1991.

Scheidle, J. 'Ultra(recht)s in Italien.' In *Tatort Stadion – Rassismus, Antisemitismus und Sexismus im Fußball,* edited by G. Dembowski and J. Scheidle. Köln: PapyRossa Verlag, 2002.

Schulze-Marmeling, D. *Der gezähmte Fußball – Zur Geschichte einer subversiven Sportart.* Göttingen: Verlag Die Werkstatt, 1992.

Schulze-Marmeling, D., ed. *Die Geschichte der Fußball Nationalmannschaft.* Göttingen: Verlag Die Werkstatt, 2004.

Schulze-Marmeling, D. and H. Dahlkamp. 'Deutsche Tugenden.' In *Die Geschichte der Fußball Nationalmannschaft,* edited by D. Schulze-Marmeling. Göttingen: Verlag Die Werkstatt, 2004.

Skrentny, W. 'Fußballstadien im Ruhrgebiet – Von der Kampfbahn zur Arena.' In *Im Land der tausend Derbys – Die Fußballgeschichte des Ruhrgebiets,* edited by H. Hering. Göttingen: Verlag Die Werkstatt, 2002.

Taylor, I. 'Soccer Consciousness and Soccer Hooliganism.' In *Images of Deviance,* edited by S. Cohen. London: Penguin, 1971.

Williams, R. *The Long Revolution.* Harmondsworth: Pelican, 1961.

Football Fans and Football History: A Review Essay

Russell Hargrave

Simon Kuper, *Ajax, the Dutch, the War: European Football During the Second World War* (London: Orion, 2003). Pp.256. £7.99 (paperback). ISBN 0752842749.

David Winner, *Those Feet: A Sensual History of English Football* (London: Bloomsbury, 2005). Pp.288. £14.99 (hardback). ISBN 0747547386.

Football and History

It is a commonplace to point out that in football, the greatest power resides with those institutions that have the most money: the richest clubs, the large international federations, and the television companies who have, over the last decade and a half, injected millions of pounds into the sport (although it should also be noted that football has always, to use a famous phrase, followed the money). Equally common is the related anxiety about the disenfranchisement of fans. Higher prices, we are constantly reminded, have frozen 'ordinary fans' out of the game, even as varying kick-off times have made attending these games more and more inconvenient.[1]

Less often commented upon, however, is the control that these big institutions can exercise over telling the history of the game. Football history never looks so attractive as when it is packaged up for sale in the club shop. Under this somewhat top-heavy system, fans are assumed to be little more than passive recipients of stories from the past, siphoned down to them in the form of glossy 'One Hundred Years of ...' books, grainy DVDs of great games from the past, and facsimile copies of match programmes that have somewhere along the line been deemed 'classic'. Football history has a downward trajectory, as the institutions that run the game also take control of its traditions, dictating to fans an officially-sanctioned history organized around what is most amenable to the paying customer. For their part, fans are invited to integrate themselves into this pre-existing, proud historical narrative.

The value of both books looked at in this review essay – Simon Kuper's *Ajax, the Dutch, the War: European Football in Europe During the Second War* and David Winner's *Those Feet: A Sensual History of English Football* – lies in a mutual suspicion of the football history made available in the club shop, and the attempt to construct in its place historical narratives drawn from fan culture. Both authors make sustained use of fans' voices, and allow alternative national football histories to emerge from disparate fragments of interviews, letters and anecdotes. Football history this time flows upward, derived from the curious and sometimes disturbing experiences of fans themselves.

To some extent, of course, all accounts of history have to delineate between what will be emphasized and what will be quietly passed-over, and it should be no surprise that football's 'official' historians too have pruned the past for whatever information proves most relevant to a given situation. But on what grounds are such decisions made? A quotation from Winner's book stands equally well for the inquisitive standpoint taken by both writers: 'Both in football and in wider culture the public, which prides itself on its collective memory, actually forgets important things and people all the time'.[2] The attempt to recover those 'important things and people' expediently forgotten from the public sphere is accompanied by an enlightening account of the sometimes very murky moral ideals served by forgetting them in the first place. The promotion of some stories to representative status, and the suppression of others, can be seen to enable the continuation of certain dangerous national myths. Every nation likes to believe in its own greatness – certainly, it seems to be the duty of any modern politician running for office to remind the nation's electorate that they want to *carry on* living somewhere great. Official football history can provide the perfect vehicle for this belief; but in these books Holland and England emerge as societies badly damaged by the events of the twentieth century, countries whose myth-making about the footballing past is marked by the struggle to deny the effects of war, and the pathos of imperial collapse.

Football under Occupation: Simon Kuper

Ajax, the Dutch, the War begins by recounting a disturbing rumour. In fact, two equally disturbing rumours. Firstly, that anti-Semitic chants and songs are becoming increasingly apparent among Dutch football fans during games featuring Ajax Amsterdam; and secondly, that Ajax itself was responding by 'hotly denying' any suggestion of a Jewish past with unseemly haste.[3] For Kuper, the very heat of the denial is intriguing in itself; asking around about Ajax and its Jewish connections has clearly touched a nerve. The primary task Kuper duly sets himself is to patiently unravel an alternative war-time history of the club, in which the Jewish culture at its heart is restored to its rightful place. Through evidence provided by letters, first-hand testimony and contemporary newspaper coverage, Kuper is able to reconstruct the experience of 'dozens' of fans who would leave the Jewish quarter of the city every Sunday during the 1920s and 1930s, loading themselves onto trams and heading for the Ajax stadium on the outskirts of town. At that time the only Jewish player at the club was an American outside-right called Eddy Hamel whose crosses, one fan recalls, were 'something like David Beckham's now'. The fourth chapter of the book traces Hamel's story, concluding with his murder at Birkenau concentration camp in 1943. Ajax's official publication for their 2000 jubilee season records instead that Hamel died before the war.

As I have already suggested, one type of football history, the 'official' one, can do much to suppress other versions of the past, which might contain stories less palatable to football fans today. In the case of Ajax, Kuper sees the club pandering to the casual anti-Jewish sentiments among opposition fans. Ajax's response to the anti-Semitism directed at them – that it is wrongheaded because Ajax has never been the 'Jewish club' that they suppose – simply plays into the hands of those who would rather see Holland's Jewish history denied. Kuper's tone is understated throughout, but here he states his opinion categorically: 'whenever Ajax denies its Jewish links, or tries to apologise for them, it is denying people who have been murdered'. The greatest achievement of this extraordinary book is the exposure of those lives and stories which lie just beneath the surface of a sustained cultural effort, across the Netherlands and elsewhere in Europe, to paper over the most unpleasant aspects of the past. Kuper is at pains to point out that football clubs are more or less the same as any other cultural institution in this sense. Fans, like consumers, will respond to ideas of 'heritage' and 'tradition' with great enthusiasm, provided that this heritage is sanitized into something easy to digest and morally uncomplicated. The modern history of occupied Europe is far from morally uncomplicated, however, and a little tweaking of the historical facts has often proved a useful way to sidestep difficult questions.

The subject of Jewish history – the very thing that Ajax has tried to 'tweak' out of history – is sometimes treated with light humour. In a recent book about the Jewish traditions inherited by his newborn son, Jonathan Freedland wonders 'what did it mean to make my son a part of a minnow people that had somehow produced some of the defining figures of Jewish history, from Moses to Jesus, Marx to Einstein and Freud?',[4] and it is entertaining to find a football fan in Israel using an almost identical statement on behalf of claims that Johann Cruijff is an 'honorary Israeli': 'We had Moses, Jesus, Freud and Einstein, so if something like that happens in football it has to have come from a Jew'. But it is the war-time suffering of Holland's Jews which lies at the heart of *Ajax, the Dutch, the War*, not least because the myth of timeless Dutch tolerance and liberalism has become such a durable piece of the nation's own official history. In the only chapter that dispenses with discussing football entirely, Kuper makes unflinching use of Hannah Arendt's *Eichmann in Jerusalem* ('the most intelligent piece of journalism I know'), and its groundbreaking research into the Netherlands's pitiful record on protecting its Jewish population.

The book nonetheless moves far beyond the myths sustained by Ajax and the Netherlands alone, and develops its comparison of official and unofficial football history in other contexts. The game between Germany and England in Berlin in May 1938, for example, has been long established in the English mindset as a moment of English triumph over German arrogance. Those remembering the game in this way have had to negotiate the tricky fact that the English players gave a Nazi salute before kick-off – 'that infamous photograph' is reproduced here – but having 'thumped' the home side 6-3, the publicly disseminated version of this match in history has transformed it into a day of pre-emptory resistance. Kuper quotes from Stanley Matthews's autobiography, in which a hostile crowd of SS thugs were silenced by the glorious performance of the English. Len Goulden scored an early volleyed goal: '"Let them salute that one," Len yelled as he carried on running, arms aloft'. But newspaper accounts of the game published in both Britain and Europe immediately afterwards, assiduously collected and presented by Kuper, contradict almost the whole story. The crowd was casual and friendly rather than partisan (as was normally the case during the 1920s and 1930s), and the minutes of the FA meetings about the game suggest that the salute was sanctioned and even encouraged by the English officials. By contrast, Matthews and his captain Eddie Hapgood tell of shouting-matches between officials from the two countries, in which the English backed down only with the determination to beat Germany even more soundly. On top of which, Germany simply weren't much good at football during the 1930s. It was their smaller neighbours Austria who dominated European football – Germany had lost to Scotland and then minnows Norway in the two games preceding the England match. They were not the scalp that Matthews and Hapgood later suggested.

The 'official' version of the game seems to mask a less attractive (and less dramatic) reality: a good English side travelled to Berlin and beat a less-than-average side very comfortably, in front of a generous and good-natured crowd. The English decided to salute Hitler, not in an outraged spirit but with no real idea of what else to do. But stories of English dogged resilience, especially in the face of adversity, have long dominated the official history of the English game (a topic dealt with in much more detail by David Winner). *This* version of events, however unsupportable in light of empirical evidence, has become the received wisdom about European football that day, according to which England's footballers took on the mighty Germans in their own backyard and proved mightier, prefiguring similar heroics in the war-years ahead.

One of the reasons this version of events has endured for so long is its quality as a story. It has all the right ingredients for being repackaged for future generations of England fans: age-old conflicts between good and evil in which – against the odds and to the despair of those who would oppress them – good wins through. But if this is an example of how football can construct for itself an official history quite unconnected to reality, Kuper also recounts scores of equally gripping but previously untold narratives from around European football and its fans. There are scores of stories weaved through *Ajax, the Dutch, the War* which collectively constitute an alternative history of

European football full of incredible but long forgotten events. One particularly memorable anecdote is that of an elderly Jewish fan called Herman Menco who, during 1942, risked his life once a week by leaving his bolt-hole in Rotterdam to watch Feyenoord play. Knowing that identification as a Jew would mean incarceration and in all likelihood death, he tried to melt into the crowds, relying upon the hope that no-one would trouble to identify one fan among so many. Few stories can make a comparable claim to fan-loyalty.[5] Among other fleeting figures are those who have achieved astonishing things on a football pitch (like the Polish footballer Ernst Willimowski who swiftly declared himself German when the Nazis invaded his country, and scored an unlikely-sounding 37 goals in five games for a German police team); or plain weird things off the pitch (an unnamed Israeli, a friend of Kuper's friend Shaul, who paid a Dutch prostitute to wear a Maccabi Tel Aviv shirt and let him beat her). One of Kuper's strengths is never to stray too far from the universally recognizable fabric of the game, and the incredible goal-scoring potency of Willimowski features as the sort of anecdote endlessly exchanged between fans. But football also enters into any number of social arenas besides its own – it is never limited to the pitch alone – and the complex blending of sex, exploitation and football in the Amsterdam red-light district is a sure reminder of the game's prodigious reach.

Much of Dutch football's ignored war-time history is, as one might expect in the chaos of an occupied country, an unsettling combination of the tragic and the absurd. Kuper quotes an extract from a letter by a man called J. Kleerekooper, written to the board of the Amsterdam football club Neerlandia in November 1945. 'Honourable gentlemen', Kleerekooper writes:

> I am aware that in many areas there are great shortages, which on occasion force us to take all sorts of emergency measures.
>
> However, what I observed at your ground today seems to me somewhat to exceed the common terms of 'boundaries'. The question to which I refer is the corner flags that mark your ground.
>
> These consist of parts of prayer clothing as used by Israelites.
>
> Personally I regard myself as a free-thinker yet I nonetheless find the solution that you have found at the least inappropriate, certainly when one considers where this clothing comes from and why it is no longer where it ought to be.

An exemplary instance of the way in which the most brutal facts of the Second World War infiltrated and disfigured everyday life, this was hardly an episode of their history that Neerlandia were likely to boast about in the future. With remarkable patience, the letter-writer acknowledges the pragmatic need for a mend-and-make-do mentality after so many years of war; but even for this 'free-thinker' the recycling of discarded Jewish clothing into makeshift corner flags demands a polite but insistent letter of complaint. The letter-writer chooses not to articulate the terrible images that underlie his letter, but they are there all the same, an unmistakable ghostly presence in the last, understated questions: where *did* 'this clothing come from', and why was it 'no longer where it ought to be'? Certainly, once the 'inappropriate' solution to their shortage of corner-flags had been pointed out to them, the directors of Neerlandia seemed to

understand the offence caused. Kuper quotes from their letter in return, hastily promising to replace the prayer-clothing.

The displacement of the 'Israelite clothing' onto a football field demands questions
of the private moral code of that club, but the pile of clothes also penetrate deep into
the national psyche of a country that, according to Kuper, has dozed too long under the
myth of its own tolerance, historical and contemporary. Should anybody have *wanted*
to find it, at the time or since, evidence against this myth was scattered, quite literally,
all over the place. That it should fall to Kuper to scour long forgotten football archives
for such evidence nearly 60 years on may be the most poignant fact of all.

Ajax, the Dutch, the War does not make use of footnotes, doubtlessly a sensible decision given the broad, popular audience that it deserves. This will nonetheless prove frus-
trating to the academic reader, especially given the quantity and variety of sources used
(where, for example, does Goebbels write that football could be useful for the Nazi party
as a 'game of mass suggestion'?). However, it is a small frustration borne out of the bril-
liance of this book, in which Kuper has made a profound and lasting contribution to
the way in which the history of football, as well as the social history of a nation, is written.

Strength not sleight: David Winner

Near the beginning of *Those Feet*, David Winner quotes Richard the Lionheart, as he
appears in Walter Scott's *The Talisman* (1825): 'what we cannot do by sleight', Richard
explains, 'we eke out by strength'. By 'we', he means the English race, and Winner adds:
'No more concise definition of English football exists'.

It quickly becomes clear that what this definition captures is not actually some
essential truth about English football through the ages, but the reputation that has
become firmly attached to the game through the stories told about it. Like Kuper,
Winner has written a book about how a nation has come to perceive its football and
itself, and how certain myths have become imbedded in the national consciousness.
English football has had its fair share of native mavericks and tricksters – if Paul
Gascoigne is the most obvious candidate of modern times, we might add the likes of
Matthew le Tissier, John Barnes, Ian Wright – but English football has been promoted
for decades as the natural home of hard work and determination. The typical English
footballer, according to the nation's most enduring stereotypes, is ill at ease among
mavericks. An illuminating example of this perception can be drawn from another
source. Researching the history of Real Madrid in 2002, Phil Ball went to see the
galacticos take on Las Palmas in the Spanish League. At half-time, and with increasing
trepidation, Ball watched fellow Englishman Steve McManaman warming up with his
Spanish and Brazilians colleagues:

> The Liverpudlian looks skinny and undernourished, like a young boy who has
> borrowed the club tracksuit and sneaked onto the pitch to play with his heroes … As
> their game [of keepie-ups] continues, I tense every time the ball floats across to him
> because I am convinced, after several years of watching Spanish football, that English
> players have inferior technique, and I am horrified that McManaman may illustrate
> this every time it is his turn to deal with a pass.[6]

As it turns out, McManaman acquits himself perfectly well. But Winner would immediately recognize Ball's very English *expectation* of technical inadequacy, and the looming sense of humiliation present when an Englishman appears on a pitch with his foreign team-mates. As Winner points out, the aftermath of England's defeat to Brazil in the semi-finals of World Cup 2002 was dominated by a feeling of embarrassment that was inseparable from an equal feeling of inevitability. The match was viewed by many England fans 'as one more instalment in a long-running saga of decent, dull English footballers humiliated by technically superior foreigners', as if the defeat came with all the predictability of a bad soap opera (this is a comparison that Winner makes more than once). At the World Cup, England weren't just seen to be hapless and boorish. They were seen to be hapless and boorish *again*.

The rest of the book is dedicated to exploring the cultural origins of this expectation. In each of its ten chapters, Winner explores an historical moment or period through which the English have come to associate football with discipline, graft and toughness (and disassociate it from those more continental characteristics of flair and trickery). This covers some fascinating ground. Like *Ajax, the Dutch, the War, Those Feet* makes generous use of interviews with fans, and cashes in on a number of memorable anecdotes. These include the Middlesbrough supporter who rebuilt Ayresome Park in his back garden and convinced the club's onetime hero Bernie Slaven to recreate his goal celebrations there for the local news, and the Aston Villa defender of the 1920s who turned up to negotiate a pay-rise with two large, armed friends. But it is the depth and breadth of Winner's reading that is most impressive. We read about the sporting ethic instilled in Edwardian private schools as a measure to strengthen boys to resist the degenerative risks of masturbation (if you were playing with a football, you couldn't be playing with yourself). Or the uniquely English affection for extraordinarily muddy, strength-sapping playing surfaces, on which it was often difficult to stand, let alone do anything as fancy as dribble. While English football fans were raised on stereotypes of Brazilian footballers playing soccer like they samba, or Dutchmen immersed in the incredible versatility of Total Football, the game at home entered the consciousness as a way to run off sexual urges, or a kicking competition with a quagmire instead of a midfield. Through examples of this kind, Winner does an excellent job of arguing why English fans might think it impossible to compete with the technical abilities of other nations. Two chapters deserve a more detailed assessment, however, one for its thrilling representation of the very best aspects of Winner's work, and the other for posing some extremely problematic questions about the project as a whole.

Italy has long been the 'principal yardstick' against which England measures its success as a nation. This is how Winner opens his argument in an excellent chapter on Anglo-Italian relations, called (predictably enough) 'Italian Job'. Thus as the fortunes of one nation diminishes, the other increases, fixing Italy in the English imagination as something that is endlessly *other*, a powerful reminder at any given moment of what England is not. We are taken back as far as 218 BC, and Hannibal invading Turin, for the first example of Italian resistance to invasion from the north; and in Turin we find a city that has played host to the pendulum swings of national success and failure throughout the twentieth century. The Italian team that lost 4-0 at home to England in 1948 were playing in a country suffering post-fascist isolation and depression, whereas English society was enjoying reassuring (if dreary) stability. By the 1970s and 1980s, the Italian economy was soaring as England's entered a recession, and Italy beat England at football for the first time, in Turin and then again in London. It was in Turin in 1990 that England suffered the first of the four high-profile penalty shoot-out defeats that would haunt the national team through the decade. Italy didn't win that World Cup, but they did beat the English in the third place play-off.

This succession of football matches alone make a riveting story – whatever happened to Toto Scillachi? – but Winner introduces a miscellaneous range of characters to help situate this footballing rivalry in a wider Anglo-Italian context. Discussion of the 1969 film *The Italian Job* is accorded plenty of space, and its depiction of plucky Brits putting one over on hapless, rather cardboard Italians is picked through in detail. But Winner also makes a very entertaining case for seeing Machiavelli's ghostly presence in the way the English talk about Italian football ('If you want to understand *catenaccio* read *The Prince*', one journalist tells him). E.M. Forster and Lawrence Olivier are also drawn into the argument for their part in entrenching certain stereotypes of the England's relationship with Italy. As one might expect by now, each example provides a variation on the same theme: the English are presented as no-nonsense, hard-working and honest; the Italians are (in a memorable couple of phrases) 'mother-fixated' and 'bottom-pinching'.

The sheer range of references used in 'Italian Job' is remarkable, as it is in the chapter 'Roys, Keens and Rovers'. Manchester United's recently departed midfield-captain Roy Keane is a figure who invokes all sorts of imagery, much of it related to the ongoing story of tough, uncompromising and slightly dangerous English football. As Winner indicates through a truly astonishing foray into 150 years of comic-book adventures (and the odd children's novel), the same name has been repeatedly used down the ages for just this sort of ultra-manly, patriotic battler. 'Royston Keene' was a Crimean War hero in the 1859 novel *Sword and Gown*; 'Royal Keene' crops up as the bad-guy in a 1909 Buffalo Bill novel; 'Barry Keene' would box his way to glory in the *Boys Realm of Sports and Adventure* during the 1920s. No wonder, it is argued, we attach such terrible power to the modern-day footballer Keane. That name brings with it an imposing history of hardness and greatness, and Roy Keane is merely the latest embodiment of what Winner calls 'Roy-ness', 'that distillation of essential British footballing manliness through the ages'.

There is a profound difficulty with the question of nationality that arises from that last sentence. It is troubling enough that Winner feels able to hop between the national tags of 'English' and 'British', as if they represented the same thing. But Roy Keane is Irish, a fact so inconvenient to Winner's argument that he simply (and irresponsibly) elides it. As other reviewers of this book have been quick to point out, this has disastrous consequences for the coherence of this chapter.[7] This is an unfortunate lapse by Winner, taking his book into extremely sensitive political territory. It leaves the reader a little uncomfortable, and it invites, too, reflection on other sections of the text in which Winner either gets his facts wrong or seems to hit slightly the wrong tone. The number of fans killed in the 1989 Hillsborough disaster was 96, not 89 as the book states – this is another blunder in a sensitive area. The odd statement also contains unnecessary exaggeration. Chelsea could hardly be said to have 'regularly' fielded teams that include no English player (it happened once or twice during the late 1990s). Sometimes the author just seems to be wildly, optimistically deluded: it seems astonishing to argue that England 'were just a game away from winning [the World Cup] in Japan (had they got past Brazil, would Turkey or Germany have stopped them?)'. And Winner occasionally gives conveniently partial versions of well-known events, in a style that is reminiscent of more 'official' versions of football history: 'When Basil Boli of France cynically head-butted Stuart Pearce during a Euro '92 game, Pearce made no fuss', he states, failing to mention the enormous plaster that Pearce ostentatiously wore under his eye for the rest of the tournament.

There is one final, important point that arises from a reading of 'Roys, Keens and Rovers'. In one way or another, the various incarnations of Roy Keane are all fighters: the war hero, the cowboy, the boxer. As one expert on boys' own stories suggests, 'the image of the warrior is still the most powerful heroic icon for boys and young men'. The subject of war acts as a background from which other arguments are advanced – when, for example, the all-male bonhomie of private school life is compared to that expected of a regiment of troops during the First World War – but any visceral sense of *actual* fighting on the world stage is curiously absent from Winner's history of English football. The obvious sites of interaction between England, football and war – the 'Christmas Day match' on no man's land, the Berlin game of 1938 covered so exhaustively in Kuper's book – go unmentioned. For those who have been intrigued by the connections made in these areas by *Ajax, the Dutch, the War*, to treat the war as nothing more than an occasional context of national life is an omission that is hard to understand. One explanation might be available in the long chapter 'The Phantom Limb', which explores the pessimism of England's football fans as a symptom of post-imperial declinism, and the embarrassed acknowledgment that English military power all over the world (and again Winner seems to writing about Britain here) has dwindled away to nearly nothing. It is often a convincing argument, maybe because in ignoring England's involvement in the century's two world wars, Winner is confirming his own thesis. In *Those Feet*, warfare appears only as metaphor. It is the rhetoric of violence from a nation whose potential for real violence is redundant; it is aggression without the teeth. The essential difference between Kuper's book about a nation under occupation, and Winner's about a nation obsessed with the language of war, might be summed-up by the fact that only Winner can confidently write that 'unlike war, football isn't an arena of life and death'.

Those Feet is an entertaining book, and it combines irreverence with incisiveness. A book of this kind about England is particularly valuble, as so much of the best recent football writing has ignored the English game because of the same utilitarian reputation that Winner places at the heart of his book. But the all too casual elisions and exaggerations that scatter through the work undermine the otherwise impressive achievement of researching and exposing the myriad stories at the root of England's footballing heritage.

Notes

[1]   For accounts of this disenfranchisement, see Hornby's prescient fears in *Fever Pitch*, 196–7; and the excellent study by Dempsey and Reilly, *Big money, Beautiful Game*.

[2]   Winner, *Those Feet*, 96.

[3]   Kuper, *Ajax, the Dutch, the War*, 10.

[4]   Freedland, *Jacob's Gift*, 9.

[5]   The nearest parallel to Herman Menco's story, albeit one in which deportation is risked rather than death, is provided in Kuper's earlier book *Football Against the Enemy*, and the account of matches held on American soil that feature South American national sides. A local newspaper report is quoted: 'Get all the illegal aliens into one stadium and swoop, that was the idea' (157).

[6]   Ball, *White Storm*, 20.

[7]   Will Buckley, writing in *The Guardian*, is politely scathing of this chapter of *Those Feet*: 'The Roy Keane conceit, though nice, is flawed. Having been born and brought up in Cork it is unlikely Roy Keane will be thrilled to find himself playing a significant part in a history of English football, sensual or otherwise. Winner tacitly admits this by including no mention of the defining moment of Roy's career, the argument with Irish manager Mick McCarthy, which led Keane to walk out of his national team' (9 April 2005).

References

Ball, Phil. *White Storm: 101 Years of Real Madrid*. Edinburgh: Mainstream, 2002.

Dempsey, Paul and Kevan Reilly. *Big Money, Beautiful Game: Saving Football from Itself*. London: Nicholas Brealey, 1998.

Freedland, Jonathan. *Jacob's Gift: A Journey into the Heart of Belonging*. London: Hamish Hamilton, 2005.

Hornby, Nick. *Fever Pitch*. London: Indigo, 1992.

Kuper, Simon. *Ajax, the Dutch, the War: Football in Europe during the Second World War*. London: Orion, 2003.

Kuper, Simon. *Football against the Enemy*. London: Orion, 1998.

Winner, David. *Those Feet: A Sensual History of English Football*. London: Bloomsbury, 2005.

Riot in the Curve: Soccer Fans in Twenty-first Century Italy

Matthew Guschwan

On 22 March 2004, fans threw two flares onto the field during the bi-annual soccer match between Rome's rival teams, SS Lazio and AS Roma. The referee halted the game while firemen rushed to the field and removed the flares. After the smoke had cleared, the game did not resume. A rumour had been spreading throughout both ends of the stadium that a child had been run over and killed by a police vehicle before the start of the game. Amidst growing unrest in the stands, two fan leaders forced their way onto the playing field and demanded to speak to the AS Roma captain and native son, Francesco Totti. These fans insisted that if the game did not cease, the entire south section of the stadium was prepared to charge the field. Meanwhile, stadium officials announced over the public address system that the rumour of the accident was false. Nevertheless, Totti was convinced that the fans were seriously aggravated and that the game must be abandoned. After a few phone calls between the referee, team officials and league officials, the game was officially suspended. Fans slowly filed out of the stadium in a relatively calm manner.

The event became headline news as journalists and commentators speculated on the motivation for this fan-initiated disruption. Some media pundits speculated that this incident was an organized protest against the failure of a state-sponsored bailout of financially struggling soccer clubs, of which both Roma and Lazio would qualify. The newspaper *Il Messaggero* theorized that this incident was an organized show of power agreed upon by the two *ultra* groups.[1] What is known for certain is that the fan leaders who rushed onto the field were arrested. They subsequently appeared in court, and were punished with minor fines and bans from the stadium.

A year after the incident described above, a match between Lazio and Livorno became a demonstration of the fans' radical politics. A few Lazio fans waved Nazi flags while the Livorno fans waved their red 'hammer and sickle' Communist flags. A few days later, another fan disturbance caused the suspension of the European Champions league match between intra-city rivals, Internazionale (known as Inter) and AC Milan (Milan). After a controversial referee decision, Inter fans threw enough flares onto the field to force the suspension of the match. This essay about Italian soccer fan culture is anchored by description and analysis of these three recent crowd disturbances that occurred between March 2003 and April 2004. These dramatic events are a starting point to discuss modern Italian soccer fan culture within the broader context of modern Italian culture.

Soccer as Cultural Performance

The defining act for soccer fans that I discuss in this essay is going to soccer games to cheer for their team. Italian soccer fans have earned approbation for their passion and grandiose displays as well as admonishment for their violent behaviour. At their best and at their worst, Italian soccer fans are as much participants in the soccer event as they are observers.

In this essay, I will treat Italian soccer matches as cultural performances. I will focus specifically on the ways in which the fans make the cultural performance, rather than the players or the soccer club management. The concept of cultural performances draws from the disciplines of anthropology and folklore as well as from the hybrid discipline of performance studies. Borrowing from the work of performance studies scholars Milton Singer and Richard Bauman, I define cultural performance as a temporally and spatially bounded event that is literally or figuratively staged by members of a society. Performances involve skilled performers, and are marked by society as events to be looked at and examined by audiences. A cursory examination reveals that Italian soccer matches easily satisfy these criteria. Professional soccer matches have a reserved time and place, and are most certainly regarded as something to observe and examine.

Bauman argues that cultural performances are compelling subjects of study because they have the following attributes[2]: 1. They are artful or at least have an aesthetic aspect; 2. They are reflexive. Cultural performances represent and comment upon the values and ideas of the society that stages the performance; 3. Cultural performances are performative in the sense defined by J.L. Austin. As explicated in his book, How to Do Things with Words,[3] performances do social 'work' and accomplish social ends; 4. Cultural performances combine the traditional and the emergent; they repeat old ideas while enabling the expression of new ideas that sometimes contest older ideas. In the course of this essay, I will highlight the ways in which the Italian soccer match is artful, reflexive, performative and serves to accomplish social ends.

Viewing soccer matches as cultural performances allows us to examine the ways in which cultural performances reach beyond the confines of the performance event itself to become influences upon, and reflections of, communal identities. In the words of John J. MacAloon, cultural performances 'are more than entertainment, more than didactic or persuasive formulations, and more than cathartic indulgences. They are occasions in which as a culture or society we reflect upon and define ourselves, dramatize our collective myths and history, present ourselves with alternatives, and eventually change in some ways while remaining the same in others.'[4] The cultural performances that occur in Italian stadiums every week are not merely spontaneous events that last for two hours a week. Instead, they are tied to the long history of Italian culture as well as to the immediate conditions of contemporary life.

The Italian soccer fans create the cultural performance by bringing elements of everyday life into the stadium. The stadium atmosphere magnifies these elements and puts them on display for the immediate public as well as the larger media audience. The passion, beauty, humour and elegance of Italian life are intensified and performed by the fans in the form of choruses, banners, flags and demonstrations. The fans use these same forms to display the ugliest, anti-social aspects of contemporary Italian life: xenophobia, racism, violence and divisiveness.

I will demonstrate how the fan performances inside the stadiums are closely tied to daily Italian life and to the robust history of Italian culture. Though some of the specific behaviour that occurs within the stadium is undoubtedly spontaneous and improvised, fan expression relies upon and draws from the traditions of Italian social life. The entire soccer event cannot happen without a significant amount of 'behind the scenes' work and the organization of committed fans. Implicitly, I argue against any analysis that finds the Italian soccer stadium to be a source of trouble in society. Rather, I argue that the fan performance inside the stadium is intertwined with Italian social and political reality. Any analysis of the anti-social expressions in the stadium should consider broader Italian culture as well.

The fan disruptions that I will discuss occurred in Rome and Milan, two of Italy's major urban centres. Massive media exposure has given these incidents a large social significance. I draw many examples from the Roman fans because it is the fan culture I am most familiar with. In the first part of this essay, I will discuss the importance of soccer in Italian culture and describe the history of organized fan groups, called *ultras*. *Ultra* groups contribute to the cultural performance of soccer matches more than any other fans. Next, I will describe prominent features of modern Italian history that directly affect soccer fan culture and their in-stadium displays. Finally, I will return to the three episodes that started this essay, and discuss them as expressions of societal anxieties about modern life, consumerism and globalism.

Soccer infiltrates daily Italian life in myriad ways. In Rome, one cannot walk through the streets without seeing the yellow and red graffiti for the team AS Roma (Roma), or the sky blue and white graffiti of their local rival, SS Lazio (Lazio). Every other shop has a picture of Roma's star and native son, Francesco Totti, or Lazio's hero, Paolo Di Canio. Cafes buzz with the rants of old men discussing the trials and tribulations of the local soccer team. On TV, soccer players are shown training and playing, or selling shoes, cars and hair-care products. In addition to the pages of coverage in the regular newspapers, two daily national sports newspapers devote most of their coverage to soccer.

The Italian soccer match has replaced historic festivals, such as the Palio horse race in Siena[5], as a primary source of civic identity. In the major urban centres of Milan, Rome, Turin, Genoa and Naples, as many as 80,000 fans cram the soccer cathedrals every Sunday, while churches are almost empty. Anthropologist Amalia Signorelli has described Italian soccer as a 'secular religion'. Signorelli writes that soccer provides, 'An elementary symbolic universe, fixed and pliant at the same time, within which it is possible for very different people to define themselves, and themselves in relations to others'.[6] For nearly a half century, soccer fandom has been an axis for social organization. Rocco De Biasi and Pierre Lanfranchi argue that these organized soccer groups derive from 'the tradition of local associations, religious and political, which are deeply rooted in Italian culture'.[7] Beginning in the early 1960s, soccer groups formed for the purpose of distributing tickets and arranging trips to away games, but now they serve as major social outlets in Italian culture.

That is not to say that politics and soccer occupy exclusive spheres; on the contrary, soccer is firmly enmeshed in national politics. Media magnate, and two-time Prime Minister Silvio Berlusconi owns one of Italy's most successful teams, AC Milan. Berlusconi used the success of his team in the early 1990s and the power of his media empire to boost his visibility and launch his political career. The centre-right political party that he founded, Forza Italia, takes its name directly from a soccer cheer that means, roughly, 'Go Italy!'. Berlusconi appealed to voters by carrying soccer (football) metaphors into the political realm. BBC journalist, David Willey, describes Berlusconi's approach to win votes.

> Using the language and slogans of the football field, Berlusconi created a new simplistic political language which immediately won over many Italians used to the deliberately obscurantist terminology of the fusty old political parties. He talked incessantly about 'coming out onto the field', 'players' and 'winning the game'. He seemed to have a magic touch.[8]

After his first election as Prime Minister in 1994, Berlusconi's soccer team won the domestic championship prompting him to declare that he 'would do for Italy what he had done for his team'.[9]

Soccer is such a fundamental component of Italian culture that people who do not like the game itself often identify with a local team. In this way, they connect to a set of orientations and values, such as local pride and political affiliation, which exceeds the notion of soccer as a game. Once a side is chosen, supporters are expected to stay loyal. In an article about Roman fans, sportswriter James Eve remarks, half-jokingly, 'Marital infidelity is one thing. Switching your football team is in a higher league of villainy altogether.'[10] In Rome, AS Roma fans consider themselves to be the true Romans from the heart of the city. Historically, they have been associated with leftist politics. Traditionally, Lazio has drawn fans from a few affluent neighbourhoods within Rome and from Rome's outlying areas. Lazio was the preferred team of fascist dictator, Benito Mussolini. The association with right-wing politics continues into the present day.

When Italian fans go to the stadium, they go not only to watch the match, but to participate in the event. Fans choruses echo throughout the stadium. Their scarves turn the stands into a sea of colour. Their banners bare the hostility that lets visiting fans and players know that they are not welcome. These are the aesthetically rich parts of the soccer cultural performance. Every game, fans compete to be the loudest, cleverest and most passionate supporters. They feel that the soccer match is as much their responsibility as that of the players or of the owners. Italian fans are nicknamed tifosi, a name that equates their passion to the madness of typhoid fever. Rather than being set apart as a space for pure leisure, Italian soccer stadiums have long reflected the anger, joy and grief of everyday life. The stadium is a place to meet with friends and to enjoy the game, and also to remember the dead, or to protest against social or political issues. Many banners memorialize the dead or protest specific legislation. As historian Paul Ginsborg wrote, 'Sunday afternoon at the stadium was sometimes a political, as much as a sentimental, education of a pretty disturbing sort.'[11]

History of Italian Ultras

Throughout Italy, many of the most committed tifosi become *ultras*. *Ultras* are organized groups of fans committed to supporting their team and are a significant element of youth culture throughout Italy and Europe. *Ultras* meet during the week to socialize, to raise money, to arrange travel to away games, and to choreograph the demonstrations and songs that they perform inside the stadium. *Ultra* groups are usually responsible for the violence and intimidation that makes the news. The *ultra* mode of participation is encoded in the notion of La Mentalitá (the mentality or mind). La Mentalitá dictates that the *ultra* must be an active spectator, overtly display identity, and confront authority and other *ultras* within the limits of an honour code.

Organized trips to away matches at even the most remote locations have been a primary function for *ultras* groups. These trips have become a major area of concern for authorities. For the *ultra*, one of the goals of going on these trips has been to fight the opposing *ultras*. Often the *ultras* would stir up trouble en route by besieging petrol station urinals and stealing food and drink from the Autogrill roadside fast food/convenience stores that dot Italian highways.

There are significant similarities between English hooligans and Italian *ultras*, but the particular social history of Italy distinguishes the two groups. Researchers Carlo Balestri and Carlo Podaliri point out that the term 'hooligan' stems from the name of a thuggish gang in England and was later applied to groups of extremely aggressive English soccer fans.[12] The name '*ultra*' was borrowed from radical leftist political groups of late 1960s Europe. From the start, *ultras* have been connected to a broad spectrum of political movements operating in Italy. Another difference between *ultras* and hooligans is that the consumption of alcohol was never a major part of the *ultra* experience, as it has been with English hooligans.

Podaliri and Balestri schematize the history and development of the *ultra* groups into four distinct phases. The first *ultra* group, named 'La Fossa dei Leoni' (the Lion's Den) was formed in Milan in 1968. In 1971, Sampdoria fans were the first to use the term '*ultra*' to refer to their group. In this first phase, *ultra* groups were firmly tied to the national political and social movements that evolved in Italy and Europe after the Second World War. In Italy, there was a national struggle between the remnants of the far right, fascist regime, the emerging leftist and communist parties, and the US-backed movement for democratic capitalism. In this highly charged atmosphere, everyday social events, including soccer fandom, adopted political and ideological significance. *Ultras* were particularly influenced by student protest movements and by English hooligan groups.

Within the stadiums, the *Ultras* began to dress alike and mark their territory within the curve (curved ends of the stadiums), the cheapest seats available. *Ultras* chanted continuously and watched the game without ever sitting down. Outside the stadium, groups developed networks of rivalries and friendships with politically like-minded *ultra* groups in other Italian cities. In general, party politics were the central organizing principle for the *ultras* fan clubs.

By the second phase of *ultra* history, from 1977–83, *ultra* groups had spread throughout Europe. In Italy, the level and organization of violence increased concomitantly with the rise of politically motivated terrorism. The optimism that had bolstered mass political movements of the late 1960s and early 1970s was replaced by the desperation of radical groups on both the left and right wings. These groups resorted to violence and terrorism that peaked with the kidnapping and killing of Prime Minister Aldo Moro, by the left-wing Red Brigades in 1978.

At the soccer stadiums, increased police surveillance forced rival *ultra* groups to arrange clashes away from the stadiums. This unstable time was marked by the death of a Lazio *ultra* from the discharge of a flare gun during the Roma-Lazio derby in 1979. The organizational structure of *ultra* groups expanded in order to manage a growing membership, and to maintain relationships with the club management as well as to arrange away trips, and to sell t-shirts and scarves to fund the entire enterprise. Struggles for control of the curve erupted among a growing number of *ultra* groups that had diverging goals. The *ultra* groups as a whole became more organized and more militant.

In the third phase of *ultra* history, from 1983–89, local and regional pride replaced national politics as an organizing principle. Regional rivalries and historical hostilities became more important than left-wing and right-wing political affiliation. *Ultras* began to refer to the curve as 'mother country' rather than as a liberated space. At this time, the first generation of *ultras* was yielding to a new generation that had no understanding of mass politics, but was interested in mass violence. Balestri and Podaliri write, 'Civil society was dominated by hedonism, exhibitionism, and disaffection for political and social commitment'.[13]

Tensions between the older left-wing groups and the younger right-wing supporters threatened to tear apart the entire curve culture. As a compromise, fan groups started to renounce political affiliations in order to maintain unity. Right-wing attitudes and xenophobia were growing in society in general. Umberto Bossi's Lega Nord (Northern League) perpetuated territorial discrimination and called for the separation of the wealthier northern part of Italy from the poorer southern part. The rise in internal regionalism was accompanied by the rise of discrimination against poor immigrants, a phenomenon already prevalent in Europe. New and violent *ultra* groups adopted as their symbol the image of Alex, leader of the *ultra*-violent thugs in Stanley Kubrick's 'A Clockwork Orange' (1971). The image of Alex replaced the image of leftist revolutionary, Ché

Guevara, in the stands throughout Italy. This change in imagery from Ché to Alex symbolized the turn away from national politics toward crude violence.

The fourth phase of *ultra* development started after the killing of an *ultra* member outside the stadium in Genoa in January, 1995. During a clash against Genoa *ultras*, a member of a group of AC Milan *ultras*, led by a right-wing accountant, stabbed and killed 24-year-old Vincenzo Spagnolo. The event drew massive criticism from every corner of society. This led to a meeting of leaders from *ultra* groups throughout Italy. The leaders issued a behavioural code condemning the use of knives in fights. After an unofficial truce, violence and racism returned to the stadiums the following year. One of the worst incidents happened in Bologna. A group of *ultras* attacked a group of black immigrants. The attack split the Bologna *ultras* into those who wanted to adopt a socially progressive attitude, and those who wanted to continue violent behaviour. The ideological split occurred throughout Italian *ultra* culture and still has not been completely mended. There are still *ultra* groups that support the team and leave politics and violence behind, and there are groups that continue to defy all rules of civility.

Podaliri and Balestri's historical analysis ends with the description of two pan-*ultra* developments in the mid-1990s. First is the Progetto *Ultra*, the organization founded by Podaliri and Balestri for the purposes of understanding and documenting *ultra* culture, and to work against racism from within these groups.[14] The second development that Podaliri and Balestri identified was an emerging resistance to the 'modernization' of soccer. Many *ultras* feel that modern soccer has been ruined by expensive tickets, police repression, greedy players and greedy owners. They look back fondly to the days when fan groups were more unified and the players and owners made the fans feel more important.

The financial landscape of European soccer has changed completely in the last ten years due, in large part, to the decision of a European court in 1995. A previously obscure professional player named Jean-Marc Bosman went to court demanding the right to play for the soccer club of his choice.[15] Backed by the Belgian national soccer association, the club management refused to allow Bosman to move to another team even though his contract had expired. In winning his case, Bosman won free agency for himself and for every professional soccer player in the European Union. This ruling intensified the international market for players, and dramatically increased players' wages. In an increasingly competitive player market, many unscrupulous owners have put their desire to win over fiscal responsibility, thus bankrupting their own teams. Fortunately for the remaining teams, satellite television provided an influx of money. Satellite broadcasters paid hundreds of millions of dollars into leagues and individual teams for the rights to beam games all over the world. This elevated players' wages again, and a new cycle of increased competition and financial ruin began.

In the mid-1990s, many *ultra* groups shied away from national politics as an organizing principle and began focusing on fighting the alienating aspects of the modern soccer industry. The website of AS Roma *ultra* group, Brigata G.G. Belli, states, 'We believe that now the most important battle is that against the soccer industry and modern soccer: these are our true enemies, who violate our passion and our game in order to do business.'[16] The Italian website 'No al Calcio Moderno' (No to Modern

Soccer) documents both in-stadium and on-the-street demonstrations for the cause.[17] In the stadiums, scores of fans wear 'No to modern soccer' t-shirts that list the negative elements of the modern game: expensive tickets, mercenary players, doping, false passports and police repression. Some representative banners within the stadium read, '*Ultras* No Profit' or 'Pay TV: We can't take these hours anymore'. The latter banners protest the Wednesday evening games that are very difficult for visiting fans to attend. Many fans have become nostalgic and conservative. They hope to reinvigorate the 'old ways' of fan participation.

As described in Podaliri and Balestri's account, *Ultra* fan culture operates within, and responds to, the prevailing Italian culture. To better understand what is occurring within the stadiums today, we must look at what is happening in the society in general. Contemporary *ultra* culture operates within a weak Italian state that is struggling to succeed in a globalizing world. The current economic downturn and significant demographic changes threaten traditional notions of Italian culture. The next section of this essay describes some major trends in the contemporary Italian cultural and social landscape.

Italy in the Twentyfirst-Century

Italy's current problems have roots that precede the foundation of this relatively young nation. At the Congress of Vienna in 1815, Prince Metternich of Austria insisted that the area that Italy now occupies be referred to as merely, 'a geographic expression'. During the next half century, the process of unification gradually overcame centuries of regional autonomy and conflicts. In 1861, the Kingdom of Italy was established as a result of the patriotic efforts of Count Camillo Cavour, Giuseppe Garibaldi and Giuseppe Mazzini. Though the border of the nation had been established, the people were not unified. Immediately following the founding of the nation, the Marchese d'Azeglio commented, 'Unfortunately, Italy is made, but Italians are not made'.[18] His comment underscored the deep economic, linguistic and cultural divisions among Italy's regions that have endured into the present day.

The project of making a unified Italian population has never been completed and as a result, there has never been a strong, centralized, national government. There are dramatic economic disparities between regions, and especially between the prosperous north and the struggling south. This so-called 'southern problem' has fuelled regional antipathy and vocal sentiment for northern secession. Umberto Bossi's Northern League garnered support among northern separatists who feel that the south is nothing but an economic drain. In the early 1990s, Angela Zanotti wrote, 'Now, for the first time in the history of the Republic, there is an attempt to spell out the problems of the Italian state on the basis of [regional] ethnicity.'[19] She notes how this unique region-based cultural and ethnic differentiation echoes the kinds of colour-based racism found in other parts of Europe. The current centre right government under the leadership of Prime Minister Silvio Berlusconi's has subsumed the separatist threats of the northern league, but Italian identity continues to deal with obstinate regionalism.

In addition to the difference between northerners and southerners, Italians have had to cope with the influx of poor foreigners that have migrated to Italy in the last thirty years. According to Emilio Reyneri, in the late 1970s labour shortages in Europe 'pulled-in' immigrant labourers.[20] In the 1980s, as the labour shortages subsided, immigrants came to Europe because unfavourable economic and political conditions in their home countries 'pushed' them out. Italy has become a popular place for refugees, due more to its relatively relaxed border patrols than to any job surplus. In the last five years, Italian economic growth has been slow and unemployment has been high among Italians and immigrants alike. The conversion from the Lira to the Euro led to inflation that has affected the elderly and poor disproportionately. There are growing tensions between Italians and immigrants as some Italians blame immigration for these economic and social problems.

The influx of immigrants and Italy's extremely low birth rate are causing drastic demographic shifts.[21] The Italian population may not replace itself, and immigrant labour will be necessary to maintain the current economic structure. Some Italians feel that the Italian way of life is threatened by these demographic changes. For example, the reactionary political group, Forza Nuova, vocally opposes immigration. They hand out flyers that read, 'Defend ourselves from the Chinese invasion', and call for a boycott of Chinese products and businesses.[22] The symbol of Forza Nuova (an encircled cross) and Nazi swastikas are common graffiti.

The Roman Derby

Against this background, soccer remains one of the major expressions of Italian social life. Many of the negative aspects of Italian society are carried into the stadium, where they are amplified and intensified. The large crowds, heightened emotions, and intense media attention create an atmosphere in which the best and worst aspects of Italian culture are expressed. The interrupted Roma-Lazio derby described at the outset of this essay is a primary example.

The bi-annual derby game between Rome's two teams, Roma and Lazio, is a battle for city pride and bragging rights. Roma and Lazio share the same stadium, the Stadio Olimpico (Olympic stadium), but as any Roma or Lazio *ultra* will tell you, that is where the similarities end. In the derby, the AS Roma fans (Romanisti) sit in the south curve because it is closer to downtown Rome. The Lazio fans (Laziali) sit in the north curve. This arrangement enables the *ultras* from both teams to monitor the *ultras* on the other side. Fans dress in the colours of their team and wear scarves with messages sewn into them that are displayed toward their enemy. A typical Roma scarf reads, 'Roma, you do not discuss, you love'. For Lazio, a typical scarf reads, 'Irreducible', which is the name and motto of their main *ultra* group.

Though the team uniforms are devised by team officials, the in stadium demonstrations are definitively folk-oriented. Both teams draw from the recent and distant past in developing symbols and demonstrations that represent them. Romanisti wear the red and yellow, the official colours of the city of Rome. Laziali wear light blue and white, the official colours of the Lazio region (which includes the city of Rome). The official symbol of AS Roma is the she-wolf and the suckling Romulus and Remus, the mythical founders of Rome. The Lazio fans have the eagle, a symbol that served as one of the official symbols of Mussolini's fascist regime. *Ultras* sing songs before, during and after every match. AS Roma fans start every match by singing, 'Roma, Roma, Roma, heart of this city, the only great love'. Lazio fans start every game by twirling their scarves above their heads and singing a hard rock oriented song, 'Non mollare mai' (Never back down).

The *ultras* save their best choreography for the derby. A typical display fills an entire end of the stadium with collared smoke; red and yellow for Roma, blue and white for Lazio. Lazio choreography flaunts the fact that their team was founded in 1900, 27 years before Roma. Romanisti unfurl banners that use the traditional symbols of imperial Rome such as the coliseum and the pantheon. The derby is the most important game of the year for both sets of fans.

During one of these derby games, *ultras* were at the center of a fan-initiated disruption. As described at the beginning of this essay, on 22 March 2004 false rumours spread throughout the Olympic stadium that a child had been run over by a police vehicle. After a period of flare throwing and confusion, two *ultra* leaders made their way onto the field, and the match was cancelled. Security officials opened emergency exits at the bottom of the stands, and fans filed out of the stadium in a calm and orderly way. The end of the match was notable for the lack of significant violence outside the stadium.

Immediately following the match, TV newscasts plastered the image of Italian football league President Adriano Galliani across the screen as he tried to explain the rationale for his decision to postpone the game. 'I took the decision because I was convinced that the conditions had made it impossible to play on … I told the referee to suspend that match and the game will definitely be replayed.'[23] Galliani's promise to replay the game was important for the integrity of the Italian league both because of the significance of this particular game and because of Galliani's role within Italian soccer and politics. Galliani is vice-president of the soccer club AC Milan, and is one of Prime Minister Berlusconi's closest confidants. At the time of this game, Roma was in second place to Galliani's first place Milan. With his announcement, Galliani tried to combat any perceptions that Roma was being treated unfairly due to Galliani's professional ties.

While the Roma spokesperson officially endorsed Galliani's decision, Lazio President, Ugo Longo said that he saw no reason why the match should not have continued, 'I think that somebody got their wires crossed, as nobody could work out why the match was stopped … If anything, I believe the suspension created tension and sparked these violent scenes.'[24] Longo's position put him in the minority. Several commentators evoked the memory of the Heysel stadium tragedy of 1985 where 39 Italian fans were killed during a European Cup final match. A rush of Liverpool fans caused a barrier within the stadium to collapse. The ghost of this incident has loomed in the background of all media coverage of every stadium disruption in Europe ever since.

In the days following the Rome derby, politicians, journalists and numerous ex-players shared their opinions. Interior minister Giuseppe Pisanu said, 'On Sunday at Olympic Stadium, we came very close to a tragedy. It is not acceptable that sportsmen and police officers are exposed to such risks …We are determined to use all the means at our disposal to prevent a repeat of similar incidents.'[25] Pisanu's strong words were followed by small fines imposed by the soccer league. Roma was fined roughly $3,000, while Lazio had to pay $67,000. These relatively small sums demonstrate the reluctance of league officials to hold the clubs responsible for the actions of their fans.

Despite intense media investigation, the intentions of these fans have never been definitively determined. The circumstances surrounding the game have fuelled speculation on the part of journalists and sport commentators. Many Italian soccer clubs, including Lazio and Roma, have taken on huge debts in the last decade that threaten their existence. As part of his soccer-based populist political strategy, Prime Minister Silvio Berlusconi, introduced legislation to allocate $500 million of tax cuts and subsidies into the professional game. This controversial initiative, nicknamed 'salva calcio' (save soccer), met fierce political resistance. For example, one union head demanded to know why 'This government cuts our pensions, while, to the millionaires of soccer, [he] cuts their taxes'.[26] Eventually, the initiative failed, much to the dismay of Roma and Lazio *ultras*. The timing of these incidents led pundits to consider the disruptive actions taken by the *Ultras* to be a reaction to the defeat of this legislation. The most convincing explanation was expressed by a long-time Roma fan who said that the *ultras* stopped this game as a brute show of force. The *ultras* sent the message that they had the power to say if the game will be played or not.[27]

Politics in the Stands

This episode exposes the burgeoning restlessness in the stands and demonstrates the *ultras'* new guerrilla tactics. Assuming that this fan disruption was organized beforehand, we see the willingness of the fans to disrupt what was once thought to be sacred. *Ultras* were successful in interrupting the soccer spectacle, but only at the price of the game itself.

Roughly one year later in the same Stadio Olimpico, a regular season game between Lazio and Livorno resembled a radical political rally from the 1960s. A group of Lazio fans waved Nazi flags and unfurled a banner that read (in translation), 'Rome is fascist'. Livorno is a small city in Tuscany known throughout Italy for its support of the Communist party. The Livorno fans demonstrated their communist attachments by arriving in Rome looking like the red army. The fans dressed in dark green battle fatigues, and waved red hammer and sickle flags. While a strong police presence maintained order inside the stadium, scuffles between the fans before and after the match led to minor injuries and several arrests. Miles away from the stadium, fans gathered and fought each other at the San Pietro train station. In total, 85 policemen were injured, and there were 17 arrests and 259 subpoenas.[28] Lazio was fined 25,000 Euros by the league.

In response to this stadium demonstration, Riccardo Pacifici, a spokesperson for the Rome Jewish community said, 'This is not just anti-Semitism, this is pure violence by people who probably don't even know any Jews'.[29] Pacifici's remarks accurately describe the widespread renunciation of national politics in preference for offensive symbols and language meant to be purely provocative, and not meant to promote any coherent political agenda.

For years, Lazio management had been trying to quell racist chants and racist banners in the stands. Lazio fans used to sing anti-Semitic songs, and have, until present time, greeted black skinned players with monkey-like grunts. In response to widespread criticism in the late 1990s, Lazio management went out of its way to introduce a black player into the team. Though it appeared that Lazio was making progress, several incidents demonstrated the attitudes of some of the fans. In 1998, the Lazio fans displayed a banner, 'Honor to Arkan, One of us', in memory of a deceased Serbian war criminal linked to genocide.

In the weeks leading up the Livorno game, fan favourite and team captain Paolo Di Canio celebrated a goal against archrival Roma by showing the straight-armed fascist salute to the Lazio *ultras* in the north end of the stadium. This action was widely criticized by politicians and the media. Italy's Minister for EU affairs, Rocco Buttiglione said, 'The Roman salute brings back painful memories for many Italians. Sport should bring people together, but the symbols of that terrible civil war can only divide. He should think about the offspring of those who were killed and what it would be like for them to see that.'[30] Despite the fact that Di Canio has a tattoo of Mussolini, and that his gesture earned praise from Mussolini's daughter, Di Canio disavowed any political meaning to his gesture. He said, 'I am a professional football player, and my celebrations had nothing to do with political behavior of any kind'.[31] The Italian Football League disagreed ruling that Di Canio had, 'Immediately and unequivocally recalled a precise political ideology', and added that players should not 'engage in any gestures indicating any kind of political ideology…which could potentially provoke a violent reaction from fans'.[32]

Within a week of the Lazio-Livorno episode in Rome, the Champions League semi-final match between AC Milan and Internazionale was suspended because fans threw dozens of lit flares onto the pitch. This intra-city derby game was halted 21 minutes into the second half when a controversial call by the referee riled the Internazionale (aka Inter) fans, whose team was losing 1-0. Faced with the fact that their team was almost certain to drop out of the tournament after losing the previous match, the referee's fateful decision (which on TV was widely considered incorrect) prompted Inter fans to throw a barrage of flares and plastic bottles onto the pitch. One of these flares hit Milan goaltender, Nelson Dida, who suffered minor burns. As firemen went to put out the flames, the fans continued to throw dozens more flares. After a 25 minute delay, the referee decided to abandon the match.

This particular match between Inter and Milan was part of the incredibly lucrative UEFA Champions League. The governing body of European football (UEFA) sponsors a made-for-TV tournament among Europe's top professional teams. These matches are played in addition to domestic league matches. Teams that advance to the later rounds of the tournament expect to make tens of millions of dollars in prize money and ticket revenue. Inter's foe in this match was none other than Prime Minister Berlusconi's AC Milan. Since the stakes were so high, the Inter fans may have felt that the referee was biased in favour of Milan.

Soon after this match ended, the made-for-TV investigation began. Milan Police Chief, Bruno Ferrante believed that this incident was organized in advance. He said, 'I think it was all premeditated and, thus, preventable … We searched the fans and confiscated lots of flares and other objects. Something like this took an exceptional amount of organization. This was not just fans angry about a refereeing decision. That was an excuse.'[33] The Inter players were more sympathetic to the fans' reaction. Juan Sebastian Veron called it 'understandable' while Ivan Cordoba and Esteban Cambiasso blamed the referee's decision for the crowds' reaction.[34] Milan player Clarence Seedorf said, 'The government, the whole country, must understand that something must be done'.[35]

While few could argue against Seedorf's point, just what should be done was another matter. Berlusconi's office issued a statement warning: 'There is a clear risk of even more serious incidents in future, a risk which must be avoided by all possible means. Resorting to the most drastic measures available should not be ruled out if necessary.'[36] As punishment for these fan actions, Inter forfeited the game 3-0, was fined $75,000, and will be forced to play four future European Cup home games in an empty stadium. Once again the real motivation behind this fan disruption has not been uncovered, though it seems that the Inter fans, like the Roman fans, wanted to take control away from the officials and dictate the conditions of the match.

Conclusion: Calcio in Transition

Italian soccer is changing on many different levels. On one side, Italy's top teams are truly world class and are marketing themselves all over the world. For example, in the same week of the interrupted match between Inter and Milan, Milan announced a new marketing deal with Warner Brothers. Milan Vice-President, Adriano Galliani said, 'I am really emotional … It represents the realization of a dream. Anyone who knows me knows that I hoped that one day A.C. Milan would become a major player and my model was Warner Bros. Like them we produce something spectacular and want to entertain.'[37] While reports of such a deal is good news for the front office, it is not good news for fans. As a smaller and smaller proportion of revenue comes directly from ticket sales, clubs have less pressure to please their ticket buying fans. This translates into less power for the *ultra* groups. International marketing deals are contributing to the growing economic disparity between Italy's top few clubs and the rest of clubs. This year, several teams were excluded from the top league due to financial problems. Parma and Lazio, formerly two of Italy's bigger clubs, are now fighting to stay in the top division after the economic collapse of their former owners, Parmalat and Cirio.[38]

As worldwide soccer becomes more business oriented, *ultra* groups want more recognition from the clubs, cheaper tickets and less police interference. At the same time, soccer stadiums reflect the tensions and anxieties of modern Italian society. These two factors combine to form an emerging restlessness in reaction to organized fan protests which are part of an Italian fan culture that is threatened to the point of self-destruction.

While the *ultras* are, in some ways, fighting the alienating effects of globalization, they are losing credibility and bargaining power from their own violent and racist actions. State and club authorities must not tolerate the racism that appears all too often in the curve. While most *Ultras* are not racist, there is too much tolerance from all of the *ultras* for racist displays. If the *ultras* do not regulate themselves, the government will likely play a larger role within the stadiums.

Soccer matches are already more heavily regulated and more militarized events than they were before. In summer 2005, interior Minister Giuseppe Pisanu sponsored controversial legislation that has increased vigilance at the stadiums. The most palpable effect of this legislation is that every ticket sold for a soccer match in Italy must have the ticket holder's name printed on it. Fans who wish to sit in the visitors' section cannot buy tickets on the day of game. This seemingly innocuous legislation has caused major disruptions throughout Italy. For example, in Rome, it is impossible to buy tickets at the stadium because the ticket booths do not have printers. Because of the immense security forces with their armoured vehicles, the environment around stadium now resembles a battleground. At the October 2005 Roma-Lazio derby, the security force included municipal police, military police and treasury guards all dressed in riot gear. At the entrance gates of the stadium, two rows of armed guards patted down everyone twice, in search of flares, fireworks and dangerous objects.

Police have taken a proactive, if repressive, approach to preventing trouble from *ultras* travelling to away matches. In recent years, police have escorted all *ultra* buses from their point of origin to the gates of the stadium. Along the way, they act as chaperones when the *ultras* stop to use the restroom or to buy refreshments. The police escort to Livorno slowed a four-hour drive into a seven-hour journey. In Livorno, Roma *ultras* were greeted by rows of military police that had lined the side streets leading up to the stadium. There were over 30 police vehicles leading up to the visitors' gate. Roma fans rushed through the gates as the game was already ten minutes underway by the time that they had arrived.

Increased police presence has not stopped acts of racism and violence in the stadiums. In a November, 2005 match between Inter and Messina, Messina player Marc Kpolo Zoro grabbed the ball and marched around the field in protest of the racist remarks that the crowd had been chanting throughout the game.[39] With his act of defiance, Zoro drew national attention to a problem that is more often ignored. Italian authorities responded with cries of outrage and little action. On October 16, 2005, a young Ascoli fan launched a small rocket into the opposing stands. The rocket hit a fifty year-old woman in the head, just above the eye, narrowly avoiding serious injury.[40] The woman's sixteen year-old son was shown on TV in tears, vowing never to return to another soccer stadium. The boy's words speak for a growing number of fans that are dissatisfied with the soccer event because of violence and chaos. For instance, a long-time Roma fan that I interviewed refuses to go back to the stadium after being clubbed in the side by a police offier who mistook him for a hooligan after a soccer match.[41]

The conflict between fans and the police led to tragedy in February, 2007, when a fan riot outside of the stadium in the Sicilian city of Catania resulted in the killing of police officer, Filippo Raciti.[42] As a result of this violence, the season was suspended for a week, while the government searched for ways to respond. After a week of public debate, league officials decided to strictly enforce regulations that were supposed to have been enforced a year earlier. Several stadiums were deemed unsuitable to host matches while other stadiums were not allowed to sell tickets to visiting fans.

Until recently, the recurring violence, racism, and various scandals that have plagued Italian soccer have not stopped fans from filling the stadiums. Decreasing ticket sales in 2005–06 and 2006–07 may finally provide the necessary motivation for a major overhaul of the soccer industry.[43]

Soccer matches are one of the few cultural performances that consistently bring together masses of Italians. The soccer match reaches well beyond the stadium to play a major role in the construction of communities, but contemporary Italian fan culture is under threat both from forces within and from outside the stadium. While *ultras* have organized resistance to change, the actions of some *ultras* undermine their efforts. Fans are resisting the commoditization of sport that has already occurred in the United States and England. It is nearly unthinkable for American fans to behave like the *ultras* because American stadiums are so highly regulated. In England, soccer officials imposed much stricter regulations in the aftermath of stadium disasters that occurred 20 years ago. English football has succeeded in making stadiums safe, as fans do not wave flags and banners and everyone is compelled to sit down, but the stadiums lack the expressive flair and vibrancy that the Italian stadiums retain.

The difficult task facing Italian government, soccer league and fans is to balance the requirements of safety and civility with the passion and expression that makes Italian soccer matches so compelling. The manic chanting and flag waving that now fill Italian stadiums may succumb to the forces of business and modernization that call for a family-oriented atmosphere. If this scenario is what the future holds, the *ultras'* will surely draw upon their formidable power rooted in Italian culture to resist any change. They will not go quietly.

Notes

[1]   Mario Menghetti, 'La Polizia: "C'Era un Piano per Far Saltare La Partita"', *Il Messagero*, 22 March 2004, 21. Reprinted in Marchi, *Il Derby del Bambino Morto: Violenza e Ordine Pubblico nel Calcio* [The Derby of the Dead Child: Violence and Public Order in Soccer], 49.

[2]   Bauman, 'Informing Performance: Producing the Coloquio in Tierra Blanca', 255.

[3]   Austin, *How To Do Things With Words*, 5.

[4]   MacAloon, 'Introduction: Cultural Performances, Culture Theory', 1.

[5]   Dundes and Falassi, *La Terra in Piazza: An Interpretation of the Palio of Siena*. The Palio is a bi-annual festival in Siena, Italy that is centred on a horse race in the city's central piazza. Each neighbourhood in Siena sponsors a horse and maintains its own set of symbols, colours and traditions. Authors Dundes and Falassi argue that the Palio acts as a robust metaphor for Siennese life.

[6]   As quoted in Ginsborg, *Italy and Its Discontents: Family, Civil Society, State 1980-2001*, 113.

[7]   De Biasi and Lanfranchi, 'The Importance of Difference: Football Identities in Italy'.

[8]   David Willey, 'Reign of two halves for Berlusconi', *BBC Online*, 14 May 2001 http://news.bbc.co.uk/2/hi/europe/1325122.stm/ (accessed 21 November 2005).

[9]   Ginsborg, *Italy and Its Discontents*, 132.

[10]   James Eve, 'Roma triumph confirms sense of superiority', *The Times* (London), 30 October 2001, Sport Section.

[11]   Ginsborg, *Italy and Its Discontents*, 117.

[12]   Podaliri and Balestri, 'The Ultras, Racism and Football Culture in Italy'.

[13]   Ibid., 95.

[14]   Progetto *Ultra*, http://www.progettoultra.it.

[15]   For a concise summary, see http://www.en.wikipedia.com/wiki/Bosman_ruling.

[16]   Brigata G.G. Belli, http://www.brigataggbelli.it.

[17]   No al Calcio Moderno, http://www.noalcalciomoderno.it.
[18]   Doyle, *Nations Divided: America, Italy, and the Southern Questions*, 39. As Doyle explains, this quote is frequently mis-quoted as, 'Now that we have made Italy, we must make Italians'. Doyle insists that d'Azeglio's attitude toward Italian unification was not optimistic.
[19]   Zanotti, 'Undercurrents of Racism in Italy', 182.
[20]   Reyneri, 'Immigrants in a Segmented and Often Undeclared Labour Market', 72.
[21]   Ibid., 74.
[22]   Forza Nuova, publicly distributed flyer.
[23]   Stephen Blin, 'Rome's Day of Shame as False Rumour Sparks Riot', *Agence France Presse* (English) 22 March 2004, Sports.
[24]   Ibid.
[25]   Ibid.
[26]   Federico Monga, 'Berlusconi Insiste: Il Calcio Va Salvato' [Berlusconi Insists: Soccer Will Be Saved], *La Stampa*, 21 March 2004, Sports Section.
[27]   Personal interview with 'Gianni' on 17 October 2005.
[28]   Lisa Palmieri-Billig, 'Swastikas Anti-Jewish Chants Mar Rome Soccer Match', *The Jerusalem Post*, 14 April 2005, 6.
[29]   Ibid.
[30]   Denis Campbell, 'Italian Fury at Di Canio's Fascist Salute', *Guardian Observer*, http://football.guardian.co.uk/News_Story/0,1563,1386176,00.html (originally published 9 January 2005).
[31]   'Di Canio's Fascist Salute Splits Italy', *Reuters*, 10 January 2005.
[32]   'Di Canio Fined for Fascist-Style Salute,' *World Soccer*, http://worldsoccer.com/news/di_canio_fined_for_fasciststyle_salute_news_62257.html, 10 March 2005.
[33]   Gabriele Marcotti, 'Inter Flare-Up Premeditated', *The Times*, 15 April 2005, 29.
[34]   James Richardson, 'The Italian Disease', *The Daily Mail* (London), 14 April 2005, 76.
[35]   Stephen Blin, 'Madness in Milan', *Daily Telegraph* (Sydney Australia), 14 April 2005, 74.
[36]   Jim White, 'Italians Must Pay for the Hooligans', *Daily Telegraph* (London), 14 April 2005.
[37]   'Calcio: Milan; Accordo Commerciale con Warner Bros.' *ANSA*, 5 April 2005
[38]   Sophie Arie, 'Parma FC Face Ruin as a Dynasty Crashes', *Guardian Unlimited*, http://football.guardian.co.uk/News_Story/0,,1120567,00.html, 11 January 2004.
[39]   'Racist Chants Almost Halt Serie A Game', ESPN Soccernet, http://soccernet.espn.go.com/news/story?id=350458&cc=3888, 27 November 2005.
[40]   Benito Malacoda, 'Hopeless but not Serious, the Italian Madness', http://www.sportnetwork.net/main/s342/st83804.htm, 4 November 2005
[41]   From personal interview with 'Paolo' on 4 November 2005.
[42]   Rob Hughes, 'Italy Issues Orders on Soccer Violence', *International Herald Tribune*, 8 February 2007, 22.
[43]   Roberto Maida, 'Stadi Vuoti: Interveniamo' [Empty Stadiums: We Will Intervene], *Corriere Dello Sport*, 24 September 2005, 2, and A. Serie 'Crowds Fall to 40-Year Low', *Agence France Presse-English*, 7 November 2006.

References

Austin, J.L. *How To Do Things With Words: The William James Lectures delivered in Harvard University in 1955*. London: Oxford University Press, 1962.
Bauman, Richard. 'Informing Performance: Producing the Coloquio in Tierra Blanca.' *Oral Tradition 9*, no.2 (1994): 255–80.
De Biasi, Rocco and Lanfranchi, Pierre. 'The Importance of Difference: Football Identities in Italy.' In *Entering the field: New perspectives on world football*, edited by Gary Armstrong and Richard Giulianotti. Oxford: Berg, 1997: 87–104.

Doyle, Don H. *Nations Divided: America, Italy, and the Southern Questions.* Athens, GA: University of Georgia Press, 2002.

Dundes, Alan and Alessandro Falassi. *La Terra in Piazza: An Interpretation of the Palio of Siena.* Berkeley, CA: University of California Press, 1975.

Ginsborg, Paul. *Italy and Its Discontents: Family, Civil Society, State 1980–2001.* New York: Palgrave, 2003.

MacAloon, John J. 'Introduction: Cultural Performances, Culture Theory,' In *Rite, Drama, Festival, Spectacle: Rehearsals toward a Theory of Cultural Performance,* edited by John J. MacAloon. Philadelphia: Institute for the Study of Human Issues, 1984: 1–13.

Marchi, Valerio. *Il Derby del Bambino Morto: Violenza e Ordine Pubblico nel Calcio.* Rome: Derive-Approdi, 2005.

Podaliri, Carlo and Carlo Balestri. 'The Ultras, Racism and Football Culture in Italy.' In *Fanatics!: Power, Identity and Fandom in Football,* edited by A. Brown. New York: Routledge, 1998.

Reyneri, Emilio. 'Immigrants in a Segmented and Often Undeclared Labour Market.' *Journal of Modern Italian Studies 9,* no.1 (2004): 71–93.

Zanotti, Angela. 'Undercurrents of Racism in Italy.' *International Journal of Politics, Culture and Society 7,* no.2 (1993): 182–7.

The Realm of the Possible: Remembering Brazilian *Futebol*

Marcos Natali

In June of 1994, the Brazilian national team won the quadrennial football World Cup. The World Cup finals – the most important and prestigious international football competition – have been held since 1930, with an interruption only during the Second World War. Although this was the fourth time a Brazilian national selection had earned the coveted trophy, 24 years had passed since Brazil's previous triumph. After the period between 1958 and 1970, when Brazilian teams won three of four World Cups held, Brazil had brought together teams which were often widely respected, yet none had done better than reach third place in the finals. For a substantial portion of the Brazilian population – indeed for an entire generation – the 1994 triumph was the first World Cup victory they had witnessed.

Such a confluence of factors, in a country where football is treated as an extremely serious issue, arousing passions rarely matched in other arenas, would lead one to expect high-spirited and extended celebrations following the Brazilian victory. This was not the case, however, and the reaction to the triumph was, according to many accounts, relatively tepid. Throughout the undefeated campaign which preceded the final game popular support for the team had been hesitant and at best lukewarm. Furthermore, not long after the end of the World Cup, Brazilian commentators were already suggesting that the victorious 1994 team could not match other teams – Brazilian or not – which had won previous World Cups, and, what is perhaps more striking, that it was less worthy of admiration than previous national teams which had been unsuccessful in the World Cup. In a roundtable discussion held in 1997, newspaper football critic Armando Nogueira said that he 'would prefer to sleep with the 1950 Brazilian team, with the 1954 Hungarian team, the 1974 Dutch team, and the 1982 Brazilian team [all of which were not victorious] than with the victory of the Brazilian team in the United States'.[1] When Mário Jorge Lobo Zagallo, then coach of the Brazilian team, remarked bitterly that Nogueira enjoyed sleeping with defeat, Nogueira agreed. In the roundtable his position was seconded by Tostão, a respected player from the 1960s, and in other spaces it was not difficult to find defenders of similar opinions. Some fans and observers even disregarded the 1994 victory altogether, counting as legitimate only Brazil's previous three World Cup victories.

The dissatisfied football fans have been accused of being romantic, unrealistic, archaic and, of course, nostalgic. Yet why does the discontent arise? Why so much disappointment over a victory? Why this insistence on siding with defeat? This essay will dwell on these questions, in the process touching on issues linked to bodily and historical memory and debates about the possibility of constructing and preserving local ways of being.

Inventing Football

Although a number of ancient societies practiced games which involved moving a spherical object to a goal of some sort, and a few specified further that this was to be done with the added difficulty of not using one's hands,[2] the game of football in its modern form arose from an agreement between English gentlemen in 1863, when the sport was effectively unified. As with other activities, the game would accompany the British in their travels to various parts of the world throughout the nineteenth century. In Latin America around the turn of the century, football was one among many activities with English origins which could be practiced in major towns. Participation was often restricted to English expatriates, however, so that the introduction of organized football in different South American countries followed a similar pattern: Englishmen founded the first football clubs in Argentina in 1867 (Buenos Aires Football Club), Uruguay in 1893 (Albion) and Chile in 1889 (Valparaíso Football Club).[3]

In the first decades of the twentieth century, local elites gradually began to join the Europeans in the segregated spaces where football was played in Buenos Aires, Montevideo, Santiago, São Paulo and Rio de Janeiro. Official games at this time were elegant affairs attended by members of select families, and presence on the field or the stands was a sign of refinement and social belonging.[4] Whether or not the stories about natives imitating the game after seeing British sailors playing at docks in Latin American ports are to be trusted, what is certain is that football was gradually appropriated by the lower classes. The spread of the game was aided by its very nature, more than once described as ideally suited for the lower classes: the space in which it is practiced can easily be improvised, on grass, dirt, sand, asphalt, or cement surfaces, with objects of various sorts temporarily playing the role of goal posts at each end of a field whose dimensions may vary considerably. (In informal games played on beaches, one of the sidelines may be marked by the ocean, demonstrating that the dimensions of the playing field need not even be fixed, expanding and contracting with the coming and going of the waves.) Of the minimal equipment which may be used, only a ball is indispensable, and even this has been improvised in a variety of ways, from socks tied together to bags of paper. Finally, the rules of the game are famous for their simplicity and sparsity and do not excessively privilege particular physical characteristics.

Football's adaptability allowed it to gain popularity as a leisurely activity in Latin America during the early decades of the twentieth century, but the history of the entrance of lower class players – and disenfranchised blacks, mulattos and mestizos in particular – into professional club teams in Latin America was riddled with conflict. According to historian Eduardo Galeano, Uruguay was the first country to include black players in its national team, and when it beat Chile in the first South American championship of 1916 with a team that included two black players – Isabelino Gradín and Juan Delgado – Chile asked that the game be annulled, claiming the opposing team had 'two Africans'.[5]

In Brazil similar incidents indicated the tension which resulted from the entrance of the lower classes into spaces previously reserved for the elite. When a black player was hired by Rio de Janeiro's América team in 1923, nine 'white' players left in protest. Mulattos and mestizos thus often disguised their ethnic background, whenever possible, in order to be allowed to play. In the 1920s, Brazilian football's first great idol, Arthur Friedenreich – son of a German immigrant and a woman of African descent – allegedly painstakingly straightened his hair before games, while Carlos Alberto – the only mulatto playing for Fluminense in 1916 – is said to have whitened his face with rice powder before entering the field.[6]

This physical masking found its equivalent in bodily practice with players like Domingos da Guia, a working-class black player whose reserved and supposedly upper-class style of playing in the 1930s and 1940s made him, in football, a figure not unlike the Brazilian mulatto writer Machado de Assis; the phrase used by sociologist Gilberto Freyre to describe the latter – 'an Englishman in the tropics' – could perhaps also apply to the former. At times no mask was sufficient, however, and after a heated national debate had considered whether blacks should be allowed to represent Brazil in the South American Championship in Buenos Aires in 1921, Brazilian president Epitácio Pessoa in effect intervened and prohibited the inclusion of blacks, declaring that it would not be in the interest of Brazil's image for non-whites to represent the country in international competitions.

The competitive pressures that followed professionalization in the 1930s made it increasingly difficult for local club teams to resist drafting talented non-elite players, and as early as the third World Cup, in 1938, some of the most admired players in the Brazilian team – like Leônidas da Silva and Domingos da Guia – were black and poor.

National and international admiration of black and mestizo Brazilian players, however, was not enough to dispel the racist ideology which claimed that Brazil would never be successful when facing European teams or whiter South American teams. After Brazilians were defeated in the World Cups of 1950 and 1954 – by Uruguay and Hungary, respectively – racist explanations were quickly summoned to explain Brazil's ineptness, and nineteenth-century theories condemning miscegenation as racial and cultural degeneration were recycled. The following was written after Brazil's defeat to Hungary in 1954:

> The Brazilian players lacked what is lacking for the Brazilian people in general ... The causes ... touch on the foundations of social science in the comparative study of races, environment, climate, eating habits, spirit, culture, and individual and common living processes ... They go back to genetics itself. It is undeniable that Hungary has a better predisposition, like so many other countries, arming its respective all-star team with the best positive attributes. Our people's psychosocial state is still *green* ... Given the state of the Brazilian people, only by chance or contingency might we become world football champions and establish hegemony in this sport ... In Brazilian football, flashy trim lends artistic expression to the match, to the detriment of yield and results. *Exhibition* jeopardizes *competition*. It would be easy to compare the physiognomy of a Brazilian all-star team, made up mostly of blacks and mulattos, with that of Argentine, German, Hungarian, or English football ... [I]t does not meet up with the *olympic aristocracy*, destined to remark itself periodically.[7]

Among the things to be noted here is the way in which the national team was already seen as a condensation of society at large. Its perceived faults, then, mirrored more general faults in the Brazilian nation itself.

Gradually, however, and in particular after the extremely successful and talented teams of the late 1950s and 1960s, Brazilian teams and players came to be acclaimed both nationally and internationally. In addition to the Brazilian national team's exceptional record in World Cups,[8] local professional teams such as Santos, Botafogo, Flamengo and São Paulo have also been successful internationally. Two of the players generally considered among the best in the history of football – Pelé and Garrincha – are Brazilians; both had their international debuts in the 1958 World Cup and played into the 1960s and 1970s. Other Brazilian players who are widely admired for their exceptional skill are Leônidas da Silva (from the 1930s and 1940s), Didi (1950s and early 1960s), Gérson, Tostão, Rivelino and Carlos Alberto Torres (who, along with Pelé, formed the base of the remarkable 1970 Brazilian team), Zico, Sócrates, and Falcão (1980s) and, most recently, Romário, Ronaldo, Rivaldo and Ronaldinho (all of whom were at some point chosen best player in the world). Admiration for these players and teams has been based not only on their competitive success, but also on the perception that there is something unique and extraordinary about the way in which Brazilians play the game, a way of playing which is believed to have developed as it did only after the game emigrated from restricted elite clubs to more marginal locations.

The process through which football was localized may be compared with similar developments in Latin American carnivals; in both cases, an elite form of recreation with European origins was slowly appropriated by the lower classes and then profoundly transformed. Thus, at first the obsession with all things English in Brazilian football included such absurd chapters as uniforms being imported – in a sport in which clothing is irrelevant – and, according to some accounts, Brazilian players asking one another in English for pardon after committing a foul. Yet the movement toward the localization of the practice was accompanied by a vernacularization of the language used not only on the pitch but also around it, by observers and fans, in a process apparently similar to the indigenization of Indian cricket around the same time, as described by Arjun Appadurai.[9] Native clothing eventually was accepted even for official games, and the English terms 'shoot', 'half-back', 'goal-keeper', and 'offside' were slowly less commonly heard around Brazilian fields. In some cases the English words were adapted by participants and observers with minor alterations ('shoot' became *chutar*, 'back' became *beque*), while in others rough Portuguese translations were used (*escanteio* for 'corner' and *atacante* for 'forward').

New terms had to be invented, however, for ways of moving the body and the ball which were seen for the first time on Brazilian fields and involved what was seen as very un-English embellishment. *Folha seca* (dry leaf), for instance, referred to a type of kick coined by Didi in the 1950s which mimicked its namesake by first rising slowly to then fall unexpectedly. Both Brazilians and Chileans claim authorship of a move which involves doing a backwards somersault, with one's back to the goal and the ball, and kicking the ball as it passes over one's head; Brazilians – who insist it was invented by Petronilho de Brito in the 1920s and perfected by Leônidas da Silva – call it a *bicicleta* (bicycle), while Chileans claim authorship belongs to Ramón Unzaga and call it a *chilena*.[10] In Brazil, then, with the vernacularization of both bodily practices and the language associated with them, 'football' slowly became *futebol*.

That the story of the practice of football in Brazil begins with this vernacularization of a foreign language and may be told as a chapter in the narrative of the spread of European influence, might lead one to expect the type of origin anxiety expressed by Richard D.E. Burton when discussing cricket in the Caribbean. Burton claims that the game, also created by the English, can best be described as 'fantasy'. Playing cricket in the Caribbean – and in particular playing against former colonial rulers – creates an illusion of power, one similar to the ephemeral inversion of hierarchies in carnival. The illusion prevents people from seeing 'the truly significant fact', which is 'not that they regularly beat Massa at his own game and regularly make him look foolish, but that they are playing his game in the first place'.[11]

The fundamental point in such criticisms is that the origin of the practice is foreign, and in Brazil some early critics of football made similar laments over what was perceived as the mimicry of a European game. Among the fiercest critics was novelist Lima Barreto, who considered football a form of modernization as baneful as the skyscraper, cinema and republicanism. In a series of newspaper articles written between 1919 and 1921, Barreto condemned the imitation of a foreign sport and founded a League Against Football. What is most notable about Barreto's protest, however, is that his was virtually a lone voice in Brazil; a vast multitude of football enthusiasts from the most diverse backgrounds applaud the ease and ability with which Brazilians adopted and transformed the game. Writers Olavo Bilac and Henrique Coelho Neto, for instance, among the first members of the exclusive Brazilian Academy of Letters, fervently supported football in Rio de Janeiro at the turn of the century. Novelist José Lins do Rêgo, author of *Menino de Engenho*, praised the national selection which represented the country in a 1932 championship and called it a reflection of Brazil's social democracy.[12] A remark by playwright Nelson Rodrigues in the 1960s summarized the situation well: it was as shocking, he claimed, for a Brazilian writer to ignore players Pelé and Garrincha as it would have been for Portuguese poet Camões to ignore the sea.[13]

Today, football is criticized in Brazil for a number of reasons, yet it is unlikely that even the most ardent critic of football would add to the argument the fact that the sport did not originate in Brazil. This might be in part because the question of origins is complex in cultures which define themselves through mixture. The Brazilian tradition of cultural 'anthropophagy', for instance, seeks to appropriate the foreign in such a way that its origins are obscured. And in fact two works of fiction would actually locate the invention of football in Brazil itself. In the mythical time in which Mário de Andrade's 1928 novel *Macunaíma* takes place, the protagonist Macunaíma mischievously hides a bug in his brother Maanape's coffee grounds. The next time Maanape drinks coffee, the bug bites his tongue and he throws it as far as he can. Macunaíma then transforms a cotton wad into a white bug and leaves it in a hammock for it to bite Jiguê, who also throws the bug into the distance. As revenge, Maanape and Jiguê magically transform a brick into a leather ball and kick it at Macunaíma's face; he in anger kicks the ball away. The two bugs land near the city of Campinas, while the ball kicked by Macunaíma lands in a vacant field. Thus, the narrative claims, coffee, cotton and football – 'three of the main pests in the country today' – were created in Brazil.[14]

In Carlos Diegues's 1984 film 'Quilombo', another possible site for the invention of football is imagined. The film is based on the story of the *Quilombo dos Palmares*, a sixteenth-century maroon community which, after being established by runaway slaves in north-eastern Brazil, developed into a self-governing collection of villages and survived a number of government attacks until its final defeat in the seventeenth century. In the film, children in Palmares are often seen practicing the Afro-Brazilian dance and martial art *capoeira*, and in one brief scene three boys play with a ball, throwing it to each other and catching it with their hands. One of the boys suddenly exclaims, 'We could play with our feet, no?' and begins to juggle the ball with his feet.[15] In both the film and the novel, then, football arises from an apparently autonomous space in the Brazilian past, indigenous in the novel and black in the film. Football is felt to be a Brazilian game in a very profound way, and the claim which begins Ashis Nandy's wonderful book on cricket in India could be modified to describe football in Brazil: football is a Brazilian game accidentally discovered by the British.[16]

Ways of Playing, Ways of Being

Such interest in reflecting on, and discussing, football in Brazil comes from the conviction that in the practice of the game something of critical importance is perceived. As Heidegger wrote about Van Gogh's painting of peasant shoes, 'This does not mean that something is correctly represented and rendered here' but, rather, that its being is taken 'into protective heed'.[17] In *futebol*, what is unconcealed is, perhaps, a possible way of being in the contemporary world. Although this specific way of being will here be primarily called 'Brazilian', there is nothing about this mode of existence which precludes it from being referred to by other names. ('Colombian', 'Caribbean', 'African-American' or 'Baroque', for instance, would be neither less nor more exact.) Antonio Benítez Rojo circumvents the impossible search for a name; he finally calls a Caribbean way of being a 'certain kind of way'. This provides an opening which allows Benítez Rojo to indicate the relation between 'a dance movement and the baroque spiral of a colonial railing',[18] even though the Caribbean dance is primarily a result of African influences (although it is also other things) and Baroque architecture is primarily a result of European influences (although it too is other things).

That a particular way of being is captured in *futebol* has been widely accepted throughout the game's history. It is, in short, a mode of existence based on pleasure, play, improvisation, excess and the appreciation of the aesthetic. This traditional *futebol* is based on short rather than long passes; players are more likely to dribble and pass the ball up the field towards their opponent's goal than to send a long kick into their half of the field. Once near the opponent's penalty area, a long cross or lob resulting in a header by a forward is rarely the preferred play, and players usually attempt to dribble or pass the ball into the area, maintaining the ball close to the ground. Short passes and dribbles, then, are plentiful, and collective strategy is secondary to individual technique. Improvisation is both praised and expected. Traditionally, offence is privileged, and the most popular players among Brazilian fans have always been attackers. Furthermore, Brazilians and foreigners alike have recognized the importance of the aesthetic dimension for Brazilian players and public.

In competitive games, winning is certainly important, and fans will often demand it with ferocity. Yet the lukewarm reaction to the Brazilian victory in the 1994 World Cup is a sign of the importance of the aesthetic for the Brazilian fan. A great player is not only one who is efficient, but one who plays in a particular way; the judgment of a player is not only, and not even primarily, quantitative.[19] Thus what other schools of football consider superfluous moves, irresponsible showmanship and irreverent flair, in Brazilian *futebol* is essential. Garrincha, considered by many to have been the most faithful incarnation of the Brazilian way of playing, is remembered for many plays without any immediately apparent objective – such as dribbling past the same player more than once, returning after having past him – rather than for goals scored.

The criticism local fans commonly direct at European players – that is, what they are thought to lack – further highlights what in Brazil is considered desirable. In popular discourse, Europeans are said to be unable to move in certain ways. Their bodies, in other words, are not capable of moving in certain ways that in Brazil are admired. These ways of moving involve flexibility and the ability to bend certain parts of the body with ease and grace. Europeans are said to have a *cintura dura* (a stiff waist) and *pernas-de-pau* (wooden legs) and to lack *jogo de cintura* (the ability to move the waist and, figuratively, to improvise).

All of the above suggest lack of flexibility and difficulty moving. In a word, Europeans are said to lack *ginga*, a word that cannot be translated into English in any simple sense. It has traditionally been used to refer to a swaying, back-and-forth motion central to *capoeira*, yet today it refers to a way of moving not only in *capoeira* but also in football, dance and everyday walking. In those teams that play with *ginga* – and this could include not only the Brazil of the 1960s but also teams such as Colombia in 1994 and Nigeria in 1994 and 1998 – not only are bodies moved in flexible, rhythmic ways, but the ball is also made to take surprising twists and turns. In a description of English team Arsenal's visit to Brazil in 1957, the English goalkeeper was said to have stared incredulously as a ball made an improbable curve and entered the goal as if it had a life of its own. The English, the newspaper account claimed, were accustomed to a 'mathematical' and 'logical' football without these surprises and protested following the improbable goal.[20]

* * *

The scene in the film 'Quilombo' in which a group of boys invents football takes place in a moment of leisure, when the entire community is involved in activities such as singing or dancing. That those involved in the ball game are children further accentuates the distance of the activity from the world of labour. This version of *futebol's* origin, then, mirrors the introduction of the game as play to many Brazilian males during the course of their childhoods, with the sign of play remaining with the game in its future incarnations, from informal street games to professional competition. Anthropologist Roberto da Matta has suggested that for Brazilians football is therefore not a sport, as it might have been for the English, but a game: 'This is because it is born as a plaything, as playing with a ball, and later play is not given up but is associated with dexterity … It is exactly because we live under the imperative of play that carnival and football are national passions.'[21] The value of the game, then, is judged by the pleasure and joy it elicits, far from the nineteenth-century English schools where football was considered a means of instilling moral values in boys, encouraging discipline, respect for rules and dedication to the Protestant work ethic. The idealized way of playing celebrated in Brazilian culture recognizes the possibility that the disciplinary and pedagogical impulse of English sports might be for a moment dribbled by a body which seeks to be the site of pleasure.

In *futebol* play is ritualized in the 'useless' dribble. The dribble performed in the middle of the field, without an objective aim and without contributing to progress towards the opponent's goal, exists for its own sake. The player and the audience derive pleasure from the beauty of the moment, regardless of its consequences. This is the territory of baroque excess, of circularity, of improvisation. To it belong dances of the Americas such as *samba*, *merengue* and *salsa*, and carnival is its most spectacular manifestation. In its 'uselessness' it becomes essential for living in certain kinds of ways. A similar argument was made by the playwright and occasional football critic Nelson Rodrigues in a Rio de Janeiro newspaper in 1977:

> The Brazilian player will not give up beauty. A simple victory will be much less if it is not beautiful. Nonetheless, the other day one of our fundamental fools was saying to me, 'Football has nothing to do with art.' The man said this, and then I thought of Mané.[22]

The 'Mané' referred to by Rodrigues was Mané Garrincha, and the article continues with the description of a few of Garrincha's plays before the 1958 World Cup. Garrincha would dribble past defenders, then stop and wait for them to return, so he could dribble them again. On at least one occasion, he stopped in front of the goal, without an opponent in sight, and instead of shooting into the open goal took the ball back to dribble other players. These were the plays which Garrincha would be remembered for, and, for Rodrigues,

> That is how we play. We don't discard that superfluous but fundamental thing which is beauty. Only yesterday I told the distinguished novelist Perminio Asfora, 'What is essential for our players is the superfluous...' I recounted this incident in order to define Brazilian football and demonstrate the profound abyss which exists between our players and the Europeans.[23]

Players and teams are therefore not judged by the public primarily for their competence and efficiency.

The reaction in Brazil to the 1994 World Cup can perhaps now be understood. The defensive stance implemented by coach Carlos Alberto Parreira created a team devoted to preventing the opponent from scoring any goals, rather than scoring them itself. Only two of the eleven members of the starting team could be categorized as pure offensive players, and, according to Parreira, even they were to have defensive responsibilities. Discipline and collective coordination, then, were essential, and improvisation and embellishment were to be discouraged. Parreira insisted that the team 'play in the way today's football demands. Magic and dreams are finished in football. We have to combine technique and efficiency.'[24] The Brazilian national selection advanced to the finals without a single loss, but also without a spectacular victory. The final game, played against an aging Italy, ended in a scoreless tie after ninety minutes of play and even after overtime neither team had been able to score a single goal. For the first time in the history of the World Cup, the championship was decided by penalty kicks.

Even before the final victory was met with timid celebrations, during the preparation for the final tournament, Parreira's defensive tactics had already provoked the fury of fans. His tactics, which enforced efficiency at all costs, were opposed with such enthusiasm not because they seemed odd but precisely because they were easily recognizable. The coach's imposition of a standard based on efficiency and productivity mirrored people's experiences as they negotiated the demands of capitalism in their daily lives. *Futebol*, however, was a space in which the homogenization of the individual labourer through the imposition of norms of efficiency was not expected to be victorious. The quality of *futebol* was therefore not to be judged by efficiency or competence – quantitative standards – but by the pleasure it provided to those watching and playing, and this pleasure, in turn, was closely tied to *futebol*'s ability to approximate in a way of playing a particular way of being. Contrary to common interpretations, then, the passion provoked by traditional *futebol* in Brazil does not result from the fact that it mirrors the local society but, rather, that it presents an image of that which is lacking in most people's everyday lives.

In such a context, fulfilment, redemption, salvation, rapture, pride, contentment and satisfaction come not primarily from watching players work and improve, but from seeing them subvert the laws of the market while playing. In many areas of Brazilian popular culture – most notably carnival and music – rather than the suspicion of play found in the Protestant work ethic, one finds, in effect, this profound mistrust of labour. Matthew Shirts has made this argument about Brazilian popular music:

> The sphere of labour projects itself over Brazilian popular music as a powerful *inverted image*; the systematic and radical negation of the values elevated into a positive light by work became the preferred poetic theme of our popular composer in the twenties and thirties.[25]

The disdain for work and the exaltation of play affects *futebol*'s status and the way in which it is played. This continues to be, after all, an activity which takes place overwhelmingly outside of work time. For the vast majority of those in some way touched by the game, *futebol* is either watched, played or talked about when one is not working. (Since it is work only for a fraction of the population, it is a mistake to equate local *futebol* – or football anywhere, for that matter – exclusively with professional teams.)

Professional football, and the national selection in particular, is *futebol*'s dominant local form, one which absorbs to a certain degree elements from local subaltern groups. Yet it must discipline the heterogeneity of local ways of playing, often manifested through the prohibition of spontaneity, improvisation and embellishment. The recurring struggles between authoritarian coaches and rebellious players may be understood in this light. It might be to escape this discipline that professional players often seem to project their desire for play into parallel activities such as *futevôlei* (a football and volleyball hybrid), where they might recuperate a hedonistic relation with the ball. Interestingly, when talking about the ball itself even professional players appear to rediscover joy and playfulness. Denilson, for instance – a contemporary player who many have likened to Garrincha – says the ball is among the things he most loves in life.[26] Didi, inventor of the *folha seca*, noted in an interview long after his retirement that he had always treated the ball with affection and love and recommends that others do the same.[27]

Throughout the history of Brazilian *futebol*, some professional players have been able to bend the constraints of disciplinary norms and exhibit hedonistic *futebol* even in professional teams. Invariably, these are the players who provoke the most passionate responses from the public, either praised as *artistas da bola* (ball artists) or viciously despised for their lack of professionalism. Garrincha, with his useless dribbles and disregard for tactics, was known by his contemporaries as *a alegria do povo* (the joy of the people).[28] Romário, recalled to the 1994 World Cup team in the last qualifying game, was well known for openly despising work and attempting to avoid practices whenever possible. In the many teams in which he played throughout his career, accusations of irresponsibility and laziness have often been levelled against him. Even his style of playing has been accused of not being 'modern' enough; Romário strolls around the field, never venturing too far from the opposing team's penalty area, participating in the game only sporadically, and contributing very little defensively. To the criticisms, Romário responds that he is not an athlete, but an artist. Constantly in conflict with the disciplinarian Parreira, Romário was the player from the 1994 team most admired by the fans.

Because of the deep-rooted mistrust of labour in Brazilian culture, the evaluation of play must be made on its own terms. The two main approaches to play in the critical tradition – play as opium, play as revolution – seek the value of play outside of itself, in its role as deterrent or stimulant of political activity.[29] Examples of each case may be drawn from recent Brazilian history, as in the use of the national football team as propaganda by the military dictatorship after the 1970 World Cup and, for the opposite case, the contestatory *Democracia Corinthiana* movement of the 1980s. If, however, the value of labour – including the labour of politics – is confronted with the critique of labour outlined above, then a critique of play based on its productivity is a misreading of the very nature of the activity, continuing to equate value with production.[30] It would use precisely the category which is being criticized as the basis of critique. In the celebration of play, the body is claimed as a site of pleasure rather than production. To play *futebol* – and to play it *as* play and not work – would be thus to live in a certain kind of way.

The Past and the Possible in Modernity

If, to paraphrase Derrida, one is indeed always learning to live, then there might be a thing or two to be learned about living from *futebol*.[31] Among the most urgent lessons is that there are many possible ways of living with the past. This is, after all, the central issue in the public debates regarding *futebol* outlined above. The certain way of being described above is today generally thought to belong to the past. That it is addressed in the discussions about *futebol* as a concrete possibility means that at least in this sphere this past is understood as that which is momentarily not dominant.[32] In conversations about *futebol*, we witness a hopeful way of relating to that subordinated past, one which does not deny its presence. Heidegger suggested something similar in *Being and Time*, arguing that the past could be experienced as a significant possibility in the present. One is not bound to the past, nor does one need to attempt a Micheletian resurrection of it. Rather, one may recognize 'the possibility of existence that has-been-there'.[33] In such a context, clinging to the past and seeking in it possibilities for the present are ways of criticizing both the present and the process through which what was once present was made into the past.

This is the framework into which the recurrent debates about the identity of Brazilian *futebol* must be inserted. The refusal, in 1994, to accept the death of what Parreira called 'magic and dreams' reflects the belief that the past – 1960s *futebol* – remains, in some way, a possibility in the present. Likewise, the reluctance to celebrate efficient and 'modern' football suggests that it is not the only possible way of playing. The continued affection for players like Garrincha three decades after their peak may be read in the same light. They represent an admirable moment in the struggle of human beings with the disciplinary constraints of capital.[34]

The same impulse claims the victorious 1994 team should be forgotten and stresses the need to remember the beautiful and graceful but ultimately defeated *futebol-arte* of Zico, Falcão, Sócrates, Júnior, and others in the 1982 Brazilian team coached by Telê Santana. In other spheres, a loss in such an important international forum would suffice to elicit demands that tradition be abandoned altogether and modern techniques be adopted instead. Thereafter, the incident would be guaranteed to be looked upon with shame. This did occur after the 1982 defeat, and in fact many of the changes subsequently implemented in Brazilian *futebol*, under the guise of a 'modernization programme', which would make teams more competitive, were a revival of 1950s theories which claimed that Brazilian teams would only be successful if they played like Europeans. Yet the fact that the 1982 team is now often remembered fondly – to the extent that some would claim that they would rather sleep with it than with other teams – is an auspicious sign. It is the recognition in the popular imagination that there are certain victories which may in fact be civilizational defeats. In Nandy's words, once again, 'mortgaging [the] future to a unilinear theory of history' and

> the vision of certain victory over the white man which goes with it, may turn out to be a prescription for a civilizational defeat if pushed to its logical conclusion. But then, I am also aware that seeing a victory as a camouflaged defeat, for reasons which have to do with the means employed to win, requires a cultural self-confidence which is increasingly available only at the peripheries of Indian society.[35]

In Brazil this rare cultural self-confidence, I venture, emerges in *futebol*. It suggests that it is possible to live without renouncing one's self and, at the same time, rejects those supposedly universal standards which determine victory and loss. The self-confidence provided by *futebol* allows certain ways of being to be embraced while they are shunned in other areas of society. Thus people might speak fondly of Garrincha's playfulness in the 1960s and praise Denilson and Romário's exuberance in the 1990s while playfulness and exuberance are repressed in their own everyday lives.

The past is here an inspiration for productive creativity and the basis for a critique of the present. It is because of this that, drawing from past modes of existence, the realm of the possible – that which may be imagined – is expanded when *futebol* is played. The 'old-fashioned' way in which players like Djalminha, Denilson, Romário, Ronaldinho and many non-professionals play today is evidence of this possibility. Djalminha has claimed that he does not admire any contemporary players and instead attempts to play like his idols from the 1960s. His attachment to the past, then, drives him to action and inspires him to play in a certain way, distancing him from the hopeless nostalgia of those who long for a game which was once practiced with romantic amateurism and lament that now everything is controlled by the market and corporate interests.[36]

These are things which are possible in *futebol* but are nearly inconceivable in other areas. Brazilians involved in *futebol* – in practice or in theory, while playing, talking or thinking about *futebol* – engage with the modern world with a critical perspective that can barely be imagined in other arenas. The self-confidence with which they negotiate modernity through drawing from the past is rare in contemporary Brazilian society. Much more common is the shame which, in a recent article, Jorge Caldeira ties directly to the control of historiography by the post-1964 military dictatorship: the 'average Brazilian imagines he is living in a country composed of a despicable elite exploiting a despicable people … Any decent character from the past appears as suspect to the highest degree.'[37] As we have seen, this is dramatically *not* the case with the characters who inhabit the history of *futebol*.

It is most likely also not the case when this 'average Brazilian' thinks about the Brazilian present through the lens of *futebol*. For a sense of the extent to which this is exceptional, consider the fate of a traditional Brazilian saying. The saying – *Deus é brasileiro* – claims nothing less than that God is Brazilian. The good fortune of having such a compatriot is often used to explain the occasional benefits befalling the country's inhabitants. Yet an amendment has recently been added to the saying, so that one may now hear that God is, indeed, Brazilian, but has moved to Miami. The celebratory pride of the original saying is tempered in its modified version by a resigned bitterness. The supreme deity honoured only one place, of the many in the world, by adopting its nationality, yet he leaves the country – in the migratory wave of the 1980s, perhaps – and settles in the United States. If even God has abandoned Brazil, one is lead to ask, who would wish to stay? If we follow the tendency of this chapter and think of the nation-state in South America as only one of the many things referred to by the word 'Brazil', then 'leaving Brazil' can be done in a number of ways, only one of which involves physical travel outside of certain geographical boundaries – and thus the full force of the saying becomes apparent.

More often than not, deciding to leave Brazil is seen not as the choice between two coeval situations, but as a historical leap out of the past and into the present – from the archaic to the modern. To fully enter modernity, then, one must abandon not only the local past but also the local present. If for a Frenchman modernization is seen as leaving pre-modern France for modern France, in Brazil the move is generally understood as leaving Brazil altogether for modern France (or England, the United States, et cetera.).

This fracture in the prevailing narrative of Brazilian modernization implies a type of self-hatred which is absent in European accounts of the arrival of modernity. If modernity is understood as a story which begins in Europe – as it usually is told – then a value may be ascribed to Europe's past, at least insofar as it made the present possible. European pre-modernity can in this narrative be celebrated in the same way that Marx celebrated the rise of the bourgeoisie: it would eventually create its own gravediggers. Outside of Europe, however, the narrative of modernization is usually thought of as the imposition of an exterior model on a pre-existing surface whose characteristics hinder the model's comfortable fit.

In Brazil, the sense that what is *most* Brazilian is archaic and obsolete is widespread, and it is not uncommon to hear that it must be buried once and for all. Versions of this narrative are present in a variety of areas, ranging from economics to cinema, and in each the general idea is that Brazil must shape itself into a likeness of Europe and the United States in order to survive. This was also once the dominant view in *futebol* in the 1940s and 1950s, and it still occasionally resurfaces. During the dictatorship the military government's attempt to have increased control of the national team resulted in Claudio Coutinho's 'scientific football' of 1978, which emphasized discipline and attempted to curtail hedonism. The dribble, significantly, was defined by Coutinho as 'a waste of time and proof of our weakness'.[38]

In general, however, this self-hatred is remarkably *not* dominant in *futebol*. Here, the belief in the desirability of a Brazilian way of being prevails, and there is an inversion of the mode of thinking described above. Maintaining Brazil's 'certain kind of way' is not suicidal but, rather, necessary precisely in order to survive. Consider, for instance, the way in which the first World Cup victory by the Brazilian team in 1958 was greeted in two newspapers:

> With the 1958 victory, Brazilians changed even physically. I remember that after the game between Brazil and Sweden ended, I saw a small black woman. She was the typical slum dweller. But the Brazilian triumph transformed her. She walked down the sidewalk with the charm of a Joan of Arc. The same was true for black men, who – attractive, brilliant, luxurious – seemed like fabulous Ethiopian princes. Yes, after 1958, the Brazilian was no longer a mongrel [*vira-lata*] among men and Brazil was no longer a mongrel among nations.[39]

Or else:

> We no longer have reason to envy anyone … You [the players] were Brazilian and, as Brazilians, without borrowing anything from anyone, won the world championship, the most arduous, the most competitive, the most difficult ever … Brazilian football was doubted, and thus Brazil was doubted. And you swept away that doubt, elevating Brazil in the eyes of the world. Not only are we brilliant, not only are we acrobats, not only are we circus artists: we are world champions … Thank you very much, Brazilian players: you showed the world a perfect Brazil.[40]

The two passages stress a perceived change in self-confidence, even among the most disenfranchised members of society, resulting from a triumph which is achieved by players who were able to succeed without ceasing to be Brazilian.

*   *   *

One might wonder why it is precisely in a non-verbal bodily practice that this certain way of being is encountered and the presence of the past is manifested. The answer lies in the fact that what I have described as an aesthetics of pleasure, improvisation, excess and mistrust of labour, is also a subaltern mode of existence. As such, its power to inscribe its past and present on paper is severely limited. (The vulnerability of the traces of the subaltern past in Brazil was rarely clearer than in 1890, when Rui Barbosa ordered that all archives pertaining to slavery be burned.) Such a situation has led to the habit among intellectuals of lamenting the 'silence of the people'. Yet the problem might be, instead, the narrow definitions of communication, tradition and history. In Brazil, bodily practice became a sort of subaltern historiography, and *futebol* was one of its preferred genres.

Notes

All translations from the Portuguese and Spanish are mine except where otherwise noted.

[1]   'Um encontro de craques', *Jornal do Brasil* (May 1997).
[2]   For an episodic history of football, see Galeano, *El Futbol a Sol Y Sombra*.
[3]   Mason, *Passion of the People?*, 2–8.
[4]   Lopes, 'Successes and Contradictions in "Multiracial" Brazililan Football', 56.
[5]   Galeano, *El Futbol a Sol Y Sombra*, 42.

[6]   For an account of these contentious incidents, see Lopes, 'Successes and Contradictions', 60–7.

[7]   Lyra Filho, quoted in Lopes, 'Successes and Contradictions', 83–4.

[8]   Brazil is the only country to have qualified for every edition of the World Cup and, with five victories (1958, 1962, 1970, 1994, 2002), has won the Cup the most times. In number of victories, it is followed by Italy (1934, 1938, 1982, 2006), Germany (1954, 1974, 1990), Uruguay (1930, 1950), Argentina (1978, 1986), England (1966) and France (1998).

[9]   Appadurai, *Modernity at Large*, 89–113.

[10]   Football chronicler Mario Rodrigues Filho created the character of a nostalgic fan in his newspaper columns and imagined his reminiscences about the days when moves were still being invented. The author had a sort of copyright of the move, he claimed, and had the right to name it. In Rodrigues Filho, *O sapo de Arubinha*, 102–3.

[11]   Burton, *Afro-Creole Power*, 185–6.

[12]   Quoted in Levine, 'Sport and Society: The Case of Brazilian Futebol', 239–40.

[13]   Carlos Haag, 'Futebol e arte formam um grande time', *O Estado de São Paulo*, 13 July 1998.

[14]   de Andrade, *Macunaíma*, 41–2.

[15]   'Quilombo', dir. Carlos Diegues (CDK Produções Ltda, 1984).

[16]   'Cricket is an Indian game accidentally discovered by the British,' Nandy writes in *The Tao of Cricket*, 1.

[17]   Heidegger, 'The Origin of the Work of Art', 181.

[18]   Rojo, *The Repeating Island*, 4.

[19]   According to Burton, the same is true in Caribbean cricket: with the batsmen it is not just a question of scoring heavily and fast but of scoring with style, panache and bravado. In Burton, *Afro-Creole Power*, 181–4.

[20]   Rodrigues Filho, *O sapo de Arubinha*, 138.

[21]   Roberto da Matta, quoted in Mason, *Passion of the People?*, 124.

[22]   The article, entitled 'O essencial é o supérfluo' (The essential is superfluous), was later published in Rodrigues, *A pátria em chuteiras*, 186–7.

[23]   Ibid., 187.

[24]   Carlos Alberto Parreira, quoted in *New York Times*, 1 July 1994.

[25]   Shirts, 'Sócrates, Corinthians, and Questions of Democracy and Citizenship', 100, 102.

[26]   'Jogadores paulistas criticam qualidade das bolas', *O Estado de São Paulo*, 31 July 1997.

[27]   Galeano, *El Futbol a Sol Y Sombra*, 121.

[28]   That Garrincha has been loved with such intensity and for so long suggests which ways of being are admired in Brazil; that his life ended tragically, with premature retirement and financial hardship, indicates the fate many encounter under capitalism when bending its laws.

[29]   Johan Huizinga lists some of the functions which have historically been attributed to play: the discharge of excess energy, training for the young, the fulfilment of an imitative instinct, an outlet for aggressive impulses and the satisfaction of the will to compete. All these hypotheses, Huizinga suggests, 'have one thing in common: they all start from the assumption that play must serve something which is *not* play'. (Huizinga, *Homo Ludens*, 2.) In capitalism, play becomes codified as part of leisure, or that which one does when not working.

[30]   See Rojo, *The Repeating Island*, 19.

[31]   Derrida, *Specters of Marx*, xvii–xviii. Albert Camus, remembering his days of playing football in Algeria, wrote that in football he learned that the ball never comes from the direction one expects it to, a lesson he would find useful later in his life. He also claimed that everything he knew of morality he had learned from football. See Camus, 'Lo que de debo al futbol', 373–6.

[32]   The fact that this way of being may now be called by such different names as Baroque, African or Brazilian, as I have suggested, illustrates how they have all been defined, from within modernity, as different versions of modernity's other.

[33]   Heidegger, *Being and Time*, 352–3.

[34]   A similar argument is made in Lopes and Maresca, 'La disparition de "La Joie du Peuple"'. It must also be said, in this respect, that it is precisely the difference in the Brazilian style of

playing that has recently become attractive to companies and marketing campaigns. Illustrating, perhaps, a shift in the workings of capitalism, or at least in advertising, straightforward efficiency and pragmatism have been supplanted in much contemporary advertising by vague suggestions of a desirable lifestyle. In this sense, Brazilian players such as Ronaldinho Gaúcho become marketable precisely because of their apparent lack of discipline and excess.

[35]   Nandy, *The Tao of Cricket*, 122.
[36]   For an example of this sort of lament, see Galeano's *El Futbol a Sol Y Sombra*.
[37]   Jorge Caldeira, 'Imagens do Brasil', *Bravo! 2*, no.17 (February 1999), 20.
[38]   Quoted in Mason, *Passion of the People?*, 154.
[39]   Nelson Rodrigues, *A Pátria em Chuteiras*, 118.
[40]   Rodrigues Filho, *O sapo de Arubinha*, 241.

References

Andrade, Mario de. *Macunaíma*. Translated by E.A. Goodland. New York: Random House, 1984.

Appadurai, Arjun. *Modernity at Large: Cultural Dimensions of Globalization*. Mineapolis: University of Minnesota Press, 1996.

Burton, Richard D.E. *Afro-Creole Power, Opposition and Play in the Caribbean*. Ithaca: Cornell University Press, 1997.

Camus, Albert. 'Lo que de debo al futbol'. In *Hambre de gol: Cronicas y estampas del futbol*, edited by Juan José Reyes and Ignacio Trejo Fuentes. Mexico City: Cal y Arena, 1998.

Derrida, Jacques. *Specters of Marx: The State of the Debt, the Work of Mourning, and the New International*. Translated by Peggy Kamuf. New York: Routledge, 1994.

Galeano, Eduardo. *El Futbol a Sol Y Sombra*. Madrid: Siglo Veintiuno de Espana Editores, 1995.

Heidegger, Martin. *Being and Time*. Trans. J. Stambaugh. New York: State University of New York Press, 1996.

Heidegger, Martin. 'The Origin of the Work of Art'. In *Basic Writings*, edited by David Farrell Krell. San Francisco: Harper Collins, 1993.

Huizinga, Johan. *Homo Ludens: A Study of the Play-Element in Culture*. Boston: Beacon Press, 1955.

Levine, Robert. 'Sport and Society: The Case of Brazilian Futebol'. *Luso-Brazilian Review 17*, no.2 (1980): 239–40.

Lopes, José Sérgio Leite. 'Successes and Contradictions in "Multiracial" Brazililan Football'. In *Entering the Field: New Perspectives on World Football*, edited by Gary Armstrong and Richard Giulianotti. Oxford: Berg, 1997.

Lopes, José Sérgio Leite and Sylvain Maresca. 'La Disparition De "La Joie Du Peuple". Notes Sur La Mont Du; Un Joueur De Football'. *Actes de la Recherche en Sciences Sociales, 79* (1989): 21–36.

Mason, Tony. *Passion of the People?* London: Verso, 1995.

Nandy, Ashis. *The Tao of Cricket*. New Delhi and New York: Viking, 1989.

Rodrigues Filho, Mario. *Os Anos De Sonh Do Futebol Brasileiro*. Sao Paulo: Cmpanhia das Letras, 1994.

Rodrigues, Nelson. 'O essencial é o supérfluo'. In *A Pátria em chuteiras: Novas cronicas de futebol*, edited by Nelson Rodrigues. Sao Paulo: Companhia das Letras, 1994.

Rojo, Antonio Benitez. *The Repeating Island: The Caribbean and the Postmodern Perspective*. Translated by James E. Maraniss. Durham, NC: Duke University Press, 1996.

Shirts, Matthew. 'Socrates, Corinthians, and Questions of Democracy and Citizenship'. In *Sport and Society in Latin America*, edited by Joseph L. Arbena. New York: Greenwood Press, 1988.

I think that the A league represents an example of soccer on a professional level. Problems surrounding ethnicity in soccer have long been documented. Although it is a new competition, early indications are that uniting cities to follow one team has lead to a decrease in crowd hooliganism. Soccer is fast becoming more popular among children and my daughters have recently started to play.

Unfortunately, it appears that the local competition is still being used as a vehicle, to express hooligan behaviour. Therefore, I am more inclined to support the A-League competition to enable my children to gain a perspective of the game which encourages a family friendly environment.

I believe the nationalisation of the soccer competition is a step in the right direction for progression of soccer in this country. Uniting the local fan bases who were largely opposed through race and rivalries into one supporter base is great. It gives a sense of unity to the city's soccer lovers. It also gives strength to the competition in this country, with success and money attracting bigger and better players. It takes a step in the right direction in making the World Cup and overall giving strength and identity to soccer in this country. Go Victory!

Soccer has been seen as an ethnic game by the predominant Anglo-Saxon section of Australian society and a received reflection of the problems of the immigrant communities. This is not so, for it is a great game and is for all people. This is why it is referred to as the world game. I watch the Melbourne Victory team play rather than a local Serbian, Greek etc. club for it is the state team and does not alienate anyone who is not of that club's particular heritage. The Melbourne Victory will be a reason for the expansion of soccer in Victoria and Australia.

The A-League is a great inclusion into the sporting agenda in Australian sport. Although I have never been to a soccer game, I feel that a premier league is also what has been missing from Australian soccer. With increasing demand on Australia to qualify for the World Cup, a top class, well organised, well-promoted elite competition will only strengthen the position of grass roots soccer as it will allow more people access to top class soccer without necessarily needing to be associated with a particular cultural group within Australia. The A-League is not connected with any other nationality groups therefore it has its own identity as an Australian soccer competition.

Having a soccer team that embraces *all* ethnic backgrounds is great for the longevity of soccer in Australia. Yes it may detract from the enjoyment of the rivalries between local teams, but it eliminates violence in crowds. I believe the A-League sparks interest from other sports followers which has to be a positive for soccer.

The cornerstone of the new A-League is undoubtedly its clear departure from the ethnic supporter bases that have characterized Australian soccer for so long. The mono-cultural rhetoric that is embedded within the A-League constitution is not dissimilar to the current position on multiculturalism articulated by the political leadership of Australia. Indeed, in what is likely to become a landmark address, the Deputy Prime Minister, Peter Costello, drew on the example of Socceroos' qualification to 2006 World Cup to claim that Australian identity is a singular notion and that becoming an Australian citizen means relinquishing pre-existing cultural affiliations:

> I was reminded of this recently when watching the Socceroos play in the World Cup Qualifier against Uruguay. A television commentator was moving amongst the crowd that was lining up to come into the ground. He came across an elderly woman with a heavy accent. He asked her where she came from, and she replied, 'I come from

Uruguay to Australia twenty years ago.' The reporter said, 'So you're barracking for Uruguay.' The woman was outraged. 'No!' she yelled back at him. 'I go for Australia!' and looked incensed that he would think otherwise. Whether she went on to say 'Australia is my country' I can't be sure but that is what she meant.[14]

For Costello the lines are drawn quite simply. Irrespective of a person's place of birth or ethnic background, if they are an Australian then they are obliged to support Australian sporting teams. This is not a particularly new stance for a conservative politician to take. In 1990 the British Tory politician Norman Tebbit posed the question to Britons of Indian and Pakistani background, 'whom [do you] cheer for?' when England plays international cricket. He claimed that many Asian immigrants failed his 'cricket test' of British identity because they supported their former country – or parent country – against their adopted homeland.[15] Should Costello be aware of Tebbit's cricket test, he would no doubt agree with it and see its applicability to the Australian context – to cricket and soccer alike. Those who condone allegiances of mixed cultural identity are guilty of what Costello refers to as a 'confused, mushy, misguided multiculturalism'. The Prime Minister John Howard is also non-accepting of unchecked cultural diversity. In support of Costello's speech, Howard declared that living in Australia means accepting a 'core set of values' that are intrinsically Australian in that they are rooted in that country's Anglo-Saxon cultural tradition.[16] Howard has long been a critic of multiculturalism. In the late 1980s, when on the opposition benches, he advocated a 'One Australia' policy against the perceived ethnic pluralism of the Hawke Labor Government.[17] The constitution of Australian soccer's new A-League appears to have diluted the multicultural character of Australian soccer in favour of a 'one Australia' sporting domain, of which the Prime Minister must surely be supportive.

Ethnicity on the Margins – The Example of Serbian Soccer

The de-ethnicising agenda has been pursued in Australian soccer not only at the premier national level, but also in regard to state competitions. The New South Wales Soccer Federation imposed the banning of 'ethnic' team names in June 1992 before the then Australian Soccer Federation had formally moved on the recommendations of the Bradley Report in regard to the NSL. Therefore, we must avoid giving an impression that the administrators in the state leagues do not have a vision of 'de-ethnicised' soccer beyond the national level. Our case study in this section of the paper focuses on the Springvale White Eagles, a club affiliated with Melbourne's Serbian community. While the supporters of this club manage to keep the link between soccer and ethnic identity they do so against the odds and in defiance of an agenda which seeks the complete removal of 'non-Australian' expressions of allegiance from the nation's sporting culture.

Soccer in the state of Victoria is organized in the following way – from the bottom up – according to a series of tiered league levels and separate divisions:

- 2nd Division – the North and South East (SE) sectors are run as separate home and away competitions
- 1st Division

- Victorian Premier League (VPL)
- 'Hyundai' A–League

The Springvale White Eagles are based in south-eastern Melbourne. They are one of several Serbian based clubs in the Melbourne metropolitan area. The others are: Westgate 'Sinjelic': State League 2 North West; Fitzroy City 'Srbija': State League 2 South East; Noble Park United 'Drina': Provisional League 1 South East; Berwick Kings 'Krjna': Provisional League 3 South East. Although they played the past season in the Victorian State League Division 2, they have also played in the Victorian Premier League. By winning the State League Division 2 last season, they were promoted and will play in Division 1 in the upcoming season. They play at the Serbian Sports Centre in Keysborough. As an entity, along with other so-called ethnic-based clubs, they represent the antithesis of the spirit, values and objectives of the Hyundai A-League. However, the club has recently completed building a grandstand and has a flourishing membership base. It won promotion to State League 1 and averaged the highest crowds in the league, matching many VPL clubs.

It is difficult to be precise about the presence of Serbians in Australia – particularly before the establishment of Serbia-Herzegovina. Many Serbs in Australia trace their home to what is now Croatia and Bosnia-Herzegovina. As such they tend to refer to themselves as Yugoslavs. However, it is estimated that approximately 60,000 Serbs now live in Australia and that they generally arrived in three waves and in two of those instances primarily as refugees. The first large group were those who sought refuge after being displaced during the Second World War. The second refugee wave was a result of the humanitarian crisis in the former Yugoslavia in the early 1990s where many had been expelled from their homes, and were also subjected to imprisonment in concentration camps. Those that arrived in Melbourne were absorbed into one of the two established Serbian communities. The northwest community is based around St Albans and a second larger community is based around Dandenong/Noble Park/Keysborough in the south east. All of these areas are within the category known as the most affordable districts. According to an informant, 'Soccer and church are the easiest ways for us to get together. First thing that happens when they get here is to get introduced to the church by the Migrant Centre in Dandenong so they've got somewhere to socialise and then the schools. Then they all know each other, then word travels fast "come to soccer".'

The White Eagles were founded in 1984 and were in the Victorian Premier League from 1997–99 before being relegated and falling all the way down to State League 2 SE. However, the team won the League in season 2005 and played Division 1 in 2006. Leaders from competing clubs attribute success of any team to the ability of each club to purchase better players. For the White Eagles, they say, this is much easier because of a relatively large support base. The White Eagles average 1,500 spectators per game whereas most other clubs average 200 – except when the White Eagles visit. The White Eagles ethnic affiliation is not necessarily welcomed although as one president of a rival club told us, 'they're not too bad – the Croats are nuttier'. The White Eagles were clearly welcomed for gate revenue and beverage sales. The club was also envied for its capacity to seriously outbid competition clubs when signing players. Said one rival club president, 'You won't see this on the books, but I'll bet some of these clubs (like the White Eagles) have set aside $5,500 for some players.'

Method

Fieldwork provides data about the lives of specific people and allows us to see alternative realities which can modify our culture bound theories of human behaviour.[18] According to Hallinan and Hughson, ethnographic-based fieldwork projects 'offer the most accessible means of getting to the heart of the questions about why and how groups of people do what they do in particular social contexts and settings.'[19] This approach employs descriptive methods such as observation and interview, allowing rich data to be collected. The ethnographic-based method offers an opportunity to gain an in-depth understanding of other cultural groups, showing cultural differences and how people with diverse perspectives interact.[20] Embracing an ethnographic approach, approximately 30 hours of observation were undertaken during the 2005 season and directly involved most home games and two away games. While this occasionally involved conversation, in-depth interviews with selected participants were not undertaken until the season's end. We decided to study the White Eagles because the Serbians are an ethnic group with a parochial investment in soccer support that has been largely overlooked in academic studies, the work of Rob Lynch and colleagues notwithstanding.[21] We were given friendly access by a relevant section of Melbourne's Serbian community, an important dimension to any ethnographic work on groups that are likely to be suspicious of outside observers.

Despite the welcome, it became immediately obvious that being an inconspicuous observer at the ground was unlikely. Initially, there were attempts to make notes whilst the matches were in progress. Only two or three people from the club knew about the researcher presence and our reason for being there. Many others deduced that being 'outsiders' and co-incidentally wearing dark green jackets (on very chilly nights) that we were present as monitors: 'He's from the Federation' (governing body). In both the formative and conclusive stages of the project, we were mindful of the need for credibility and thus shared our work with supporters, academics, and in the case of the White Eagles, with non-affiliated Serbians.

At the Ground

The White Eagles ground is on the fringe of an outer suburban area. The most obvious aspect when arriving at the ground for the first time is its relative remoteness. Like all other spectators it was necessary to obtain private motor vehicle transport as there was no public transport and the ground was situated several kilometres from the nearest housing estate, and well out of walking distance from any bus stop. The entire space including clubhouse, parking areas, playing field and practice field is owned by the club. Club officials estimate its real estate worth as $A8million. 'The ground – we 99 per cent own it. We have a very small loan on it. The site was selected years ago – I was just a young kid then. It was bought under the regime of Yugoslavia and everyone was there. Then when the war broke out, the Serbs took it over [in 1994 the club changed from Springvale United to White Eagles] and the Croatians left. We took out loans to fix up the grounds. It was just a shed.'

Club members maintain that everyone that came out in the 1990s was a refugee from war. Most people moved to where there was a church. DMG Plastics in Keysborough employed a lot of refugees who had come out and did not require any qualifications. 'They get jobs for each other which is easier in low paid factory work.' From there on, once people get the language skills and experience, they tend to move somewhere else. 'DMG employs the most that I know of. Where do they move? It varies. Most people have settled within the Keysborough area but there's a lot of people who've moved out to Narre Warren, Berwick. Hampton Park is a big area, too.'

The soccer club has continued to serve as the social focal point for Serbian émigrés in the Keysborough and surrounding area. The clubhouse and its surrounds are have undergone some renovation and, although somewhat basic compared to the facilities of fully corporate sports clubs, are a source of pride for the community. Attendance of the club – for an outsider – provides a unique sense of stepping into a Serbian domain in the Australian suburbs. The most obvious aspects of the sensual experience are the smells and tastes of Serbian cuisine, cevapi rolls being the centrepiece of the menu.

Sponsors

All clubs rely on sponsorship for a portion of income. The general view is that more money brings better players and more wins. One opposition club official was clearly envious of the White Eagles ability to raise income. 'They get plenty of money and can afford to buy quality players.' The White Eagles were sponsored by Endeavour Sidings (second team shirts), Savoy Industrial Cleaning (the Director is Serbian and a supporter – the White Eagles are the sole beneficiaries of any sponsorship from this company), and Wellington Carpets (first team shirts). The perceived yield to each sponsor is not at all clear. The link between soccer club and business has another significant dimension. According to sources in the White Eagles club, many refugees were offered employment by DMG Plastics in Keysborough. The reason for the owner's enthusiasm to employ Serbian refugees is uncertain, and remains somewhat unquestioned in the community – 'he likes to employ the refugees'. However, the company is not an official sponsor of the White Eagles: 'DMG they are not a sponsor, but when we have dances they'll occasionally give something or if we need to fix up the hall, he'll help out.'

The club has a budget which enables stipendiary remuneration for certain staff: Coach, Players, Assistant Coach and Manager. A minimum of two security guards at each game are also paid but they are paid at standard rates. The majority of the club workers are volunteer staff: Gate and Ticket Box (sellers and collectors), Bar (2 men), Kitchen (3–4 men and women), Parking attendants (men), Greenkeeper (resident manager), Security for Race/Tunnel (men), and Dressing Room attendants. In a sense, these members comprise a separate supporter group. As one put it to us 'I'm too busy to watch the game but I try and keep up'.

Supporter Groups

The Ultradox

This is the self-chosen name for a group of approximately 200 mostly young adult males who congregate for home and away matches. For home games, the Ultradox occupy the upper right-hand side of the stand. Whilst members do not arrive en masse, they do not arrive alone either. Each group with drums begins banging from arrival in the car park until departure. The Ultradox are endorsed by the club who paid for the drums and supplied T-shirts (white with red ULTRADOX on the front with a large same red coloured Adidas logo on the back. The Ultradox name was a thoughtful creation in so much as it was carefully chosen to replace the 'ethnic' nickname banned by the governing body. 'It's a new word that they've created to stop people from thinking that they're ethnically based – which we are not allowed to be. But it's basically Orthodox (reference to the traditional Serbian Church).' The very name of the club is also potentially provocative given that the double-headed white eagle is the distinguishing feature of the Serbian coat of arms. We asked a club official if the Ultradox group was officially part of the club. 'They're not a formal group like they're not organised by the soccer club. We got them t-shirts and bought their drums. We have to keep in communication because if it's a tough game – like the one against Chelsea (Croatian) they have to know that they have to behave.'

Ultradox is not perceived as an 'ethnic' derivative by the soccer authorities and is therefore a surreptitious means of symbolic ethnic identification, a blend of key Serbian cultural markers – the Ultra supporters group of FC Red Star Belgrade and the Serbian Orthodox Church. This is reminiscent of similar symbolic creativity exhibited by the young Australian Croatian soccer supporters in the mid-1990s, discussed by Hughson as 'keeping ethnicity in on the sly'.[22] At each game, the Ultradox banner is displayed above the group high on the back wall of the grandstand. Whilst the Ultradox group is, in general, glad to be regarded as a valuable asset by the club management and many of the players, a number of group members express frustration at the passiveness of the other supporters of the White Eagles. They speak enviously of the atmosphere they witnessed first hand when attending games in Serbia. They desired a more intimidating atmosphere at the White Eagles. One provided us with a photocopy of an article from an English-based football magazine which was titled 'Get Down on Your Knees before the Serbs'. The roving English reporter had concluded that the Belgrade supporters were to be the most feared in Europe. Several of the Ultradox expressed frustration that, despite their efforts, the overall atmosphere at White Eagles games was tranquil compared to those in Belgrade. A lust for such missed excitement flamed their desire to travel to Serbia and, in the meantime, to live out a 'long distance nationalistic' soccer support on the local terrace.[23]

The Regulars

According to a club committee member, 'The Ultradox organised themselves to support some of the players who were their friends. The rest are just general supporters.

We've had Macedonian and Turkish clubs in the area come to the ground. We let anyone through the gate – no matter who it is.' The 'regulars' comprise those who attend most if not all matches – 'My dad is 75 and he goes to all the games in the area he can – Krina, White Eagles, all the away games. His pensioner group amaze me how they organise themselves – where is it, we'll go. The old people still manage to get around each Saturday without fail.' According to another supporter, 'I went to every single away game last year, and we had more of our people than the local people. We went to Eastern Lions and there were signs everywhere saying 'Cevapi For Sale Today' and their President said "we love it when you guys come – the only day of the year when we make money".'

Other supporters might be influenced by the weather or the attractiveness of the fixture. 'It's hardest to get a crowd when it's raining. Lowest crowd we got was 800.' For the home game against Chelsea (Croatian) the crowd was 2,500. For many though, attendance was associated with a routine social engagement. 'I have grown up around Serbian soccer games and have enjoyed them immensely. I saw many examples of nationalistic conflict with games resulting in fights of all sorts. I think local soccer is the basis of 'A' League soccer. Overall, I would say that I support local soccer due to the great food (cevapi) and the social aspects.'

Supporter Behaviour

Whereas the club supporters could readily be sorted into two distinct categories, the fan behaviour was influenced slightly by position on the ladder/table but more so by the affiliation of the opposition. There were three very different responses: matches against the Croatians, the other Serbian team, and the remaining teams.

According to a committee member,

> (The Croatians) brought flags that were confiscated. They also had a photo of one of their ex-political leaders which they put up in the club room – the change room. It got taken down pretty quickly. We did that [removal/confiscation] – when it's at our ground. There are representatives of the soccer federation present but they're incognito. We don't know who they are. It's our responsibility to make sure our ground is all quiet and smooth.

Club committee members insisted that the residual tension with Croatian supporters is not highly problematic. A typical response in this regard:

> We deal with them as professionals – like we do with everyone else. You don't have choices. It's not their fault. It's not my fault. Supporters! You'll never get them to mix. Our very first game of the season was at Chelsea [Croatian] and we'd organised a bus for our people. I didn't actually go. I don't like to go if there's the possibility of violence or to witness. The president's gone with a couple of committee members and when they got there, Chelsea hasn't got any security – no fencing, no gates. There were more of our supporters there but they [the Croatians] were more verbal and abusive. Look they were really no trouble here. Everyone left the ground without incident. Once you get them into the car-park, no-one knows who's who, anyway.'

Said another,

> I was involved a couple of years ago with Fitzroy Serbia when we played St Albans [Croatian]. I think it's cooled down some, but they are always going to hate each other, I think. More in young males who get taught by their parents but look, the war is still too fresh. A lot of people lost a lot of family members and, in the end, it was all for nothing.

The match against the other Serbian team somewhat resembled a family gathering or re-union. Very apparent was the number of people engaged in friendly conversation whilst the game was in progress. This continued throughout and the queues for food and drinks were noticeably busy. However, towards the end of the match, the mood turned rapidly sour. The scores had been tied throughout but the White Eagles scored an apparently lucky late goal. The Fitzroy club was deep in the relegation zone. A drawn result or win was vital. The tension was palpable. Fitzroy were decidedly agitated by the outcome. Being unsure of the heated language exchanges, we were informed later by a White Eagles club official that 'they were upset with us because we didn't throw the game – let them win so that could avoid relegation'. This match also illuminated some of the tensions within the Serbian supporters as a whole. Whatever the catalyst, comments ensued which highlighted the apparent hierarchal demarcation within the Serbs. Our follow up conversations were instigated by a comment that they (Fitzroy) were 'not real Serbs, anyway'. We sought clarification on this contention. In essence, it was put to us that Bosnian Serbs and Krina Serbs were not as 'true' as Serbs from Serbia. We were told (by a Serbian Serb),

> Krina? Even though they call themselves Serbs, I would not classify them as Serbs – there's a distinction. When I speak of Serbs, I only refer to those from Serbia. For example, I would never classify those who come from Croatia as real Serbs. They are of Serbian background but not true Serbs. Also, the people from Krina don't actually speak Serb. They speak a dialect.

This was strongly refuted by a club official, 'My husband's from Krina – a region around Dalmatia. They are all still Serbs. Serbs are defined by religion so whatever information she gave you is incorrect. Most people go to both churches even though they are from different sides.'

We also determined that several of the younger supporters were very cautious and hesitant about assisting as informants. We sensed that they had some divergent views about Serb identity. 'I'd really like to help but I'm worried that I might get offside and get in trouble with the club. I can't afford to be associated with anything critical [of Serbs].' A couple of our informants indicated that they preferred to keep 'a low profile' and not mention their identity because of the negative associations assigned to Yugoslavia, Serbia primarily linked to the reported actions of Slobodan Milosevic. Sekulic has discussed the consequences to Serbs about the West's opinion of Serbs in so much as they have been vilified as the enemy and the culprits for the war.[24]

Conclusion – One Australia/One league

The original national soccer league was established at a time when Australian politics was embracing 'multiculturalism' and various governments had established departments and agencies which accommodated the diversity of language and cultural heritage of Australian residents. Nevertheless, sport remained a bastion of conservatism and the conventional coaching management and selection methods were inherently assimilationist. Not long after the commencement of the national league some commentators touted the dropping of 'ethnic names' for soccer clubs. This prompted an accusation of 'reverse multiculturalism' from one of the earliest academic writers on Australian soccer.[25] Over time, conservative commentators maintained a strongly negative view of the persistent 'ethnic' affiliations within the sport. By the 1990s this rhetoric went largely against the political mainstream, in which multiculturalism generally enjoyed bi-partisan support, maverick voices such as Howard's notwithstanding. However, it is an interesting coincidence that in the current day when Australia has a Prime Minister and Deputy Party Leader who have both spoken publicly against multiculturalism and its underpinning philosophy of cultural diversity, that a 'de-ethnicised' national soccer league has finally emerged. The constitution of the Hyundai A-League articulates with Howard's formerly mooted 'One Australia' policy – in the Prime Minister the league should find its leading patron.

A different story continues on the suburban margins of Melbourne and other Australian cities. Our case study has looked at the example of how a particular collective Serbian Australian identity is maintained through a social network with soccer in pivotal place. Soccer has long been a key dimension of the social experience of certain migrant groups in Australia and an undoubtedly thorny issue within the contested terrain of multiculturalism. Should the corporate driven A-League succeed – given the responses of followers and attendance rates at matches the indicators are positive in this regard – it is unlikely that ethnic affiliations will re-emerge at the national level of soccer competition in Australia. However, as long as soccer is played out in the suburban backblocks it is equally unlikely that the ethnic roots will be severed; the link between soccer and migrant settlement is an important part of Australian cultural history, a *fact* disregarded by those who maintain that there is no place for 'un-Australianness' in Australian sport.

Notes

[1]   Australian Bureau of Statistics, 2004.
[2]   Hughson, 'Australian Soccer: "ethnic" or "Aussie"?', 14–15.
[3]   Ibid.
[4]   Stoddart, *Saturday Afternoon Fever*.
[5]   Mosely, 'Balkans Politics in Australian Soccer'; Mosely, *Ethnic Involvement in Australian Soccer* and Roy Hay, 'British Football, Wogball or the World Game?'
[6]   Moseley, *Ethnic Involvement in Australian Soccer*.
[7]   Mosely, 'Balkans Politics in Australian Soccer'.
[8]   Hay, 'British Football, Wogball or the World Game?'
[9]   Hughson, 'Australian Soccer: "ethnic" or "Aussie"?', 13–14.
[10] Hallinan and Krotee, 'Conceptions of Nationalism and Citizenship among non-Anglo-Celtic Soccer Clubs in an Australian City'; Miller, 'The Unmaking of Soccer'; Hughson, 'Football, Folk Dancing and Fascism'.
[11] Danforth, 'Is the "World Game" an "Ethnic Game" or an "Aussie Game"?'.

[12]   Mosely, Entry for 'Soccer', *The Oxford Companion to Australian Sport*, 322.
[13]   http://www.a-league.com.au/default.aspx?s=league accessed 19 January 2006.
[14]   Costello, 'Worth Promoting, Worth Defending'.
[15]   Marquesee, *Anyone But England*, 137.
[16]   David Humphries, 'Live here and be Australian, Howard declares', *The Sydney Morning Herald*, 25 February 2006.
[17]   Kelly, *The End of Certainty*, 422.
[18]   Lincoln and Guba, *Naturalistic Inquiry*.
[19]   Hughson and Hallinan, *Sporting Tales*, 3.
[20]   Lincoln and Guba, *Naturalistic Inquiry*.
[21]   Proctor and Lynch, 'The Uses of Soccer by Serbian Australians in the Expression of Cultural Identity'.
[22]   Hughson, 'The Bad Blue Boys and the "magical recovery" of John Clarke', 255.
[23]   cf. Hughson, 'Football, Folk Dancing and Fascism', 177.
[24]   Sekulic, 'Foreign Press Writing about Disintegration of Yugoslavia and Culprits for War'; Sekulic, 'Are the Serbs Recognized as the Enemy in Western Public Opinion?'; Sekulic, 'Stereotypes about Serbs in Public Opinion of Some Western Nations'.
[25]   Allan, 'Ethnic and Race Politics'.

References

Allan, L. 'Ethnic and Race Politics: Reverse Multiculturalism and the Politics of Australian Soccer.' *Soccer Action 2* (September 1982): 2.
Australian Bureau of Statistics, 2004.
Bush, Jane R. 'Rhetoric and the Instinct for Survival.' *Political Perspectives 29* (March 1990): 45–53.
Costello, Peter. 'Worth Promoting, Worth Defending: Australian Citizenship, What it Means and How to Nurture it.' Address to the Sydney Institute, Thursday 23 February 2006. http://www.treasurer.gov.au/tsr/content/speeches/2006/004.asp
Danforth, L.M. 'Is the "World Game" and "Ethnic Game" or an "Aussie Game"? Narrating the Nation in Australian Soccer.' *American Ethnologist 28, no.2* (2001): 363–87.
Hallinan, C.J. and J.E. Hughson. *Sporting Tales: Ethnographic Fieldwork Experiences.* Sydney: ASSH Inc., 2001
Hallinan, C.J. and M.L. Krotee. 'Conceptions of Nationalism and Citizenship among non-Anglo-Celtic Soccer Clubs in an Australian City.' *Journal of Sport and Social Issues 17* (1993): 125–33.
Hay, R. 'British Football, Wogball or the World Game? Towards a Social History of Victorian Soccer.' *Australian Society for Sports History: Studies in Sports History 10* (1994): 44–79.
Hughson, J. 'Australian Soccer: "ethnic" or "Aussie"?: The Search for an Image.' *Current Affairs Bulletin 68, no.10* (1992): 12–16.
Hughson, J. 'Football, Folk Dancing and Fascism: Diversity and Difference in Multicultural Australia.' *Journal of Sociology 33, no.2* (1997a): 167–86.
Hughson, J. 'The Bad Blue Boys and the "magical recovery" of John Clarke.' In *Entering the Field: New Perspectives on World Football*, edited by G. Armstrong and R. Giulianotti. Oxford: Berg Publishers, 1997b: 239–59.
Kelly, Paul. *The End of Certainty: Power, Politics and Business in Australia.* St.Leonards, NSW: Allen & Unwin, 2nd ed. 1994.
Lincoln, Y. and E. Guba. *Naturalistic Inquiry.* Newbury Park, CA: Sage, 1985.
Marquesee, Mike, *Anyone But England: Cricket and the National Malaise.* London: Verso, 1994.
Miller, Toby. 'The Unmaking of Soccer: Making a Brand New Subject.' In *Celebrating the Nation: A Critical Study of Australia's Bicentenary,* edited by T. Bennett, P. Buckridge, D. Carter and C. Mercer. Sydney: Allen & Unwin, 1992: 104–20.

Mosely, P. Entry for 'Soccer'. In *The Oxford Companion to Australian Sport,* edited by W. Vamplew, K. Moore, J. O'Hara, R. Cashman and I. Jobling. Melbourne: Oxford University Press, 1992: 316 and 321–3.

Mosely, P. 'Balkans Politics in Australian Soccer.' *Australian Society for Sports History: Studies in Sports History 10* (1994): 33–43.

Mosely, P. *Ethnic Involvement in Australian Soccer: A History 1950–1990.* Canberra: Australian Sports Commission, 1995.

Procter, N. and R. Lynch. 'The Uses of Soccer by Serbian Australians in the Expression of Cultural Identity.' In *Proceedings of the Second ANZALS Conference,* edited by C. Simpson and B. Gidlow. New Zealand: Lincoln University, 1995: 182–88.

Sekelic, N. 'Foreign Press Writing about Disintegration of Yugoslavia and Culprits for War (January 1991–April 1992).' *Sociologija 3* (1997): 401–23.

Sekelic, N. 'Are the Serbs Recognized as the Enemy in Western Public Opinion?' *Sociološki Pregled 1* (1998): 3–31.

Sekelic, N. 'Stereotypes about Serbs in Public Opinion of Some Western Nations.' *Nova srpska politicka misao 1–2* (1999): 27–57.

Stoddart, B. *Saturday Afternoon Fever: Sport in the Australian Culture.* Sydney: Angus & Robertson, 1986.

A Victory for the Fans? Melbourne's New Football Club in Recent Historical Perspective[1]

Roy Hay and Heath McDonald

In 2005 a completely new football (soccer) team, the Melbourne Victory, was created in Victoria, Australia to play in a new national league, the A-League.[2] Within a year it was drawing 50,000 fans to a regular season home game against Sydney FC in a league whose eight participants stretch from Perth, Western Australia to Auckland in New Zealand.[3] This was the third time in less than a decade that a new soccer team had been launched in a city which is best known for its devotion to Australian Rules football, cricket and horse racing.[4] The other two, Collingwood Warriors and Carlton, lasted one season and three seasons and eight games respectively before collapsing in acrimony and debt. Collingwood and Carlton began with on-field success. Collingwood won the National Soccer League (NSL) cup in 1996–97, while Carlton lost narrowly by two goals to one in the NSL Grand Final in its first season in 1997–98.[5] Collingwood drew a 15,000 crowd for its first game, which if sustained, would have underpinned financial survival, but neither it nor Carlton was able to hold the fans in anything like adequate numbers.[6] Collingwood and Carlton were associated with the Australian

Rules football clubs of the same name, played their home games on the football ovals and sought to benefit from what were seen to be the superior administrative capacities of the clubs in the dominant code.[7] Yet both failed spectacularly. Is there any likelihood that the Victory will go the same way or is this a victory for the fans?

The Collingwood and Carlton Experiments

The introduction of Collingwood and Carlton was predicated on clear synergies in trying to combine Australian Rules and football in the new clubs. Soccer had switched to a summer season in 1989, largely to avoid competition for media coverage and sponsorship with Australian Rules and rugby league. Also the revenue from the pools companies in England for the use of Australian fixtures during the northern hemisphere summer break which had been a small but steady source of income had now declined in relative terms. Some of the suburban Australian Football League (AFL) clubs in Melbourne were under increasing pressure as the AFL seemed to be intent on reducing the number of Melbourne clubs and promoting teams in other states. Football clubs faced high costs associated with running suburban home grounds as more and more games were switched to the Melbourne Cricket Ground (MCG) or interstate. So attracting soccer clubs to play at their venues in the off-season seemed to outweigh the risk of boosting a rival code. From the soccer viewpoint links to football could be seen as fitting into attempts by its then leadership under David Hill to 'mainstream' the game. Teams associated with football clubs could not be described as ethnic, unlike Melbourne Croatia or South Melbourne Hellas. This foreign or ethnic image had become counterproductive in the eyes of Hill and his administration. Individual entrepreneurs and business groups noted the rising popularity of soccer as qualification for the 1998 World Cup gathered momentum and public attention.[8] The growth in junior participation in soccer relative to Australian Rules raised the issue of future markets for the codes and the possibilities of cooperation rather than conflict.

However the Collingwood and Carlton ventures were flawed in conception and execution. The historical antipathy between the codes did not help.[9] Collingwood was really the former NSL participant, Heidelberg Alexander Soccer Club, in disguise and when footie fans found out they stayed away in droves.[10] Collingwood threatened to withdraw from the league before the season was completed and players were not paid, but under pressure from Soccer Australia, Heidelberg patron Jack Dardalis helped the club to complete its on-field obligations.[11] Carlton was more inclusive and did extremely well on the field but could not attract enough support to succeed. The soccer fans did not socialize or spend as much in the club during or after games as their Australian Rules peers. The backers of the club had somewhat divided aims. Instead of concentrating solely on domestic success, they were hoping to develop young Australian players and then sell them to top European clubs, as Melbourne Knights did with Mark Viduka. A serious injury to the first of these youngsters, Simon Colosimo, knocked that plan on the head and changes to the transfer compensation system in Europe compounded the problems.[12]

New Clubs in other States

New soccer clubs have been created in other states, for example, Perth Glory was started as an NSL club in 1996. Perth innovator, businessman and club owner Nick Tana and his colleagues set out to establish a single team to represent the city, explicitly appealing to all football supporters of whatever heritage to join the new entity.[13] Initially it was very successful on and off the field, drawing crowds in excess of 15,000 to Perth Oval, where temporary movable stands were used to form an oblong stadium, with just one circular terrace area at one end which was quickly colonized by fans brought up on a diet of English Premier League football. In a series of articles Tara Brabazon has recounted the rediscovery of a form of Englishness at Perth Glory.[14] In practical terms this gave the club a strong spectator base for home games, but Tana complained that the Australian Soccer Federation (ASF) did not fulfil its promises to him to market the code and set up similar teams and clubs in other states. When the ASF was finally replaced by a new regime under Frank Lowy in 2004 following government intervention and the Crawford Report, the way was cleared for a more rational organization of the game at national level.[15] By that time Perth had lost momentum and the resources which Tana had poured into promotion in Perth and he withdrew his support. At time of writing the club's ownership had passed to the FFA, which remained unable to find a buyer for it.[16]

Northern Spirit and Parramatta Power were introduced as new entities in Sydney in 1998 and 1999 respectively. Both just managed to survive into the final season of the NSL in 2003–04 after relatively undistinguished playing performances and poor crowds after promising starts.[17] Spirit reached the top six play-offs in its first and fourth seasons going out in the first elimination final on the first occasion. In 2003–04 both the Spirit and the Power took part in the top six home and away series.[18] Despite some investment by former Australian international players and a cadre of capable and enthusiastic volunteers, the Spirit had effectively gone before the NSL was terminated, while the Leagues club behind the Power had announced that it would not continue to support the team before the demise of the league.

In Adelaide two clubs, Adelaide City Juventus, drawing on Italian-Australian support and West Adelaide Hellas, with Greek-Australian backing had performed creditably in the NSL. Hellas won the NSL championship in 1978 and Adelaide City was champion in 1986, 1991–92, and 1993–94 but the club collapsed in 2003 just as what was to be the final NSL season was about to commence. In a hurried rescue effort the South Australian Soccer Federation and a commercial partner formed a new club, Adelaide United, again appealing to all local soccer fans to support the new entity. So far the club has survived with reasonable crowds and was the leading team at the end of the home and away matches in the inaugural A-League season 2005–06, losing narrowly to Central Coast Mariners in the Preliminary Final. In both Adelaide and Perth it could be argued that a one club-one city policy was appropriate and effective, but for a larger metropolitan centre like Melbourne and Sydney, which historically had at least two, and sometimes several more, national league clubs, the concept of a single club to represent the city was untried and risky.

So the precedents for the Melbourne Victory were not encouraging. Though it is unusual in Australia to set up a completely new league and several clubs it is not unprecedented, as Australian Rules and rugby league have gone through major transformations including the foundation of new clubs since the 1980s.[19] Overseas, complete new leagues and the clubs to take part in them have been created in the United States (Major League Soccer), Japan (J-League) and South Korea (K-League). In Australia it had become clear to nearly everyone inside and outside the game that the current structure and governance of the game had become dysfunctional by the early years of the new millennium.[20] Repeated failure to qualify for the World Cup, especially that in Japan and Korea in 2002, the effective bankruptcy of the governing body, Soccer Australia, its National Soccer League and many of the leading clubs, and the political infighting at the highest levels in game had brought the code into disrepute.[21] Approached by the Chair of Soccer Australia, Ian Knop, in 2002, the Federal Minister for Sport, Rod Kemp, with the backing of the Prime Minister, John Howard, set up an inquiry into the governance of the game which led to recommendations for wholesale change and the appointment of a new interim board with Frank Lowy of the Westfield Group as Chair.[22]

After a hiatus during which the main focus was on putting a new structure in place, recruiting high quality administrative personnel, planning for qualification for the World Cup in Germany in 2006 and achieving a switch from the Oceania Confederation of FIFA to the Asian one, attention turned to forming a new national soccer league. The model developed was for a smaller number of teams, initially ten, but later eight as against eleven in the final year of the NSL, one club per city and one per state, with the exception of New South Wales, which eventually had three, Sydney FC, Central Coast Mariners based in Gosford and Newcastle Jets.[23] Reasons for the small number of teams included the desire to concentrate the available talent to raise standards; to return to clear geographic locations rather than ethnicity as the basis for support: and to have a short domestic season so that leading teams could take part in international competitions, such as the Asian Champions League and the World Club Championship. Partly as a consequence there was no national competition in 2004–05 and the new A-League only began late August 2005.

Melbourne Victory: Creating and Holding a new Fan Base

Melbourne Victory emerged as the winner in a struggle to represent the city against another consortium fronted by former Socceroo, Steve Horvat. Neither group was able to raise the full $5 million dollars initial capital demanded by the Football Federation of Australia (FFA), the new governing body.[24] In the end however the Victory bid was successful in obtaining the five-year franchise to participate in the A-League, with the former chair of the Hawthorn Football Club (an AFL team), Geoff Lord, the founder of the Belgravia Group, as chair. Belgravia Soccer Management owned between 50 and 100 per cent of the shares in the Melbourne Victory Limited, an unlisted company, which gained the FFA Licence. The FFA also invested in the Melbourne Victory. By 2007 the Victory shareholding had been diversified and there were approximately 50 shareholders with interests ranging from $500,000 to $10,000.[25]

So Melbourne Victory, as the new franchised team taking part in the Australian A-league football (soccer) competition in 2005 had to create an instant fan base for a single team to represent Melbourne and Victoria in a national competition.[26] This is something rugby league had to do with the Melbourne Storm and which the Australian Football League faced when it expanded nationally at last (in the 1980s, a decade after soccer established the first national league of any of the football codes in 1977). The Storm began in a blaze of publicity and drew excellent crowds, though these have fallen away since despite excellent on-field performances.[27]

What made the Melbourne Victory task particularly difficult was not just the competition from the other codes of football, particularly Australian Rules, but the recent history of the round ball game. Successive administrations, most notoriously that under David Hill, made strenuous attempts to undermine the ethnic basis of support for many of the successful clubs in the previous National League.[28] Making the game 'mainstream' was the aim, but the methods flew in the face of Australia's professed commitment to multiculturalism and showed a total lack of awareness of the role of soccer clubs in helping successive generations of migrants to this country to become Australians.[29] As the A-League kicked off Frank Lowy, the President of the Football Federation of Australia, appealed to the 'old' fans to come along to support the new team. Yet in the end a new demographic has emerged in support of the Victory.

Deprived of national league football for the best part of two years, following the Crawford Report into the organization of Association Football in this country, the fans returned in numbers to support the various State League competitions. In Victoria, the Premier League attracted more than a quarter of a million people to games in 2005, even before its final series started. Many of these teams are still strongly based in local ethnic communities, even though they have given up the previous ethnic identifiers.[30] Nevertheless, as the Crawford Report insisted, there was 'passionate latent public support' for the game in Australia.[31]

Four thousand or more fans turned up for the Victory's matches in the pre-season Cup competition in August 2005, despite an almost complete lack of advertising. The club needed to triple that number to be financially viable in the new and expensive A-League. Worries remain about the club's financial backing. Sponsorship at national level is good, including Korean car making giant Hyundai, and until 2006 Victory struggled to win high-profile local corporate backing, though it did snare the consumer electric giant Samsung as major sponsor in November 2005.[32] Financial stability, clear and transparent financial dealings, and better treatment of sponsors remain absolutely necessary to maintain current, and attract future, corporate support.

Soccer has several advantages as it tries to re-establish its national league. Participation rates for boys and girls are higher than for any of the other football codes, though there is a sharp drop off in adulthood. There have been huge attendances for World Cup qualifiers and similar competitive games against top-class foreign opposition. However, even though Melbourne is still regarded as the sporting capital of Australia, translating that support into tribal loyalty for a single Melbourne team is not guaranteed. These high participation rates were not translated into high attendance rates as spectators in the past.

The long-term goal for Melbourne Victory is to create a new fan base among the youngsters who have grown up on a diet of superstar European players, some of whom are Australians such as Harry Kewell, Tim Cahill and Lucas Neill. The A-League clubs have been allowed to sign marquee players, European, South American or Asian stars who are reaching the end of their career in the hope that they will attract supporters who remember their exploits and also pass on their knowledge and example to the next generation of local heroes. So Adrian Leijer, at 19, found himself in direct opposition to his childhood hero, Dwight Yorke when Victory played Sydney in the first round of the A-League in the harbour city. Yorke played for Manchester United when it won the European Champions League, the English Premier League and the FA Cup in 1999.

Reactions

Following the first Melbourne Victory home game in the A-League in 2005 it was clear that some of the goals had been met, though there were some flaws in the presentation of the game. There was a great crowd and atmosphere and finale to the match. The pre-match activities were generally good. Some fathers and their children were involved in a half-time penalty kick exhibition. Former Socceroos and the Joeys, the Australian Under-17 national squad, were introduced before the game.

It is important to remember the history of football in Melbourne in recent years. There is no problem drawing a crowd for the opening game, but then a sharp decline often occurs as people find they are not getting what they wanted. The Victory is certainly making an effort. There was a great deal of work done by players and officials prior to the game, as they visited clubs and organisations and tried to establish credibility with fans and potential fans. Tickets were given away or supplied to numerous junior football clubs, for example.

Preliminary Evidence

In the season 2005–06 Melbourne Victory claimed 6,000 members, though by the start of the 2006–07 season this had been apparently reduced to 5,000. Within a few weeks of the start of the 2006–07 season however the Victory was boasting that it had signed its 10,000th member.[33] Even the earlier figure was much higher than for other A-League clubs according to David Friend, who was charged with promoting membership of the new club. He pointed out that Victorians are habituated to the concept of membership of a football club since all the AFL clubs are still membership based. They are prepared to pay a relatively high fee which guarantees entry to games and other privileges.

In New South Wales, however, people tend to regard their small fee for joining a social and gaming club as their contribution to a sporting organization. The Leagues Clubs finance the sporting teams and their clubs through their gaming revenue rather than memberships as such. So a new habit has to be inculcated in the northern states if the soccer clubs are to attract large memberships.

In 2005 Melbourne Victory attracted an attendance at pre-season games of around 4,500 and 17,960 for the first league game, effectively the full capacity of its Olympic

Figure 1   Melbourne Victory fans at Olympic Park in 2005.
Source: Melbourne Victory website.

Park stadium. Another 13,831 turned up for the second game against Newcastle Jets. They made plenty of noise but caused absolutely no trouble.[34] Fan groups were beginning to emerge already, judging by websites and distribution on the ground. Atmosphere was building and it was coming from the fans themselves.[35] The Union Rebels were founded by Peter Cass who modelled his group on the Leeds United Ultras. This group is completely independent of the Melbourne Victory club but provides away game travel, social activities and country supporters links.

The author spent much of the period before the second home game against Newcastle Jets talking to the fans in the outer including members of the Blue and White Brigade, one self-started group of fans who lead the chants from the North-East corner of the ground under the pylon. The Union Rebels inhabit the same area. The former group are 40 strong already, have sold 60-odd professionally-designed T-shirts and were handing out song and chant sheets to newcomers. A group from Epping on the northern outskirts of Melbourne represent the ethnic groups whom David Hill and others were trying to weed out. Despite this they were determined to come and support the Victory. They said they just wanted to see good standard football and would welcome visits by top class European teams to show comparisons. Another group were from Frankston and Carrum in the South East, who said they were footy, not soccer, fans but had come along and had enjoyed the atmosphere and had returned in greater numbers this time. A girl from Geelong thought the prices and the space to watch were better than for AFL, while an Indonesian lad had taken out a Victory membership. He had previously only been to an Oakleigh Cannons match in the Victorian Premier League. So the new fans are a mixture of old and new and they are in the process of creating their own culture, not simply being manipulated by the media and the club. It is to be hoped that they find reasons to stick it out and provide a long-term backing for this new entity. At national level, the FFA head of operations, Matt Carroll claimed crowd numbers already exceeded expectations with average crowds of 11,500 above the aim of 10,000 and people in their 20s driving the growth.[36]

Heath McDonald Membership Survey

As part of its attempt to understand its supporters the Melbourne Victory commissioned a survey of its membership by Dr Heath McDonald of Deakin University. The survey covered members of the Melbourne Victory who had given email addresses to the club and had agreed to be contacted by it. McDonald's report outlined the findings of an embedded email survey conducted with Victory football club members during May 2006. In total, 1,142 members completed the questionnaire within the two-week timeframe, or 41 per cent of those contacted, and roughly 19 per cent of the total claimed membership for the 2005–06 season. The questionnaire aimed to identify the level of member satisfaction with membership services, and give guidance to the club on how that satisfaction level could be managed.[37] The demographic profile of Victory members which emerged is one of young, professional males. 'The membership is significantly younger than most AFL clubs, which augurs well for the club's future. However, female membership seems low, and this represents a strong opportunity for the club, given the reported "family friendliness" of both the venue and the club itself.' For reasons which are discussed below it is not clear that the fan or supporter base of the club precisely mirrors this demographic profile. It could be argued that the members who supplied email contact details would be more likely to be young adult males in white-collar employment than any other demographic group. The total membership for 2005–06 was around one-third of the capacity of the club's stadium, or 42 per cent of average attendance at home games.

Outgrowing its Home Stadium

> Well as a second year Melbourne Victory member, I have to say the only thing the club has been lacking is a stadium to match the awesome atmosphere and excitement of the games. Bring it on! It's surely a sign of things to come for the fast maturing A-league.[38]

By the start of the second, 2006–07, season of the A-League it was becoming clear that Melbourne Victory had reached the capacity of Olympic Park. The stadium, originally completed for the Olympic Games of 1956 and partially refurbished to accommodate rugby league's Melbourne Storm, still has a running track around the playing area and standing terraces at both ends of the ground. It is within walking distance of the Central Business District. Parking is limited close to the stadium and there are major problems if another event is taking place at the Melbourne Cricket Ground, or the Rod Laver or Vodaphone arenas which are close-by on the other side of Swan Street. Though it has an excellent playing surface, unless cut up by a rugby league match immediately prior to a football game, and is liked by the players and many fans, Olympic Park is reaching

Figure 2   Artist's impression of the new stadium planned for the Melbourne Sports Precinct.
Source: Melbourne Victory website.

the end of its useful life without major investment.[39] The State government plans to replace it with a 25,000 capacity oblong stadium in 2009.[40]

The size is set not by the expressed demands of the football, rugby league and rugby union codes who may be its major tenants, but by an agreement when the Docklands stadium, Telstra Dome, was completed that no stadium larger than 25,000 would be built in the central area for ten years.[41]

After a number of fans and members were turned away from early season matches in 2006, an agreement was reached with the operators of Telstra Dome for the match between the Victory and Sydney FC to be switched to that venue in September. A record attendance for a non-finals match between Australian football teams was set when 39,730 people passed through the turnstiles, significantly higher than the organizers had predicted. Subsequently two more matches were switched to the Telstra Dome drawing 25,921 and 32,368 spectators and in the light of this spectacular growth the rest of the Victory's home games were to be played there with the exception of that against the New Zealand Knights in December. Since the Knights remained tailed off on the A-League ladder this would not be expected to be a high drawing attraction, but it was claimed that Telstra Dome was unavailable on 17 December because of another booking.

While it is too soon to be certain that this is not a flash-in-the-pan, there is no doubt that it is a huge increase in match attendances taking the Victory into comparison with the English Premier League and the top competitions in Germany, Spain and Italy (see Table 2).[42]

After seven rounds of Serie A in Italy in 2006 average attendance was 19,511.[43] In the English Premiership the average was 34,084. The Victory average was 26,589 for its first six home A-League games, two of which were played at the limited capacity Olympic Park.[44] The demographic of the attendance remains to be closely studied, but it

Table 2   Association football attendances selected countries

Country	League	Season	Average Attendance
Germany	Bundesliga	2005–06	40,775
England	FA Premier League	2005–06	33,875
Spain	La Liga	2005–06	29,029
Italy	Serie A	2005–06	21,968
Japan	J-League	2005	18,765
Argentina	Primera Division	2003–04	17,363
Scotland	Scottish Premier League	2005–06	16,174
USA	Major League Soccer	2005	15,108
Australia	A-League	2005–06	11,627
Australia	A-League	2006–07*	12,166
South Korea	K-League	2005	11,258
Australia	Australian Football# League	2006	35 250
Australia	National Rugby League	2006	16 485

*   Season in progress.
Source: Football Federation Australia statistics. http://www.a-league.com.au/
\#   Australian Rules football, does not include finals series.
Source: Wikipedia,   http://en.wikipedia.org/wiki/Sports_league_attendances#Domestic_professional_leagues,
accessed 3 November 2006. Individual sources for each league are cited on this website.

is clear that it is quite different from that indicated by the first membership survey reported above. Families, theatre-goers, fans of Victorian football clubs and Australian Rules teams have joined the ranks that have flocked to the 55,000 capacity dome with its retractable roof, which has been closed for part or all of these matches.

Originally designed as part of Melbourne's bid to host football matches during the Sydney Olympics in 2000, when the premier of Victoria, Jeff Kennett, was developing a major events strategy and was Honorary Executive President of the Victorian Soccer Federation, the stadium was planned to accommodate the rectangular codes.[45] It has retractable seating which enables a conventional football shape to be created, though these have not been brought into use so far for Victory games. It is located adjacent to the Central Business District, next to the major railway station, formerly Spencer Street, now Southern Cross, and the bus terminal. It has ample parking, much of it under the stadium. The stadium itself is designed for very effective television viewing and has all the modern amenities expected by fans. They have responded to the availability of the comfort and space which allows for effective concentration of young adult males in chanting bays behind the goals while other family groups can spread around the almost circular viewing area on three levels. The higher levels are quite steeply raked keeping fans relatively close to the action, given that there is significant unused space around the perimeter of the football pitch. There is little doubt that the availability of this venue, well known as it is to Australian Rules spectators, has contributed significantly to the increase in attendances at Victory home games.

This growth in the popularity of the game in Melbourne is partly a result of changes in the administration of the game and the success of the national team, the Socceroos, in qualifying for the FIFA World Cup in Germany in 2006 and performing well in the finals. The A-League has seen a concentration of talent and a rise in the standard of matches, and the Victory has been very competitive in the first half of the 2005–06 season and in 2006–07. Media coverage of the games has increased significantly, with, for example, the Fairfax-owned Melbourne newspaper, *The Age*, becoming a sponsor of the Victory. A pay per view television channel, Foxtel, has contracted to broadcast all the A-League matches in return for a substantial cash injection into the code. Though there have been complaints that the absence of the national competition from free-to-air viewing is disappointing, the short-term financial boost for the clubs has been essential. Several of the eight clubs in the A-League had to have major financial and ownership reconstructions after substantial losses in 2005–06. At time of writing, Perth Glory remained under the ownership of the league, the New Zealand Knights was tailed off in last place in both seasons and drawing derisory crowds, and Sydney FC was in breach of salary cap rules in winning the inaugural championship.

The switch from the uncompetitive Oceania Confederation to the much more attractive Asian Confederation with its huge audiences for football has been very important in underpinning the potential for the game in the next generation. What also differentiates this growth in popularity from all previous cases is that it is not driven by, or at least closely associated with, a wave of inward migration of people from football playing countries. This is the first domestic-inspired football boom in Australian soccer history. It is also based on a much wider demographic than the largely ethnic-group-related teams which dominated the National Soccer League for most of its existence from 1977 to 2004.

The Fans in 2006

The fan groups are growing and becoming differentiated in 2006–07. The Blue and White Brigade (BWB) seems to have become the largest and most organized supporters' group, at least in its own estimation. Its website indicates that it is run by a former university student, now an employee at Australia Post, Adam Tennenini. He was also a player with Brimbank in the Victorian Provisional League.

The different groups reflect a range of styles of support. The BWB congregates at the north-eastern end of the terrace at Olympic Park and the southern of Coventry end of Telstra Dome. It usually organizes a collective march from the ground to the CBD after a home game. It claims to espouse a European style of support in contrast

Figure 3   Banner from the Blue and White Brigade website.

to the Union and some other groups who are seen to favour an English and Welsh style as many members of the latter group support teams in the English Premier League and the Football League. Some of the self-attributed names M7C (May 7 Crew) and SDC (Southern Death Crew) may simply be a post-fan parody of the more nefarious types of hooligan gangs which frequented the terraces of English football grounds before the Taylor Report, but it would be worrying if some members began to take them seriously. For the game against Adelaide United on 15 October 2006, for the first time, a significant number of vociferous away fans appeared at the Telstra Dome. While this created a lively atmosphere during the game and some inventive chanting, it also produced some very foul mouthed and apparently aggressive behaviour from the Victory end, which was not assuaged when the captain of the Melbourne Victory, Kevin Muscat, clashed with the Adelaide United coach, John Kosmina, towards the end of the game.

The Victory was facing its first defeat of the season, being a goal down with a few minutes left to play. Muscat went to retrieve a ball which had gone out of play at the technical area of the visiting team. In his haste to pick it up, he slipped and collided with Kosmina, who was sitting down and whose chair was upended as a result. The coach sprang to his feet and seized Muscat briefly by the throat, before being disengaged by his assistant, former Socceroo Aurelio Vidmar. After the match, all the participants tried to make light of the incident but the authorities took a much dimmer view. Kosmina was banned from coaching from the technical area for six matches and an undisclosed fine was imposed. The last two games and the fine were suspended for the rest of the season.[46] His club also sanctioned him and required that he attend counselling sessions. Given the ease with which Australian soccer can be associated with violence in the media and by its critics, and by other codes of football, this was a salutary warning.[47] The number of column centimetres devoted to the Muscat-Kosmina incident in the next few days far exceeded those devoted to the game, for example. It is quite clear that family fans do not want to be involved in an unsafe environment so it is incumbent on the Melbourne club to follow the example of the League and crack down on any incidents involving its own players or spectators.[48]

This seemed to happen at the following home game when the public address system broadcast several polite warnings to fans to moderate their language and there was a low key but visible police presence in the young crowd behind the goals. In the match itself Victory had two players sent off and was 2–3 down at half-time, but the fans helped lift the team with its constant support and the nine men scored a dramatic late equalizer. In the virtually complete absence of away team supporters, the opposition was from the central coast of New South Wales, fans at either end of the stadium engaged in coordinated chanting and singing throughout the second half.[49]

Criticisms aside, the support of the fans so far has been very impressive. Up to 400 Victory fans have travelled to away games. Given that the A-League has teams from Perth in the west, 3,000 kilometres from Melbourne and Auckland in New Zealand, three hours flying time away, it is interesting to see this modest disclaimer on the BWB

Figure 4   Victory fans in full voice.
Source: Blue and White Brigade website.

website. 'Due the distances involved large numbers of fans tend only to travel to cities close to Melbourne like Sydney and Adelaide.'[50]

In 2006 the A-League remains precarious, despite exceeding its targets for crowds and obtaining significant sponsorship. The New Zealand Knights from Auckland, the New Zealand franchise, is in dire straits. It is tailed off at the bottom of the league for the second season, has been unable to attract more than an average of 2,000 supporters to home games and remains at loggerheads with the New Zealand football authorities. The Perth club at the time of writing is wholly owned by League which cannot so far find a buyer. Sydney FC and Melbourne Victory have substantial investment by the FFA. Victory did not meet the FFA financial criteria at the time of the launch. All clubs lost money in the first season. It is not clear whether any, even the Victory with its staggering crowds, are breaking even in the second year. Without the short-term injection of funds from the pay-per-view broadcaster Foxtel it is doubtful whether the competition could have survived in its current format. In England, Rupert Murdoch's BSkyB used Premier League football as the means to establish the market penetration and profitability of pay-per-view television. It is unlikely that the same dynamics will be successful in a country where Association football remains the second code in all states.

Conclusion

In most parts of the football world, the stability and longevity of clubs in the major leagues since the early twentieth century is very impressive. There have been relatively few new foundations in England and new entrants to major leagues have to fight their way up through the promotion and relegation system usually over a period of decades. In recent times the Wimbledon club moved to Milton Keynes and renamed itself as the Milton Keynes Dons. The vacuum in Wimbledon was filled by a team which claimed the original name. When Manchester United was taken over by an American tycoon, a group of fans formed a new club, FC United, to retain what they considered to be the essence of the original spirit.[51] In Italy there has been much more volatility, though even there clubs survive financial and other scandals and resultant relegations, fines and bans to reappear in the top divisions.[52]

So to appear in a national league and go from zero to around 50,000 supporters in little more than a season is very rare, though not unique since large initial crowds marked the foundation of some of the clubs in Major League Soccer and the J-League in Japan. There have also been big one-off crowds for soccer finals in Perth and Brisbane, but these were not repeated in subsequent seasons. There is a risk that this might happen to the Melbourne Victory. The other football codes are in a very strong relative position and likely to fight back. The AFL media contract with the Channel Seven television network dwarfs that made between Foxtel and the FFA. However, the basis for growth and stability is being laid in Melbourne. The fan base is certainly there. The 11,000 members provide a very good springboard for the club. Word of mouth is spreading around the city and further afield, with many fans travelling hundreds of kilometres to attend home games. As has been noted above, this boom in the game is driven by the domestic population, not inward migration. The organization of the game has been significantly improved. Entry into Asian competitions and qualification for the World Cup have improved the profile and public awareness of the sport. So the Victory can build on these changes in the football environment to maintain and even increase its current spectacular level of support.

Notes

[1]   This article draws on a paper presented to the Footy Fever Conference in Melbourne in 2005 and its subsequent published version, Roy Hay, 'Fan Culture in Australian Football (soccer): From Ethnic to Mainstream?'. I am indebted to Bill Murray for helpful critical comments.

[2]   For an interesting discussion of the differences between the A-League and its predecessor the National Soccer League, see Booth, 'The A-League: A New League for Australia, from Old Soccer to New Football', paper presented to the Football Fever: Identities and Allegiances Conference, Victoria University, 25 September 2006. An abstract appears in *Bulletin of Sport and Culture 26* (September 2006): 17. The background to the formation of the National Soccer League and its chequered history are covered in Murray and Hay, *The World Game Downunder*, 113–31, and Thompson, *One Fantastic Goal*, 90, 92–3, 106–10.

[3]   Also from Melbourne in the south to Brisbane in the north. In European terms this is the equivalent of Portugal to the Ural mountains and Iceland to Athens or more than the whole of continental United States of America.

[4]   See Table 1 for Melbourne Victory attendances, 2005–07. Australian Rules football crowds average just over 35,000, with over 90,000 for grand finals, cricket tests at the MCG can draw 50–80,000 spectators and the spring racing carnival at Flemington has set a record of 129,000 on Derby day in 2006.

Table 1   Melbourne Victory attendance

Date	Comp	Opponent	Venue	H	A	Crowd	Average
30.07.05	PreS Cup	Perth Glory	Olympic Park	0	0	4,528	
6.08.05	PreS Cup	Adelaide United	Olympic Park	0	0	4,687	
12.08.05	PreS Cup S F	Central Coast Mariners	Olympic Park	1	3	3,781	4,332
4.09.05	H A L 2	Perth Glory	Olympic Park	2	2	17,960	
25.09.05	H A L 5	Newcastle Jets	Olympic Park	1	0	13,831	
10.10.05	H A L 7	New Zealand Knights	Olympic Park	3	0	11,010	
16.10.05	H A L 8	Sydney F C	Olympic Park	5	0	18,206	
28.10.06	H A L 10	Adelaide United	Olympic Park	0	1	16,201	
4.11.06	H A L 11	Queensland Roar	Olympic Park	0	1	13,239	
11.11.05	H A L 12	Newcastle Jets	Olympic Park	0	0	12,407	
18.11.05	H A L 13	Central Coast Mariners	Olympic Park	0	2	13,892	
29.12.05	H A L 16	Perth Glory	Olympic Park	2	2	14,754	
4.02.06	H A L 21	New Zealand Knights	Olympic Park	2	1	10,078	14,157
16.07.06	Pre S Cup	Adelaide United	Launceston	0	1	6,834	
29.07.06	Pre S Cup	Central Coast Mariners	Olympic Park	1	3	6,593	
11.08.06	Pre S Cup	Queensland Roar	Epping Stadium	0	0	2,117	
18.08.06	Pre S Cup	Perth Glory	Olympic Park	1	0	2,215	4,440
25.08.06	H A L 1	Adelaide United	Olympic Park	2	0	15,781	
2.08.06	H A L 2	Sydney F C	Telstra Dome	3	2	39,730	
17.09.06	H A L 4	Central Coast Mariners	Olympic Park	1	0	17,617	
1.10.06	H A L 6	Queensland Roar	Telstra Dome	4	1	25,921	
15.10.06	H A L 8	Adelaide United	Telstra Dome	0	1	32,368	
3.11.06	H A L 11	Central Coast Mariners	Telstra Dome	3	3	28,118	
9.11.06	H A L 12	Perth Glory	Telstra Dome	1	0	22,890	
26.11.06	H A L 14	Newcastle Jets	Telstra Dome	0	1	27,753	
8.12.06	H A L 16	Sydney F C	Telstra Dome	0	0	50,333	
17.12.06	H A L 17	New Zealand Knights	Olympic Park	4	0	15,563	
12.01.07	H A L 20	Queensland Roar	Telstra Dome	1	2	28,937	
4.02.07	H A L MSF	Adelaide United	Telstra Dome	2	1	47,413	
18.02.07	H A L GF	Adelaide United	Telstra Dome	6	0	55,436	31,376

Notes: PreS Cup   Pre-Season Cup
   H A L #   Hyundai A League Round
Source: FFA website, http://www.a-league.com.au/default.aspx?s=fixtureresults, accessed 5 November 2006.

[5]   Andrew Howe, *National Soccer League, Official Season Guide 2003–04*, 182–4 has the playing records of both clubs.
[6]   Carlton only succeeded in attracting around 5,000 for its first game against Perth Glory and seldom exceeded that number thereafter apart from finals matches and Melbourne derbies against South Melbourne and the Melbourne Knights.
[7]   Thompson, *One Fantastic Goal*, 132–3.

[8] Lou Sticca, a corporate member of the Carlton Football Club and a long-time soccer fan was the driving force behind the Carlton team. Solly, *Shoot Out*, 101.

[9] Hay, '"Our wicked foreign game"'; Murray and Hay, *The World Game Downunder*. See also Walsh, 'Understanding the Spectator: The First 50 Years of the *Football Record*', paper presented to the Football Fever: Identities and Allegiances Conference, Victoria University, 25 September 2006. An abstract appears in *Bulletin of Sport and Culture 26* (September 2006): 25.

[10] Heidelberg Alexander was backed by the Greek community of the northern suburbs of Melbourne around its home ground at the Olympic Village of 1956. It played in yellow and black stripes, whereas Collingwood wore black and white stripes. Trying to combine the strips with yellow, black and white proved unsatisfactory to both sets of fans. Relations between Greek-speaking and English-speaking groups remained tense if not hostile.

[11] Thompson, *One Fantastic Goal*, 133.

[12] Solly, *Shoot Out*, 101–2.

[13] Tana initially linked with another businessman with political connections in Perth, Paul Afkos, but the two eventually split very acrimoniously. Solly, *Shoot Out*, 99–100.

[14] Brabazon, 'What's the Story Morning Glory? Perth Glory and the Imagining of Englishness', 53–66.

[15] Hay, '"Our wicked foreign game"', 182, notes 53 and 63; ('Sports Factor', ABC Radio National, 11 March 2005).

[16] Hill, 'Perth Glory's tenth anniversary deserves to be applauded by anyone who respects the game's history', 26.

[17] The Spirit often drew around 15,000 fans to North Sydney Oval, but the players had been signed on highly unrealistic contracts which meant that even that number did not cover costs. Solly, *Shoot Out*, 103; Thompson, *One Fantastic Goal*, 139.

[18] Howe, *NSL Guide*, 2003–04, 183–5.

[19] Hay, 'Fan Culture in Australian Football', 92.

[20] FIFA used this excuse to reverse an earlier decision to award the Oceania Confederation a direct entry for one team to the World Cup in 2006. The excuse hardly covered up the political pressure from CONMEBOL, the South American Confederation, which would have surrendered half a place as a result.

[21] David Crawford, *Report of the Independent Soccer Review Committee into the Structure, Governance and Management of Soccer in Australia*, 1–5. Hereafter, Crawford Report.

[22] The processes, analysis and the proposals can be found in the Crawford Report. The politics is discussed in Solly, *Shoot Out*, 217–32. Lowy's career is recounted in Margo, *Frank Lowy*.

[23] Thompson, *One Fantastic Goal*, 150–1.

[24] Though it was never explicitly stated, the fact that Horvat had been a key player at the Melbourne Knights, a Croatian-backed club, might have counted against the other bid.

[25] The Belgravia Group, founded in 1990, employs over 3,000 people in a wide variety of operations, and is one of the largest operators of golf courses and fitness centres in Australia. Wikipedia, http://en.wikipedia.org/wiki/Geoff_Lord, accessed 25 October 2006. See also 'Michael Lynch, 'Lord among masters of Victory bid," *Age*, 22 October 2004; additional financial information supplied by Geoff Miles, Chief Executive Officer of Melbourne Victory.

[26] Roy Hay, 'Melbourne Victory needs instant fans,' *Geelong Advertiser*, 3 September 2005, 33.

[27] The Melbourne Storm was minor premier and grand finalist in 2006, only losing to Brisbane in the grand final.

[28] Hay, '"Our wicked foreign game"', 173–9.

[29] Despite the deliberate marginalization of ethnic supporters, Simon Colosimo's brother has been a regular attendee in the outer at the Victory games in Melbourne.

[30] South Melbourne has dropped the Hellas name which the fans still shout. Melbourne Knights are still greeted by chants of Croatia.

[31] Crawford Report, 2.

[32]   Melbourne Victory chair Geoff Lord claimed on 24 November 2005 that the club had attracted investment of $750,000 in the last two weeks and now had between $4.25 million and $4.5 million in total, still short of the $5 million required by the FFA which itself had taken a stake of $1.25 million in the club. Michael Lynch, 'Goals dry up but cash is pouring in for Victory,' *Age*, 25 November 2005.

[33]   By the beginning of November 2006 the claimed membership had reached 11,000. Tony Ising, '11,000 reasons to celebrate Victory,' Melbourne Victory Media Release, 2 November 2006.

[34]   A few toilet rolls but no flares were thrown towards the end of the match against the Queensland Roar on 4 November when 13, 239 supporters turned up.

[35]   James Willoughby, 'Victory's Twentieth Player,' *Australian and British Soccer Weekly*, 1 November 2005, 19.

[36]   Julia Medew, 'Full strength beer and cheap tickets make for an A-League night out,' *Age*, News, 23 November 2005, 5.

[37]   McDonald, *Melbourne Victory Football Club, 2005–06 Club Member Satisfaction*. Kindly supplied to Roy Hay by Dr McDonald.

[38]   Posted by: Glen at September 1, 2006 02:38 PM, Balls Up, *The Age* Blog, http://blogs.theage.com.au/ballsup/archives/2006/09/under_the_dome.html, accessed 29 October 2006.

[39]   Olympic Park rated over 7 out of 10 for its feeling of being a home ground, for being family friendly and for the ease of getting to the ground, in the McDonald membership survey. The standard of facilities, quality of entertainment and especially value for money food and beverages supplied rated much lower.

[40]   The new stadium will be close to Olympic Park on Swan Street and hence part of the major sporting precinct which includes the Melbourne Cricket Ground and the Tennis Centre at Flinders Park. It thus maintains an Australian pattern of grouping sporting facilities in close proximity. See Haig-Muir, Mewett and Hay, *Sporting Facilities in Victoria*; Hay, Lazenby, Haig-Muir and Mewett, 'Whither Sporting Heritage', 367–70.

[41]   The stadium was originally named Docklands after the former dockyards site on the west of the CBD where it was being developed. Telstra, the telecommunication company, then became its naming rights sponsor.

[42]   Paolo Bandini, 'Why are Serie A attendances on the slide?' *Guardian Unlimited Football*, 28 October 2006, http://blogs.guardian.co.uk/sport/2006/10/25/why_are_serie_a_attendances_on.html

[43]   Attendances in Italy were affected by the match fixing scandal which resulted in the demotion or penalising of a number of leading clubs, including Juventus, AC Milan and Fiorentina and Lazio. Dunne, 'Hearts of Darkness', 70–6.

[44]   Table 1, based on official FFA figures.

[45]   Bert van Bedaf, 'Victorian Soccer's dry dock,' *Soccer Australia*, 31 January 1998, 70–3.

[46]   Michael Cockerill, 'Kosmina given six-game ban,' *Age*, Sport, 19 October 2006, 9.

[47]   Hay, 'A New Look at Soccer Violence', 41–62.

[48]   The coach and the Chief Executive Officer are aware of the problems and share the concern expressed here. 'The CEO is liaising with the support groups regarding their language and behaviour.' Information from an informed source at Melbourne Victory, 3 November 2006.

[49]   Roy Hay, 'It didn't end in the victory, but it was a hell of a game', *Geelong Advertiser*, 4 November 2006, 103. The author was not responsible for the headline.

[50]   Blue and White Brigade website, http://www.bluewhitebrigade.tk/, accessed 28 October 2006. Sydney is approximately 1,000 kilometres away and Adelaide over 700 km, but this is Australia not Europe.

[51]   Football Club United of Manchester, www.fc-utd.co.uk. The club runs on a membership basis and is progressing through the lower leagues.

[52]   Foot, *Calcio*, 4 89–500.

References

Booth, Ross. 'The A-League: A New League for Australia, from Old Soccer to New Football.' *Bulletin of Sport and Culture 26* (September 2006) 17.

Brabazon, Tara, 'What's the Story Morning Glory? Perth Glory and the Imagining of Englishness.' *Sporting Traditions 14,* no.2 (May 1998): 53–66.

Crawford, David. *Report of the Independent Soccer Review Committee into the Structure, Governance and Management of Soccer in Australia.* Canberra: Australian Sports Commission, 2003.

Dunne, Frank. 'Hearts of Darkness,' *FourFourTwo 146* (October 2006): 70–6.

Foot, John. *Calcio: A History of Italian Football.* London: Fourth Estate, 2006.

Haig-Muir, K.M., Mewett, Peter and Hay, Roy. *Sporting Facilities in Victoria.* Final Report to Heritage Victoria on the history of sporting sites in the state, 2000. Unpublish ed. Available from the Heritage Victoria Library, Melbourne.

Hay, Roy. 'A New Look at Soccer Violence'. In *All Part of the Game: Violence and Australian Sport,* edited by Denis Hemphill. Sydney: Walla Walla Press, 1998: 41–62.

Hay, Roy. 'Fan Culture in Australian Football (soccer): From Ethnic to Mainstream?' In *Football Fever: Moving the Goalposts,* edited by Matthew Nicholson, Bob Stewart and Rob Hess. Melbourne: Maribyrnong Press, 2006: 91–105.

Hay, Roy. '"Our wicked foreign game": Why has Association Football (soccer) not become the Main Code of Football in Australia?' *Soccer and Society 7,* no.2–3 (2006): 165–86.

Hay, Roy, Colleen Lazenby, Marnie Haig-Muir and Peter Mewett. 'Whither Sporting Heritage: Reflections on debates in Victoria about Waverley Park and the Melbourne Cricket Ground'. In *Twentieth Century Heritage: Our Recent Cultural Legacy,* edited by David S. Jones. Adelaide: Proceedings of 2001 Australia ICOMOS National Conference, 2002: 367–70.

Hill, Simon. 'Perth Glory's tenth anniversary deserves to be applauded by anyone who respects the game's history.' *Australian FourFourTwo* (December 2006): 26.

Howe, Andrew. *National Soccer League, Official Season Guide 2003–04.* Soccer Australia, Homebush, Sydney, 2003: 182–184.

McDonald, Heath. *Melbourne Victory Football Club, 2005–06 Club Member Satisfaction.* Melbourne: Melbourne Victory Football Club, 2006.

Margo, Jill. *Frank Lowy: Pushing the Limits,* Sydney: Harper Collins, 2001.

Murray, Bill and Roy Hay, eds. *The World Game Downunder.* Melbourne: Australian Society for Sports History, ASSH Studies in Sports History,no.19, 2006.

Solly, Ross. *Shoot Out: The Passion and the Politics of Soccer's fight for Survival in Australia.* Milton, Queensland: John Wiley, 2004.

Thompson, Trevor. *One Fantastic Goal.* Sydney: ABC Books, 2006.

Walsh, Melissa. 'Understanding the Spectator: The First 50 Years of the *Football Record.*' *Bulletin of Sport and Culture 26* (September 2006): 25.

Football Hooliganism in the Netherlands: Patterns of Continuity and Change

Ramón Spaaij

Introduction

The academic discourses on football hooliganism have attracted scholars from various disciplines and localities. The distinctive, mostly English, theoretical and methodological approaches represent a number of opposing academic factions. There has long existed a tendency to avoid cross-cultural comparisons except in the most general of terms.[1] The development towards a more internationalized research community, starting in the late 1980s and early 1990s with a number of international conferences and some non-English research publications on football fan behaviour, partly changed this tendency.[2] The internationalization of academic research on football hooliganism appears to have gained momentum in the late 1990s and early 2000s. Some edited volumes have certainly advanced comparative research into football culture and hooliganism,[3] and scholars from a variety of countries have published relevant papers in journals such as *Soccer and Society*, the *International Review for the Sociology of Sport* and the *Sociology of Sport Journal*.[4] Despite these signs of growing cross-cultural comparison, historical and sociological accounts of the level and forms of football hooliganism outside Britain remain relatively scarce. This is certainly true for parts of Eastern Europe and Latin America, but also for some Western European countries. A striking example of the 'many opinions, few facts' rhetoric is, arguably, the case of football hooliganism in the Netherlands. Foreign journalists and scholars regularly refer to the 'organized battles' of Dutch hooligans as a cause for international concern. In the build-up to Euro 2000, *The Guardian* reported that, 'Hooliganism has declined in Britain in recent years, but in the Netherlands it has got worse … After gun battles in Rotterdam, Dutch police fear Orange disorder will wreck the Euro 2000 tournament.'[5]

The case of Dutch football hooliganism is of considerable theoretical relevance to the contemporary debate on football fan behaviour, in particular to discussions of the social organization and social sources of football hooliganism. In this essay I examine the emergence, development and dominant characteristics of the phenomenon on the basis of qualitative as well as available quantitative data. I try to show the major patterns of continuity and discontinuity in the evolution of football hooliganism in the Netherlands. The paper is divided into four parts. The first part examines the emergence of football hooliganism in the Netherlands and the process of national diffusion. I then turn to the development of football hooliganism in the 1980s and 1990s. In the third section, I analyse the recent patterns and developments in Dutch football hooliganism. Finally, I briefly examine some central features of the persistence of football hooliganism in the Netherlands.

Football hooliganism is viewed in this paper as a specific form of spectator violence at football matches. It is defined as the competitive violence of socially organized fan groups, principally with opposing fan groups.[6] Football hooliganism is essentially other-directed: for violent rivalries to develop and persist, the existence of at least one oppositional fan group is necessary. It is important to note that the native term for this type of behaviour is *voetbalvandalisme* (football vandalism). The use of this term became common among politicians, media and academics from the mid-1970s onwards due to initial official and media focus on the train wrecking exploits of Dutch football supporters.[7] Most academic studies of the time adopted a similar terminology, using 'vandalism' as an umbrella term for activities as diverse as missile throwing, fighting and verbal abuse.[8] From the mid-1990s, these types of behaviour have been more regularly referred to by academics and journalists as 'football violence', 'football crimes' or 'hooliganism'.[9] The Centraal Informatiepunt Voetbalvandalisme (CIV; Dutch National Football Intelligence Unit) and other government institutions continue to use the term *voetbalvandalisme*. These labels are, to varying degrees, all misleading since they group together distinctive types of offences caused by football supporters, including what I have defined as football hooliganism.

The Emergence of Football Hooliganism in the Netherlands

British terrace culture has historically been a major influence for Dutch football supporters. Dutch fans have introduced various elements of this football culture into their own styles of support, such as songs, chants and the display of scarves and flags. In the 1970s, Dutch football grounds witnessed the emergence of so-called 'sides', first in country's four main cities: Amsterdam (F-Side), Rotterdam (Vak S), The Hague (North Side) and Utrecht (Bunnikzijde). These sides had much in common with the British youth ends and emerged as a result of a similar process of internal differentiation. The sides predominantly consisted of young supporters in their teens and early twenties who congregated in specific areas of the ground, usually in the cheaper sections behind one of the goals. These areas were soon transformed into the exclusive territory of the young fans attempting to create a passionate atmosphere through vocal (chants) and visual (display of flags and scarves) support.

The emergence of the sides marked the beginning of an important discontinuity in the level and forms of spectator violence in Dutch football. The level of spectator violence at professional football matches in the Netherlands before the 1970s appears to have been comparatively low and there are no indications of an early tradition of football hooliganism. Throughout the history of Dutch professional football some inter-fan fighting has occurred, but this fighting does not seem to have involved more than uncommon, spontaneous outbursts of spectator violence.[10] Early incidents of spectator violence usually took the form of missile throwing or assaults on players or the referee. Spectator disorderliness was only occasionally directed at rival supporters. Incidents were usually triggered by events on the pitch, such as a controversial refereeing decision or defeat.[11] This pattern gradually changed in the mid-1970s as a result of the emergence of the sides and their increasingly violent inter-group rivalries. Spectator violence at football matches became increasingly detached from the match itself.[12]

Some sides were already the cause of some official and public concern by the early 1970s. FC Utrecht's Bunnikzijde obtained some degree of notoriety for its violent behaviour. The violence provoked by FC Utrecht fans encouraged rival sides to respond to these aggressions in similar ways, setting in motion the development of an early network of inter-group rivalries. The early incidents provoked by the sides were relatively spontaneous and unorganized. The fan groups attended football matches without planning violent confrontation, but they usually did not refrain from the use of violence when challenged by their rivals.

> In those days [the early 1970s] you wouldn't go out looking for trouble. Rather you would firm up for away travel because you knew about their reputation. I mean, I had seen dozens of Utrecht fans waving bicycle chains above their heads saying, like, 'you're going to get your head kicked in'. That was unheard of back then. It both frightened and fascinated me.[13]

The behaviour of English supporters on Dutch soil played an important part in the transformation of (the mediated image of) spectator violence in Dutch football. English supporters were responsible for the first widely reported incident of football hooliganism on Dutch territory. During the UEFA Cup final between Feyenoord and Tottenham Hotspur, on 29 May 1974, visiting supporters attacked home fans in adjacent sections of the ground. Over 200 people were injured. The incident is widely regarded as the Netherlands' first genuine experience with football hooliganism and has been dubbed 'the day Dutch football lost its innocence'.[14] Apart from shocking the authorities and the wider public, the incident stimulated the interest of many young supporters in British terrace culture and, in particular, football hooliganism. Supporters of several Dutch clubs travelled to cities such as London, Manchester and Liverpool to personally experience the atmosphere of English football. Visits of British clubs to the Netherlands were viewed with enthusiasm and anticipation. This was certainly the case for members of the F-Side who attended the annual pre-season tournament in Amsterdam, witnessing the infamous hooligan groups of Manchester United and Leeds United.[15]

In the early stage of football hooliganism in the Netherlands, the four main sides were involved in the vast majority of incidents. They provoked an upward spiral of competitive violence which revolved around establishing their hegemony over rival groups by invading their home territories and fighting them. It is important to note that only a section of the sides were actively involved in the violent incidents. Many young fans were drawn to the sides by their atmosphere inside the ground rather than by the increasing propensity to violence. The behaviour of the sides was increasingly noticed by journalists condemning their 'mindless' violence. The first televised domestic football riot, on 24 October 1976, showed FC Utrecht supporters challenging and chasing Ajax fans with bicycle chains. FC Den Haag and Feyenoord hooligans established a similar reputation for producing home-made bombs. In 1982, following the club's relegation to the First Division, Den Haag fans set fire to their own stadium, something which other sides considered an incomprehensible act.

The behaviour of the four sides and the related media attention set off a process of national diffusion. Fan groups throughout the country began to organize themselves in sides and imitated the behavioural patterns of the pioneering sides. In many cases, this process of imitation became particularly visible after young home supporters were attacked by members of the four main sides. The reputations of the pioneering sides also had an impact on some Belgian and German supporters, who, parallel to British influences, began to import certain elements of the Dutch hooligan scene. Young fans of Belgian Club Bruges, for example, created their East Side after having personally observed the misbehaviour of Feyenoord hooligans during a friendly match between the two teams in 1980.[16]

The emergence of football hooliganism in the Netherlands should be understood as a continuation of fights between rival (youth) groups in other contexts.[17] Such fighting initially took place between youths from different city districts and from different villages. From the mid-1970s, these inter-group rivalries were partly displaced to the football context as the different groups began to jointly occupy the terraces of their local or favourite team.[18] Local inter-group rivalries were temporarily suspended at match days and recreated along the lines of football affiliation, mirroring in many respects the 'Bedouin syndrome' (the enemy of my enemy is my friend, et cetera).[19] They now jointly fought their common rivals (rival sides) in the name of their club or city.

The Development of Football Hooliganism in the 1980s and 1990s

Football hooliganism became a prominent subject on the Dutch political agenda in the second half of the 1980s. The Heysel disaster (1985) heightened fears over the potential lethality of football hooliganism and resulted in the introduction of the European Convention on Spectator Violence and Misbehaviour at Sports Events.[20] Domestically, the level and seriousness of football hooliganism increased substantially due to the continuing national diffusion of the hooligan subculture and the radicalization of some inter-group rivalries. Live television broadcasting of a UEFA Cup match between Feyenoord and Tottenham Hotspur, on 2 November 1983, brought to people's homes the serious fighting between opposing supporters on the terraces of De Kuip. More than 50 supporters were treated for minor injuries and three English fans were taken to hospital for treatment of stab wounds. The stabbing of one English supporter by a home fan was repeatedly broadcast on national television. The Dutch television network NOS described the disorder as 'degrading scenes that have absolutely nothing to do with football'.[21] In March 1987, riot police cleared the home terrace of the Zuiderpark stadium in The Hague following attacks by home fans on visiting Ajax supporters. An international fixture between Holland and Cyprus in October 1987 was suspended after a Dutch fan threw a bomb onto the pitch, injuring Cyprus' goalkeeper. In September 1989, an Ajax fan was arrested after throwing an iron bar onto the playing field during a European Cup match between Ajax and Austria Wien. During a league match between Ajax and Feyenoord in Amsterdam, on 22 October 1989, two Feyenoord hooligans threw home-made bombs into a home section of the ground. The bomb contained fireworks and small bullets, injuring fourteen Ajax supporters. One home fan suffered an arterial haemorrhage. Riot police immediately cleared the entire away section and all 500 visiting fans were searched at the exit.[22] The incident was widely reported by national and international media. The BBC concluded that Holland was 'fast taking over as Europe's most troubled footballing nation'.[23]

The Dutch authorities introduced several security measures in reaction to the (perceived) growing threat of football hooliganism. Early containment strategies concentrated mainly on the segregation of home and away supporters and the deployment of larger numbers of police officers at 'high risk' matches. Fences were erected inside football grounds and clubs invested in the development of a security organization. More recently, the renovation, rebuilding or relocation of several Dutch football grounds in the early 1990s advanced compliance with post-Hillsborough requirements. Similar to developments in Britain, the post-Hillsborough approach to managing Dutch football features the recognition that security and safety are two separate issues and emphasizes the improvement of customer services and fans' experiences.[24] In 1989, the Dutch Football Association (KNVB) agreed with the clubs, in accordance with UEFA regulations, to gradually convert the football grounds to all-seater stadia by the end of the 1990s. Clubs also improved their ticketing procedures and controls, installed closed-circuit television (CCTV) and began to invest in the improvement of steward organizations.[25] It is important to note, however, that the shift towards a more customer-oriented approach to the management of football sits uneasily with the continuing emphasis on the containment of football supporters (for example, the introduction of an identity card scheme and compulsory travel arrangements).[26]

The repressive and techno-preventative containment strategies did not so much eradicate football hooliganism, but rather changed its dominant forms. Opportunities for fighting inside grounds diminished, but hooligans responded to these changes by displacing their fighting to locations outside the stadia, such as city centres and train stations. Containment strategies also failed to prevent the occasional train vandalism and looting of shops and gas stations.[27] In the second half of the 1990s it became painfully clear that football hooliganism had not been reduced to any real degree. On 16 May 1996, Feyenoord and PSV hooligans confronted each other in Rotterdam's city centre forcing police officers to fire warning shots. After a match between FC Utrecht and Feyenoord, on 26 October 1996, rival hooligans pelted each other and the police with stones. Seven police officers were injured. On 17 May 1998, hooligans of Ajax, PSV and Feyenoord fought before and during the Cup Final between Ajax and PSV in Rotterdam. The celebration of Feyenoord's national championship, on 25 April 1999, escalated into a full-scale riot. Four fans were injured by police bullets.

The radicalization of the violent rivalry between Feyenoord and Ajax hooligans accounted for much of the political and public concern over football fan behaviour in the 1990s. Spontaneous and pre-planned encounters between the two groups took place at several locations. On 21 May 1995, for example, a group of 60 Ajax hooligans attacked a television studio seconds before the start of the talk show *Lief & Leed* featuring hooligans of Feyenoord and FC Utrecht. They smashed the windows of the studio canteen with stones. The Feyenoord hooligans immediately began to chase their rivals and vandalized the canteen and bar with objects such as iron bars. They roamed the environment in search of the Ajax hooligans, who had retreated after the initial attack.[28] The determination of Feyenoord and Ajax hooligans in seeking violent confrontation culminated in 1997. The encounter between the two groups on 16 February 1997 constituted a new element in the development of Dutch football hooliganism. Feyenoord and Ajax hooligans pre-arranged a fight near the A10 highway and maintained frequent phone contact in the week leading up to the event. The pre-planned confrontation never really materialized. The Ajax hooligans retreated after observing the larger, heavily-armed group of Feyenoord hooligans. The police arrived at the scene and forced the Feyenoord hooligans to return to their cars.

The intended confrontation finally came into being a month later, on 23 March 1997. On this occasion, there had been no prior arrangements. Feyenoord played away at AZ in Alkmaar, while Ajax played in Waalwijk against RKC. Although a revenge attack by the Ajax hooligans was expected, none of the Feyenoord fans knew exactly where and when. On their way to Alkmaar, on the A9 highway, the Feyenoord hooligans spotted a group of 100 to 150 Ajax fans in a distant field. The hundreds of Feyenoord hooligans abandoned their cars rushing towards their rivals. The first confrontation lasted only twenty to thirty seconds before the Ajax hooligans retreated. A minute later they fought their rivals once again, but were eventually forced back by a larger group of Feyenoord hooligans. A 35-year-old Ajax hooligan died after being beaten with various objects. In the aftermath of the incident, 45 Feyenoord and eight Ajax hooligans were imprisoned or banned for up to four years for their part in the riot. Although the confrontation at Beverwijk was generally perceived as a 'victory' for Feyenoord hooligans, with the benefit of hindsight most hooligans deeply regret the event. Football hooliganism, in their opinion, should not be about killing people.

I had a very bad feeling about what was going to happen. But basically you had no choice: we had to show up in order not to lose face. Looking back, I deeply regret the fight because someone died. It was never my intention to kill him, you know. You just want to fight and humiliate the opponent, that's all.[29]

The Current Shapes of Football Hooliganism in the Netherlands: Some Qualitative and Quantitative Clues

The violent incidents in the second half of the 1990s suggest that football hooliganism in the Netherlands has far from disappeared. The quantitative data compiled by the CIV seem to confirm the idea that spectator 'violence' at football matches is not on the decline. Table 1 shows that the arrest rates at professional football matches in the Netherlands have not changed much over the last three seasons, but are higher than in the 2000/01 season. Recent arrest rates are also significantly higher than in the late 1980s, when the CIV first began to register the number of arrests at football matches (in the 1988/89 season there were 1,021 arrests; in the 1989/90 season a total of 950). It is difficult to determine the precise meanings of this increase since it may be indicative of changes in registration capacity rather than changes in the 'real' level of spectator violence. Furthermore, the listed arrest rates do not distinguish between different types of offences and, therefore, tell us nothing about the development of *specific forms* of spectator disorderliness (that is, football hooliganism).[30]

A closer examination of the arrest rates per club reveals that a small number of clubs account for a comparatively high percentage of the total amount of arrests per season. The seven clubs listed in Table 2 account for between 54 and 69 per cent of the total number of arrests at professional football matches in the Netherlands (36 clubs in total). It is difficult to draw conclusions from these figures. With the exception of ADO Den Haag, the listed clubs are among those drawing the largest crowds, particularly Feyenoord, Ajax and PSV. It is thus logical that more arrests are made at these clubs. Moreover, the arrest rates may reflect more policing strategies at high-profile matches than the actual problems these clubs are faced with. Finally, the arrest rates fluctuate significantly per season, partly due to the large number of arrests at certain single incidents.[31]

Table 1   Number of arrests at professional football matches in the Netherlands, 2000/01 to 2003/04*

Season	No. of arrests
2000/01	1107
2001/02	1840
2002/03	1558
2003/04	1617

*   Including league, cup, European Cup and friendly matches. Excluding arrests at matches of the Dutch national team and foreign supporters arrested at European Cup matches in Holland.
Source: Data provided by CIV.

Table 2   Number of arrests per club, 2000/01 to 2003/04*

Club	Season			
	00/01	01/02	02/03	03/04
Feyenoord	134	347	246	147
Ajax	90	497	147	226
FC Utrecht	79	97	159	331
PSV	161	115	157	72
NEC	63	63	25	158
Vitesse	46	103	88	47
ADO Den Haag	29	53	120	81
Total	602	1275	942	1062
% of (total no. arrests)	54% (1107)	69% (1840)	60% (1558)	66% (1617)

* Clubs with the highest number of their fans arrested (on average).
Source: Data provided by CIV and elaborated by the author.

A third type of statistics compiled by the CIV is the number of registered 'incidents' (Table 3). The CIV defines an incident as

> an event requiring additional police deployment whereby the behaviour of a group of supporters aims at the following: (a) seeking a confrontation or; (b) causing damage or; (c) committing public violence or; (d) making discriminatory remarks or; (e) violent behaviour by supporters directed at the police and club security personnel (e.g. stewards).[32]

This broad definition frustrates a more sophisticated analysis of the development of football hooliganism since the registered incidents include both physical and verbal offences and fail to distinguish between qualitatively distinctive types of violence (for example, fighting; vandalism; missile throwing).

Due to the serious limitations of the statistical data presented above, in the remainder of this paper I examine the current shapes of football hooliganism in the Netherlands in a more qualitative manner. Recent studies have claimed that contemporary football hooliganism in the Netherlands is more complex and less surveyable and predictable than in the 1970s and 1980s.[33] Within this development, five dominant patterns can

Table 3   Number of registered incidents at professional football matches in the Netherlands, 2000/01 to 2003/04*

Season	No. of registered incidents
2000/01	-
2001/02	117
2002/03	96
2003/04	98

* The CIV only registers 'incidents' since the 2001/02 season.
Source: Data provided by CIV.

be distinguished: (a) the partial displacement of hooligan confrontations; (b) increasing levels of planning and coordination; (c) violence against the police; (d) alternatives to physical violence; and (e) the heterogeneous social composition of hooligan groups.

Partial Displacement of Hooligan Confrontations

Large-scale confrontations between rival fan groups inside Dutch football grounds became relatively rare from the 1980s onwards. Spectator violence in and around grounds has, however, not been completely eradicated. Adang has made the important point that:

> Violence or the damage that results from it outside grounds is valued differently. Inside the ground visolence is often less threatening and risky (apart from the use of bombs) than outside, because inside the stadium opposing supporters are always separated by fences. Moreover, they have been searched before entering the ground.[34]

Occasionally, serious fighting takes place inside Dutch football grounds. On 5 November 1997, a Champions League match between Feyenoord and Manchester United was marred by a violent confrontation between Feyenoord hooligans and visiting supporters inside the ground. A cup match between the Ajax Reserves and FC Utrecht in March 2002 was overshadowed by fighting between rival hooligans and between hooligans and the police. A total of 122 fans were arrested.[35] On 28 February 2002, several smaller fights occurred during the UEFA Cup match between Feyenoord and Glasgow Rangers, resulting in 40 arrests.[36] Journalists have occasionally used such examples to argue the 'comeback of hooliganism inside football grounds'.[37] Small-scale disorder inside football grounds is relatively common, including vandalism and assaults on stewards.

Instead of reducing the level and seriousness of football hooliganism, containment policies have had the unintended consequence of (partially) displacing inter-fan fighting away from the grounds. Hooligan groups may go to great lengths to circumvent pervasive official controls and confront their rivals at unexpected times and locations, either spontaneously or pre-planned. Hooligans sometimes defy compulsory travel arrangements by arriving in the city where the away match is played the night before the match, or by turning up at matches which do not involve their team with the sole intention of provoking disorder. Police officers and journalists have recently suggested that this type of behaviour is currently on the increase.[38] One newspaper went as far to suggest that 'the risk of a second Beverwijk is growing rapidly' and 'the relative quietness in and around football grounds is only an appearance'.[39] In the late 1990s and early 2000s, hooligan groups increasingly confronted each other at pre-season or mid-season friendlies, occasionally involving temporary inter-group alliances. FC Twente supporters fought a joint combination of Club Bruges and ADO Den Haag hooligans in August 1999. In January 2002, NAC hooligans were attacked by an alliance of FC Groningen and Belgian Germinal Beerschot supporters.[40]

Another source of potential conflict between rival hooligans is the nightlife, in particular the dance events and raves organized throughout the country. Rival hooligans have occasionally confronted each other at such venues, for example at Dance Valley in 2004.[41] Finally, the deep-seated hostility between Feyenoord and Ajax hooligans has twice been contested at matches between the two clubs' reserve teams, mainly due to the absence of pervasive security measures at these matches. Recently, on 15 April 2004, dozens of Ajax hooligans intimidated and attacked players and managers of the Feyenoord Reserves after a match in Amsterdam. One player was treated in hospital for concussion.[42]

Increasing Levels of Planning and Coordination

As part of their attempts to circumvent police controls, Dutch hooligan groups have become more coordinated and purposeful in their activities. Hooligans make use of mobile phones and, to a lesser extent, Internet to arrange confrontations. Several Dutch hooligan groups maintain instrumental 'liaisons' with rival groups, which allow for a more effective coordination of pre-arranged confrontations (prior agreement on a location, time, format), despite fears of being tapped by the authorities. Such confrontations often take the form of 'hit and run' fights; brief but serious disorder after which both groups disperse to avoid apprehension. Such assaults do not necessarily involve rival hooligans, but may also be directed at the police or security personnel.[43]

The increasing levels of planning and coordination of football hooliganism in the Netherlands should not be understood as signs of formal organization or hierarchical structures.[44] Attempts to convict hooligans as members of a 'criminal organization' have all failed. The Dutch Supreme Court concluded that there was insufficient evidence to sustain the prosecution's claims that the disorder at Beverwijk was the result of a structured criminal organization rather than initiatives of individuals or incidentally cooperating persons or groups of people. On the other hand, the judges sustained that the events had 'an organized character'.[45] A recent court case against alleged Ajax hooligans had a similar outcome; all charges of membership of a criminal organization were dismissed by the judges.[46] The social organization of football hooliganism does generally not exceed basic forms of coordination and synchronization within hooligans' own ranks and, occasionally, with rival hooligan groups. Hooligan confrontations do not result from formal structures but from a combination of common interests (i.e. in fighting), opportunities for rapid resource mobilization, inter-group contacts established over the years and familiarity with certain urban spaces (i.e. football grounds, routes to stadia, railway stations, city districts). The social cohesion of the larger hooligan groups appears to be limited. They consist of a variety of smaller, autonomously operating sub-groups or individuals that may merge in anticipation of violent confrontation.[47] There regularly exists some degree of conflict between the different sub-groups. During large-scale disorder, these more-or-less identifiable sub-groups are joined by individuals who do not belong to the hard core but who identify with the 'group' under specific circumstances and behave accordingly. These dynamics feature a process of self-selection, especially when disorder is more-or-less 'expected' (for example, at high-profile matches): (young) fans who tend to identify with the group are likely to be present, whereas others will not.[48]

There is no evidence of formal leadership within Dutch hooligan groups. Influential informal leaders or 'regulators' usually derive their position from their seniority, prestige or organizational skills.

> There is no formal hierarchy or anything. Of course there are people who coordinate certain activities, who say 'we go there at this time'. There is always someone who first mentions that, but they are different people. Sometimes it's one person and the other time it's others. You cannot pick anyone as the leader of the group. The only hierarchical structure is in terms of seniority. Long-standing hooligans usually have more prestige than younger ones. That's logical, isn't it? I mean, that's how it works in companies too.[49]

Rather than being formally organized, experienced hooligans are street wise and have developed a practical understanding of the opportunity structures for football violence and policing strategies.[50] During confrontations they often remain in the background while younger hooligans more eager to 'prove' themselves engage in the actual fighting or missile throwing. The latter category is therefore more often arrested that the more matured hooligans.[51] More generally, certain 'regulators' within the hooligan groups focus predominantly on logistic and organizational tasks, such as obtaining tickets for specific sections of the grounds, travel arrangements or disseminating temporary behavioural codes (for example, verbally or through leaflets). Their organizational skills are also perceptible in the organization of dance parties and funerals for deceased hooligans. On such occasions hooligans may cooperate with the police, issue and enforce certain behavioural codes or create a temporary unit of ushers.

Alternatives to Physical Violence

Experienced hooligans are aware of the fact that the opportunities for collective violence at football grounds are more limited than in the past. They regularly attempt to utilize certain alternatives to physical confrontations which, at times, may generate the same excitement or fun as physical violence.[52] Hooligans sometimes force authorities to take draconic security measures by spreading false information on upcoming events and potential confrontations. Experienced hooligans also consciously attempt to disrupt or circumvent undesired security measures using their bureaucratic networks and skills to appeal to banning orders, ticket pricing or travel arrangements. Moreover, hard-core supporters and hooligans alike have used their experience and networks to protest against disproportionate policing strategies. Feyenoord supporters lodged an official complaint against the Amsterdam riot police in 2002 for the disproportionate use of violence and the infliction of injury on a number of visiting fans. The accusation was sustained by the Commission for Police Complaints.[53] In 2004, FC Utrecht's official supporters' club protested against the aggressive policing of its members by displaying a photo of one of the riot police officers allegedly involved in the incident on the internet.[54] These types of 'fan activism' have blurred the ideal-typal distinction between hard-core (non-violent) supporters and hooligans since both categories may be similarly involved in the protests, which occasionally take on more threatening or violent dimensions. Examples of the latter are the blocking of railway tracks by FC Utrecht supporters in March 2002, the threats directed at cinemas throughout the country to prevent the broadcasting of the Ajax documentary *Daar hoorden zij engelen zingen* in December 2000 and, in March 2001, the intimidation of actors participating in the play *Hooligans* which, consequently, was suspended.[55]

Violence Directed at Police

Hooligans do not merely fight each other but may also confront the police, especially when the latter is attempting to separate the warring parties. Some hooligan groups view the police as a legitimate opponent, as part of the violent inter-group rivalries.[56] Violent behaviour directed at the police takes on different forms ranging from small to large scale. In the early 1990s the police first observed a process of polarization in their interactions with hooligan groups. Regular police officers perceived their influence on hooligans to be on the decline and, to avoid further endangerment, they were increasingly substituted by riot police.[57] More recently, hooligans have occasionally attacked police officers and riot police *en masse*. FC Utrecht hooligans fought the riot police after an away match at Ajax on 29 February 2004. Earlier that month, ADO Den Haag supporters forced back riot police after the latter had charged the away section of the Amsterdam Arena following away fans' vandalising of seats. The most widely reported incident of attacks on the police took place after a match between Feyenoord and Ajax in Rotterdam, on 17 April 2005. Hundreds of Feyenoord supporters attacked riot police officers and pelted them with stones and bottles, injuring 42 officers. In the aftermath of the incident the police displayed photographs of suspected Feyenoord fans on television and the Internet. Conflicts between hooligans and the police have also emerged as a consequence of the fan projects and intelligence-led policing strategies carried out at a local level. The *Hooligans in Beeld* (Hooligans in View) project, which closely monitors known hooligans in and outside the football context, has been introduced in several police districts and will soon be implemented at all professional football clubs in the Netherlands. A secondary consequence of the project has been the polarization of the relations between hooligans and the police. On some occasions police officers involved in the projects have been the victims of intimidation and physical violence.[58]

The Heterogeneous Social Composition of Hooligan Groups in the Netherlands

The historical development of the social composition of Dutch hooligan groups features both continuities and changes. The emergence of football hooliganism in the Netherlands, in the early 1970s, should be located within the context of post-war social changes. Youth began to emerge as a distinct social category with its own cultural practices and styles, and were increasingly influenced by British youth subcultures. In the country's main cities large numbers of working-class youth from different districts and suburbs began to attend football matches.[59] The football hooligans were characterized by their relatively low levels of education.[60] Van der Brug has argued that in the Dutch situation 'there is a relationship between individual downward mobility and participation in football hooliganism, a situation which is quite different from the pattern in Britain, where the explanatory factors are much more collectivistic and highly related to social class'.[61] At this relatively early stage of football hooliganism in the Netherlands there were signs of significant variations in the social backgrounds of hooligans. In their early analysis of the Z-side at FC Groningen, Veugelers and Hazekamp contend:

> There are a number of differences between the social position of the inner-city group and the various district groups … They [members of the inner-city group] more often have lower educational levels or quit their studies, are more often unemployed and have more experiences with correctional institutions and prisons. Youths from the district groups usually live with their parents, have a paid job or are at school.[62]

There is evidence to suggest that, in recent years, the social composition of football hooligans in the Netherlands has become more heterogeneous, though there are important variations.[63]

I will illustrate this point by a brief examination of the social backgrounds of hooligans at two Dutch football clubs: Feyenoord and Sparta Rotterdam.[64] The majority of Feyenoord hooligans grew up in working-class areas, but in recent years the group's class composition has become somewhat more heterogeneous. Very few hooligans are long-term unemployed and the vast majority earn a moderate income. Many older hooligans are skilled manual workers employed as builders, dockworkers, carpenters, bouncers, and so on. Although certain older hooligans have experienced a degree of upward social mobility, they are not beyond their cultural roots and male friendships networks. Their involvement in football hooliganism as well as, for many hooligans, their involvement in the club constitutes a major source of excitement and identity in their lives. The younger hooligans either work or are still in school. Many of them have a relatively low level of education. They tend to dislike school and experience problems with teachers and fellow students. Their parents often do little to prevent their sons from engaging in delinquency and hooliganism. Parental neglect is in several cases related to the disruption of families or to drug or alcohol abuse. Several young hooligans grow up in a social environment (family, school, neighbourhood, football club, nightlife) in which aggression and the threat and use of violence are part of everyday life. Their reputation for physical prowess provides them prestige among peers and is used to intimidate other young men in everyday life. Within their friendship groups physical prowess, risk taking and the ability to 'look after yourself' are dominant values. 'Sissy' behaviour is viewed with disdain. The quest for risk and excitement features centrally in their activities.

The social backgrounds of Sparta hooligans differ substantially from those of their counterparts at Feyenoord. Many Sparta hooligans are enrolled in universities, while some have already completed their university degree. Full-time occupations vary from teaching in primary or secondary schools to health care professionals and a printing-office employee. Only one of the group's core members is a builder.[65] Most hooligans can be characterized as 'middle-class'. Although Sparta hooligans celebrate a hard masculine identity based on physical prowess, their collective identity is also constructed in relation to Feyenoord hooligans and certain other Dutch hooligan formations. Whereas the latter are portrayed as 'rough, hard-core criminals', the Sparta hooligans view themselves as a more sophisticated, fashionable 'fighting crew' and hooliganism is commonly regarded as a temporary lifestyle. As one hooligan put it:

> "Feyenoord hooligans have very different backgrounds. I mean, many of them have no education, both parents on drugs, brought up in a culture of violence. Our group is completely different. We come from stable families, quite well-off, have certain values in life, an education. They will probably still be doing their business when they're 35. I certainly won't. I have others goals in life, you know.[66]

Sparta hooligans claim to be 'addicted' to the pleasurable emotional arousal associated with football hooliganism. They take pride in engaging in violent confrontation with rival hooligans before, during or after football matches.

An ethnographic study of core members of FC Haarlem's hooligan group FCH Fanatics conducted by one of my students, Jeroen Korthals, reached very similar conclusions. Six out of ten study at a university level or have a university degree (BA, BSc or MA). The vast majority (around 80 per cent) of the self-declared hooligans claim neither to perceive themselves as 'working class', nor to have been raised in an environment conducive to aggression or the use of violence. In fact, they reject the use of violence in everyday life, but are hooked to the adrenalin rush they get from engaging in, organizing and fantasizing about football-related violence.[67]

Football Hooliganism in the Netherlands: Some Concluding Remarks

The dominant developments and characteristics identified in this paper suggest that football hooliganism in the Netherlands has changed rather than disappeared. Though stressing its persistent nature, I should mention that the lethality of Dutch football hooliganism is often over-estimated. Over the last three decades only two football-related deaths have been reported; one during the Beverwijk riot in 1997, and one in Enschede in 1991, where a FC Twente supporter was stabbed to death by a Feyenoord hooligan the night prior to a match between the two teams. By way of conclusion, in this final section I briefly examine two inter-related features that may enhance our understanding of the persistence of the phenomenon. The first characteristic is the changing age range of Dutch football hooligans. Several older hooligans (30 to 45 years old) have been part of their groups since the late 1980s or before. Some are still centrally involved in football hooliganism, while others are part-time participants mainly 'turning up' for high-profile matches. Their maturity and experience has enabled them to develop a practical knowledge of the opportunity structures for football violence and policing strategies as well as to establish instrumental or affective 'relations' with other groups. Besides being 'addicted' to the 'buzz' of football violence, some older hooligans have certain economic interests for continuing their involvement in hooligan groups (for example, drug trade; merchandising). At the other end of the age continuum, in the late 1990s and early 2000s new hooligan youth groups emerged at several Dutch football clubs. These youth groups are either integrated into the established hooligan groups or operate autonomously (with their own names and symbology). Their members are mostly young males between 15 and 23 years old. There is generally high usage of hard drugs (cocaine, speed, ecstasy) among young hooligans. Their behaviour is viewed by many older hooligans as violating, in some ways, the unwritten 'codes of conduct', for example by attacking non-hooligans. For many young supporters, identifying with or engaging in football hooliganism appears to be a fashionable way of life closely related to the media attention and entertainment industry surrounding the hooligan experience (private video footage, books, documentaries, clothing). The Internet plays a central role as a site for socialization and 'cyberhooliganism'.[68] National and international hooligan confrontations are chronicled on special hooligan web sites. Many self-declared young hooligans are not physically violent but rather attempt to manifest themselves through verbal warfare (threats; abuse; bragging) on the Internet.

The second feature that provides insight into the persistence of football hooliganism are the psycho-social pleasures its participants derive from the hooligan experience. Accounts of hooligans reveal how they experience an overpowering 'buzz' or adrenalin rush when confronting their opponents.[69] In the Dutch case, the 'buzz' of football hooliganism does not appeal exclusively to young working-class males. The seductions of football violence should not be understood as merely an epiphenomenon of social class – even though this may certainly be the case in specific situations, such as at football clubs located in areas with strong working-class traditions and legacies (see my description of the hooligan group at Feyenoord). The pleasures derived from the intense emotional states of the hooligan experience are closely related to hooligans' anticipation of 'disorder' and 'chaos'. Hooligans routinely describe their 'battles' as a war scenario in which 'all hell breaks loose'. They regularly evaluate previous clashes or fantasize about upcoming events. In reality, most fights are quite brief and comparatively few people are seriously injured. Instead of asking why football hooliganism occurs, one might ask: why does it not occur more often? Most spontaneous fights do not escalate into serious collective violence and the vast majority of pre-arranged confrontations never materialize, for instance because one group (or both) fails to 'show' or runs away, or because police disrupt their plans. The 'buzz' of football hooliganism is not only intimately connected to anticipation, but also to (overcoming) fear. Courage, in this sense, is not the absence of fear but rather the sufficient discipline to perform when one is afraid.[70]

Police measures against football hooliganism have reduced the opportunities for experiencing the 'buzz' in and around football grounds, but the hooligan experience (real or mediated) remains 'highly desirable to large numbers of prospective participants'.[71] Playing into this demand, a transnational market in the reproduction or simulation of football hooliganism – in print, film, video games and clothing – has emerged. Websites such as www.hardcorehooligan.nl offer a range of material on the subject of football hooliganism, such as press reports, real-time video clips and a messageboard. Similar modes of reproduction and interaction can be found in some football 'fanzines'. Some Dutch fanzines contest the cultural properties of 'regular' football fans, emphasizing instead the hard masculinity celebrated by football hooligans.

Notes

[1]   Moorhouse, 'Football Hooligans: Old Bottle, New Wines?', 490.

[2] Notably: O'Brien (ed.), *European Conference on Football Violence*; Giulianotti, Bonney and Hepworth (eds), *Football, Violence and Social Identity*; Roversi, 'Football Violence in Italy'; Giulianotti, 'Scotland's Tartan Army in Italy'; Peitersen, 'Roligan. Un Modo d'Essere dei Tifosi Danesi'; Horak, 'Things Change'; Bromberger, Hayot and Mariottini, '"Allez l'O.M., Forza Juve"'.

[3] Armstrong and Giulianotti (eds), *Football Cultures and Identities*; Armstrong and Giulianotti (eds), *Fear and Loathing in World Football*; Dunning, Murphy, Waddington and Astrinakis (eds), *Fighting Fans*.

[4] For example: Pilz, 'Social Factors Influencing Sport and Violence'; Andersson, 'Swedish Football Hooliganism, 1900–1939'; Spaaij and Viñas, 'Passion, Politics and Violence'.

[5] *The Guardian*, 2 May 1999.

[6] For an elaborate conceptualization, see Spaaij, 'The Prevention of Football Hooliganism'; cf. Giulianotti, 'A Different Kind of Carnival'.

[7] For example, in the first official inquiry into the matter, Hartsuiker, *Rapport van de Projectgroep Vandalisme door Voetbalsupporters*.

[8] Siekmann (ed.), *Voetbalvandalisme*; van der Brug, *Voetbalvandalism*.

[9] Adang, 'Van Voetbalvandalisme naar Voetbalcriminaliteit?'; Ferwerda and Gelissen, 'Voetbalcriminaliteit. Veroveren Hooligans het Publieke Domein?'; van Gageldonk, *Hand in Hand*.

[10] Miermans, *Voetbal in Nederland*.

[11] Van der Brug, 'Football Hooliganism in the Netherlands' p.176.

[12] Van der Brug, *Voetbalvandalisme*, 223.

[13] Interview with Feyenoord supporter, February 2005.

[14] *Rotterdams Dagblad*, 20 April 2002, 43.

[15] Pieloor, van de Meer and Bakker, *F-Side is Niet Makkelijk!*, 22.

[16] Verleyen and de Smet, *Hooligans*, 16.

[17] Stokvis, 'Voetbalvandalisme in Nederland'.

[18] Custers and Hamersma, 'De Genese van het Fenomeen Hooliganisme in Nederland', 23; Köster, 'Weer Trekken Wij Ten Strijde', 71.

[19] Harrison, 'Soccer's Tribal Wars', 604.

[20] Council of Europe, *European Convention on Spectator Violence and Misbehaviour at Sports Events and in particular Football Matches*.

[21] *NOS Nieuws*, 2 November 1983.

[22] *NOS Nieuws*, 22 October 1989.

[23] *BBC News*, 22 October 1989.

[24] Tummers, *Architectuur aan de Zijlijn.*; COT, *De Amsterdam Arena*, 8.

[25] KNVB, *Handboek Veiligheid*; Heijs and Mengerink, *Stewarding in Nederland*.

[26] This dilemma cannot be elaborated on here to a full extent due to lack of space. The issue is discussed to some length in Bormans, *'Feyenoord Bedankt!'*.

[27] Van der Brug, 'Football Hooliganism', 177.

[28] Van Gageldonk, *Hand in Hand*, 94–7; *NOS Nieuws*, 21 May 1995.

[29] Interview with Feyenoord supporter, November 2001.

[30] For an analysis of the flaws of statistical data on football-related arrests, see: Spaaij, 'Het Succes van de Britse Voetbalwet', 4–5; Spaaij, 'Hooligans, Politie en Informatie', 139–43.

[31] CIV, *Jaarverslag Seizoen 2003–2004*, 36–41.

[32] CIV, *Jaarverslag Seizoen 2002–2003*, 11.

[33] COT, *Voetbal en Geweld*, 31.

[34] Adang, *Hooligans, Autonomen, Agenten*, 32.

[35] *Korpsbericht Politie Amsterdam-Amstelland*, 2 April 2002.

[36] CIV, *Jaarverslag Seizoen 2001–2002*, 46.

[37] See, for example, *BN De Stem*, 2 April 2002; *De Gelderlander*, 2 April 2002.

[38] CIV, *Jaarverslag Seizoen 2003–2004*; *Eindhovens Dagblad*, 26 February 2005; *De Gelderlander*, 23 February 2005.

[39]   *BN De Stem*, 1 March 2005.
[40]   *Trouw*, 3 August 1999; *Drentse Courant*, 8 January 2002.
[41]   *De Volkskrant*, 23 August 2004; *Haagsche Courant*, 2 March 2005.
[42]   Auditteam Voetbalvandalisme, *Audit Jong Ajax.*
[43]   Van der Torre and Spaaij, 'Harde-kern Hooligans', 31.
[44]   Adang, 'Collectief Geweld tussen Voetbal – "Supporters"', 180.
[45]   Hoge Raad, 10 July 2001.
[46]   Rechtbank's Gravenhage, 6 July 2006.
[47]   COT, *Openbare Orde,* 125.
[48]   Adang, 'Collectief Geweld tussen Voetbal – "Supporters"', 180; van der Torre and Spaaij, *Rotterdamse' Hooligans*, 44.
[49]   Interview with Feyenoord supporter, October 2004.
[50]   Van der Torre and Spaaij, *Rotterdamse' Hooligans*, 27.
[51]   Interviews with senior police officers and security officers, January 2001 to November 2004.
[52]   Van der Torre and Spaaij, *Rotterdamse' Hooligans*, 75–7.
[53]   *Rotterdams Dagblad*, 11 November 2003; Jagan, 'Informatie op "Tien"', 65–6.
[54]   *RTV Utrecht*, 28 September 2004.
[55]   Spaaij, 'Hooligans', 6.
[56]   Ferwerda and Gelissen, 'Voetbalcriminaliteit', 92–3.
[57]   CIV, *Jaarverslag Seizoen 1990–1991.*
[58]   CIV, *Jaarverslag Seizoen 2003–2004*, 4; interviews with senior police officers, October 2004.
[59]   Stokvis, 'Voetbalvandalisme', 181.
[60]   Van der Brug and Meijs, *Effect-evaluatie Project Voetbalvandalisme en Jeugdbeleid*, 26.
[61]   Van der Brug, 'Football Hooliganism', 179–80.
[62]   Veugelers and Hazekamp, *Inside Z-side*, 22.
[63]   Ferwerda and Gelissen, 'Voetbalcriminaliteit', 87; de Haan, Nijboer, Bieleman and Meijer, *Nieuwe Aanwas Voetbalsupporters*, 10; Spaaij (ed.), *Supportersgedrag en Hooliganisme in het Nederlandse Voetbal.*
[64]   See, for example, Spaaij, 'Hooligans'; Van der Torre and Spaaij, *Rotterdamse' Hooligans*; Spaaij, 'The Prevention of Football Hooliganism'.
[65]   The analysis is based on my fieldwork among Dutch hooligan formations between 2000 and 2005. See for example: Spaaji, 'Understanding Football Hooliganism'.
[66]   These data were gathered in 2003 and 2004 and may therefore be somewhat dated.
[67]   Personal interview, July 2003.
[68]   Van der Torre and Spaaij, *Rotterdamse' Hooligans*, 77; Hulsteijn, 'Voetballen op het Internet'.
[69]   Giulianotti, *Football: A Sociology of the Global Game*, 52–3.
[70]   Collins, 'Gewelddadig Conflict en Sociale Organisatie', 189–90.
[71]   Giulianotti, *Football: A Sociology of the Global Game*, 53.

References

Adang, O.M.J. 'Van Voetbalvandalisme naar Voetbalcriminaliteit?' *Tijdschrift voor de Politie 59*, no. 11 (1997): 26–30.
Adang, O.M.J. *Hooligans, Autonomen, Agenten. Geweld En Politieoptreden in Relsituaties.* Alphen aan den Rijn: Samsom, 1998.
Adang, O.M.J. 'Collectief Geweld tussen Voetbal – "Supporters": Organisatie, Groepsprocessen En Sociale Identiteit.' *Tijdschrift voor Criminologie 46*, no.2 (2002): 172–181.
Andersson, T. 'Swedish Football Hooliganism 1900–1939.' *Soccer and Society 6*, no. 1 (2001): 79–96.
Armstrong, G. and R. Giulianotti, eds. *Football Cultures and Identities.* London: Macmillan, 1999.
Armstrong, G. and R. Giulianotti, eds. *Fear and Loathing in World Football.* Oxford: Berg, 2001.

Auditteam, Voetbalvandalisme. *Audit Jong Ajax – Jong Feyenoord D.D.* Den Haag, 2004.

Bormans, R. *'Feyenoord Bedankt!' De Supporters En Hun Club.* Nijmegen: SUN, 2002.

Bromberger, C., A Hayot and J.M. Mariottini. '"Allez l'O.M., Forza Juve": The Passion for Football in Marseille and Turin.' In *The Passion and the Fashion: Football Fandom in the New Europe,* edited by S. Redhead. Aldershot: Avebury, 1993: 103–51.

Brug, H. van der. *Voetbalvandalisme: Een Speurtocht Naar Verklarende Factoren.* Haarlem: De Vrieseborch, 1986.

Brug, H. van der. 'Football Hooliganism in the Netherlands.' In *Football, Violence and Social Identity,* edited by R. Giulianotti, N. Bonney and M. Hepworth. London: Routledge, 1994.

Brug, H. van der and J. Meijs. *Effect-evaluatie Project Voetbalvandalisme en Jeugdbeleid.* Amsterdam: Het Persinstituut, 1989.

CIV. *Jaarverslag Seizoen 1990–1991.* Utrecht: CIV, 1991.

CIV. *Jaarverslag Seizoen 2001–2002.* Utrecht: CIV, 2002.

CIV. *Jaarverslag Seizoen 2002–2003.* Utrecht: CIV, 2003.

CIV. *Jaarverslag Seizoen 2003–2004.* Utrecht: CIV, 2004.

Collins, R. 'Gewelddadig Conflict en Sociale Organisatie. Enkele Theoretische Implicaties Van De Sociologie Van De Oorlog.' In *Hoofdstukken Uit De Sociologie,* edited by J. Goudsblom, B. van Heerikhuizen and J. Heilbron. Amsterdam: Amsterdam University Press, 1997.

COT. *De Amsterdam Arena: Evaluatie Van De Veiligheidsorganisati.* Amsterdam: Politie Amsterdam-Amstelland, 1998.

COT. *Voetbal En Geweld.* Alpen aan den Rijn: Samsom, 1999.

COT. *Openbare Orde: Ernstige Verstoringen, Ontwikkelingen, Beleid.* Alphen aan den Rijr: Kluwer, 2002.

Council of Europe. *European Convention on Spectator Violence and Misbehaviour at Sports Events and in Particular Football Matches.* Strasbourg, 1985.

Custers, T. and S. Hamersma. 'De Genese van het Fenomeen Hooliganisme in Nederland.' In *Supportersgedrag En Hooliganisme in Het Nederlandse Voetbal,* edited by R.F.J. Spaaij. Amsterdam: Universiteit van Amsterdam, 2005.

Dunning, E., P. Murphy, I Waddington and A.E. Astrinakis, eds. *Fighting Fans: Football Hooliganism as a World Phenomenon.* Dublin: University College Dublin Press, 2002.

Dunning, E., P. Murphy and J. Williams. *The Roots of Football Hooliganism: An Historical and Sociological Study.* London: Routledge and Kegan Paul, 1988.

Ferwerda, H. and Gelissen, L. 'Voetbalcriminaliteit. Veroveren Hooligans het Publieke Domein?' *Justitiele Verkenningen 27,* no.1 (2001): 84–95.

Gageldonk, P. van. *Hand in Hand: Op Stap Met De Hooligans Van Feyenoord.* Amsterdam: Nijgh & van Ditmar, 1996.

Giulianotti, R. 'Scotland's Tartan Army in Italy: The Case for the Carnivalesque.' *Sociological Review 39,* no.3 (1991): 503–27.

Giulianotti, R. *Football: A Sociology of the Global Game.* Cambridge: Polity Press, 1999.

Giulianotti, R. 'A Different Kind of Carnival.' In *Hooligan Wars: Causes and Effects of Football Violence,* edited by M. Perryman. Edinburgh and London: Mainstream, 2001.

Giulianotti, R., N. Bonney and M. Hepworth, eds. *Football Violence and Social Identity.* London: Routledge, 1994.

Haan, W.J.M. de, J.A. Nijboer, B. Bieleman and G. Meijer. *Nieuwe Aanwas Voetbalsupporters. Een Vooronderzoek Naar Mogelijkheden, Wenselijkheden En Beperkingen Van Onderzoek Naar Nieuwe Aanwas Van Problematische Voetbalsupporters.* Groningen: Intraval, 2001.

Harrison, P. 'Soccer's Tribal Wars.' *New Society 29,* no.622 (1974): 604.

Hartsuiker, J.F. *Rapport van de Project-groep Vandalisme door Voetbalsupporters.* Den Haag: Ministerie van Justitie, 1977.

Heijs, L. and A. Mengerink. *Stewarding in Nederland.* Apeldoom: VUGA, 1993.

Horak, R. 'Things Change: Trends in Australian Football Rom 1977–1990.' *Sociological Review 39,* no.3 (1991): 531–48.

Hulsteijn, G. 'Voetballen op het Internet. De Rol Van Fansites Binnen De Subcultuur Van Het Hooliganisme.' In *Supportersgedrag En Hooliganisme in Het Nederlandse Voetbal*, edited by R.F.J. Spaaij. Amsterdam: Universiteit van Amsterdam, 2005.

Jagan, A. 'Informatie Op "Tien": Over Hoe Informatie Voetbalgeweld Kan Voorkomen.' Erasmus Universiteit Rotterdam, 2004. Unpublished MA dissertation.

KNVB. *Handboek Veiligheid*. Ziest: KNVB, 2003.

Korthals, J. 'Fanatieke Supporters. Een Onderzoek Naar Uitingsvormen En Drijfveren.' In *Supportersgedrag En Hooliganisme in Het Nederlandse Voetbal*, edited by R.F.J. Spaaij. Amsterdam: Universiteit van Amsterdam, 2005.

Köster, M. 'Weer Trekken Wij Ten Strijde. Onderzoek Naar De Opkomst, Ontwikkeling En Huidige Situatie Van Nec's Harde Kern.' In *Supportersgedrag En Hooliganisme in Het Nederlandse Voetbal*, edited by R.F.J. Spaaij. Amsterdam: Universiteit van Amsterdam, 2005.

Miermans, C. *Voetbal in Nederland: Maatschappelijke En Sportieve Aspecten*. Assen: Van Gorcum, 1955.

Moorhouse, H.F. 'Football Hooligans: Old Bottle, New Wines?' *Sociological Review 39*, no.3 (1991): 490.

O'Brien, T., ed. *European Conference on Football Violence*. Lancashire Polytechnic, 1987.

Peitersen, B. 'Roligan. Un Modo d'Essere dei Tifosi Danesi.' In *Calcio E Violencia in Europa*, edited by A. Roversi. Bologna: Il Mulino, 1990: 169–86.

Pieloor, R., B. van de Meer and M. Bakker. *F-Side is Niet Makkelijk*. Utrecht: Het Spectrum, 2002.

Pilz, G.A. 'Social Factors Influencing Sport and Violence: On the "Problem" of Football Hooliganism in Germany.' *International Review for the Sociology of Sport 31*, no.1 (1996): 44–66.

Roversi, A. 'Football Violence in Italy.' *International Review for the Sociology of Sport 26*, no.4 (1991).

Siekmann, ed. *Voetbalvandalisme*. Haarlem: De Vrieseborch, 1982: 311–332.

Spaaij, R.F.J. 'Hooligans, Politie en Informatie: Een Vloeiende Combinatie?' Universiteit Leiden, 2001. Unpublished MA dissertation.

Spaaij, R.F.J. 'Het Succes van de Britse Voetbalwet: Kanttekeningen En Best Practices.' *Tijdschrift voor de Politie 67*, no.1 (2005): 4–8.

Spaaij, R.F.J. 'The Prevention of Football Hooliganism: A Transnational Perspective.' In *Acts Del X Congresso Internacional De Hostoria Del Deporte*, edited by J. Aquesolo Vegas. Sevilla: CESH, 2005.

Spaaij, R.F.J., ed. *Supportersgedrag en Hooliganisme in het Nederlandse Voetbal*. Amsterdam: Universiteit van Amsterdam, 2005.

Spaaij, R.F.J. and C. Viñas. 'Passion, Politics and Violence: A Socio-Historical Analysis of Spanish Ultras.' *Soccer & Society 6*, no.1 (2005): 79–96.

Stokvis, R. 'Voetbalvandalisme in Nederland.' *Amsterdams Sociologisch Tijdschrift 18*, no.3 (1991): 165–88.

Torre, E.J. van der and R.F.J. Spaaij. *Rotterdamse' Hooligans: Aanwas, Gelegenheidsstructuren, Preventie*. Alphen aan den Rijn: Kluwer, 2003.

Torre, E.J. van der and R.F.J. Spaaij. 'Harde-Kern Hooligans: Verder Dan Geweld.' *Tijdschrift voor de Politie 65*, no.7 (2003): 28–33.

Tummers, T. *Architectuur aan de Zijlijn. Stadions En Tribunes in Nederland*. Amsterdam: D'ARTS, 1993.

Verleyen, K. and S. de Smet. *Hooligans*. Leuven: Davidsfonds, 1997.

Veugelers, W. and J. Hazekamp. *Inside Z-Side. 'Voetbalvandalen' in Woord En Beeld* Groningen: Xeno, 1984.

Accidental Racists: Experiences and Contradictions of Racism in local Amsterdam Soccer Fan Culture

Floris Müller, L. van Zoonen and L. de Roode

Introduction

Soccer fan cultures around the world are renowned for their potential to bring people together and produce a positive sense of collective identity. Paradoxically, their potential to function as a public arena for the expression of racism has become equally notorious. At first glance, some recent statistics seem to suggest that this notoriety is increasingly unjustified. In the Netherlands, for example, only 2.2 per cent of all reports of racist incidents made to the official anti-discrimination agencies were related to soccer and other forms of 'sports and recreation'.[1]

It would, however, be premature to conclude that soccer racism is gradually disappearing. Many authors writing on racism in soccer have started to adopt new paradigms that define racism in much wider, cultural terms and to document racist aspects of soccer culture that were previously ignored. It is now increasingly accepted that expressions of racism can take many forms in the various domains of soccer culture: collective racist chanting on the terraces is only the most visible.[2] Racism, it is argued, often insidiously structures the interactions and decisions in soccer culture from the terraces, locker rooms and playing fields up to the boardrooms, soccer media and patterns of financial endorsement. From this perspective, a (temporary) decrease in collective forms of racism during soccer matches cannot be taken as a straightforward indication that racism is retreating from soccer culture as a whole. Moreover, the low numbers of complaints and lack of discussion about daily racism at soccer clubs and matches might be an indication of processes of 'ignoring and silencing' rather than a genuine absence of abuse and inequality.[3]

Despite considerable academic attention to the field of soccer racism, only a handful of empirical studies have been published that substantiate and deepen our understandings of the ways racism is being expressed and experienced within local soccer fan cultures. This paper aims to do just that, by discussing the forms in which racism manifests itself locally in Amsterdam soccer culture and analyzing how these forms are experienced by soccer fans and players. Our results show that fans and players draw on one particular discourse to make sense of their experiences of racism in soccer culture. However, the positions they take up in this discourse are different, as are the ways that they deal with racism when they experience it.

In the following pages, we will first present a short outline of the new paradigm that has emerged for the study of racism in soccer. We then discuss the research design of our study and the ways in which various concepts were applied during data analysis. After that we present the results of our analysis, followed by a conclusion and a discussion of the relevance of our results for the further empirical study of racism in soccer culture.

Theories of Soccer Racism

Proponents of a more cultural perspective on soccer racism have argued that many conceptualizations of racism tend to suffer from an unduly limited analytic framework. In both academic writing and in the minds of the general public and their representatives, racism in soccer is often exclusively associated with the aggressive behaviour of groups of hooligans in and around the stadium.[4] However, racism has also been documented amongst ordinary soccer fans,[5] between players,[6] amongst referees and coaches [7] and in the institutional sector of soccer associations and soccer media.[8] Back, Crabbe and Solomos have argued that most of the literature on soccer and racism ignores this variety by reducing the problem to a clearly identifiable, problematic 'racist/hooligan' group.[9] They propose instead that soccer racism should be considered as an aspect of wider soccer culture.[10]

Back *et al.* have argued that studying the expressions and processes of radicalization in soccer is facilitated by the subdivision of soccer culture into four domains.[11] They refer to these domains as 'the vernacular', 'the occupational', 'the institutional' and 'the culture industry'. The 'vernacular' domain roughly corresponds to those contexts and forms of racist behaviour that are generally recognized as a problem within soccer. Collective racist chanting amongst fans falls under this domain, as well as the excesses of 'neighbourhood nationalisms' in which soccer club identities give rise to racist behaviours within and outside the stadiums.[12] The 'occupational' domain draws attention to the forms of racism that professional players experience at their own clubs during matches and at the training grounds, including the racist expectations and the processes of 'stacking' black players in particular playing positions that correspond to racist expectations of performance.[13] It also includes racialized interactions and exclusions in places like the locker rooms and sports club's bars. The 'institutional' domain involves issues of racialized access to decision making in the club, racialized patterns of club ownership, and a lack of representation of different ethnic groups on club boards. It also involves the shapes of social networks that can constitute racialized networks of patronage, which obstruct access of certain minorities to the world of professional soccer.[14] The fourth domain, 'culture industry', covers the racism involved in biased representations of soccer players from different ethnic backgrounds in the popular media and patterns of commercial endorsement that support them.[15] This domain also covers racialized discourses in sports programs and match coverage.

As this short list illustrates, the shapes and locations in which racism may be expressed and needs to be challenged and studied has expanded tremendously from the older focus on mere excesses of spectator violence. For our present research, we focused on the ways in which racism was experienced and expressed in the vernacular and occupational domains of soccer culture in particular.

Racialization

The focus on different cultural domains and interactions outlined above has particular consequences for the way racist behaviour is interpreted, and its reproduction theorized. Overt and instantly recognizable 'racist' acts can no longer be taken as shorthand to classify a person as belonging to a deviant group of soccer fans that is characterized by moral degeneration (that is, 'racist/hooligans'). They should rather be seen as expressions of a larger 'racialized' culture of soccer.[16] Thus, the key to understanding racism does not lie exclusively in the study of the content, consequences and intentions behind the overt racist act itself. It also requires taking into account the cultural context in which such acts become meaningful expressions.[17]

The cultural context of racism is reproduced through contingent processes of 'Racialization',[18] which are contained in the unobtrusive, sub-conscious minutiae of everyday practices. Such everyday practices can range from jokes about black players in the locker room to differential racist expectations on the training grounds and the formation of mono-ethnic sub-groups of players within mixed soccer clubs and teams.[19] These practices do not necessarily produce *overt* racism, nor may people recognize these interactions as rooted in racialized perceptions of reality. However, by reproducing a racialized context they do constitute the necessary *potential* for overt racist abuse to occur in meaningful ways.

Since the potential for meaningful expressions of racism lies in sets of racialized practices and interactions of wider soccer culture, the usual focus on the 'perpetrator' and 'victim' of the racist act needs to be complemented with a similar rigorous attention for the culture in which the act was expressed. Because Racialization implies a set of differentially racialized cultural contexts it also constitutes a move away from the common assumption that such a context is formed by a single, coherent racist ideology. Instead, it allows for an understanding of the contradictions and incoherencies within and between the expressions of racism in different domains of soccer culture.

For example, white soccer fans can racially abuse black players of the opposite team whilst supporting those on their own team,[20] and racist abuse is also common between different non-white ethnic groups and in situations where the white majority is underrepresented.[21] The terms of racism, moreover, may in some situations also be reversed and lead to phenomena that are difficult to grasp without a sense of the inherent contradictions of contingent Racialization. For example, it has been noted that a racialized black identity can have a number of advantageous connotations within a masculine culture like soccer. In some circles, the mythical dimensions of the black body (of physical, sexual and athletic prowess) may even make a black identity preferable over a white one in terms of its ability to signify a powerful masculinity.[22]

As a result, such racialized identities may sometimes be sought out for short term gains as a kind of 'strategic essentialism'.[23] Without doubt, the contingent admiration of racialized black bodies and men is not only a source of possibility within soccer culture, but also one of restraint. Racialized expectations of 'black performance', for example, position black players mostly in attacking roles, and much more rarely as key defenders or goalkeepers.[24] Moreover, this particular black identity is not available to all black players. In contrast to players of British-Caribbean descent, those of British-Asian descent are rarely perceived as potentially talented professional players in any position at all. The latter ethnicity, as Burdsey has shown, is stereotypically taken as effeminate and too frail for soccer.[25]

Minorization

Anglo-American authors have developed this cultural perspective on soccer racism with a particular focus on black minorities. However, while a considerable number of Dutch minorities are from the African Diaspora, the Dutch debate on discrimination and racism has centred much more on the abuse of specifically Muslim (Turkish and Moroccan) immigrants and their offspring.[26] The concept of 'Racialization' is only partially relevant to their situation as religion is also a key part of the discrimination and abuse they are faced with.

Jan Rath has therefore argued that some of the racism in the Dutch situation is better described as shaped and enabled through processes of 'minorization'. Within a context of racism against 'Dutch minorities', the victims' cultural otherness is not defined as a fixed, biological difference. Instead, such abuse often carries the connotation of a strong imperative on behalf of the 'ethnic other' to erase their difference and assimilate into the Dutch culture.[27]

In wider Dutch society, processes of minorization have been institutionalized in government programs for enculturation of new immigrants ('inburgeringscurssusen') and the renewal of programmes that up to the 1950s aimed to civilize the problematic groups of the white working (under) class but are now meant to guide problematic groups of migrants in their cultural and moral assimilation into society.[28] Although the concept has not been yet been applied to soccer culture, we would expect processes of minorization, although not as institutionalized, to be applicable there too.

Both Racialization and minorization discussed here specify the specific theoretical starting point of our empirical study of soccer racism in Amsterdam. In what follows, the method of this research will be presented, followed by a presentation of the results.

Method

For this research, we used 20 in-depth interviews that were carried out with soccer fans and players as part of a larger soccer research programme conducted by the Centre for Popular Culture of the University of Amsterdam. The soccer fans were interviewed as part of a thesis project about fan behaviour and expressions in the so-called Ajax F-side: the hardcore supporters of the Amsterdam club.[29] All of these supporters were of a white ethnic-Dutch background. The soccer players that were interviewed were players from local Amsterdam clubs that varied in terms of their geographical location, ethnic diversity in the club and the size of their membership. The players that were interviewed for this study were of Turkish, Moroccan, Surinamese, Afghani, Pakistani and white Dutch backgrounds.

Interviews were held at the soccer grounds, cafés nearby or at the respondents' homes and usually lasted about one hour. During these interviews respondents were asked to reflect on their experiences with ethnicity in the context of soccer culture. The interviewers worked with a topic list that provided thematic pointers, but did not contain any standardized questions. The interviewee was given as much freedom as possible to reconstruct their own experiences with racism and soccer in ways that were meaningful to them. Working from the paradigm of Racialization outlined earlier, we defined racism in this study as an integral aspect of both the practices and discourses in soccer culture. This meant that we focused not only on the overt expressions of racism but also on the racializations of interactions and personal narratives of the people we interviewed. We also looked at the wider context of soccer culture and its masculine codes of conduct, in order to understand the ways people experience and narrate their experiences of soccer racism. This focus on discourses and practices allowed us to focus on both fans and players simultaneously, as differently positioned actors within the same cultural field, and to investigate the dynamics that ensued from these different discursive positions.

The interviews were transcribed and analyzed with the help of computer software for qualitative data analysis. The analysis was carried out in three phases. In the first phase of analysis, the interviews served to develop insights into the different forms of racism that were expressed in local Amsterdam soccer culture. In a second phase, our analysis focused on the discourses of racism that were used to describe different kinds of racism and on the kinds of racialized practices these forms of speaking ignored or silenced. In the third phase, a synthesis was made of the ways the results of the first two phases positioned soccer fans and players differently in relation to expressions of racism in soccer culture.

We will first discuss the different forms in which racism presents itself locally in local Amsterdam soccer and the dominant discourse with which our respondents reflected on their experiences with these phenomena. Then we will discuss the ways fans draw on this discourse and take up a particular position within it when discussing their participation in racist abuse. Finally, we briefly discuss the ways soccer players deal with different forms of racism while drawing on the same dominant discourse as the fans.

Forms of Racism in Amsterdam

Despite the common assertion that racism in Amsterdam is rare and insignificant, our research showed that it is frequently expressed in many of the complex and contradictory forms that are reported in the literature. An example of this contradiction is found in the following quote, from a young black player for a soccer club with a white upper class history.

> We had to play another team, who had a Surinamese striker, and then [my team mates] just go like um … well, 'break that nigger', and what did they say again, um, well, 'that fuckin' nigger, I'm going to stand on his head', you know, that kind of stuff […] but I also have that colour, so basically it's also about me. Because he makes that remark about him means that he really thinks that way about me and he makes those remarks about me when I'm not around. But to my face he hardly ever says it.

As this quote illustrates, it was possible for white team mates to express overt racism towards a black player on the opposing team without it immediately constituting, for them, an attack of the black player on their own team. This particular experience, however, did offend the black player on their team and led him to question their loyalty and respect for him.

The contradictory nature of contemporary racism also means that it is not restricted to expressions made by white people. Our respondents explained that racism was also expressed between different minority ethnic groups or even within the same ethnic group. As the following quote illustrates, in particular contexts racist hierarchies are even inverted so that, as in this case, a black player can be accused of being white by his black opponents.

> Another thing I've encountered a lot, is that when we played a team with many people of dark skin, they insulted me for being white, and being a bounty, those kind of remarks, so it works both ways, I don't mean to say that it is only them, I was insulted by everybody, so actually there is no difference between white and black. They all do it.

The term bounty in the above constitutes a racist metaphor of a chocolate candy bar with white coconut filling. To call a black person a 'bounty' effectively accuses them of excessively assimilating to white culture and therefore placing themselves outside of the black community. The quote therefore illustrates that racist behaviour is found even within ethnic groups that have traditionally only been accorded the role of victim within discourses on racism.

Racialization

When discussing their experiences with racism, most interviewees only considered overt racist abuse to be 'racism'. Their experiences with racialized soccer culture in general were therefore usually absent in their discussions of racism. In many cases processes of Racialization were simply not immediately recognized as such because they occurred in the context of friendly and joking interactions. This finding is illustrated by the following quote, in which a black soccer player can be seen to struggle with calling an experience in which a racist joke was made racist because it is expressed without the intention to hurt.

> [At that soccer club] There were more jokes about me being dark skinned. I mean not hateful, or not being racist, but um … well I know a joke which is really stupid, which I've known for a long time, which actually is pretty racist, like why are my hands so white? Because I stood like this [*making a gesture of standing with his hands against the wall, FM*] when they painted me black. So yes, that kind of stuff [...] and when I said something about it, then sometimes people listened, but they were always jokes that referred to the colour of my skin.

Apart from this issue of recognizing racism illustrated by the quote above, discussions of Racialization are further complicated by the fact that, in some contexts, Racialization can be accompanied by friendships, intercultural exchanges and carry unexpected benefits in a masculine culture. For the black player quoted above, the racialized masculine context of the locker room did not only result in 'stupid jokes' but also opened up an enjoyable position of a hyper-sexual black male.

> Well you've got jokes about the genitals. Those are also flattering (laughs), and, yes, well I find that, yes, there is kind of more interest in the sense that I am also asked how I'm doing, in my culture, like, hey, how does that work, how do you do that?

Anti-Muslim Racism and Minorization

For Muslim players in Amsterdam such positions of hypersexual Racialization are unavailable. Instead, they are faced with new emerging forms of racism and minorization in the growing anti-Muslim climate in the Netherlands. Much of this racism took the form of overt derogatory nationalistic remarks such as 'shit Moroccan', 'dirty Turk', et cetera. This repertoire of racist abuse has become so common that it is even directed at players who merely look like they are from Morocco or Turkey. One Turkish respondent reflected on this phenomenon in the following way:

> We've had [...] a game lately, last week, our goalkeeper got insulted for being a fuckin Moroccan and things. He isn't a Moroccan, but he looks like it, so they threw that at him.

Much anti-Muslim racism is coded in such a way that it may not be immediately recognized as such. For example, a collective chant about the facial hair of a players' mother

('Boussatta, your mother has got a moustache') signifies as anti-Muslim abuse specifically, because it is read as a marker of deviant Islamic gender norms for appearance in the Dutch context. Other coded forms of racism are contained in references to sheep and shoplifting. These relate to the image of the 'backward Muslim immigrant' made popular through the assassinated Theo van Gogh's use of the term 'goat fuckers'. Generic insults directed at family honour can also be perceived as specifically anti-Muslim racism by soccer players with a Muslim background, as is illustrated by the following quote of a 19-year-old Turkish soccer player who ignores biological difference altogether when giving his defining of racism in soccer: 'Yeah, [racism] is when they just try to antagonize you and then it's about where you're from or about your family.' Apart from explicit forms of racist expressions, processes of minorization also seem to result in practices that are often too subtle to brand as racism. For example, discussions about 'where you're from' were read by one of black soccer player as offensive if they were asked for the wrong reasons.

> I am Dutch, I feel Dutch sometimes, sometimes not; that's mostly because of remarks, then you think like…, like that question 'where are you from'. That's just a nasty question I think, because basically I am … and then they say 'oh you speak Dutch so well' and I'm like 'yeah, hello, I was born here, and have grown up here'.

This quote illustrates the breadth of practices in which the difference from the Dutch white norm can be emphasized and can function to exclude and minorize certain participants of soccer culture. Such insidious and innocent practices as discussing your heritage at the soccer club may thus be linked with the reproduction of racism in Amsterdam at least. However, many seemed reluctant to put such experiences into words, let alone to challenge them. Our analysis showed that one important reason for this was the general discourse with which both fans and players made sense of their experiences with racism.

Discourses of Racism

Our analysis showed that the dominant discourse in local Amsterdam soccer culture constructs racism as an expression of individuals who stand outside the decent morality of reasonable and tolerant people. Such 'racists' are assumed to have a fixed and coherent ideological racist belief system that is impossible to challenge or change within the confines of the soccer stadium. This discourse corresponds to what Back *et al.* have called a discourse of the 'racist/hooligan' folk demon.[30] In many racist incidents it leads to the conclusion that, since it is a problem caused by an extremist minority that will never change its ways, the best strategy is to simply ignore it. As one of the respondents said:

> Um … I think that time is wasted on a person with this kind of opinion. Because you just don't change anymore when you've reached a certain age and still have an opinion like that. I wouldn't know what might trigger you to get a book or something and just change all of a sudden and then think like, well, all of a sudden I'm interested in all the other cultures here.

Since this discourse of the 'racist/hooligan' folk demon holds that racism is an expression of a coherent set of racist values and beliefs, it cannot deal with the myriad of coded and contradictory expressions of racism and Racialization within soccer culture that we discussed earlier. As a result, it becomes possible for those expressing and experiencing racism to deny its importance by claiming that the perpetrator is in fact, not a 'real' racist, because he or she does not adhere to a racist ideology, but is swept away by emotions or the atmosphere at the stands.

> Well soccer is ummm, two things I think, you've got emotion, as a result of which you just say stuff you don't mean and there are those guys that really hate foreigners, who really are racists. Look, in the heat of the moment it is hard to distinguish one from the other

As this quote illustrates, the discourse of the 'real racist' at first seems to distinguish only between 'innocent' people and racists. However, it also opens up the discursive position of the person who is not really a racist but nevertheless engages in sporadic racist activity. The distinction between the two lies in the intention and 'true' values and beliefs of the offender, which are usually very hard, if not impossible, to determine in the context of soccer culture.

Both fans and players discussed many contextual factors that may cause a person to express themselves in racist terms while they actually 'didn't really mean it', such as emotion, stupidity, group pressures or the need to affect the outcome of the game. This discursive position was very common in the accounts of both fans and soccer players. We call this the position of the 'accidental racist', since it involves admitting to past racist behaviour while simultaneously claiming that it was never intended as such. When the person committing a racist act is perceived as such an accidental racist, the act is emptied of its political meaning and reduced to an expression of abuse that is no different from other common forms of abuse in soccer culture. The offender thus manages to avoid the stamp of a 'real' racist and the moral consequences that would have. In the following quote, a Turkish soccer player constructs racism directed at Turks as insults that 'don't matter' to him and his team mates because they are mere emotional expressions: 'No, I mean, they say fuckin' Turk occasionally, but you might as well say fuckin' redhead. This is how we all see it, you know. It's all, yeah, it doesn't matter. And, yeah … it's all just emotion.' To this particular player, racism need therefore not be seriously and systematically challenged if it was the product of emotional involvement in the game. As such, his account opens up discursive space from which to claim innocence but simultaneously engage in racist behaviour.

As a result of this shared discourse on 'true' racism, offenders and victims take up complementary positions in relation to racist behaviours based on whether it was perceived as 'real' or 'accidental'. These positions have different consequences for soccer fans and soccer players, which we will now discuss in turn.

Fans and Racism

Before discussing the ways soccer fans talked about their experiences with racism, it should be emphasized that we will be discussing those instances in which racist expressions of soccer fans were openly discussed. We have done so to illustrate the dynamics of the positions that soccer fans take up in relation to soccer racism in dominant discourses about its meaning. It would be a mistake, however, to assume that such open discussions are part of everyday interactions. One of the most common responses to explicit questions about soccer racism was therefore, unsurprisingly, to downplay its frequency and significance, despite the fact that all of the fans and players interviewed for our research at some point argued that they had witnessed, experienced or engaged in racism personally in various intensities and locations. One typical comment is listed below, which was made by a black respondent before he went on to discuss a wide range of experiences he had had with racism at his local soccer club: 'All of us had the same experience – that it occurred occasionally, but it's only two or three people, so basically it isn't really that bad.' The dominant position of soccer fans talking about racism is therefore still that of the 'innocent' spectator who abhors racism, hardly ever encounters it and never partakes in it himself.

Nonetheless, many of the Amsterdam soccer fans we spoke to did openly discuss their own participation in racist behaviours at the soccer grounds. Most were acutely aware, at least in the context of interviews, of the fine line they are treading when participating in verbal abuse in the stadium. Many of the fans went to considerable lengths to maintain a discursive position as an accidental racist when discussing their occasional and contradictory recourse to racist abuse in the stadium. Two common arguments were repeatedly put forward by the interviewees to justify this position.

First of all, fans describe the sometimes racist excesses of their 'supporter' behaviour as mere instrumental acts to influence the outcome of the game. This argument also asserts that soccer players know this too and that the stadium is a context in which all participants are aware that abuse is meaningless and should not be taken personally.

> It's […] meant to put them off their game. And when you manage to do that by using [offensive] chanting then you're doing it well. I don't think that all of it is always insulting. When you're at home sitting on your couch and you hear it, you think 'that's bad'. But when you're having an experience in the stadium, those words are experienced entirely differently.

Second, shouting abuse is often constructed by the fans as an individual emotional release that has meaning only in form but not in content. The following quote illustrates how fans de-politicize their abuse by claiming that it is merely an expression of their emotional state of mind: '[I don't abuse players] to hurt them, I just do it because I'm frustrated. And then you, like, shout away the frustration. You lose your aggression. That's why you do it. Not to hurt them.'

In these accounts, the emotions evoked by the game and group processes on the terraces can sometimes cause a self-proclaimed non-racist soccer fan to partake in racist abuse by accident.

> Usually I don't really care what I sing. Mostly you just find out afterwards if it was a smart thing to do or it wasn't

> Against Van Gobbel [a Surinam-Dutch player] I've yelled all kinds of things […] 'Van Gobbel was an illegal immigrant bastard' […] In general I think about it, but sometimes there are emotional moments in which you just forget to think straight.

In many instances, moreover, racism was expressed in the form of joking remarks that were intended in the first place to amuse and not to offend. Our respondents indicated that in such a situation, it was unlikely to be interpreted as a reflection of a serious racist ideology at the same time. However, the fans were aware of the fact that there is a 'line' even an accidental racist should not cross. The ambivalence of their position is exemplified in the following quote, where a fan discusses his participation in chanting a racist slur against Moroccan player Bousatta.

> I can remember the story about Dries Boussatta very well. I sang along joyfully. Yeah … you could have a discussion about that too. Is it okay, is it racist, or is it soccer humour? How do you see it?

Because of their perceived humorous qualities, the slurs against Bousatta were therefore constructed as, at most, only ambivalently racist. During the game, such ambivalence resulted in a situation that allowed for this soccer fan's participation in racist expressions without risking the accusation of being a 'real racist' – although the ambivalence of the act, as this quote illustrates, did require some narrative work during the interview.

Soccer Players

While it might be expected that the notion of the accidental racist is a particular position taken up only by fans that try to account for their own problematic behaviour, our research showed that soccer players who suffer racist abuse discuss their experiences in the same way. Soccer players' accounts of their experiences reflected the same tripartition between an innocent majority, 'real racists' and those people who do engage in racist behaviour but don't 'really' mean it (that is, accidental racists).

However, whereas the notion of an 'accidental racist' constitutes a safe position for fans that occasionally express themselves in racist ways, it presents soccer players with a major obstacle in confronting racism. The contradictions and incoherence in the expressions of racism, coupled with a discourse which defines racism through the ideological intentions of the perpetrator but leaves room for 'unfortunate' meaningless expressions of racism, result in a situation where many racist expressions either go unrecognized or are discounted as mere attempts to influence the outcome of the game by emotionally unsettling the player.

> When people say those things to me I think, let them talk, it's just because they feel powerless, because you can't win you start talking to me. […] When you're behind they don't start jabbering. Then it's just quiet. But when you're ahead, then it's all frustrations, they want to put you off your game, and stuff like that, and yeah, they say that when they really can't win any more. I let them go.

The quote above illustrates how the intention of the person committing a racist act is essential to determine its meaning. When players are unable to 'let it go' and do get offended by racist abuse and take it personally, they are faced with the challenge of assessing motives and beliefs of the offender, and thus to determine whether they are dealing with a true racist or a mere 'accidentally racist' fool. As the following quote shows, victims can thus fail to challenge the racist act simply because they are not sure enough about the intentions of the person who offended them.

often there is a verbal aspect by which you know. Or else I don't know it and I just let it go. That's why I don't respond most of the time, especially with my own team mates. I find that difficult, how to asses that. To what extent does someone mean what he says?

In practice, the task of determining the 'true' motives of an offender often turns out to be an exceedingly difficult task within a masculine soccer culture where 'not making a fuss' about your personal grievances is valued highly. This translates into some remarkable and again intrinsically highly contradictory social practices in which experiences of racism are reworked and, to some extent, rendered meaningless.

It is really … during those 45 minutes, you almost want to kill him, you say almost everything, but some people rattle on and say these stupid things, like these racist remarks, but outside the stadium it's like 'hey mate, get a beer on me' and then it's over […] you just go along with them and it's forgotten.

However, even experiences with racism that can't be shrugged off so easily were difficult to discuss within the masculine culture of soccer. In the following quote, a half Pakistani-half Dutch player exemplifies these norms when he gives an example of the way his team would react to a black player who has been offended by crowds making monkey chants.

Well … then they would say in the dressing room 'but you ARE a monkey' or something like that. You know, and then they laugh about it. It's sort of a mentality in soccer culture, you know, actually it isn't important, it's just professional, it's about winning the game. When someone starts to argue against that culture, it's instantly silenced

Within such a masculine context, accusations of racism are thus constructed as 'making a fuss' and being preoccupied with your individual needs and emotions. The individual who still feels offended by such meaningless racist banter is constructed as weak, unable to resist the temptation of reacting to abuse and therefore endangering the victory of his own soccer team.

When you just shut your mouth and score a goal, [the racist] will start to see it differently. He'll start to think, '[racist abuse] doesn't work on him'. But there are some players that do react to these kinds of things. And this usually results in a fight. That happens so often, but it's up to the one that can't control himself.

The only generally accepted reactions to racism are therefore either ignoring it altogether or improving your playing performance to win the match and 'shut the racist up'. Our analysis indicates that these views of racism are not a matter of white versus black or Dutch versus non-Dutch individuals. Many non-Dutch players also expressed the belief that emotions aroused by racism should be used to motivate yourself to perform better and that to spend too much time dwelling on experiences of racism is undesirable and a sign of weakness. Accusing others of racism in this context was sometimes therefore read as an indication that the accuser is unwilling to put in more effort and, sometimes, even trying to abuse anti-racist regulations to his own advantage.

Conclusion

Amsterdam soccer culture in many ways reflects the old and new forms of racism that have been documented in other parts of the world. The same puzzling contradictions can be found in the expression of racism, as well as in the Racialization of wider soccer culture. Our analysis indicates that the dominant discourse of what constitutes 'racism' makes for a very poor tool to address this multilayered kaleidoscope. It is, however, the general discourse used by both fans and players.

Because their shared discourse only recognizes racism as such when it is expressed with the clear intention to injure and to reflect ideological convictions, those that commit racist acts are left with a discursive space through which they can avoid accountability. By denying any racist intentions and convictions, their behaviours are constructed as an innocent joke taken the wrong way or an unfortunate by-product of harmless emotional involvement in the game. They thus take up the position of an 'accidental racist' whose abuse does not qualify as 'real' racism and should therefore 'not be taken too serious'.

Soccer players also experience racism through the lens of this discourse. As a result, those who suffer racist abuse are confronted with the task of establishing the 'true' racist intentions of their offenders. They may thus spend much time and effort trying to prove that the abuse they suffered was 'really racist'. In most cases, however, the result is inconclusive and the racist act cannot be adequately challenged. As a result of both the efforts required to 'prove' racism and the slim chances of success, many instances of racism are accepted as a regrettable 'part of the game'.

These results confirm that a common reaction to experiences of racism in soccer culture is one of ignoring and silencing.[31] Our research contributes to the understanding of this phenomenon by explicating a number of the discursive and cultural processes through which these reactions are (re)produced. Apart from the central role of the discursive position of an 'accidental racist' described above, more general dynamics of racialized masculine soccer culture also need to be taken into account. The accusations of racism in soccer tend to be read as 'making a fuss' because of the ensuing claims and counter claims about the intentions and convictions of the offender. Moreover, an accusation of racism may backfire and result in accusations of being over sensitive and, for example, failing to appreciate racist jokes for the harmless tease they were intended to be. Within a soccer culture in which masculine codes of honour and team spirit are central, such accusations may also be read as setting your individual problems before the interests of the team. Addressing racism through official anti-racist channels may therefore simply be a bridge too far for many players who may first and foremost be looking to be a part of the team and 'one of the lads'.[32] Instead, the more viable response is to retaliate personally and anonymously. These kinds of retaliation range from playing better and winning the match when the abuse is coming from the terraces during a match, to committing verbal or physical abuse against the perpetrator directly. To react in any other way is read as a sign of weakness for which there is little room in soccer culture, let alone in the context of a soccer match.

One important step forward in the eradication of soccer racism would therefore no doubt be to ensure that racism is no longer defined by the identity and intentions of the perpetrator but rather by the behaviour itself in order to make public redress of racism more accessible. Moreover, our analysis points to importance of the cultural context through which practices of ignoring and silencing are reproduced. It is essential that the focus is also directed at the problematic masculine codes of conduct and processes of Racialization and minorization, which structure interactions along racist lines on a daily basis and limit the progressive internal dynamics of soccer culture.

These processes are responsible for the reproduction of the *potential* for racism in soccer culture and need to be challenged as well. To do so, however, will require that larger soccer culture is critically evaluated by the actors involved. The relative lack of official complaints about overt racist expressions in Amsterdam soccer culture, for example, might actually in part be explained by the fact that racialized relations and practices may not even qualify as 'accidentally racist' because none of the participants recognizes them to be structured by racist discourses at all. A critical change in soccer culture therefore requires both a redefinition of the kinds of racism that 'count', as well as a sustained critical discussion about the racialized, masculine culture of soccer that partly constitutes the potential for racism.

Given soccer's increasingly global character, it is evident that many of the studies on soccer racism that are currently being carried out from a cultural perspective will be applicable to a broad range of national contexts. However, it needs to be kept in mind that the situation of racism in local Amsterdam soccer is best characterized with the neologism 'glocal'. While the racist discourses in the Netherlands are similar to those in countries like England, the positions and background of the ethnic minorities in Amsterdam soccer are different, with the most notable being the large groups of second generation immigrants from increasingly problematized Muslim 'guest worker' communities. Not only are the forms in which racism presents itself to these groups to some extent peculiar to the Dutch context, but the processes of minorization through which this racism is reproduced can also be traced through the history of the socio-political Dutch context.[33] Any attempts to engage with racism in a specific locality will thus require attention to the global and local aspects of racism and the ways in which they find expression within any particular soccer culture. Nonetheless, it pays to be on guard in any local context for the discourses and practices we encountered in Amsterdam. As the universal proverb goes, 'accidents happen'.

Notes

[1]   Landelijke vereniging van anti-discriminatie bureaus en meldpunten (LVADB), *Kerncijfers 2004*.
[2]   Back, Crabbe and Solomos, *The Changing Face of Football*; Back, Crabbe and Solomos, 'Beyond the Racist/Hooligan Couplet'; Garland and Rowe, *Racism and Anti-racism in Football*; Jones, 'The Black Experience within British Professional Soccer'.
[3]   Back *et al.*, *The Changing Face of Football*.
[4]   Garland and Rowe, 'Selling the Game Short'; Back *et al.*, 'Beyond the Racist/Hooligan Couplet'; Jones, 'The Black Experience within British Professional Soccer'.

[5]   Brown, *Fanatics! Power, Identity and Fandom.*
[6]   King, 'Race and Cultural Identity'; Burdsey, 'One of the Lads?'
[7]   Back *et al.*, 'Beyond the Racist/Hooligan Couplet'; King, 'Race and Cultural Identity'.
[8]   Back *et al.*, 'Beyond the Racist/Hooligan Couplet'; Hermes, 'Burnt Orange'.
[9]   Back *et al.*, 'Beyond the Racist/Hooligan Couplet'.
[10]   Ibid.
[11]   Ibid.
[12]   Crabbe, 'England fans – A new club for a new England?'
[13]   Maguire, 'Sport, Racism and British Society'.
[14]   Burdsey, 'Obstacle Race?'
[15]   Hermes, 'Burnt Orange'; McCarthy *et al.*, 'Construction Realities Images and Interpreting Realities'.
[16]   Garland and Rowe, 'Selling the Game Short'.
[17]   Miles, *Racism after 'Race Relations'*; Garland and Rowe, 'Selling the Game Short'; Back *et al.*, 'Beyond the Racist/Hooligan Couplet'.
[18]   Miles, *Racism after 'Race Relations'*.
[19]   Ibid.; King, 'Race and Cultural Identity'.
[20]   Garland and Rowe, 'Selling the Game Short'; Burdsey, 'One of the Lads?'
[21]   King, 'Race and Cultural Identity'; Mercer, *Welcome to the Jungle.*
[22]   Carrington, 'Fear of a Black Athlete'; Jones, 'The Black Experience within British Professional Soccer'.
[23]   Mercer, *Welcome to the Jungle*; Spivak, *In Other Worlds.*
[24]   Maguire, 'Sport, Racism and British Society'.
[25]   Burdsey 'Obstacle Race?'; also King, 'Race and Cultural Identity'.
[26]   Van Sterkenburg and Knoppers, 'Dominant Discourses about Race/Ethnicity and Gender in Sport Practice Performance'.
[27]   Rath, 'The Netherlands'.
[28]   Ibid.
[29]   These interviews were conducted by David van der Leij; see also van der Leij, *Daar Hoorden zij Engelen Zingen.*
[30]   Back *et al.*, 'Beyond the Racist/Hooligan Couplet'.
[31]   Ibid.
[32]   Burdsey, 'One of the Lads?'
[33]   Rath, 'The Netherlands'.

References

Back, L., T. Crabbe and J. Solomos. 'Beyond the Racist/Hooligan Couplet: Race, Social Theory and Football Culture.' *British Journal of Sociology 50,* no.3 (1999): 419–42.

Back, L., Crabbe, T. and Solomos. J. *The Changing Face of Football: Racism, Identity and Multiculture in the English Game.* New York: Berg, 2001.

Brown, A., ed. *Fanatics! Power, Identity and Fandom.* London: Routledge, 1998.

Burdsey, D., 'One of the Lads? Dual Ethnicity and Assimilated Ethnicities in the Careers of British Asian Professional Footballers.' *Ethnic and Racial Studies 27,* no.5 (2004): 757–79.

Burdsey, D., 'Obstacle race? "Race", Racism and the Recruitment of British Asian Professional Footballers.' *Patterns of Prejudice 38,* no.3 (2004): 279–99.

Carrington, B., 'Fear of a Black Athlete: Masculinity, Politics and the Body.' *New formations 45,* no.4 (2002): 91–110.

Crabbe, T., 'England Fans – A New Club for a New England? Social Inclusion, Authenticity and the Performance of Englishness at "home" and "away".' *Leisure Studies 23,* no.1 (2004): 63–78.

Garland, Jon and M. Rowe. *Racism and Anti-racism in Football.* Basingstoke: Palgrave, 2001.

Garland, J. and M. Rowe. 'Selling the Game Short: An Examination of the Role of Antiracism in British Football.' *Sociology of Sport Journal 16,* no.1 (1999): 35–53.

Hermes, J., 'Burnt Orange. Television, Football, and the Representation of Ethnicity.' *Television and New Media 6,* no.1 (2005): 49–69.

Jones, R.L., 'The Black Experience within British Professional Soccer.' *Journal of Sport and Social Issues 26,* no.1 (2002): 47–65.

King, C., 'Race and Cultural Identity: Playing the Race Game inside Football'. *Leisure Studies, XXIII,* 1 (2004): 19–30.

Landelijke vereniging van anti-discriminatie bureaus en meldpunten (LVADB). *Kerncijfers 2004.* Amsterdam: LVADB, 2004.

Leij, D. van der. *Daar hoorden zij engelen zingen. Supporterskoren op de F-Side.* Amsterdam: Uva masters thesis, 2005.

McCarthy, D., R.L. Jones and P. Potrac. 'Constructing Realities Images and Interpreting Realities. The Case of the Black Soccer Player on Television.' *International Review for the Sociology of Sport 38,* no.2 (2003): 217–38.

Maguire, J., 'Sport, Racism and British Society: A Sociological Study of England's Elite Male Afro/Caribbean Soccer and Rugby Union Players.' In *Sport, Racism and Ethnicity,* edited by G. Jarvie. London: Falmer, 1991.

Mercer, K. *Welcome to the Jungle.* New York: Routledge, 1994.

Miles, R. *Racism after 'Race Relations'.* London: Routledge, 1993.

Rath, J., 'The Netherlands. A Dutch Treat for Anti-social Families and Immigrant Minorities.' In *The European Union and Migrant Labour,* edited by M. Cole and G. Dale. Oxford: Berg Publishers, 1999: 147–70.

Spivak, C. *In Other Worlds: Essays in Cultural Politics.* London: Routledge, 1988.

Sterkenburg, J. van and A. Knoppers. 'Dominant Discourses about Race/Ethnicity and Gender in Sport Practice Performance.' *International Review for the Sociology of Sport 39,* no.3 (2004): 301–21.

Football Fan Groups in Andalusia

Álvaro Rodríguez Díaz

Introduction

I analyze the Spanish spectators in Andalusia who visit professional soccer stadiums according to different categories. Among the demographic categories, there are two age groups of this kind of supporter which are classified as children and adults. The ultras are classified according to two considerations: the way they support the team and the social position of the fans. There are no clear distinctions between both types. Although they overlap, the categories are based on how they support their teams: radical and accessory. The radicals are persistent, noisy and colourful, and are integrated with the so-called ultras. These young people identify themselves with certain lifestyles which are typical to their social status, normally working class. The position occupied in the social scale, as well as the position occupied in the stadium, is secondary and subordinate.

This brief description presents some hints of the final objective: to depict the situation of young ultras in Andalusian soccer. I understand these groups as a social construction: they have been produced by public opinion. Simultaneously, they are also a social product: their members respond to a certain sort of socialization. I analyse the associations where they are integrated, from the point of view of the social transition process.

I investigate two groups, which are defined in time and space. 'Biris' (Seville FC's ultras) and 'Brigadas Amarillas' – Yellow Brigades – (Cadiz CF's). I implemented an observation plan, consisting of six phases with 26 qualitative indicators, one of which was how they supported the team. Six observers participated between 1994 and 1996.

The observation was extended to more fieldwork, including bus trips to other cities and personal and informal relationships, sometimes by means of 'participating observation'. Ten open-ended interviews and two group discussions were carried out, between ultras from the Biris and the Brigadas Amarillas. Later, we performed 150 personal surveys with closed questions. We received economic support from the Andalusian Government for this fieldwork.

Hypotheses

Public opinion has developed different labels to define gangs of young people. Even youngsters assume these labels: 'Heavies are politically defined as extreme left wing… radical Andalusian nationalists, whereas skins have Spanish flags and are racists' (I.16.C).[1] This bipolarity is a reminder of the times at the end of Francoism, when there were 'progres' (radical left wing) and 'fachas' (radical right wing). In the so-called urban tribes, we can find new identities in which the ideology is mixed with aesthetic aspects. Red Skins, for example, are left wing but wear shaved heads. In Spain, in the last decades we have been using formulas increasingly to label young people: mods, rockers, rappers, et cetera. In fact, the names refer to Anglo-Saxon commercial stereotypes, which match young people with their musical preferences. The objective is market segmentation so as to encourage new variants of record consumption; that is the reason why there is false exaggeration about the young. For Jameson the stereotype is 'the place of an illicit excess of sense'.[2]

The commercial classification of young people is introduced in the sports market, so the ultras are not only new consumers of spectacle, but also the spectacle itself. They are usually registered under the concept of 'young subculture'. Accordingly, there are too many classifications; in fact, sometimes, there are sub-groups within an original group. Youngsters can easily get all the necessary information from appearances:

> In our stands, we have basically two looks. The first look is a little bit rocker, leather jacket, jeans jacket, with the Seville anagram, long hair; and the other look, is closer to the usual ultra look nowadays, that is, those green jackets with the orange lining, soldier boots, soldier trousers, short hair. (I.20.S)

The labelling means that the individual who is labelled assumes the category as his own: 'At first, when we came here to see Cadiz CF , then, the people called me ultra…,well, that's all right now,… I'm an ultra.' (I.15.C). Giddens points out how the theories about labelling are always created from the inequality point of view:

> The labels applied to create categories of deviance thus express the power structure of society. By and large, the rules in terms of which deviance is defined, and the contexts in which they are applied, are framed by the wealthy for the poor, by men for women, by older people for younger people and the by ethnic majorities for the minority groups.[3]

The Andalusian ultra does not regard himself as a 'hooligan', which is the referent for fans in Northern Europe. This label refers to the sort of rowdy supporters who enjoy ripping up the seating and hurling them into lines of riot police, that is, what the

Spanish police calls 'erosive groups'. Buford, a North American writer, joined these groups and related a clear example:

> Those moments when conscience stops really appeal to me, moments when all you can think of is surviving... There, in the streets of Fulham, I felt, as the group exceeded the abysmal metaphor, as if I literally was weightless... in an adrenalin euphoria state... And for the first time, I was able to understand the fans' words to describe that experience. That massive violence was their drug.[4]

For Buford, soccer violence is a new type of 'popular culture'. In this sense, I propose some hypotheses: Was hooliganism a circumstance that was boosted by the British power to turn aside the Scottish, Irish or Welsh nationalisms? Does this phenomenon have anything to do with the discipline of English education? Gaviria, a Spanish sociologist, says that the fights of Anglo-Saxon supporters are a problem provoked by their education being much better than their jobs.[5] Undoubtedly, the Andalusian reality is very far from the patterns we can find in the north of Europe and in some other regions of Spain, where there is senseless and obvious violence.

On the other hand, Vinnai observes how soccer is becoming increasingly technical. He compares the organization of professional sport with the organization of any ordinary work. Players are more specialized now and they even have to optimize their skills: 'The 22 athletes provide the crowd of the stadium with activities regulated by rules which are very similar to those of an ordinary job'.[6] In fact, the workers' specialization is parallel to the fans' specialization. Thus, the different spectators in the stadium choose their own level of consumption, according to how people make use of these entertainment services. Both sportsmen (producers) and supporters (consumers) have become more specialized.

Elias and Dunning argue that the first modern sport games were created to control students in English public schools, in the middle of the nineteenth century.[7] These were boarding schools, where the young upper class and nobility were educated. The young students' free time was devoted to the popular, atavistic and rural games. Those sports had hardly any rules and were violent and even cruel. There were too many accidents, violent encounters and injured people despite the fact that the community wanted to be industrious and well-managed. Educators were actually the creators of modern sports by turning traditional games into non-violent and regulated sports.

Free time has been closely related to the birth of sport. Foucault defines sport as body control within certain premises and with fixed and productive rules.[8] That civilization process matches the industry and the market process that was in progress. Fair play was a new value, a gentlemen's agreement, applicable to both commerce and sport. Norbert Elias analyzes the civilization process that developed in courteous Europe, where wars between gentlemen were avoided. That truce is carried out by means of pacts, parliaments, political rules.[9]

Thus, cruel games were suppressed in the socialization of young English men mainly because newspapers supported the elimination of those practices. The reformist policies in the nineteenth century replaced the vulgar games that the students of the British elites played: they rationalized them, they delimited them, and different institutions were created to regulate them. Competition appears now as a fundamental value in the same way as in economics. The record is the new measure, and everything is gauged in terms of rank and production.

Elias explains the origins of football in Spain. In 1904 the Spanish government passed the Sunday Rest Act, an old aspiration of trade unions. The newspaper reports were ironic about how bored workers were, since they had 'nothing to do'; they drank in the pubs, which caused an increase in alcoholism and public disorder. The first sport championship was created in that year. Competitions were held on Sundays (the number of bullfights also increased at week-ends). Before, only the elites were involved in sport. Now, the leisure of the working class brought about the creation of clubs in the factories which were supported by the employers. The football league (liga) was born a few years later and so unhealthy leisure was replaced by sport. Elias' pacification processes are Foucault's disciplinary control processes of the space. However, this process is not over yet because the absence of fixed rules among many spectators and players is causing this pacification process to be still in progress.

Soccer is fed by the values of society. The crowd of people in the stadium shares the same values for both games and work: compete and win. Violence in soccer comes from the supporters who do not assume these values in sport. They identify the show with competition, ignoring the ludic or educative aspects. There are groups who cannot understand the metaphor and the difference between sport and real life.

The crowd can be a shelter for any irregularity. The relationship between anonymity and crowd has been studied by a great many authors with very different ideologies. For example, Fromm [10] and especially Le Bon, who was a fascism defender: 'A crowd is a febrile, delirious body, in hypnosis state'.[11] Freud also felt intellectual inclinations for the gregarious instinct: 'The crowd is a resurrection of the primitive hordes'.[12]

The ultras pay to see the match but unconsciously they have not given up participating in the game. In the origins of soccer there was a continuous interchange between players and spectators.[13] But now the ultras are customers, as well as part of the show. They practice a parallel game to the one played on the ground, although it has more arbitrary rules. They consider their game to be fun and they look down on the rest of the public because they do not represent 'the real thing', everything is fake for them. Lorenz affirms that some adolescents are people who do not adhere to social rules as in the times of the prehistoric hordes:

> The instinctive necessity to be a member of a united group who fights for common ideals is so strong that it is secondary to know what those ideals stand for as well as their intrinsic value. From my point of view, this explains why youngsters form gangs whose social structure is surely very similar to the one in primitive societies.[14]

There are other theories which downplay the importance of instinct in understanding aggression in young people. Fromm, for example, highlights the relevance of learning and points out that prehistoric groups did not succeed by violent attitudes, but by full cooperation: 'Just by increasing the productivity and work division, and also when hierarchies and elites are constituted, destruction and cruelty appear in large scale.'[15] Also Montagu, although he does not rule out the instinctive element, gives a prominent role to learning: aggression is learned and is a consequence of frustration.[16] Vázquez and Varela state the following on this subject:

> How to explain aggressiveness in sport then? Doubtlessly it is a safety valve not of the aggressive instinct of man, but of the pressures that a certain organization of life provokes so that a latent aggressiveness must be repressed. This aggressiveness clearly appears among supporters and football fans.[17]

Different approaches highlight the social interaction in football hooliganism, rather than a predisposition to violence.[18] From these perspectives, we can see that in sport competitions the social and economic organization causes imbalances, inequality, adversity, et cetera. The need for success in sport is closely related to the degree of insecurity of the social structure of the community where the match is played.

Comments about Violence

In the first contact with the young people, they all said they had nothing to do with violence: 'we are not violent' (I.18.S). That classification as non violent arose spontaneously without any mention by the interviewer about the subject. However, they were resigned to the fact that both public opinion and the mass media identify ultras with violence. 'After the program of the other day on TV2, the people who see you in the street consider that you are a delinquent; so, sure, it is very difficult to say: I am a Biri.' (I.17.S). This kind of message also appears in their own families: 'My mother always tells me not to get in trouble' (I.19.C).

According to the Dictionary of the Royal Spanish Academy, the first meaning of 'violent' is: 'Out of his natural state or situation'. The interpretations for this definition are open:

> We arrived at Valence, and the first thing we saw was the police car... they make us get off [the bus] and they take us away; then we go to the police station although we haven't done anything; so they photocopy our IDs; That is what I call provoking and incitement. (DG. S)

They have had few confrontations with the security forces. Somehow, it is positive for police to know that the problem is identified: on match days they only have to watch a specific area of the stadium. Ultras are escorted and guarded, and to some extent all this paraphernalia make them feel even more important because they can demonstrate in a disciplined way. This situation is even stressed when the clash is against opponent supporters.

> We're going to have a 'nice welcome' in Malaga, because when they were here [in Seville], many people were after them, so we know that they are waiting for us. We need to stick together. The police are going to escort us, and thus we won't have experience of what happened in other years; nobody will get his head broken. If they go for us, let it be one hundred or two hundred against one hundred of us. (DG.S)

Every year there is a violent retaliation to previous aggressions. Therefore, it is not easy to know which group began the fight. There is a vicious circle that reproduces the hostility year after year. It is a mutual, revengeful and historical reaction, which is absolutely assumed by everybody: 'I can't conceive, for example a Sevilla-Betis match or Malaga-Seville or something like that, without any confrontation. It would be impossible, I think it is impossible' (I.21.S).

Nowadays all spectators must remain seated. This directive was intended to control the supporters behind the goals. Accordingly, two objectives are accomplished. On the one hand, violence may be prevented, and on the other, there is a stricter control of the sale of tickets so that clubs cannot sell more tickets than they are allowed to. However, the real purpose is to avoid anonymity by making supporters stay in one place without jumping or moving about. When tickets were not numbered, ultras were closer to the players. When people were able to move freely in the stands, the influence on players was stronger because the group worked as a whole. The tendency in professional soccer is currently to keep fans away from players and from the violence of the game, which, in turn, stands for a symbolic violence, a sublimation of the fans' violence.[19]

Ultras are always surrounded by the police, particularly when they go to other cities. Paradoxically, this way they are more easily quantified and identified. The security measures have favoured the delimitation of the group. Thus, they have fostered the social construction of radical groups, on the one hand, because they have defined the group, and on the other, because they offer the necessary images to the mass media for their legitimacy. These young people know they are observed when they are within the police cordon. Some of them even cover their faces, assuming the role they have been given. Thus, unlike in other places (family, school, et cetera), they can feel like protagonists. The strict control are under favours their identity and their common pride and moreover, they are always eager to show that off in front of the cameras. Apart from that, some actions of the police hinder the helpful response of the fans. Magnane points out that the more immobile the supporters are, the more hostile their attitude will be.[20] In addition, sometimes the presumed violent actions are actually expressions of joy: 'That ritual of jumps, the tumult... I do not believe that this has anything to do with violence... Hands up, leather jackets, fists,... I do compare it with a rock concert' (I.22.C).

All these exhibitions disappear as they grow older. When they are 24 or 25 years old, they move little by little away from the central nucleus to occupy more peripheral positions. They move away when they have already experienced sufficiently anti-social behaviour. That is why it is easy to explain why they quit when they have a girlfriend, not to mention a family or a steady job. In the same way, they believe that 'it is better not to get any more risks just in case the police get a file on you' (I.17.S).

Official reports state that the mass media highlight the repercussions of ultras.[21] In this way, the real news is not the results of the game, but the extra-sport incidents. The best example is in the United Kingdom, where hooliganism goes hand in hand with the popular papers. News about the riots stops the sociological analysis from being fully objective. Some authors point out how the treatment of the so-called gutter press fosters the dangerous image of hooligans. The media propose hard measures to tackle the problem, and as a consequence, people become distanced from the problem.[22]

Taylor has also analyzed how the mass media demanded extreme measures, which soon began to be implemented by the respective governments. He describes the process as a 'cycle of stimulus and response between the press and the government'.[23] The press did not analyze vandalism from a social perspective, taking into account the poverty of the communities of the English working-class, but from a penal perspective. On the other hand, Mason highlights the coincidence, at the end of the nineteenth century, of the emergence of the popular press together with the emergence of soccer supporters.[24]

Notwithstanding, we cannot find as many cases of violence in Andalusian soccer as there are in Europe, and furthermore, the figures are very similar to the ones for the rest of Spain. For example, every year since 1987, at least one bus is attacked with stones and there are usually riots after some matches between neighbouring teams. The most serious incident took place in Cadiz in 1985, when a spectator died having been hit by a flare. It was a unlucky accident, and two fans were condemned for lack of judgment. In comparison to the problems in other areas, the situation here is not so worrying: according to the local statistics in Seville, there are more than 5,000 acts of vandalism every year, in other words, about 14 a day. The point is that acts of vandalism in football matches are usually magnified by the mass media, although they only represent a small percentage fo the total. However, these violent acts in the stadium are witnessed by many people and are broadcast all over the world in full detail and everybody is aware of these incidents. All the information is biased and accordingly, we can find some distorted opinions such as those of the *Movement against Intolerance* (Spanish youth association): 'Among the ultras groups in Andalusia 90% are skinheads. Most of them are men between 15 and 30 years old.'[25] These simplistic and superficial opinions try to connect the Andalusian problem to the Anglo-Saxon label once again: soccer and racism.[26] These types of messages have been criticized by John Bale, when he compares the English press alarmism with the reality of smaller incidents. He underlines that people do not always consider that certain facts are anti-social, for example, graffiti: 'Whereas some people see it as some kind of vandalism, others see it as art'.[27] The tendentiousness of the press in Andalusia is not so pronounced. However, in Seville's local press almost every couple of weeks there is negative news about ultras. It is undeniable that vandalism is a problem, but the information is always overstated. We have only found one positive article in all the data we have compiled.[28]

The Antiviolence Commission (attached to the Spanish Soccer Association) admits that violence is implicit in daily life: 'Violence is everywhere in society…, not only in youth, although it is especially conveyed by the young'; 'There is a violent subculture within society'.[29]

Many authors have established a certain parallelism between war and soccer. Such warlike representation is expressed in the language of the sport tactics: rear, firing, counterattack. Even trainers and managers use expressions such as 'fight to death'… 'no quarter to the enemy', 'blood, sweat and tears'. In the Spanish press files, there is ample documentation on the matter. Many of these phrases have become songs of the ultras, repeated by them every Sunday. The atmosphere on the days leading up to the match gets rather rough sometimes as the mass media usually give full coverage of the statements of everybody involved in the match. If violence is considered 'to be outside the natural state', then many directors, journalists and fans behave this way. In this sense, in a nationwide survey carried out by the Gallup Institute in 1988, two out of ten professional footballers declared that they were urged by managers during the half-time of some matches to act violently.[30]

Ultras also practice simulated violence. The avalanches, shouts, flags or drums, not only symbolize their support of the players, but also demonstrate the group's force. Soccer history reflects a progressive separation among the public in the stadium; the more people, the more segregation in more heterogeneous places.[31] Ultras are an intermediate group between the mass of supporters and the players. They are the greatest participants in the show, the closest actors to the game, and that is why they are entitled to make the victory theirs.

The Social Construction of Ultras Groups

The groups were born at the beginning of the 1980s from some traditional groups of supporters, who acted in an unorthodox and jubilant way. After several public order problems, those groups are replaced by the first Andalusians ultras. At the end of the 1980s, clubs built up their capital as an initial step to the creation of the Sport Public Limited Companies in 1992. Then there was an explosion of professional sport, where spectators became clients, the number of ultras increased and many women joined the world of football.

For Acosta and Rodríguez, one of the reason that young people were attracted to soccer was the low price of the tickets.[32] It was in the years of the democratic political transition in Spain when the population in general moved away from soccer. In addition to the economic crisis, the spectacle became less and less interesting, mainly for young people. Furthermore, the democratic opposition had related soccer to Francoism.[33] For that reason, the clubs offered very cheap season tickets for the youth. Club executives supported ultras at the end of the 1970s: 'In order to stop the decrease of the average age of spectators and the supporter desertion from football grounds, [the clubs] paid for their trips, gave tickets, flags.' [34]

Another factor was the mimicry of the hooligan phenomenon. In 1985, the general public was shocked by the Heysel tragedy in Belgium during the final of Europe's former League Champions. This fact amplified the problem, the term eurohooliganism was created and there were all kinds of international connections, articles, reports, talk shows about ultras' violence, et cetera. Paradoxically, the consequence was the export of the model to many countries, including Spain. Real Madrid FC's *Ultra Sur* and FC Barcelona's *Boixos Nois* recreated that European pattern broadcast on television. They imitated the dramatic appearance of the radical fans of opposite teams. The season 1985–86 was marked by the beginning of serious confrontations between ultras of Real Betis and Seville FC (the two clubs in the city of Seville). The supporters had never previously been enemies but the confrontations have not stopped ever since. Generally speaking, according to Canter and Comber, the appearance of young supporters recreated a different psychological climate for the spectators, who were not so homogenous any more. Summing up, radical groups imitated each other in their social strategies, and the mass media in their information.[35]

Ultras means 'extreme', much more than a fan: an unconditional supporter, who goes further than any other supporter: 'We the ultras are the radical fans' (I.16.C). In this way, there is a clear separation with respect to most of the fans. To be an ultra is a matter of honour, as they belong to a very exclusive spirited minority: 'We are not too many ... but we are the real radical fans' (DG. S). Of the youngsters interviewed, 90 per cent go to all or almost all the matches when the team plays at home. Many subgroups consisting of three or four friends go together. Several small groups can constitute what they call sections, ten or twelve people, who identify the section with the districts where they live. This structure is flexible and arises from the base, without any clear hierarchies or stability.

Rookies try to demonstrate their courage through various exploits, as an initiation ceremony for their entrance and acceptance. The youngest (14 or 15 years) usually embrace direct and unconditional militancy. They just want to be noticed. It is self-initiation, nobody makes decisions or sets standards. You are an ultra just for the sake of being in the stands and melting chorally with the others. One of the active members, a 22-year-old male with a university degree, which is exceptional, describes the phases they undergo. The rookies have to earn it, then they become 'leaders' and finally they leave when they are 'established': Each phase roughly corresponds to certain ages:

> A group of people, from 13–14 years, even 12 years, to 17–18 years, in general. This is a generalization that has many exceptions, but you know, there are people who are a little more aggressive, perhaps people who have been going to the stadium for one year; they discover the ultra stuff a year before, the chants. They want the people to know them immediately, they are eager to be protagonists, or even become a legend. This kind of person is usually a little bit more aggressive. Soon there is a group of people that are older than 23–24, who are normally working and already have some money, so they can afford to go on all the trips. These people do not care too much about the ultra stuff, organization, banners and all that. They go in order to have some fun and they sometimes get stoned. There is also an intermediate group of people between 18 and 22–23, who are the people you really can rely on. I think that in general the people who are doing all the stuff are actually pretty normal. When there are problems going on, they are much more reliable than the younger; on the other hand, the older are more 'established' and are a little afraid of losing their jobs as they are not supposed to be into this 'silly' stuff of ultras. (I.22.S)

There are about 4,000 ultras in the Andalusian cities. There are about 800 Biris, about 100 of which are active, and about 10 are leaders. As for the Brigadas Amarillas in Cadiz, there are about 300 of them. The archetypical Andalusian ultra is an 18-year-old man who goes to every soccer match; he has got a season ticket. The majority are students, mainly studying vocational subjects. Only 6 per cent are older than 23 years old, and 10 per cent are younger than 14 years old. I have even noticed 11-year-old ultras, the so-called 'pitufos'. The circumstances are still very far from those in other north European countries. In our case, almost eight out of ten said they were students (77 per cent), which is a similar ratio to that of the rest of the Andalusian population of those ages. However, the number studying vocational subjects is four times the Andalusian average. The rest are working (13 per cent) and unemployed (10 per cent).

Almost 75 per cent of these fans have a season ticket and most of them have had one since they were about 13. In order to get the ticket, they must be helped by adults, normally parents or relatives. They remain loyal for purely economic reasons. Season tickets holders pay less, and there are usually reductions for teenagers. This is important as young fans have little disposable income and, apart from that, this fosters their attendance habits. Still, the violent social image does not allow them to appear as ultras. That activity is hidden in their daily life. There are parents who do not know that their sons participate in these groups. The secrecy, sometimes like a game, facilitates that participation.

The groups fulfil some of the formal requirements of any ordinary 'association': logo, fanzine, membership card, scarf, web page, small fees. In any case, it is an informal association and the objectives are short term: organization of trips, preparation of *tifos*,[36] establishing relationships with fans of other clubs, et cetera. The fact that they are very informal does not imply that they are less dynamic than traditional supporter groups, which are actually more passive and bureaucratic. However, due to certain behaviour it is necessary for someone to be responsible for the group:

> Because in the trips we may stop in a bar, and somebody does not pay or steals something as if it were the typical joke in a school end-of-year trip, a study tour... Then, of course, if you organize the trip, that entails assuming certain responsibilities and sure, you are responsible for everybody, including the bunch of wankers who make all the trouble... You are the scapegoat, and if they ask the bus driver, he will always say: that is the guy who has organized everything. (I.23.C)

The Same and Different at the Same Time

After the match as a 'sacred meeting',[37] the young supporters are scattered during the week all over the districts and schools. They are no different to other boys of their age or background: 'we do not see each other, but on Sunday everybody meets in the stadium. There everybody knows everybody and so on.' (I.18.C). They are the same as the rest of the people, but at the same time, they are also different. They are linked to a soccer emblem, but they think they are more 'authentic' supporters.

When they become less dependant on their families, their social life becomes more open to different activities. They study or at least they try, they work or look for a job, they participate in the Holy Week processions[38] of their districts, go to their casetas[39] in the April Fair, rehearse their 'chirigotas'[40], they hang around with their mopeds, they go to the cinema on the discount days, play the guitar and sing flamenco at home... still, the day of the match is their great day; they become collective protagonists, without any hierarchies, and they do not let that fleeting opportunity escape.

Their social position is the same as that of their mates, sharing their light and shade, as well as their contradictions. The majority used to go to the stadium with their families, and then they joined a different way of participation that, in principle, seems more motivating: to belong to a group of young people who are more dynamic and more up-to-date with what it is going on there, that is, to support the local team. In other cases, teenagers join the ultra group very naturally by accepting the invitation of a friend. The transition is sometimes opposed by their families: 'I used to enjoy going to the trips with my father; but he said that all the new hooliganism was turning football into nothing but violence' (DG.C). As a result, youngsters quit going with their families and prefer having fun with ultras. An official report defines ultras as 'teenagers' gangs'.[41] On the other hand, they do not have many prospects for the future and they fear that they will always be a subordinated class with no chance for leadership in the long term.

> What the working class, the unemployed, really like is soccer… My father is a crane driver, and he works wherever he can.

> Sometimes we speak about work and I must say that I am worried about that.

> Right, most people are worried about the future… we think that there is no future; now I can eat at home every day, but there will be a time when things will change… you think that this is never going to happen, but if you think for a minute, you realize that sooner or later I would have to find my own way.

> The problem turns terrible if you are thinking of buying or even renting a flat. Nowadays to buy or to rent a house is impossible, and the young people of Seville have to live with the parents, although many people would like to become independent and they can't. (DG.S)

They do not have an articulated system of beliefs. A teenager admits: 'It is very difficult that a 15 year old lad may have political ideas' (I.15.S). They have a certain system of ideas, with the necessary contradictions, sometimes surreal, for example, the walls of their rooms have posters of both Che Guevara and the image of the Virgin of their brotherhood. Moreover, they say they have no interest in politics and yet they sing the Andalusian anthem carrying the Basque flag, or they enjoy punk music at the same time as they are brethren of the brotherhoods in Holy Week. Still, others have more coherent ideas and try to appear as 'good boys':

> The last thing we have decided is to display a big banner against racism in the next match and to distribute 10,000 red and white balloons with phrases against racism, so as to contribute in raising conscience on this problem, and apart from that, so as to get rid of the bad reputation of everything involved with football. (I.21.S)

They fly more Andalusian flags than Spanish, but actually, the important thing is the ideology represented by the team:

> I think that violence is in society, not in soccer. The point is that soccer has more repercussions. Football is our way to forget about everything.

> You forget your problems in soccer, you forget the high school, the work, the problems with your parents, the house, the lack of money, unemployment, the troubles in the family.

> I believe that Sunday evening is useless if you don't go to the stadium, everything is closed, there are only three cinemas here in Cadiz, and so, people prefer going to have some fun watching the match, you enjoy the match, you laugh, you know.

> For example I always listen to the match on the radio when Cadiz is not playing at home.
>
> And some days we are going to the training sessions.
>
> That's right, and when I find out that there is something on the radio about Cadiz, I always listen to it.
>
> Sometimes Cadiz is our only topic of conversation when we are all together.
>
> To be a Cadiz fan is not to be a Cadiz fan for 90 minutes on Sundays. It is to be a Cadiz fan all the days. (DG.C)

The hostility between the groups reflects the rivalry between the cities: the administrative and political centralism of Seville versus the tourist periphery of Malaga, or the harbour territory of Cadiz: 'we have no problems with the people; I have Sevillian friends myself. The question is that we are against everything that Seville conveys' (I.22.C). The most determining factor is belonging to a city rather than the nationalistic and left-wing ideology that most of the groups share. The definitive element that joins them together is the club; they describe that feeling in rather emotional terms: 'It is clear that Cadiz is always the first thing because players, managers, etc will leave but Cadiz will always be there' (I.20.C). Ultras are a clan *within* each club, which is more communitarian than associative.[42] These 'youngsters of the clan' are self-identified in relation to their rivalry with 'the others': Betis supporters are above all anti-Seville FC, and the same stands for the radical Seville fans.

These differences among ultras are a post-modernist aspect in Spain. Historically, in the rural and pre-modern community, almost all the masculine population participated in sport celebrations. There were no spectators, in the present sense of the word. During a large part of the twentieth century, the spectators were uniformed as in the fordist society, protected by full employment and the security of the welfare state. After the economic crisis of the 1970s, the ultras brought about the first important split in the mass of fans. Thus, the middle-class regard them negatively, 'bloody teenagers', so they say. However, the radical groups are still there because they play a complementary role: they contribute to an ample contingent: 'we are sons of workers' (I.19.S). In addition, their support to the players is much more effective than that of the rest of the people.

The stadium is the place where the young people enjoy autonomy in spite of the security force around them. To be the focus of attention makes them feel very proud. They feel they are the best supporters, the fans that the players really need, especially when things go wrong. They are an allegory of 'the military arm' of the club. Thus, they criticize the rest of the fans, whom they call the 'old people'. For them the president's box represents the clearest example of what they despise, calm passionless public. The disposition of the spectators in the stadium is also a different exhibition of emotions.[43] At the same time, the social inequality in the city is reflected in the hierarchy of the stands. The prices of the tickets symbolize the economic position of the consumers. The cheapest stands are always those of the ultras, 'type C' according to UEFA. The most expensive prices are in the grandstand:

The people who are always cross and grumpy with the team are seated on the expensive grandstand. They are pessimistic, old, conservative people, who are always disillussioned, and complaining. (I.16.S)

Those very adults let them break certain social rules during the match. Thus, they constitute an ephemeral and travelling social space, a place of transition for young people of the Andalusian working class, a place for the socialization of young masculine people where, besides, winning is sometimes more important than observing the rules. For young supporters, who lack their own social space and freedom in the institutions, the stands turn into one of the few public premises they can take control of as well as the place where they can show off their difference.

Notes

[1]   These quotes are taken from interviews with different men in charge of sport facilities during the qualitative analysis carried out. At the end of each quote, there is a key – 'I', meaning 'interview' , or DG, 'discussion group', followed by the age of the interviewee, and finally 'S' for 'Seville' or 'C' for 'Cadiz'.

[2]   Jameson and Žižek, *Estudios culturales,* 106.

[3]   Giddens, *Sociology,* 128.

[4]   Buford, *Entre los vándalos,* 240.

[5]   Gaviria, *El buen salvaje: de urbanitas, campesinos y ecologistas varios.*

[6]   Vinnai, *El fútbol como ideología,* 32.

[7]   Elias and Dunning, *Quest for Excitement.*

[8]   Foucault, *Surveiller et punir.*

[9]   Elias, *The Civilizing Process, Vol. 2.*

[10]   Fromm, *Anatomía de la destructividad humana.*

[11]   Le Bon, *Origen de la psicología de las masas,* 25.

[12]   Freud, *Psicología de las masas,* 60.

[13]   Bale, *Sport, Space and the City.*

[14]   Lorenz, *Sobre la agresión,* 18.

[15]   Fromm, *Anatomía de la destructividad humana,* 27.

[16]   Montagu, *Anthropology and Human Nature.*

[17]   Vázquez and Varela, *100 años de deporte,* 20.

[18]   Stott and Reicher, 'How Conflict Escalates'; King, 'Football Hooliganism and the Practical Paradigm'.

[19]   Sometimes the violence created is not so symbolic: in 1968, the riots during the match between El Salvador and Honduras ended with a declaration of war between both countries.

[20]   Magnane, *Sociologie du sport.*

[21]   Spanish Senate, *Dictamen de la Comisión Especial.*

[22]   Dunning et al., *The Roots of Football Hooliganism,* 8.

[23]   Taylor, 'The Sports Violence Question', 160.

[24]   Mason, *Sport in Britain.*

[25]   Published in the newspaper *El Mundo,* (Spain) 17 January 2000.

[26]   Buford, *Entre los vándalos.*

[27]   Bale, *Sport, Space and the City,* 115.

[28]   'An applause for the Biris', *Diario 16,* (Seville) 16 September 1991.

[29]   Spanish Senate, *Dictamen de la Comisión Especial,* 48, 44, 59.

[30]   Ibid., 190.

[31]   The new modern trend is for the spaces to be clearly delimited. Annett *et al.*, 'El desarrollo del estadio moderno de fútbol'.

[32]   Acosta and Rodríguez, *Los jóvenes 'ultras' en el fútbol sevillano.*

[33]   Shaw, *Fútbol y franquismo.*

[34]   Acosta and Rodriguez, *Los jóvenes 'ultras' en el fútbol sevillano*, 37.

[35]   Canter and Comber, *Football in its Place.*

[36]   *Tifo* is an Italian word which is used to describe the scenography that the ultras tifosi display when the players appear on the pitch. *Tifos* usually consist of huge banners, mosaics or flags together with other performances with pieces of paper, flares, et cetera.

[37]   Regarding 'substitution' of the religious rites by the soccer spectacle, see the interesting article by Bromberger, 'El fútbol como visión del mundo y como ritual'.

[38]   These processions are very popular in Andalusia.

[39]   'Casetas' are a sort of stand made of canvas where families, groups of friends, clubs, et cetera socialize during the local spring festival of Sevilla, the so-called 'Feria de Abril'.

[40]   'Chirigota' is a kind of coral comic tune sung in Cadiz carnival.

[41]   Spanish Senate, *Dictamen de la Comisión Especial*, 204.

[42]   Tönies, *Community and Society.*

[43]   Jeu, *Le sport, l'emotion, l'space.*

References

Acosta, Rufino and Fernando Rodríguez. *Los jóvenes 'ultras' en el fútbol sevillano.* Seville: Instituto Municipal de Juventud y Deportes, Unpublished manuscript, 1989.

Annett, John, Sarah Coxon, Nichola Crilly, Scott Reid and Anna Stead. 'El desarrollo del estadio moderno de fútbol: el ejemplo inglés.' *Apunts: Educación Física y Deportes 59* (2000): 62–6.

Bale, John. *Sport, Space and the City.* London: Routledge, 1993.

Bromberger, Christian. 'El fútbol como visión del mundo y como ritual.' In *Nueva antropología en las sociedades mediterráneas,* edited by M.A. Roque. Barcelona: Icaria, 2000: 253–74

Buford, Bill. *Entre los vándalos.* Madrid: Anagrama, 1992.

Canter, David and Miriam Comber. *Football in its Place. An Environmental Psychology of Football Grounds.* London: Routledge, 1989.

Dunning, Eric, Patrick Murphy and John Williams. *The Roots of Football Hooliganism. An Historical and Sociological Study.* London: Routledge, 1988.

Elias, Norbert. *The Civilizing Process, Vol. 2: Power and Civility.* New York: Pantheon, 1982.

Elias, Norbert and Eric Dunning. *Quest for Excitement : Sport and Leisure in the Civilizing Process.* Oxford: Blackwell Publishers, 1986.

Foucault, Michel. *Surveiller et punir.* Paris: Gallimard, 1975.

Freud, Sigmund. *Psicología de las masas.* Madrid: Alianza Editorial, 1980.

Fromm, Eric. *Anatomía de la destructividad humana.* México: FCE, 1975.

Gaviria, Mario. *El buen salvaje: de urbanitas, campesinos y ecologistas varios.* Barcelona: El Viejo Topo, 1979.

Giddens, Anthony. *Sociology.* Oxford: Polity Press, 1995.

Jameson, Fredric and S. Slavoj Žižek. *Estudios culturales: reflexiones sobre el multiculturalismo.* Buenos Aires: Paidós, 1998.

Jeu, Bernard. *Le sport, l'emotion, l'space.* Paris: Vigot, 1977.

King, Anthony. 'Football Hooliganism and the Practical Paradigm'. *Sociology of Sport Journal 16,* no.3 (1999): 269–73.

Le Bon, Gustave. *Origen de la psicología de las masas.* Buenos Aires: FCE, 1975.

Lorenz, Konrad. *Sobre la agresión: el pretendido mal.* Barcelona: Grijalbo, 1974.

Magnane, Georges. *Sociologie du sport.* Paris: Gallimard, 1964.

Mason, Tony. *Sport in Britain.* London: Faber & Faber, 1988.

Montagu, Ashley. *Anthropology and Human Nature.* Boston, MA: Porter Sargent, 1957.

Shaw, Duncan. *Fútbol y franquismo.* Madrid: Alianza, 1987.

Spanish Senate. *Dictamen de la Comisión Especial de la violencia en los espectáculos deportivos con especial referencia al fútbol.* Madrid: General Courts, 1990.

Stott, Clifford and Steve Reicher. 'How Conflict Escalates: The Inter-group Dynamics of Collective Football Crowd "Violence".' *Sociology 32* (1998): 353–77.

Taylor, Ian. 'The Sports Violence Question: To Soccer Hooliganism Revisited'. In *Sport, Culture and Ideology,* edited by J. Hargreaves. London: Routledge, 1985: 152–96.

Tönies, Ferdinand. *Community and Society.* Michigan: The Michigan State University Press, 1957.

Vázquez, Manuel and Mercedes Varela. *100 años de deporte. Del esfuerzo individual al espectáculo de masas.* Barcelona: Difusora Internacional, 1973.

Vinnai, Gerhard. *El fútbol como ideología.* Buenos Aires: Siglo XXI, 1974.

Fleet Feet: The USSF and the Peculiarities of Soccer Fandom in America

Sean Brown

Introduction

> The crowd was good if you were playing for Poland. (US manager Bruce Arena)

On 11 July 2004 the Polish men's national side played a friendly against the Americans. That the match was played in Chicago was highly significant, because it represented a chance for the city's nearly 150,000 Polish residents to watch their native national side. As the *Chicago Tribune* noted in the 12 July edition, they came out 'in droves':

> Soldier Field was decked in red and white, the banners were written in Polish, and the initial goal scored by the road team was met with deafening cheers. Television spectators could easily have been fooled into thinking that the match was taking place in Warsaw rather than Chicago. The equalizer scored by the home side was met with a collective gasp, then silence.[1]

This vignette is hardly unique, as this essay will attempt to show. It represents another step in the dance that the United States Soccer Federation (USSF) shares with the foreign-born soccer fans within its borders, or simply soccer fans who would rather support a foreign side over the American one. This dance, simultaneously representing attraction and repulsion, has a great effect on American soccer fans wishing to see the national side play in meaningful contests, specifically World Cup qualifiers. In the first half of this essay, I hope to show that the USSF must operate using both push and pull factors when scheduling the national side. In the second half, I examine a specific group of fervent American soccer fans and the ways in which they are forced to support not only the national team, but soccer in general in the United States. It is an attempt to highlight the particular exigencies of soccer fandom in the United States.

The USSF and Scheduling the Men's National Team

As mentioned, the USSF is very sensitive to the ways in which it schedules matches for the men's national side. On the one hand, friendlies and regional tournaments are scheduled with the idea towards maximizing revenue, and are scheduled specifically with foreign fans in mind. On the other hand, the World Cup qualifiers are scheduled specifically in an attempt to shut out the foreign fan and maximize support for the home side. By operating in this manner, the USSF necessarily keeps some of its most important matches out of some of the most populous areas of the country, such as New York, Los Angeles and Chicago.

At the risk of sounding naive and insular, it seems that this represents a rather unique situation in world soccer. What other federation must keep its most important matches away from its major population centres for fear of saddling its team with a 'road' type atmosphere? It then becomes very difficult to provide the national team with a truly home field advantage, though it seems that Columbus, Ohio may be emerging as the city of choice for the USSF.

While this essay is hardly a look at fan culture in the ways in which it may be conventionally conceived, it is necessary to look at American soccer fandom from a macro level in order to identify its trends and particular exigencies. American soccer culture can only be understood against the backdrop of the game's immense popularity amongst certain segments of the population, and how that both enhances and hinders the efforts to promote the sport amongst other segments. The United States, as an immigrant nation, owes its vitality and its very existence to its foreign-born population. However, it is this very population that in some ways hinders the sport's development amongst the latter-day descendents of the first wave of immigrants of decades and centuries past. This is the population that looks at soccer as foreign and other which – while it certainly does not stop the from allowing their children to play it in tidy suburban parks – does seem to hinder soccer as a mass spectator sport in the United States.[2]

This essay will also take a brief look at the major indigenous pro-soccer fan group in the United States, Sam's Army. This group of devoted fans provides a brief micro-level illustration of soccer's place in mainstream American sporting culture. The ways in which the group defines itself, expresses itself, and understands its own place in the progression of American soccer will in many ways allow for a justification of USSF's tactics in scheduling its men's team.

Background

Before entering into a discussion of soccer in the United States, a crucial distinction must be made: that of spectatorship versus participation. For any analyst to simply state that soccer is not popular in the United States is not merely a gross oversimplification, it is patently false. Soccer routinely ranks in the top five participation sports in the US, generally lagging behind basketball, gridiron football, baseball and softball, and volleyball. When casual participation is removed and organized team sports are measured, soccer passes gridiron football and volleyball.[3] The phenomenon of soccer playing in the US is not particularly recent, but nearly three decades in the making. From the years 1980–95, participation rates in soccer rose in the US by over 300 per cent.[4]

Once that distinction is made, then a reasonable discussion can take place. Within the confines of this essay, the question of participation will not be at issue. Instead, when reference is made to the failure of soccer to take root in this country, the reference is made consciously with spectatorship in mind. Further, spectatorship is not simply defined in terms of who attends particular matches inside the stadium. It encompasses also the fans that choose to partake of the event either at home, in a public venue such as a sports bar, or in a more private setting outside of their own home (such as the home of a friend). Markovits and Hellerman refer to the overall presence of a sport in the collective consciousness as the 'hegemonic sports culture'. Sports in the United States that have achieved a level of consciousness in the US include baseball, basketball and American football.[5]

One of the reasons put forth as to why soccer hasn't entered the national sporting consciousness in any significant way is because of a sense of 'foreignness'. Majumdar and Brown have explored this from a historical perspective vis-à-vis baseball and cricket in the nineteenth century. In that paper, the authors argued that in the early formation of the American sporting landscape, the sports that eventually 'won out' were those that were able to be separated from their British origins or, in the case of basketball, could lay claim to having a uniquely American origin. Soccer, like cricket, was a distinctly British pastime. As such, it was at a fairly insurmountable disadvantage in the emerging sporting landscape.[6]

Over the last century however, a number of changes have altered the composition of both soccer and the United States. While a comprehensive undertaking of these changes would be a Sisyphean task, focusing on two particular alterations – one to the sport of soccer and one to the composition of the United States – will serve to illustrate the particular quandary in which the United States Soccer Federation currently finds itself.

On the one hand, the face of soccer has changed dramatically over the course of the last 150 years. No longer simply a British export, soccer has truly become 'the world's game'. A look at the number of nations who are members of FIFA will show that it rivals a look at member nations of the UN. It is played and played well on every continent in the world (Antarctica notwithstanding). One need only look at the current rankings to note the diversity found in the sport. Within the top 20 teams in the world, the only continent not represented is Asia.[7] At the time of writing, the United States was ranked 35. However, the men's national team was found in the top ten for much of 2006. Clearly, soccer cannot be understood as simply a British export, or a European enclave within world sport. It *is* the world's sport. It's origins as a British invention are now largely irrelevant.

On the other hand, the composition of the United States has also changed dramatically over the last 150 years. Immigration, which hit a low in the 1930s, has now climbed back to levels not seen since the first decade of the twentieth century (see Figure 1). However, the face of immigration has changed. No longer are the majority of immigrants coming into the US from Europe. These first and second waves of immigrants generally found themselves – over the course of simply a generation or two – fully integrated into mainstream American life, their old cultures having been suppressed, muted or altogether eliminated. This was the assimilation model of immigration.

Later waves of immigrants have changed the face of America. The source of immigration has shifted from Europe to Central America, and the level and nature of their assimilation has changed concomitantly. Assimilation can be partial, segmented, or non-existent. If the later waves of immigrants are choosing to retain elements of their culture, soccer has been a large part of that retention.

We are then left with two distinct soccer cultures in the United States: recent immigrants arriving from soccer-playing nations, and the suburbanites, a curious pair to say the least, and hardly a pair at all:

> But the social exclusivity and geographical separateness of suburban football culture from these Latino communities, the dependence of recreational football on the self-organization and funding of parents and the lack of access to green space in inner-city communities were major factors in limiting the development of US football. As

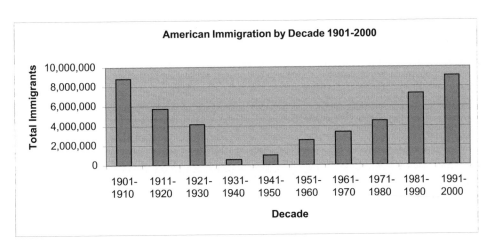

American Immigration by Decade 1901-2000

Figure 1

a consequence the Latino communities of the USA overwhelmingly chose not to engage with the football mainstream of America.[8]

Additionally, what stands out about the suburban soccer culture in the United States is the lack of carryover from participation to spectatorship, even as the kids are playing the game. Jere Longman notes in his chronicle of the 1999 Women's World Cup squad that even the best female players on the planet didn't follow the game as fans.[9] At the youth level, one of the founders of Sam's Army recounts the tale of working at a soccer workshop for coaches when one of the presenters began working with a group of 10-year old players who were scheduled to perform a drill. In order to determine first possession, the coach asked the boys to name an opponent of the US national team during the upcoming World Cup (2002). When no one could correctly name even a single team, the coach asked any one of the boys to tell where the competition was being played. Again he was met with silence.[10]

The evidence does not end at the anecdotal level. Despite the very high levels of participation mentioned above, both attendance at MLS matches and television ratings illustrate that those kids who play soccer do not go on to follow soccer once their playing days are over, and that some never follow the game even as they are playing it. An adequate explanation of this phenomenon does not seem to exist.

Wann *et al.* explain how sport fans become sport fans by turning to agents of socialization, specifically the family and peer group, with males being influenced mostly by the peer group and females by the family.[11] What this does not tell us is why there is a disconnect between the sports we play as children and the sports we follow. It seems that the answer lies in the realm of access. It is not especially easy to follow soccer in the United States, even our own domestic league. While games are shown regularly on ESPN, this type of exposure does not lend itself to producing fans, but only exploiting existing ones. Many MLS teams have a difficult time getting their games shown locally or on over-the-air television, which may inhibit their ability to reach all potential segments of their audience. On the other hand, it may be that mainstream media is simply responding to a lack of demand. It is a 'chicken or egg' type of argument. Thus the disparate soccer cultures in the US operate in differing realms as well, with the suburban soccer culture primarily a participatory culture and the immigrant soccer culture being constructed more holistically, consisting of participation and spectatorship. The USSF certainly understands this, and it helps to dictate the ways in which they schedule fixtures for the men's national team.

When the game means little in terms of formal consequence (that is, World Cup qualification), then the USSF often intentionally schedules matches in areas designed to maximize attendance, as will be illustrated. This only makes perfect sense after all. However, when the match is a qualifier, the USSF must take care to provide as positive an atmosphere for the team as possible. For example, were the USSF to schedule a qualifier against Mexico in Los Angeles, it is very likely that the US team would face an extremely hostile crowd. The USSF then must take care to schedule the team in places where a friendly crowd is likely. The consequence of this is that cities like Los Angeles, New York City and Chicago are unlikely to ever host a World Cup Qualifier. These major urban areas of high population could be key to the eventual growth of soccer in the United States, but they are not likely to see the American's most important matches, the kind that produce not merely a match but an event; the kinds of events that produce lifelong fans of a sport rather than ephemeral participants in a spectacle.

The USSF is operating with either a tacit or explicit understanding of Claude Fischer's Subcultural Theory of Urbanism, which was originally written to help explain the social effects of an urban way of life.[12] It was an explicit challenge to the understanding of urbanism as originally posited by Wirth in particular.[13] To Wirth, the social effects of urbanization were generally negative, with social alienation and isolation being the primary outcomes. This line of reasoning stretches all the way back to Tönnies in *Gemeinschaft und Gesellschaft*, perhaps the genesis of the field of urban sociology.[14] By altering the variable of size in his own study, Fischer was better able to account for the quantity and vitality of subcultures in urban areas, whose effects were hardly deleterious, though the social ties found within the urban milieu tended towards weaker and secondary ties, rather than the primary ones which marked more traditional rural societies.[15] More particularly, the work of Finke, Guest and Stark has particular applicability to the work being performed here.[16] In that study, the presence of increasing quantity and density of populations in an urban environment allow for a greater number and intensity of subcultural ties. Specifically, Finke, Guest and Stark have sought to understand why religious involvement is often positively associated with urbanism. In their analysis, increased population allows for a 'critical mass' to be built for many different expressions of religious faith, where an area with a smaller and sparser population would not allow for certain, less prominent expressions of faith. Applied to this particular work, in order to maximize revenue through gate receipt, the USSF need only schedule matches against visiting sides in areas where there exists a large enough population of first or second generation immigrants from said country to provide profit for the match. The major question left is whether or not the USSF has been successful in its push and pull of fans of foreign sides.

The Study

A convenient though highly imprecise way of dealing with the question of crowd composition is to rely on the media reports of the matches, particularly the newspapers in the cities where matches took place. They are most likely to contain more details about the match and the atmosphere surrounding it. So to that end, in order to determine the efficacy of the USSF strategy for scheduling the US men's national team, I accessed the newspaper reports of the previous day's matches, and searched them for particular mention of crowd composition. It is my belief that only crowds with particular imbalances would be mentioned, if at all. However, upon reviewing this process, I was left with a first-hand understanding of its shortcomings. Having attended the England/US match on 28 May 2005, I was well aware of the enormous presence of England supporters at the match, who were more numerous and quite a bit more vociferous than the American fans. However, upon reviewing the accounts for the match, there was no mention of the crowd in the story. Thus, this method is hardly foolproof. The particular matches I used for comparison were friendlies and

Table 1   Opponents and Locations for Friendlies and World Cup Qualifiers for the years 2004–05

Friendlies		Qualifiers	
Opponent	**Location**	**Opponent**	**Location**
England	Chicago	Panama	Boston
Honduras	Albuquerque	Mexico	Columbus
Columbia	Fullerton, CA	Costa Rica	Salt Lake City
Poland	Chicago	Guatemala	Birmingham
Honduras	Boston	Jamaica	Columbus
Mexico	Dallas	Panama	Washington DC
Haiti	Miami	El Salvador	Boston
Denmark	Los Angeles	Grenada	Columbus

World Cup Qualifiers from 2004 and 2005. See Table 1 for the opponents, and locations for those matches.

The Results

For the eight friendlies played by the team in 2004 and 2005, the media outlets in the cities of those matches reported on the crowd only twice: in the case of Poland in Chicago and Haiti in Miami. Both of these cities are known for their high populations of those respective nationalities. However, in perusing fan accounts of some of the contests as well as my own personal experience, it can be said with some confidence that the Mexico match in Dallas was at the very least bipartisan and most likely pro-Mexico, owing to the large Mexican population in the area. Additionally, the England match that took place in Chicago was also a pro-England crowd, meaning that fully half of the friendlies played on American soil in 2004 and 2005 were played in front of 'hostile' crowds. That then is the price of maximizing revenue for the sustenance of the programme.

Meanwhile, in the eight World Cup qualifying matches, four of the newspaper accounts the following day made mention of the crowd, but in doing so they were noting that the fans of the visiting side were generally in the minority, with only the Guatemala fans in Birmingham, Alabama making a showing that the local reporter termed 'bipartisan'. Thus it seems that the USSF has in fact been at least partially successful in scheduling the men's national team in a manner that protects itself financially in some cases and protects the psyche of the team in others. The idea that one should – when financial gains are at stake – plan for the maximization of crowd size is a perfectly logical assumption, and obvious to the point of lunacy once the parameters are laid out. However again the question is necessary: In what other fairly advanced soccer-playing nation (if one can assume that the United States belongs in that category, but the national team ranking and rates of youth and adult participation tend to support the argument in the affirmative) does the issue arise of where to hold matches?

In England, can the national team not play in London because of the threat that visiting fans would take up more space in the stadium than the home side? Is this an issue in Italy? Brazil? If Markovits and Hellerman are at all correct in their assessment of American soccer as the exception, then certainly this aspect is a part of that exception.

The Fans

What all of the above has accomplished, if anything, is simply another illustration of the marginalization of soccer, but particularly American soccer, in certain quarters of the country. What is important for the rest of this essay is to begin to understand and illustrate the ways in which supporters of American soccer, particularly the most loyal and fanatical supporters of American soccer, view and deal with its marginalization. Though no actual ethnographic work was attempted, it is believed that certain elements of the mission of the unofficial fan club of US Soccer (Sam's Army) are made plainly evident in its public face, its website. Through a content analysis of editorials on the official site of Sam's Army, I hope to show the ways in which the participants have created a community for themselves, and how the construction of this community is bound up in Cohen's notion of community construction. It becomes clear that Sam's Army has attempted to carve out a particular niche for itself within the larger American sporting community, specifically revolving around an 'us against them' mentality.

Community: A Particularly Problematic Paradigm

We can understand the above talk of social ties and urbanism as existing within the larger argument of community in an urban environment. A comprehensive or even introductory look at the arguments embroiling American urban sociology is far beyond the scope of this work, but I will mention them, and delve into one slightly more deeply. The three major structural positions regarding the effects of urbanization on community are generally known as: 'Community Lost',[17] 'Community Saved'[18] and 'Community Transformed' (alternatively known as 'Community Liberated').[19] Additionally, there exists a fourth argument, which is a hybrid of the Saved and Transformed arguments, known as Subcultural theory, which was particularly addressed earlier, along with the 'Community Transformed' argument.

Another significant alternative to a structural model of community comes from Anthony Cohen. For Cohen, the question of community goes far beyond its structure, but back again to the very definition of community. Cohen answers the question by making explicit his plans to avoid it. 'There is no attempt made … to formulate yet another definition. Rather, it is proposed to follow Wittgenstein's advice and seek not lexical meaning but *use*'.[20] Cohen goes on to articulate two distinctive uses of the notion of community: that those within the group have something in common with each other and that this characteristic distinguishes them in some way from members of other groups. In Cohen's terms, the notion of community then implies similarity as well as difference.

For Cohen, the community is constructed not of spatial considerations, but through symbols. Thus, when he speaks of boundaries, he is not referring to boundaries in the material sense, but the symbolic boundaries that separate one community from another. Communities are composed of similarities and differences, which presents obvious problems, first and foremost from the inherent comparative nature of this construct:

> This assumption has provided a fundamental and irresolvable philosophical problem in social anthropology for it is tantamount to the view that one culture can be descriptively and, therefore, interpretively, reduced to terms which are appropriate to another.[21]

Another significant issue with this perspective is the nature of the symbol, which does not in itself contain meaning, but rather merely contains the potential for meaning. Thus, the symbol allows different individuals within the same community to share a similar experience with a similar symbolic structure, but with entirely different understandings of the experience. This ambiguity in the use and interpretation of symbols limits the ability of the researcher to objectively understand the community of study. Meaning is then imparted only through its members' subjective understanding of participation.[22]

A further extension of the notion of community which is almost too easily and casually applied to sport fans can be found in the work of Benedict Anderson.[23] While Anderson loosely gets back to the notion of the geographically bounded community, the boundary is that of the nation state, and the community is imagined. It is imagined in Anderson's conception because it is impossible for the members of the community to all be familiar with, or even know the existence of, all or even most of the other members. However, this sense of the imagined community (more popularly understood as either patriotism or nationalism) is sufficiently pervasive and powerful that its members will often willingly not only kill but die for it. It becomes easy to appropriate the structure of the imagined community, and re-imagine it in terms of sporting fans, at least structurally.

Sport Fans and Community

While research on sport fans is often seen by sport scholars as marginalized,[24] research on sport fans that deals explicitly with the notion of community is virtually nonexistent. Gary Armstrong's ethnographic account of Sheffield hooligans, while valuable as a participant observation study, explicitly placed the fan group against the community at large, rather than within it, though the group would fit in well with Cohen's understanding of community.[25] Mark Mizruchi has noted that home court (or field) advantage is primarily an expression of community but, like the community of Anderson, this community cannot but be imagined.[26] Major professional sport teams, consistent with the subcultural theory of community as articulated by Finke, Guest and Stark, must be able to generate a critical mass of potential fans in order to make their existence economically viable. Thus, they invariably locate in metropolitan areas, precisely the types of spaces for which the entirety of the population cannot be known. This is a further illustration of the inherent difficulties of attempting to pin down notions of community. What Mizruchi calls a celebration of community, Finke, Guest and Stark would call a subculture, and Anderson, were he so interested in sport fans, would call simply imagined.

The most relevant study for my purposes was conducted by Holly Swyers.[27] Utilizing Cohen's conception of community, Swyers' study of the 'bleacher bums' that populate the outfield sections of Wrigley Field in Chicago serves as a notable synthesis of several of the themes articulated above. First, she explicitly invokes the community concept articulated by Cohen: 'The sense among bleacher regulars that they are a part of something larger than themselves is a comment on the community *consciousness* of the regulars'.[28] The sense of these particular fans' understandings of their community sentiment is embedded in larger themes of Anderson's imagined community or that of the subcultural theorists. The entireties of Cub fans are almost completely unknown to each other, and the fans that populate the bleachers of Wrigley are but a sliver of the population of Cub fans.

Sam's Army

As mentioned above, Sam's Army is the unofficial fan club of the US National Soccer Team. It is, however, more than that. It serves as a 'home base' for fans of all American soccer. Its efforts extend out from the national team and include the domestic professional leagues, from Major Soccer League (MLS) down to the semi-pro leagues operating around the country. It was, as an organization, an ardent supporter of the Women's United Soccer Association (WUSA) before its demise. This portion of this essay will explore Sam's Army from Cohen's conception of community discussed above, and the final discussion will concern the exigencies that have produced such an organization in its present form.

As mentioned, Cohen wrote that community was not defined at the core of any particular group, but at its margins. In the case of Sam's Army, much of their self description centres on what it is not, rather than what it is. A notable exception is their explicit homage to Scotland's Tartan Army, known throughout the soccer establishment for their friendliness and orderly behaviour.[29] Later on in the Frequently Asked Questions section of the website (FAQ), the positive association with the Tartan Army is contrasted with unacceptable behaviour often associated with European soccer: 'Racist and violent behavior will not be tolerated at any time. We consider ourselves ambassadors of our country and of the sport itself. We expect this at home and abroad. We pride ourselves on our good behavior and sharing that experience with an opposing fan. If you're a wanna-be hooligan, you are not wanted.'[30]

The more explicit examples of this type of self definition come within the articles written by members of the group, some of which have been cited earlier. These articles take the form of brief editorials, but – without the aid of valuable ethnographic work – give a keen insight into the ways in which members of Sam's Army view themselves, the organization, and the mission of the organization. For instance, regarding the article cited above highlighting the ignorance of players at a coaching clinic, the author continues, 'Would they have known the answer to the question if it was an NFL, NHL, or MLB question? DEFINITELY!'[31] Here, the author is simply voicing the frustration at the inability of soccer to grow out from being an activity to being a part of the American sporting culture, an unvoiced assent to the Markovits and Hellerman explanation of the failure of soccer to become a part of the hegemonic sport culture of the US (see above).

According to another contributor to the website,[32] another boundary to which American soccer fans can define themselves against is 'the media', with specific attention paid to Jim Rome, a loud-mouthed sports pundit working in radio and television for ESPN. Rome is regularly a controversial and polarizing figure throughout the American sporting scene, but his specific hatred of soccer has earned him a special place in the minds of Sam's Army members. For them, Rome represents the larger sporting media in the US, which – according to them – not only ignores soccer on a regular basis, but is actively attempting to suppress soccer from ever becoming a popular sport in the US. According to the editorial written by member Jimmy LaRoue, Rome was worried about going into the 2002 World Cup after the United States triumphed over Mexico in the qualifying round. LaRoue quotes Rome as saying, 'the fact that we're no longer the worst team in the world bothers me'. Additionally, Rome stated, 'Anything other than a last place finish in the World Cup is unacceptable'.[33] Such comments are not out of character with the types of things Jim Rome is known for saying, and certainly not out of character in the blunt and hyperbolic ways in which he expresses them. Clearly, however, he has become a figure around which Sam's Army members can direct their specific bile towards as an example of the American media's attempt to discredit the sport.

Thus, there has been an attempt to discredit Rome and his ilk, or 'some yapping head of the sports' media establishment'.[34] In this article, Sam's Army member Brian Farenell exhorts American soccer fans to ignore Rome and those like him:

> Soccer fans need to understand one thing: Jim Rome is irrelevant. He preaches to the converted. He spews anti-soccer pablum [*sic*] to people who don't like soccer … He is a shock jock, a sports' [*sic*] equivalent to Bill O'Reilly. Why should any of us care?

The attempt to discredit Rome and those like him (they are more prevalent than one might think), is a way for soccer enthusiasts in the US to band together in the face of a common enemy, thus reaffirming their own identity, in plain opposition to the outside force.

Other areas in which the establishment of an 'us against them' mentality is expressed by author Kevin Lindstrom, a particularly vociferous supporter of American soccer. In a series of articles titled 'Taking it to the Next Level', Lindstrom identifies three distinct boundaries against which Sam's Army members can distinguish themselves: particular soccer fans (Sam's Army supports soccer at every level and every incarnation in the United States),[35] casual soccer fans (Sam's Army is authentic and fanatical about their support),[36] and the American soccer establishment (Sam's Army are sophisticated fans that know more about how to support their team at a venue than do the soccer authorities in the US).[37] Lindstrom's articles invoke the spirit of Benedict Anderson every bit as much as Cohen. He is clearly speaking out to fans that he does not nor ever will know, but he speaks with a clear affinity for those fans, which is the essence of the imagined community. Like Swyers' Bleacher Bums in Wrigley Field, at the game, members of Sam's Army, through pre-game rituals such as tailgating, songs, chants and drumming, create the feeling that what they are involved in constitutes a community in the way which it is described by Cohen, but it is also imagined in the ways described by Anderson.

Discussion

The question of why soccer has not been able to become a part of the hegemonic sport culture in the US is almost a cliché by now. It has been analyzed, answered, re-answered, refuted and completely taken for granted. The explanations have been historical, structural or cultural. Certainly a meta-analysis of this question is in order, though the task would likely become a book-length problem. In the end, the analyst is left with so many answers, many if not most sounding at least plausible, that the question sometimes shouldn't be why is soccer not popular in America but how does it even exist in the first place? The goal of this essay was twofold: first, to establish the plausibility that, regardless of the reasons, soccer as a spectator sport is often a distinctly first or second-generation immigrant affair, and that the USSF must be cognizant of this fact, and that one can illustrate this knowledge by looking at how the USSF protects the men's national team from certain areas of the country in its most important matches. The second goal of this essay was to illustrate how the fans of American soccer view themselves and the sporting world around them, and attempt to set themselves apart from it in a defiant manner. These tactics illustrated in the second part of the essay are necessary exactly because of the nature of the sport's fandom illustrated in the first. Supporters of American soccer simply have more battles to fight than supporters of other national sides around the world. They fight apathy from soccer's youth participants and antipathy from sporting media as well as fans of foreign sides that keep important matches from population centres.

Despite the obstacles faced by soccer in America, its most ardent fans are still optimistic. Sam's Army member Mark Bushman writes, 'The fan base is growing, my friends. Don't let the pessimists tell you otherwise. One day at a time, one step at a time, one fan at a time.'[38] Unfortunately, it's a refrain that has been heard for decades. Participation at the youth level has been high for a long time, and it is questionable that this participation has translated into any real growth. In order for the sport to grow here, it is likely that the MLS must grow from its place as a third-rate professional league. The advantage that Major League Baseball and the National Basketball Association have over MLS is that the best players in the world play in those leagues. This is clearly not the case in MLS. The recent signing of David Beckham by the Los Angeles Galaxy seems to be less a serious run at the world's best talent and more a run at the greatest publicity splash possible. It is thus doubtful that the move has any serious impact on MLS, though it will give Beckham far more exposure in the United States. Additionally, a World Cup victory might also be necessary (and most certainly helpful) for soccer to 'catch on' in the US.

For the prescient American soccer analyst, soccer will not have arrived in this country when the television ratings start to rise or when the stadiums start to fill. By then it will have already happened. Those analysts will be looking at the final triumph, not the genesis. It will come when a group of 10-year-old soccer playing kids can not only name where the World Cup is being played or who the American opponents are, but when they can name the roster by heart, debate omissions and tactics, and start pretending to be Ronaldhino rather than Michael Jordan or Peyton Manning.

Notes

[1] *Chicago Tribune*, 12 July 2004.
[2] Brown, 'Exceptionalist America'.
[3] Association, Sports Goods Manufacturers. 'Sports Participation Topline Report 2005'.
[4] Black and Hebdige, 'Women's Soccer and the Irish Diaspora', 531.
[5] One can also, if so inclined, add National Association for Stock Car Auto Racing (NASCAR) to that discussion, though at the time of publication, Markovits and Hellerman listed ice hockey instead. Markovits and Hellerman, *Offside*.
[6] Majumdar and Brown, 'Why Soccer, Why Cricket?'.
[7] http://www.fifa.com/en/mens/statistics/index/0,2548,All-Nov-2006,00.html accessed 22 November 2006.
[8] Goldblatt, *The Ball is Round*, 784.
[9] Longman, *The Girls of Summer*.
[10] Spacone, 'Do We KNOW Soccer?'
[11] Wann *et al.*, *Sport Fans*.
[12] Fischer, 'Toward a Subcultural Theory of Urbanism'.
[13] Wirth, 'Urbanism as a Way of Life'.
[14] Tönnies, *Gemeinschaft und Gesellschaft*.
[15] Lee *et al.*, 'Testing the Decline-of-Community Hypothesis'.
[16] Finke, Guest and Stark, 'Mobilizing Local Religious Markets'.
[17] Tönnies, *Gemeinschaft und Gesellschaft*; Durkheim, *The Division of Labor in Society*; Durkheim, *Suicide*; Simmel, 'The Metropolis and Metropolitan Life'; Park, 'The City'; Wirth, 'Urbanism as a Way of Life'.
[18] Wellman, 'The Community Question; Gans, *The Urban Villagers*.
[19] Granovetter, 'The Strength of Weak Ties'; Wellman and Leighton, 'Networks, Neighborhoods, and Communities'; Hampton and Wellman, 'Neighboring in Netville'.
[20] Cohen, *The Symbolic Construction of Community*, 12, italics in original.
[21] Ibid., 38.
[22] For more on the importance of subjective understanding in subcultures, see Haenfler, 'Rethinking Subcultural Resistance'.
[23] Anderson, *Imagined Communities*.
[24] Crawford, 'The Career of the Sport Supporter'.
[25] Armstrong, *Football Hooligans*.
[26] Mizruchi, 'Local Sports Teams and Celebration of Community'.
[27] Swyers, 'Community America'.
[28] Ibid., 1087.
[29] http://www.sams-army.com/index.php?Mlist=faq. Accessed 12 January 2007.
[30] Ibid.
[31] Spacone, 'Do we KNOW Soccer?' National Football League (NFL); National Hockey League (NHL); Major Baseball League (MBL).

[32] It is important to not that these editorials are not a part of a discussion board on the site, and thus it can be inferred that they are not simply the rantings of extremist members, but rather voices for members expressed by prominent contributors to the website.

[33] LaRoue, 'Rome is Spooked, Admits U.S. Has "Good" Team.'

[34] Farenell, 'American Soccer Fans Need To Grow Up'.

[35] Lindstrom, 'Taking it to the Next Level'.

[36] Lindstrom, 'Taking it to the Next Level Pt. 2'.

[37] Lindstrom, 'A Call to Arms'.

[38] Bushman, 'The Ranks are Growing'.

References

Anderson, Benedict. *Imagined Communities: Reflections on the Origin and Spread of Nationalism.* New York: Verso, 1991.

Armstrong, Gary. *Football Hooligans: Knowing the Score.* Oxford: Berg, 1998.

Association, Sports Goods Manufacturers. 'Sports Participation Topline Report 2005: Statistical Highlights from the Superstudy® of Sports Participation.' SGMA International, 2005 Report published online: http://www.sgma.com/associations/S119/files/p286–05.pdf. (accessed October 28, 2006).

Black, Michael and D. Hebdige. 'Women's Soccer and the Irish Diaspora.' *Peace Review 11,* no. 4 (1999): 531–8.

Brown, Sean F. 'Exceptionalist America: American Sports Fans' Reaction to Internationalization.' *International Journal of the History of Sport 22,* no. 6 (2005): 1106–35.

Bushman, Mark. 'The Ranks are Growing'. In http://www.sams-army.com/index.php?Mlist= content_full&article_id=28. (2002) (accessed 10 January 2007).

Cohen, Anthony. P. *The Symbolic Construction of Community.* New York: Tavistock Publications, 1985.

Crawford, G. 'The Career of the Sport Supporter.' *Sociology 37,* no. 2 (2003): 219–37.

Durkheim, Emile. *Suicide: A Study in Sociology.* Glencoe, IL: Free Press, 1951.

Durkheim, Emile. *The Division of Labor in Society.* New York: Free Press, 1984.

Farenell, Brian. 'American Soccer Fans Need to Grow Up.' In http://www.sams-army.com/ index.php?Mlist=content_full&Article_id=43. (2002) (accessed 10 January 2007).

Finke, R., A.M. Guest and R. Stark. 'Mobilizing Local Religious Markets: Religious Pluralism in the Empire State, 1855–1865.' *American Sociological Review 61,* no. 2 (1996): 203–18.

Fischer, Claude S. 'Toward a Subcultural Theory of Urbanism.' *American Journal of Sociology 80,* no. 6 (1975): 1319–41.

Gans, Herbert. *The Urban Villagers.* New York: Free Press, 1962.

Goldblatt, David. *The Ball Is Round: A Global History of Football.* London and New York: Viking, 2006.

Granovetter, M. 'The Strength of Weak Ties.' *American Journal of Sociology 78,* no. 6 (1973): 1360–80.

Haenfler, Ross. 'Rethinking Subcultural Resistance: Core Values of the Straight Edge Movement.' *Journal of Contemporary Ethnography 33,* no. 4 (2004): 406–36.

Hampton, K. and B. Wellman. 'Neighboring in Netville: How the Internet Supports Community and Social Capital in a Wired Suburb.' *City and Community 2,* no. 4 (2003): 277–311.

LaRoue, Jimmy. 'Rome Is Spooked, Admits U.S. Has "Good" Team.' In http://www.sams-army.com/index.php?Mlist=content_full&Article_id=41. (2002) (accessed 10 January 2007).

Lee, B.A., R.S. Oropesa, B.J. Metch and A.M. Guest. 'Testing the Decline-of-Community Thesis: Neighborhood Organization in Seattle, 1929 and 1979.' *American Journal of Sociology 89,* no. 5 (1984): 1161–88.

Lindstrom, Kevin. 'Taking It to the Next Level.' In http://www.sams-army.com/index.php?Mlist =content_full&Article_id=93. (2002) (accessed 10 January 2007).

Lindstrom, Kevin. 'Taking It to the Next Level Pt. 2.' In http://www.sams-army.com/index.php?
Mlist=content_full&Article_id-98. (2002) (accessed 10 January 2007).

Lindstrom, Kevin. 'A Call to Arms.' In http://www.sams-army.com/index.php?Mlist=content_full
&Article_id=152. (2003) (accessed 10 January 2007).

Longman, Jere. *The Girls of Summer: The Us Women's Soccer Team and How It Changed the World.*
New York: Harper Collins, 2000.

Majumdar, Boria and Sean F. Brown. 'Why Baseball, Why Cricket? Differing Nationalisms, Differing
Challenges.' *International Journal of the History of Sport 24,* no. 1 (2007): 139–56.

Markovits, Andrei and Steven Hellerman. *Offside: Soccer and American Exceptionalism.* Princeton,
NJ: Princeton University Press, 2001.

Mizruchi, M.S. 'Local Sports Teams and Celebration of Community: A Comparative Analysis of
Home Field Advantage.' *Sociological Quarterly 26,* no. 4 (1985): 507–18.

Park, R.E. 'The City: Suggestions for the Investigation of Human Behavior in the Urban Environment.' In *The City,* edited by Robert E. Park, Ernest W. Burgess and R.D. McKenzie. Chicago:
University of Chicago Press, 1925.

Simmel, Georg. 'The Metropolis and Metropolitan Life.' In *Georg Simmel: On Individualism and
Social Forms,* edited by D.N. Levine. Chicago: University of Chicago Press, 1971.

Spacone, Mark. 'Do We KNOW Soccer?' In http://www.sams-army.com/index.php?Mlist=conte
Mizruchi nt_full&Article_id=16. (2002) (accessed 10 January 2007).

Swyers, Holly. 'Community America: Who Owns Wrigley Field.' *International Journal of the History
of Sport 22,* no. 6 (2005): 1086–105.

Tönnies, F. *Gemeinschaft Und Gesellschaft, Grundbegriffe Der Reinen Soziologie.* Darmstadt: Wissen-
schaftliche Buchgesellschaft, 1963.

Wann, Daniel, M.J. Melnick, G. Russell and D.G. Pease. *Sport Fans: The Psychology and Social Impact
of Spectators.* New York: Routledge, 2001.

Wellman, Barry. 'The Community Question.' *American Journal of Sociology 84,* no. 5 (1979): 1201–31.

Wellman, B. and B. Leighton. 'Networks, Neighborhoods, and Communities.' *Urban Affairs
Quarterly 14,* no. 3 (1979): 363–90.

Wirth, Louis. 'Urbanism as a Way of Life.' *American Journal of Sociology 44,* no. 1 (1938): 1–44.

All Together Now, Click: MLS Soccer Fans in Cyberspace

Wayne Wilson

The birth of the top United States professional soccer league, Major League Soccer (MLS), which began play in 1996, coincided with the rise of the Internet as a widely used information technology. The Internet and Internet discussion boards have become an important part of the soccer culture for many American fans who follow MLS.

MLS supporters, of course, are not unique in their use of the Internet. Soccer fans throughout the world and sports fans of all types in the United States use the Internet. The Internet, however, serves a function in the lives of American soccer followers that is different from the role it plays for supporters of sports such as baseball, American football, basketball and ice hockey.

Discussion boards provide a way for MLS followers in the United States to build virtual communities around a league that lacks traditions and a strong identity, and teams that have no history of generational or geographically based loyalty. They also offer a means of information exchange for American soccer enthusiasts in a country whose most influential media remain inattentive to the sport. And, boards facilitate fan networking in a geographically large country with only a small number of professional teams.

The most-used set of soccer discussion boards in the United States is on BigSoccer.com, a website launched in 1995. The website celebrated its tenth anniversary in August 2005 with more than one million user-visits for the month, 316,649 posts and 13 million page views.[1] The site had over 68,000 registered members in November 2005. The general public is allowed to read the exchanges on BigSoccer, but only members may post messages.

Computer-mediated communications systems such as BigSoccer enable researchers to examine expressions of thought and emotion 'taken from the actual life of a virtual community' with the 'peculiar advantage' of having little or no influence on the people being studied.[2] This paper will examine the way in which BigSoccer members express their allegiance to, and interest in, the league. The goal here is not to theorize patterns of communication or the socio-behavioural dynamics of the BigSoccer community, but rather to present a qualitative interpretation of the themes that arise as BigSoccer members discuss the league and its teams. That interpretation will flow from an understanding of the sporting context in which MLS exists, a context defined largely by the diversity of soccer cultures in the United States, the commercial magnitude of soccer relative to other sports and the sports media environment.

Soccer Cultures in the United States

Soccer in the United States is a sport of contradictions. Nearly 18 million people play the sport. About half play at least 25 times a year. Soccer is the fifth most-played sport in American high schools. At least four million young people also play in leagues outside the school system.[3] Yet, despite the high number of players, soccer remains a relatively minor spectator sport, as measured by attendance and other indices.

Except for a brief infatuation with the American women's World Cup team in 1999, soccer has not galvanized broad national interest in the United States. In several of the nation's urban centres, though, soccer on occasion attracts the attention of more people than any other sport.

The United States has a men's professional league playing in major markets throughout the country, and its men's and women's national teams have winning records. Yet, many of the nation's most passionate soccer fans pay them scant attention.

The mainstream English-language media provide little coverage compared to what they devote to American football, baseball, basketball, ice hockey and several other sports. On the other hand, soccer is the predominant sport in the nation's growing Spanish-language media.

Satellite and cable television, and the Internet provide a wealth of soccer media content. Fans in the United States can choose from thousands of soccer broadcasts each year, a range of television soccer news programmes and millions of Internet pages. This abundance notwithstanding, soccer rarely attracts a large national television audience.

These contradictions reflect a soccer culture in the United States composed of a mosaic of soccer spectator subcultures. A typography of these subcultures would include several overlapping yet distinct types of spectatorship that coalesce around youth soccer, women's soccer, the men's national team, MLS and minor professional leagues, and foreign teams and leagues.

The parents of children and teenagers participating in organized youth soccer are a large and overlooked spectator group. With millions of young people playing, in some cases, up to 50 matches a year, parental spectatorship easily outstrips in-person spectatorship of more commercial forms of the sport. Other elements of the youth soccer culture include magazines, newsletters, websites and even minimal television coverage.

Women's soccer, for a brief period in 1999 when the United States hosted and won the Women's World Cup, captured the attention and imagination of the American public as soccer never has before or since. An estimated 40 million American television viewers watched some portion of the final between the United States and China. The success of the Women's World Cup spawned a women's professional league called WUSA. The league lasted three seasons before going out of business in 2003. Although the women's national team no longer commands the attention of the 1999 squad, it still attracts large television audiences and respectable stadium crowds. A peak audience of 10 million viewers tuned in on a Thursday afternoon to watch the 2004 Olympic Games gold-medal match between the United States and Brazilian women.[4]

The men's national team has never had a moment that generated as much public interest as the 1999 women's team. On the field of play the team has done well. The team reached the quarter-finals of the 2002 World Cup, and in 2005 qualified for its fifth consecutive World Cup, finishing first in its region. Despite a lack of national fervour, the men's team usually attracts larger crowds than the women's national team, in part because many spectators show up to root for the United States' opponents. All the team's matches are shown on some type of national television broadcast.

MLS is the leading professional league. It began play in 1996, more than a decade after the demise of its predecessor, the North American Soccer League. The 13-team MLS has all the trappings of more established professional sports leagues in the United States – national and regional television and radio broadcasters, good stadiums and national sponsors. The season extends from April to November. The United States has no relegation and promotion system. MLS follows the lead of other United States professional leagues with geographically based divisions instead of a single table. The league champion is determined by post-season playoffs, not by total points earned during the season. In 2005, the league attracted 3.1 million spectators.[5] MLS has lost money every year and continues to be overshadowed by the so-called Big Four professional team sports leagues – the National Football League (NFL), Major League Baseball (MLB), National Basketball Association (NBA) and National Hockey League (NHL).

There are various national and ethnic groups in the United States that follow soccer originating outside the country. These groups constitute another spectator subculture. By far the largest, most consolidated group is Latinos. The assumption that Latino enthusiasm for soccer is a phenomenon confined to 'recent émigré enclaves' is misleading. The United States Census Bureau reported that there were 41.3 million Latinos in the United States, in 2004, or 14 per cent of the national population. Most Latinos were born in the country. In California, the nation's most populous state, a third of all residents are Latino.[6]

The role of Latinos in American soccer culture is complex. Part of the complexity results from the great diversity of Latinos as an ethnic group. Part of it derives from the divided loyalties of Latino soccer fans. Many Latinos support the United States national team and the MLS. According to one estimate, 50 per cent of MLS fans are Latinos.[7] That said, it is also true that soccer matches in Mexico and other Latin American countries hold more significance for millions of Latino fans than do MLS contests or United States national team games.

Among Latinos, soccer occupies a place of greater cultural importance than it does among other major ethnic groups in the United States. Univision, the largest Spanish-language broadcaster in the United States, claims that more Latino men aged 19–49 watched the broadcast of the Mexican league's championship in June 2004 than watched the 2004 Super Bowl or final game of the baseball World Series.[8]

While the mainstream English-language media routinely overlook or underreport the sport, soccer holds a pre-eminent position in United States-based Spanish-language media. Those media can reach virtually the entire Latino population. Nationally broadcast Spanish-language sports news programmes treat soccer as the most important sport. Spanish-language newspapers such *La Opinion* in Los Angeles, *La Raza* in Chicago and *Rumbo de Houston* give soccer top billing.

In urban areas with high percentages of Latino residents, soccer can become a city's most-watched sport on television on a given day, even if the Anglo population and other communities are almost completely oblivious to the event taking place. Television viewership in Los Angeles during the 2004 Copa America tournament was a case in point. All coverage was on Spanish-language television. Los Angeles audience ratings of the 18 July quarter-final match between Mexico and Brazil easily surpassed all other sports events for the weekend. One in five televisions in-use in the Los Angeles market was tuned to the game. The following weekend, the ratings of the Brazil-Argentina championship match and consolation game between Colombia and Uruguay continued to be strong. Ratings for each game trounced the English-language broadcasts of MLB, NASCAR, tennis, golf and the Tour de France.[9]

Latino interest in the sport also expresses itself in the form of attendance at live events involving national and club teams from Latin America. The Mexican national team plays often in the United States. In 2003, for example, El Tri played nine matches in eight markets, averaging 37,000 people a game.[10]

Commercial Magnitude of Soccer

Despite its popularity as a participatory activity, significance among Latinos and rare brief periods of interest among the general public, soccer is a small commercial enterprise in the context of United States spectator sport. This is evident in attendance figures, gate receipts, television audience ratings and advertising revenue.

The commercial disparity between American soccer and MLS on the one hand, and better-established sports on the other, has been well documented in previous works.[11] The gap remains essentially unchanged. *SportsBusiness Daily* estimates that attendance for all forms of commercial soccer in the United States, during 2003–04, was about 8.3 million. MLS accounted for 2.5 million. Other forms of soccer included in the total were the Women's World Cup, WUSA, CONCACAF Gold Cup, indoor soccer, minor professional leagues, European club tours and college soccer.[12]

MLS averages about 15,000 spectators a game, which is not far below the per-game average of the NHL and the NBA. The Los Angeles Galaxy led MLS attendance in 2005, drawing about 24,200 per match. The Galaxy average was higher than that of any NHL or NBA team, and six MLB teams.[13] The per-game figures, however, tell only part of the story. There were 12 MLS teams in 2005. Each played 32 regular-season games. Other professional leagues have many more teams and, with the exception of the NFL, play many more games. As a result, when attendance numbers are aggregated, MLS's 2005 total attendance of 3.1 million spectators is dwarfed by other commercial sports. MLB in 2004 totalled 74 million spectators. Minor league baseball drew 40 million. The NHL and minor league hockey attracted 37 million in 2003. The NBA and National Collegiate Athletic Association (NCAA) men's and women's basketball combined had 73.8 million spectators. The NFL and college football had 69 million. MLS attendance also ranked lower than those of golf and auto racing.[14]

The attendance differential creates a corresponding gap in gate revenues. Total soccer gate revenues, including MLS plus other forms of soccer, were less than $60 million in 2004. MLB revenues totalled $1.4 billion. The NFL and NHL had just under $1 billion each, with college football bringing in $1.3 billion, and the NBA $1.2 billion. Soccer boosters often set their sites on the NHL as the major league that MLS is most likely to overtake, but at present the NHL's gate revenue is 17 times greater than all soccer revenues combined.[15]

Media Environment

American television offers viewers a wide range of soccer choices. In addition to United States national team and MLS competitions, millions of viewers can see matches from the English, Spanish, Italian, German, French, Dutch, Mexican, Argentine and Brazilian premier leagues on one of 13 national networks showing soccer.

Definitive, comparative television viewing statistics are difficult to assemble, but there is no doubt that soccer viewership is lower than that of other professional team sports. MLS has national broadcasting agreements with ABC Sports, ESPN2, Fox Soccer Channel, Fox Sports en Espanol and HDNet. Nearly every MLS team has at least one local or regional television broadcast partner. MLS, however, fails to attract a large national television audience. The 2005 championship game drew only 854,000 television households (HHs). By comparison, the 2005 Super Bowl drew 45 million HHs; the World Series averaged 12.5 million HHs over four games; and the final game of the 2004 NBA Championship was seen in 15 million HHs.[16]

During 2005, the MLS game of the week on ESPN2 averaged about 200,000 HHs. An important NFL Monday night game gets about 15 million HHs. Regular-season MLB on Fox network averaged 2.9 million HHs. NBA regular-season games broadcast over-the-air attracted 2.5 million. On cable, the number was about 1.1 million. Bass fishing tournaments and bowling regularly beat MLS ratings by wide margins.[17]

A scarcity of publicly published ratings for regional sports networks and smaller national networks makes it impossible to precisely calculate gross cumulative viewing numbers for all forms of soccer viewing in the United States. Soccer-only networks such as Fox Soccer Channel (FSC) and GolTV offer dozens of matches weekly, but they lack the distribution of sports networks such as ESPN, ESPN2 and general-interest over-the-air networks like ABC. FSC's most popular product is the English Premier League (EPL). FSC broadcasts 230 EPL matches a year (shown 600 times), delivering HHs numbering in 'the mid-five-figure range'. Mexican league matches broadcast by Univision, in 2005, drew about 900,000 HHs per game.[18]

These numbers suggest a substantial gross cumulative viewing audience for soccer, but other sports have an even greater presence on American television, and most of them draw more viewers per game. National and regional networks broadcast more than 4,100 MLB and 2,100 NBA games annually. Regional networks alone broadcast over 3,600 college basketball games.[19]

One indication of a sport's commercial appeal on television is the advertising revenue it generates. Soccer trails not only baseball, football, basketball and hockey, but also professional wrestling, bowling and rodeo in television advertising revenue.[20]

Media reporting about soccer occurs in newspapers, television sports news programmes and on the Internet. Spanish-language sources in all three media cover soccer extensively. The most-read English-language newspapers and most-watched sports news broadcasts provide relatively little coverage of the sport. The *Atlanta Constitution/Atlanta Journal* and *Kansas City Star*, by one measure, published 18 times as many NFL articles as MLS pieces between 1996 and 2004.[21] ESPN's *SportsCenter*, the country's leading sports news show, sandwiched a brief post-match report about the 13 November 2005 MLS championship game between lengthier reports on regular-season NFL games and other news items.

The Internet has benefited soccer information consumers in the United States. There is a worldwide audience for soccer content on the Internet. The lure of this potential market combined with the ability of Internet content creators to by-pass traditional information gatekeepers has resulted in the development of millions of soccer webpages that ameliorate the imbalance between soccer information and other sports information in English-language television and paper-based journalism. The 18:1 NFL to MLS ratio cited above shrinks to 6.5:1 on the Internet. Google searches for 'soccer', 'basketball' and 'baseball' returned 116 million, 120 million and 122 million hits respectively.[22] The World Wide Web empowers the public to actively seek, rather than passively wait, for information. Given that opportunity, soccer fans take advantage of it. On Foxsports.com, for example, soccer is the fourth most-viewed sport.[23] It is in this media milieu that BigSoccer developed.

BigSoccer.com

Basic membership on BigSoccer is free. The company derives its revenue from advertising, the sale of merchandise from its online store and fees for premium memberships that provide access to restricted forums, enhanced 'surfing' capabilities and the ability to create customized screen profiles that include graphics and other identity elements.

Of the more than 68,000 BigSoccer members, approximately 90 per cent live in the United States. Between 85 and 90 per cent of unique site visits come from the United States.[24]

The fans who participate in MLS discussions on BigSoccer are a self-selected virtual community built around a strong interest in the league and it teams. While they are not necessarily representative of most MLS fans, their posts nevertheless are one expression of an evolving American soccer culture.

Content on BigSoccer is divided into forums, sub-forums and threads, representing a progression from general to specific topics, covering soccer throughout the world. Threads contain one or more posts, or individual messages. Moderators monitor threads and have the authority to edit, move or close them.

The MLS forums are the largest set of forums on BigSoccer. From mid-2002 to late 2005, BigSoccer recorded more than 60,000 threads and 1.5 million posts about MLS.[25] The site offers forums on general MLS topics and sub-forums for each MLS team. Every MLS match prompts pre- and post-game threads as well as in-game banter among members who are watching or listening to the game. The overwhelming majority of BigSoccer soccer threads concern competition and performance aspects of soccer: 'Trades and Cuts: Who should stay, who should go?', 'MLS Referees Suck' and 'MLS Goal Of The Year Voting.' These threads contain spirited expressions of fan support for their teams and a healthy antipathy of other clubs. BigSoccer recognizes and encourages such rivalries through a forum titled 'MLS: Fan Rivalries'.

There are discernable content differences among the various team boards. The differences derive from variables such as location, competitive strength and date of entry into the league. What is more significant than the differences among MLS team forums, however, are their commonalities and the extent to which issues arise that transcend the field of play. The tenuous nature of MLS as a business enterprise results in a tacit understanding among the BigSoccer MLS community that individual teams will cease to exist if the league fails to survive. Therefore, to be a committed fan of any MLS team is also to be a supporter of the league. Being a league supporter who can knowledgeably participate in BigSoccer discussions requires an awareness of business and cultural issues affecting MLS.

A reading of BigSoccer MLS posts reveals several interrelated business and cultural themes that emerge explicitly and implicitly in thousands of posts. These recurring themes, which reflect and illuminate the state of MLS and its fan base, can be grouped in four broad categories: 1) the consumer experience, including media consumption and live spectatorship, 2) soccer's place in American sport, 3) the status of the United States in world soccer, and 4) the role of Latinos in United States soccer.

The Consumer Experience

BigSoccer explores many dimensions of the soccer consumer's experience. The most salient topics are the limited amount of English-language media coverage, the nature of existing coverage, the quality of television broadcasts and the in-stadium MLS spectator experience.

The paucity of media coverage is a constant source of frustration to the BigSoccer community. BigSoccer writers resent what they regard as non-existent or poor pre- and post-match coverage in major English-language newspapers, magazine and television sports news shows. ESPN, the leading United States sports network is a favourite object of scorn, inspiring threads like 'ESPN HATES SOCCER! (part 28348)'.

If the lack of coverage annoys BigSoccer contributors, the nature of the coverage and commentary often enrages them. There are several media personalities in the United States – called 'soccer haters' or simply 'haters' – who delight in loudly disparaging the sport. Whenever this occurs there are always BigSoccer posters who rise to the bait. (All BigSoccer posts quoted here include all spelling, punctuation and grammar errors, as they appeared on the website.)

> What a jackass … It's so frustrating to hear guys like this, who'd rather watch poker or golf, rag on soccer. I'm goin to wage an email jihad against this fraud … What a loser. He is simply another loud-mouthed, ignorant fool.

> I'm sick and tired of neanderthals like Deford, with his cheesy, I-hang-out-at-casinos moustache, treating the beautiful game like it's the plague. Enough is enough.

> Korneiser has no f'in clue what he's blabbing about. He's clueless and is a 'hater'.[26]

Although, soccer is readily available on American television, BigSoccer posters, generally speaking, find the coverage to be below their expectations. They criticize the technical quality of broadcasts and the skills of announcers. While every announcer has his or her defenders, a call for opinions about any announcer almost always elicits more negative than positive responses. The following comments from a thread about an experienced announcer who commentates on MLS and international matches are typical of the genre:

> The guy is a total embarrassment.

> I've never seen nor heard a guy less prepared and ignorant … This guy is horrible.

> I cant stand him. Hes annoying as hell.

> His ability to put the emPHAsis on the wrong syLAble is uncanny … IMO, he's an idiot.

> I wish I could find a way to communicate just how much I dislike his commentary. It is embarassing. It is cloying. It distracts me from the game. Sometimes it is physically painful.[27]

Most discussions of the in-stadium experience at MLS games centre on the issue of 'passion.' Many writers view the stadium experience as overly tame: 'our games are not as "intense" as Id like'. They lament the presence of too many 'laid back' fans, children, 'soccer moms' and 'business types who got some corporate tickets and wouldn't know an offside trap from a throw-in'. While members want to see more passion at games, there is no consensus on how to achieve it. A small number of posters have suggested that spectator violence at games would generate more public interest in the league. A greater number, however, reject that view. The role of organized non-violent supporter groups in MLS stadiums is universally praised as contributing to a positive experience. On balance, writers are satisfied, but not thrilled, with the atmosphere in MLS stadiums, particularly 'when there is a reasonable sized crowd and an opponent who is a rival'.[28]

An important element of the stadium discussion is the concept of the so-called soccer specific stadium, or 'SSS' in the parlance of BigSoccer. Initially, every MLS team played in an American football stadium; nearly half still do. Putting soccer in football stadiums is condemned on a number of counts. The field stripes are visually distracting. Playing soccer in 'an environment obviously controlled by a different sport makes MLS look minor league'. The stadiums are too big. Since soccer does not draw as many fans as American football, the sight of mostly empty seats at a soccer match makes a poor impression on television. And, for in-person spectators, 'any less than 30,000' creates an 'atmospheric-death-trap'.[29]

These aesthetic considerations combined with owners' desires to control parking and concessions revenue and avoid paying stadium rent to other parties have led to a movement in the league to build SSSs. Six teams used SSSs in 2006, with the new Toronto franchise scheduled to begin play in an SSS in 2007.

The atmospherics and operations of the existing SSSs and the prospect of new soccer stadiums are popular recurring topics. BigSoccer members typically regard SSSs as absolutely essential to improving the public image of the sport and making ownership of a team profitable: 'Only when every single MLS club has their own stadium will this league realize its full potential'.

That is not to say, however, that the BigSoccer community is unanimously generous in its assessment of the league's SSSs. The Columbus Crew Stadium has been criticized for its 'overall blandness'. One writer complained that the Home Deport Center in Los Angeles 'must have the worst groundskeeper … in pro sports'. The food and drink concessions in Los Angeles and Dallas are sources of frequent complaints:

> HDC [Home Depot Center] food makes me anxious to board a 747 and sit in economy class, just for the cuisine.

> The concessions were the bane of my existence … I've never seen a concessions line go so slow. Missed the first 10 minutes of the 2nd half in that line.

> I love going to HDC, but the food vendor is just not prepared for crowds of over 20,000. I went to get a beer … the clerk was completely untrained … This awful service may discourage return visits.

The Dallas stadium includes a large stage at one end of the field built to host revenue-generating concerts. It has not been well received:

> For the love of God, do something about the stage: What an eyesore. I'm not sure if anything can take up such massive, empty space but surely they can do something that won't be 95% bare concrete.

> I **hate** that damn stage, I know the revenue, blah blah blah, but its hideous.[30]

These complaints notwithstanding, the majority of posters, including the complainers, are enthusiastic about the SSSs, with 'awesome' and 'great' being the operative adjectives.

Soccer's Status in the United States

The issue of soccer's status in the United States, and by extension MLS's place, permeates thousands of threads. Posters ask, why is soccer not a bigger commercial and cultural phenomenon? And, will MLS challenge the NFL, NBA, NHL and MLB? Typical of the threads in this vein are, 'Why doesn't the American sports public embrace soccer?', 'United States Corporate-controlled Media is determined to denigrate soccer/football' and 'This is why soccer is not as popular as the top sports in United States'.

Although not expressed in the academic dialect and very rarely developed with reference to scholarly works, the explanations put forth on BigSoccer are not unlike those found in academic literature. Markovits and Hellerman's thesis that soccer was 'crowded out' of the American sport space because 'native born Americans and immigrants' in the nineteenth century came to view it as a 'non-American activity' thus influencing immigrants to look to other sports as a means of assimilation, finds its parallel on BigSoccer:

> About a hundred years ago, football (American) and baseball was supposed to be the red-blooded, American sport that made us different from Europe ... An immigrant would arrive and their childern would learn two things in order to get accepted as an American: baseball and English.[31]

Sugden's assertion that attempts to establish soccer as a 'mainstream professional sport' suffer because soccer 'is viewed as a game for foreigners, rich white kids and women' as well as his exploration of the possibility that a media 'conspiracy' inhibits soccer's growth, are similar to many BigSoccer posts:

> soccer is seen by Americans as foreign ... It is the #1 comment I get from people who find out I'm a soccer fanatic. 'That's that foreign sport, isn't it?' ... a perception which those who don't like soccer and fear it may catch on in this country reinforce every chance they get.
>
> [soccer's image is] upper middle class people with really nice sweaters drinking evian.
>
> it's still seen as a little girl's sport. They think it's not a physical enough game.
>
> you have to realize that there is an antisoccer stablisment here in USA, and most of the members are part of the USA sports media.[32]

The status of soccer, of course, has direct implications for followers of MLS. There is a clear understanding on BigSoccer that MLS trails the Big Four in popularity. While few American sports fans ponder whether the NFL, MLB or the NBA has a future, the business condition of MLS is a pervasive issue on BigSoccer.

Even in threads not devoted directly to finance and marketing, business issues often rise to the surface. For example, MLS's end-of-season playoff system to decide the league champion inspired hundreds of posts in 2005. Threads on the topic that began as exchanges about the fairness of the play-off format and its validity in determining the champion quickly evolved into discussions of marketing and revenue generation:

The revenue missed by 6 playoff games wouldn't be that much. If necessary, add a regular season home game (from 16 to 17 to recoup the missed revenue).

It's all about how you sell it. If you market it as you are describing, people may be confused.

Switching to a single-elimination would make it a lot easier for casual sports fans to understand.

The league is in the business of making money. More tems = more playoff games = more loot.[33]

The preoccupation with the business aspects of MLS inspires a steady stream of threads dealing with ways to attract more fans and achieve profitability. There are regularly recurring threads devoted to attendance. There is a standing forum on 'expansion', that is, the league's plans to launch teams in additional cities. The balance sheets of clubs and the league are analyzed in threads such as 'MLS Financial Structure' and 'Did the galaxy make a profit this year?'.

Uncertainty about the financial stability of the league prompts a wide range of predictions about it future. Some writers express trepidation about the survival of MLS. Representative of the pessimistic position was a 2005 post that stated,

> MLS is going to fail unless it makes big changes quickly ... We are talking about the survival of a sports league ... Soccer fans are growing in number in the U.S. while MLS attendance and TV ratings are slipping into oblivion. The bitter irony is the quality of play has improved greatly. The packaging and presentation of it stinks. No wonder no one watches it on TV and you can barely give the tickets away.

Others, while not predicting the demise of the league, question the league's ability to thrive. In a thread titled 'Why MLS wont grow audience anytime soon' a writer predicted that MLS is 'destined to stay in the cellar of American Sports.' Another person in the same thread offered several criticisms, adding, 'It's not fatal, just not compatible with major-league aspirations'.

There is at the same time a more optimistic school of thought that acknowledges the existing problems with the league, but argues that MLS has 'the potential to grow huge'. One poster predicted, 'in ten years maybe the best soccer in the world will be played here why? we have $$$$$$'. And, another wrote, 'the MLS will grow into the #2 American sport in 20 yrs', trailing only the NFL.[34]

America's Place in World Soccer

Just as BigSoccer members debate soccer's place in American sport, they also examine the United States' standing in the world of international soccer. Points of departure for these discussions include the senior national team, youth national teams, careers of individual American players employed abroad and MLS.

The various men's national teams, although respectable in international competition, have not established themselves as being among the world's elite. MLS, as several writers have noted, is unique among professional leagues in the United States in that it does not represent the pinnacle of the sport. BigSoccer posters are well aware of these realities and constantly debate the quality of the United States soccer and MLS in relation to other countries, clubs and leagues.

Comparisons abound. How does the boys' under-17 team compare to Brazil's? Is the quality of MLS comparable to mid-table teams in the English Premier League? Does MLS have a better business model than the Australian 'A' League? And, could men's NCAA Division I college teams beat third division professional teams from Germany? In making their comparisons, writers introduce a myriad of causal variables including, among others, youth development programmes, talent identification methods, racial composition of the soccer-playing population, players' body types, impact of other sports on the soccer talent pool, United States geography, coaching techniques, match tactics and business structures.

What is significant, in the context of American sport, about the speculation and debate regarding the quality of United States soccer is not the percentage of writers who believe that the best team in MLS could or could not beat the weakest side from England's Premiership. Rather, it is that so many posters feel the need to measure or estimate America's place in the international hierarchy of their favourite sport. There is no other professional team sport that inspires American fans to question the quality of either the league or its individual players relative to others in the world.

Symptomatic of the realization that the United States, in the men's game, is not the world's greatest soccer nation are posts revealing a concern about how American soccer is perceived in other countries. To be sure, many BigSoccer members profess to be unconcerned about how 'they' see 'us'. Yet, there are at least as many participants whose posts suggest otherwise.

Good performances by a few MLS teams against European clubs in summer friendlies and the MLS All-Stars' easy victory over Fulham FC a couple of weeks before the start of the 2005 EPL season, generated both optimism and a search for validation by foreign sources. One poster quoted Chelsea executive Peter Kenyon's positive post-match comments about MLS. Others wrote:

> It impressed [Fulham manager] Coleman and many of the opposing fans of all the teams that played MLS competition this past month. [It] earned MLS more respect, as evidenced by the articles on Fulham's website and other fans' posts.

> people looked at it and said, 'Hmmm, maybe MLS isn't a piece of dreck after all'.

A subsequent match between another MLS select side and Real Madrid in Spain produced a very different result and set of reactions. Real's 5-0 victory prompted several threads, the largest totalling 520 posts and more than 18,200 views. The thread presented a wide range of opinions. Some posters dismissed the match as a meaningless exhibition, but others clearly were worried about the impact it would have on European perceptions: 'The way we played, the way we looked, all played into all the bad stereotypes of … american soccer'. Several posts included translated excerpts from condescending Spanish press articles. More than 40 posts contained some form of the words 'shame', 'humiliate', 'embarrass' or 'disgrace'.[35]

Latinos and Soccer in the United States

The Latino role in United States soccer elicits strong and diverse opinions on BigSoccer. The men's national team and MLS are the focal points of the discussion. In part, the intensity of opinions derives from the fact that the United States and Mexican national teams are closely matched rivals and the two strongest teams in their region. It is clear, however, that BigSoccer discussions about Latinos are about more than just soccer. They contain all the core elements of the broader social discourse about Latinos, immigration and assimilation.

Several points of contention drive the exchanges. There is a realization that Latino support is essential if the national team is ever to attract widespread public interest and if MLS is to succeed financially. This belief is coupled with a recognition that Latino soccer culture is in some ways separate from other soccer cultures in the United States. Although Latinos form important segments of the MLS, and to a lesser extent, the national team fan bases, many Latinos, citizens and non-citizens alike, prefer to follow and support Mexican and Central American national teams and clubs. This breeds resentment on the part of some MLS and United States national team fans:

> [They] live in this country, most likely even born in this country, [and] identify themselves as mexican-american. The bad thing is that they rather be more mexican than american … Why do [they] only support mexican MFL clubs and why do they not support us soccer? Seems like their alligence is not to this country or to our league.[36]

The announcement in 2004 that Club Deportivo Guadalajara, more commonly known as Chivas, would create and enter a new team in MLS accentuated the issue. The new team was to be called Chivas USA and would share the soccer-specific Home Depot Center with the Los Angeles Galaxy.

The entry of any Mexican-owned team would have created controversy. Chivas presented an especially controversial case. Throughout its history Chivas has prided itself on having only Mexican players. Its owner, Jorge Vergara, made no secret that his new MLS club was meant to appeal first and foremost to Mexican Americans, Mexicans and other Latinos living in the United States, and that Spanish would be the club's primary language of business.

The often contentious exchanges about Chivas USA on BigSoccer amplified most of the issues related to Latinos and soccer in the United States. Writers' screen names and self-descriptions indicate that Latinos, Anglos and African Americans all participated in discussions and that positions regarding Chivas USA did not breakdown cleanly along ethnic lines.

One of the first questions regarding Chivas USA was whether Latinos would switch their allegiance to the new team. In threads such as 'Is Chivas USA taking away most of our mexican/latino fans' and 'Are Mexicans going to support Chivas????', some posters predicted a wholesale abandonment of existing loyalties. Most writers, however, argued that fans of other Mexican clubs would feel no affection for Chivas USA. Furthermore, they noted, it was unlikely that Latinos with roots in Central American would follow the club. As one writer put it,

Mexicans? Very few. The rest of us latinos? NO. Like it has been said here before, not all Mexicans like Chivas, and as for the rest of us latinos, that are not Mexican, we don't give a crap about Chivas.[37]

There was considerable agitation over Chivas of Guadalajara's Mexican-only hiring policy. Despite league assurances that Chivas USA would not be allowed to discriminate, many fans took Vergara at his word when he was quoted as saying that the team would be made up of three Mexican nationals and United States Latinos, making the team 'a Spanish-speaking Chivas … a Latin Chivas'. Ultimately, the team that Chivas USA assembled was racially and ethnically integrated, but during the planning stage many posters protested what they thought would be the club's exclusionary policy: 'It is racist. Can you imagine the uproar if someone bought a team and said, I am going to make this organization all white?'[38]

In a similar vein, many writers attacked the concept of founding and marketing a team based on nationality and ethnicity.

> I don't like the fact that they are marketing the team as a 'Latino/Hispanic' team, specifically a team for Americans of Mexican descent or Mexican nationals living in the United States. It segregates the soccer community, making it a United States vs. THEM.

> This is really a terrible, terrible way for the league to 'reach out' to Hispanics – pick an owner that in fact polarizes the Hispanic community and put the team in a city that simmers with class and ethnic tensions against another team in the same city – with the new team already having a predetermined racial fan base.[39]

Vergara for his part did little to assuage those who felt threatened by the introduction of a Mexican-owned teamed. He seemed well aware of the broader implications when he provocatively told the *Los Angeles Times*, 'We're taking the U.S. back, little by little'. Nativists on Bigsoccer also attached a broader significance to the new team.

> Chivas USA [and] … illegal immigrants … Both should never be let into the country!

> Chivas are specifically made so that gringos aka white people don't support them. I am white. So I am always rootign against them. Vergara wants to make this a Mexican vs gringo thing, I am gonna do my part to help.[40]

A thread titled 'I Hate Chivas USA' ultimately morphed into a debate that had as much to do with immigration policy and the economic impact of Mexican immigrants in the United States as it did soccer.[41]

Among the most visceral posts were those debating whether Chivas USA would attract violent fans. Once again Vergara played a role in exacerbating the situation, telling a crowd of club supporters at a pre-season rally, 'The peace and tranquility is over'.[42] BigSoccer posters expressed fear for their personal safety at matches, recounted violent encounters with Chivas USA supporters and worried about whether violence would drive away other fans, especially families. It would be overly simplistic to characterize the negative posts as nothing more than examples of Anglo bigotry. Some clearly were, but many negative posts came from people who identified themselves as 'Latino' or 'black', or had Spanish screen names.

Posts predicting or complaining about violence essentially took two forms – criticisms directed specifically at Chivas USA fans and those aimed more generally at 'Mexicans'. Responding to a report of a Galaxy fan being attacked by Chivas USA fans following a match at the Home Depot Center, members wrote,

> This is going to happen anywhere they play. Here in Denver they threw bottles and cups onto the field and several scuffles broke out after the game. MLS is going to have to realize that along with the additional revenue (if any) that Chivas brings in, they also bring a fanbase that is filled with scumbags.

> This the way typicall mexican fans act when they lose, I've seen it may times, They just dont know how to react to losing. But unfortunatley were going to see this more and more as the years go bye trust me.

> i agree. mexican fans cannot handle a loss especially to a bunch of 'gueros' … they will try and start a fight.[43]

As with almost every topic discussed on BigSoccer, the exchanges regarding Chivas USA included a wide range of opinions. The negative posts that typically started threads were met consistently with strong counter arguments, insults or dismissive sarcasm. Latino and non-Latino posters alike defended Chivas USA fans and welcomed the passion they brought to the league. Several writers offered thoughtful explanations of the immigrant experience, while others took a more heated political tack. Nevertheless, the existence of such debates reveals the fractious nature of soccer fandom in the United States.

Conclusion

The community of soccer fans who follow the MLS on BigSoccer expresses a curious mixture of insecurity, resentment, passion and optimism reflecting the contradictions of the sport in the United States. Fans are insecure about the quality of the soccer they watch and the financial viability of their professional league. They resent soccer's low standing in the hierarchy of American sport. They complain that important segments of the media ignore, under-report and too often ridicule the sport. They also resent the fact that a significant percentage of soccer fans in the country do not respect or follow the MLS. At the same time, BigSoccer members have formed virtual communities of passionate team supporters. On balance, they are optimistic about the future of American soccer and MLS, believing that MLS will one day challenge the Big Four for supremacy, or at the very least become a financially secure league offering high-quality soccer comparable to the better European and South American leagues.

BigSoccer threads and posts underscore the lack of a unified soccer culture in the United States. It is not clear whether BigSoccer and other discussion boards will change that reality. The development and availability of information technologies such as the Internet, satellite and cable television, cell phones, personal data assistants and the convergence of these technologies certainly will facilitate the building of virtual communities of fans who want to follow specific teams and leagues. However, to the extent that emerging technologies make it easier for small groups of people with shared interests to form functioning vibrant cyber communities, the nation's soccer fans may become increasingly focused on their existing modes of soccer consumption and less inclined to look elsewhere. The very innovations that facilitate community building may also obviate the need for disparate groups of soccer fans to find common ground. It remains to be seen whether the Internet and related emerging information technologies will contribute to a more inclusive, more unified soccer culture in the United States, or many disconnected cultures.

Notes

[1]   Post 1, http://www.bigsoccer.com/forum/showthread.php?p=6154451#post6154451. All citations to BigSoccer.com indicate the URL preceded by the post number in the linear mode display of the cited thread. Updated membership counts are available at http://www.bigsoccer.com/forum.

[2]   Paccagnella, 'Getting the Seats of Your Pants Dirty: Strategies for Ethnographic Research on Virtual Communities.'

[3]   *The Superstudy of Sports Participation 2003, Vol. II, recreational Activities, 2004 Edition*, 92–125. *2004–05 NFHS High School Athletics Participation Survey* at http://www.nfhs.org/script-content/VA_Custom/Survey Resources/2004-05_Participation_Summary.pdf.

[4]   Peter Diamond (Senior Vice President, Programs, NBC, Olympics), in telephone conversation with author, October 21, 2005.

[5]   MLS attendance total includes regular- and post-season matches. http://www.mlsnet.com/MLS/stats/index.jsp?club=mls. http://www.mlsnet.com/MLS/mls/events/mls_cup/2005/stats/index.jsp?club=mls.

[6]   Sugden, 'USA and the World Cup', 249. Sugden's phrase 'recent émigré enclaves' may have been applicable in 1994, but it no longer is today. See http://www.census.gov/Press-Release/www/releases/archives/facts_for_features_special_editions/005338.html.

[7]   David Davis, 'Conquistador in Cleats'. *Los Angeles Times Magazine*, 13 March 2005, 10.

[8]   'Mexican Soccer Broadcasts Break Audience Records for the Univision and Telefutura Networks', Press Release, 23 June 2004, at http://www.univision.net/corp/en/pr/Miami_23062004-1.html.

[9]   Jo Laverde (Communications Manager, Nielsen Media Research), email message to author, 10 August 2004. Larry Stewart, 'Ramsey Quits Fox Over Salary'. *Los Angeles Times*, 30 July 2004, D-4. See 'What Los Angeles Is Watching' sidebar.

[10] 'About Soccer United Marketing', http://www.sumworld.net/display.php?id=20040000001.

[11] See Markovits and Hellerman, *Offside: Soccer and American Exceptionalism* and Brown, 'Can European Football Spur Interest in American Soccer?', 49–61.

[12] http://www.sportsbusinessdaily.com/index.cfm?fuseaction=article.main&articleID=90628.

[13] http://www.mlsnet.com/MLS/stats/index.jsp?club=mls. http://sports.espn.go.com/nhl/attendance. http://sports.espn.go.com/nba/attendance. http://sports.espn.go.com/mlb/attendance.

[14] 'Gate Revenues and Attendance Comparisons By Sport (By 2004 Revenue/Seat)'. *Media Sports Business*, 30 September 2005, 3–5.

[15] Ibid.

[16] Stewart, 'NBC Won't Miss a Thing at the End of the Chase', 18 November 2005, in Web-only 'Sports Extras', http://www.latimes.com/sports/custom/extras/la-spw-tvcol18nov18,1,4317723.column?coll=la-sports-extras, retrieved 22 November 2005. Brian Schecter, 'Super Bowl: Slight Ratings Dip'. *Media Sports Business*, 30 February 2005, 7. Schecter, 'MLB Post-Season Tallies Lower TV Numbers'. *Media Sports Business*, 31 October 2005, 9. Schecter, 'Playoff Hoop Ratings: A Mixed Affair', *Media Sports Business*, 30 June 2004, 7.

[17]   'Add Chivas', *AAF SportsLetter*, August 2005, http://www.aafla.org/10ap/. SportsLetter-16-3/SLhome.html. Schecter, 'MLB Post-Season Tallies Lower TV Numbers'. Schecter, 'NBA Network TV Ratings: Firing Blanks'. *Media Sports Business*, 30 April 2005, 11. http://www.sportsbusinessdaily.com/index.cfm?fuseaction=article.main&articleId=96030.   http://www.sportsbusinessdaily.com/index.cfm?fuseaction=article.main&articleId=93310.

[18]   Edward Derse (Director of Emerging Networks, Fox Sports Interactive Media), email message to author, 25 October 2005. Univision ratings are based on a 24 game sample.

[19]   Schecter, 'MLB Cable TV Carriage At Record Levels', *Media Sports Business*, 31 March 2005, 3. Schecter, 'College Basketball Regional Cable Carriage 1997–04 (Ranked By 2004 Total Games)'. *Media Sports Business*, 31 March 2005, 8. Schecter, 'NBA TV Times Are Changing'. *Media Sports Business*, 31 October 2004, 10.

[20]   'Gate Revenues and Attendance Comparisons By Sport (By 2004 Revenue/Seat)', 3.

[21]   Author's search, 17 November 2005, of Thompson Dialog (www.dialog.com) electronic files 713 and 147, using the queries 'nfl and football' and 'mls and soccer,' returned 17,718 NFL hits and 926 MLS hits.

[22]   Author's Google search, 22 November 2005, using the queries 'nfl and football' and 'mls and soccer', returned 40.9 million and 6.3 million hits respectively. The 'soccer', 'basketball' and 'baseball' comparison undercounted the amount of soccer information on the Internet because millions of Web-pages use the word 'football' to refer to what most Americans call 'soccer'.

[23]   Derse, email message to author, 19 October 2005.

[24]   Jesse Hertzberg (President and Founder, BigSoccer, Inc.), email message to author, 17 November 2005.

[25]   http://bigsoccer.com/forum/forumdisplay.php?f=958.

[26]   Post 4, http://bigsoccer.com/forum/showthread.php?p=6466644. Post 27, http://bigsoccer.com/forum/showthread.php?p=6477672. Post 6, http://bigsoccer.com/forum/showthread.php?p=6594265.

[27]   Posts 1, 8, 15–17, http://bigsoccer.com/forum/showthread.php?t=239883.

[28]   Posts 17 and 2, http://bigsoccer.com/forum/showthread.php?t=154904&page=1&pp=15. Post 2, http://bigsoccer.com/forum/showthread.php?p=4905174.

[29]   Post 34, http://bigsoccer.com/forum/showthread.php?p=6529163. Post 8, http://bigsoccer.com/forum/showthread.php?t=179485.

[30]   Post 1, http://www.bigsoccer.com/forum/showthread.php?p=4904717. Post 4, http://www.bigsoccer.com/forum/showthread.php?p=5532809. Post 15, http://www.bigsoccer.com/forum/showthread.php?t=184994. Post 1, http://www.bigsoccer.com/forum/showthread.php?p=4626870. Post 1, http://www.bigsoccer.com/forum/showthread.php?p=6101709. Post 4, http://www.bigsoccer.com/forum/showthread.php?p=5430946. Post 1 and 6, http://www.bigsoccer.com/forum/showthread.php?p=6393186.

[31]   Markovits and Hellerman, *Offside*, 52–3. Post 6, http://www.bigsoccer.com/forum/showthread.php?t=200195.

[32]   Sugden, 'USA and the World Cup', 250, 220. Post 31, http://www.bigsoccer.com/forum/showthread.php?p=3504599. Post 13, http://www.bigsoccer.com/forum/showthread.php?p=4439252. Post 3, http://www.bigsoccer.com/forum/showthread.php?p=3467876. Post 8, http://www.bigsoccer.com/forum/showthread.php?t=146662. In 2005, Nike and United States Soccer, the sport's domestic governing body, attempted to counter the perception of soccer as foreign, feminine and effete with a 'Don't Tread on Me' marketing campaign. A T-shirt advertisement on the federation's website stated,

> Join the flag-waving, apple-pie-eating, red-blooded American Soccer Campaign that shouts boldly to the World: **Don't Tread On Me!** No matter how much France looks down on us, Brazil doubts us, or England mocks us; no matter what the odds, or the situation, or the game, the American people have this uncanny, gloriously stubborn belief that if we want something badly enough, we will

achieve it. This is the desire that coursed through the veins of our revolutionaries in 1776. This is the desire that courses through the veins of Team USA as they prepare to challenge the World in 2006.

Retrieved 22 November 2005 at http://store.yahoo.com/ussoccerstore/us50205847.html. A clear majority of BigSoccer posts about the campaign were positive. See http://bigsoccer.com/forum/showthread.php?t=254793&page=1&pp=15&highlight=tread and http://bigsoccer.com/forum/showthread.php?t=254961&highlight=tread.

[33] Posts 2 and 29 at http://www.bigsoccer.com/forum/showthread.php?t=261263. Posts 4 and 8 at http://www.bigsoccer.com/forum/showthread.php?t=258981&page=1&pp=15.

[34] Posts 37, 1, 34, 10 and 11, http://www.bigsoccer.com/forum/showthread.php?t=259580. Post 1, http://www.bigsoccer.com/forum/showthread.php?t=234879.

[35] Posts 30, 26 and 28, http://www.bigsoccer.com/forum/showthread.php?t=226993&page=2&pp=15. Post 339, http://www.bigsoccer.com/forum/showthread.php?p=5919725.

[36] Post 39, http://www.bigsoccer.com/forum/showthread.php?t=104627.

[37] Post 9, http://www.bigsoccer.com/forum/showthread.php?t=169995.

[38] Post 79, http://www.bigsoccer.com/forum/showthread.php?mode=hybrid&t=110129. Post 3, http://www.bigsoccer.com/forum/showthread.php?t=79564.

[39] Davis, 'Conquistador in Cleats', 30. Post 85, http://www.bigsoccer.com/forum/showthread.php?t=110129&page=6&pp=15. Post 7, http://www.bigsoccer.com/forum/showthread.php?t=115018.

[40] Post 8, http://www.bigsoccer.com/forum/showthread.php?t=104627. Post 8, http://www.bigsoccer.com/forum/showthread.php?t=185043.

[41] See posts from 203, http://www.bigsoccer.com/forum/showthread.php?t=110129&page=1&pp=15.

[42] Paul Gutierrez, 'On Paper, Chivas Seems Ready to Go'. *Los Angeles Times*, 3 August 2004, D-3.

[43] Posts 10, 14 and 17, http://bigsoccer.com/forum/showthread.php?t=220726&page=2&pp=15.

References

Brown, Sean Fredrick. 'Can European Football Spur Interest in American Soccer? A Look at the Champions World[TM] Series and Major League Soccer.' *Soccer & Society* 6, no. 3 (2005): 49–61.

Markovits, Andrei S. and Steven L. Hellerman. *Offside: Soccer and American Exceptionalism*. Princeton: Princeton University Press, 2001.

Paccagnella, Luciano. 'Getting the Seats of Your Pants Dirty: Strategies for Ethnographic Research on Virtual Communities.' *Journal of Computer-Mediated Communication* 3, no.1 (1997). http://www.nicoladoering.de/Hogrefe/paccagnella97.htm.

Sugden, John. 'USA and the World Cup: American Nativism and the Rejection of the People's Game.' In *Hosts and Champions: Soccer Cultures, National Identities and the USA World Cup*, edited by John Sugden and Alan Tomlinson. Aldershot: Arena, 1994: 219–52.

The Superstudy of Sports Participation 2003, Vol. II, recreational Activities, 2004 Edition. Hartsdale, NY: SGMA International, 2004.

The Pub as a Virtual Football Fandom Venue: An Alternative to 'Being there'?

Mike Weed

Introduction

A sunny Saturday afternoon, the sort of day when it would be almost impossible to find a seat in the beer gardens of most of England's pubs – the English public rarely miss the opportunity to take advantage of warm weekend afternoons. However, somewhat curiously, many beer gardens are almost empty, and there's a strange set of sporadic cheers and jeers coming from inside many pubs. It is, of course, the day of a big international – a qualifier, or even a finals match, in the World Cup or European Nations Championship, with the England team, to use the war metaphor that is so often part of these encounters, battling a foreign foe on overseas soil. The exact details of the match are unimportant and, in fact, it need not be football – rugby is increasingly becoming part of what reformed football hooligan Dougie Brimson calls 'the culture of pub supporting'.[1]

There has long been a link between the English public house and football. The pub has been a place to read about football, to talk about football, and to meet with friends before going to a live match. The pub provides a place where the male holy trinity of alcohol, football and male-bonding come together. Pubs are the venues for the most vociferous of debates about the chances of the local or the national team in their forth-coming league, cup or international game, places in which to read and dispute the opinions or speculations of journalists about the team's latest signing or the identity of the next England Manager. In recent years, however, there has been a change in the role played by the pub. Its centrality in football culture certainly hasn't changed, but it is increasingly becoming clear that the pub itself is now a venue in which to watch live football.

During the 2002 World Cup in Korea and Japan, I conducted an ethnography of the pub as a football spectator venue.[2] This essentially involved spending about a month in the pub watching and talking about football! Many of my colleagues were incredu-lous, and have taken great joy in using this particular piece of research as my primary identifier in introducing me to other academics – 'this is Mike, his research involves going to the pub and watching football'. However, this piece of research provided some interesting and useful insights into the nature of the sports spectating experience, re-casting it in a different light to that in which it has often previously been understood. However, before briefly re-visiting this work prior to considering in detail the nature of the spectating experience, it is perhaps first useful to examine the genesis of the pub as a sport spectator venue.

The Pub as a Sport Spectator Venue

As noted above, there is a long-standing relationship between the pub and football. However, it is only in the last decade or so that the pub has become a significant and regular venue in which to watch live sport, and particularly in which to watch football. The number of pubs displaying boards and posters advertising the matches they will be showing is an indication that pub management companies and major brewers recog-nize the importance of this trend, but the football authorities also appear keen to promote the pub as a venue in which to watch football. In September 2003, pub management companies, brewers and the football authorities jointly promoted 'National Pub Football Week'. This initiative has continued with further Pub Football Weeks being held in May 2004 and September 2005.

The evidence from market information sources, such as Mintel and Keynote, is that the market for pub sport spectating is significant. In fact, in 2002, more people (9.1 million) watched live sport on television in a pub or a bar than paid to watch live sport at an event (8.7 million).[3] This equates to 19 per cent of the population. While the data from earlier years is a little sketchy, and thus direct comparisons or any statistical trends analysis are difficult, it does not appear to be unreasonable to say that the use of the pub as a regular venue in which to watch football and sport in general has largely emerged and grown over the last 10 to 15 years. Given this timescale, it is possible to point to three factors that have driven this trend. One of these factors is fairly straightforward, and is simply the increasingly relatively cheap availability to pubs and bars of the technology to show sport on a big screen. However, the remaining two factors are a little more complex and demand more detailed discussion. The first of these is the move of live televised Premier League football to the satellite broadcaster BSkyB in 1992. The second, is what has been referred to by some as the 'sanitisation' of Premier League football grounds as a result of the changes brought about by the 1990 Taylor Report on the safety of sports stadia.

Some authors (such as Emery and Weed) believe that the formation, in 1992, of the 'Premier League' (also referred to as the Premiership) was one of the most significant changes in the structure of top-flight football in England since the league itself was established in 1888.[4] The Premier League comprised the clubs formerly in the Football League's Division One. Formed under the auspices of the FA, it was initially largely a vehicle to facilitate a separately negotiated TV contract for the larger clubs who thought this would bring them more money. At the time, all four divisions of the Football League negotiated the TV rights contract collectively and the only way the top clubs could subvert this was to form a breakaway league. The timing of this breakaway coincided with the development of a business strategy by the satellite operator BSkyB which used football coverage as a loss-leader to sell subscriptions to their satellite service. This meant that BSkyB were prepared to pay large sums of money to obtain the TV rights for football. According to the journalist Simon Freeman, football was seen by BSkyB as the 'hook' by which people on lower incomes could be persuaded to sign up to a satellite TV subscription.[5] However, football coverage was a hook not only for private households, but also for businesses which saw the potential of live sport broadcasting:

> Demand for coverage of live football and other sport has been supported by both household subscriptions and by subscriptions from pubs, clubs and hotels. During the 1990s, live sports broadcasts were seized upon as a means of bringing men back into pubs.[6]

> [In the early 1990s] … football alone was driving the growth of Sky Sports, the main satellite channel. Sky targeted pubs, and many landlords of pubs with predominantly male clientele naturally took advantage of the big screen technology to screen live matches.[7]

In the early days, BSkyB were more effective at targeting businesses than household subscribers, and as such, the initial growth of pub football watching did not arise out of consumer preference, but out of necessity. While the arrival of BSkyB meant that many more football matches were shown live on TV, the low penetration levels of satellite and cable television in the early days of BSkyB's coverage 'led to increased numbers of consumers being forced to view live sport outside the home, with pubs and bars accommodating the bulk of this market'.[8] Contemporary estimates of non-terrestrial television subscription are of around 47 per cent of households in the UK, with around 50 per cent of these subscribing to sports channels.[9] However, penetration levels in the early to mid-1990s were much lower. As satellite and cable TV was in its infancy at this time, exact figures are difficult to come by, but extrapolations from figures suggested by Mintel and Keynote lead to an estimate of between 8 per cent and 10 per cent of households having access to non-terrestrial channels in 1993, and between 14 per cent and 17 per cent in 1995.[10] Clearer estimates show that this had risen to 27 per cent in 1998 and then to 32 per cent in 2001.[11] While the percentage of sports subscribers at this time can be little more than a guess, it is reasonable to estimate that between 5 per cent and 8 per cent of the population would have been able to access the first year of BSkyB's Premiership coverage at home.[12]

While the low levels of access to live football at home drove many football fans to the pub, other factors relating to the live football spectating experience may also have had an impact. A range of problems with the behaviour of football spectators during the 1980s, and an incident, not related to any form of misbehaviour by fans, at the FA Cup semi-final at Hillsborough between Liverpool and Nottingham Forest in 1989 (at which 96 fans died) led to an inquiry under Lord Justice Taylor, with the remit to, 'inquire into the events at Sheffield Wednesday football ground [Hillsborough] on 15 April 1989 and to make recommendations about the needs of crowd control and safety at sports events.' The Taylor Report, published in January 1990, identified football clubs as having prime responsibility for the safety and comfort of spectators, and included, as the primary recommendation in the report, the conversion of all first and second division grounds to all-seater stadia by 1994, and of all Football League grounds by 1999. While the requirement for lower league clubs has since been relaxed, all Premiership grounds are now all-seater stadia.

There are those who argue that the move to all-seater stadia has destroyed the traditional atmosphere of football that was a product of the terraces where fans were allowed to stand: 'Fans no longer have the ability to choose where they watch the game as they did in the era of open terraces, something that certain fan groups believe has been detrimental to the atmosphere of British football.'[13]

In fact, in recent years there has been a campaign by a fan lobby group called SAFE (Safe-standing Areas for Football in England) to have some standing re-introduced at Premiership grounds because it generates a better atmosphere. This has been supported by Gordon Taylor, the Chief Executive of the Professional Footballers Association, who believes that 'without a doubt one of the differences in the game with all-seater stadiums has been the consequent lack of atmosphere'.[14]

However, it is unlikely that it is purely the presence of seating that suppresses the atmosphere inside modern football stadia. Undoubtedly, the 'spectre of football hooliganism'[15] has also had an impact. The idea that seating has helped to address the problem of hooliganism is one that is popular with many commentators, among them former Secretary of State for National Heritage, David Mellor:

> The beneficial impact on crowd behaviour and the diminution of racist chanting can also be ascribed in part to football grounds becoming family friendly, an impossibility when we had the terracing. That's because terraces play to the old aggressive male stereotypes that football post-Hillsborough has been surprisingly successful at suppressing, at least most of the time.[16]

Yet, along with the suppression of football hooliganism can go the suppression of atmosphere, with many in the press and among the football authorities and government confusing the two. In fact, the Football (Disorder) Act incorporates a wide-ranging definition of disorder, which includes: 'using threatening, abusive or insulting words or behaviour or disorderly behaviour; displaying any writing or other thing which is threatening, abusive or insulting' (Schedule I, 14C[2]). However, Armstrong and Young note the problems that such a widespread definition can cause in criminalizing those elements of football support for whom chanting and singing are a significant element of the football experience but who would certainly not consider themselves to be involved in 'disorder'.[17] In fact, almost all football chants could be defined as 'insulting', indeed to be such is almost their *raison d'être*. Consequently, the provisions of the Act could allow for the banning of anyone who has ever chanted or sung at a football match: 'An involvement in the songs, chants, and the ribald and witty badinage [becomes] sufficient to generate arrests and help classify and sustain the idea of a hooligan problem.'[18]

Therefore it would appear that the 'spectre of football hooliganism' alongside the introduction of all-seater stadia has created an atmosphere inside football grounds that makes the pub a more attractive place in which to watch football: 'Sky also offers young male fans, at least, the prospects of collective and participatory pub TV coverage, the "new terraces" in an age of what are, for them, "sanitised" and allegedly atmosphere-free all-seater grounds.'[19]

The development of a 'culture of pub supporting', has found also its way into popular culture writing, with Dougie Brimson, in his book *The Geezers Guide to Football* writing that:

> The shift towards a culture of pub supporting has already started. It is cheaper and easier to simply go down the pub and watch the game while having a few beers. In most cases it will be with the same group of geezers and so the atmosphere will be as good if not better than at the actual game.[20]

While a 'culture of pub supporting' appears to have developed largely out of necessity as a result of a lack of access to live televised football matches in the home, it has now developed into an activity that is attractive in its own right. Despite the increased penetration of non-terrestrial television in recent years, pub sports spectating is growing in popularity, with Keynote estimating that over a third of men regularly go to pubs to watch sport.[21]

The 2002 World Cup in Korea and Japan

The 2002 Football World Cup presented an ideal opportunity to investigate the extent to which pub spectating had developed into an attractive activity in its own right, as opposed to a necessity in order to watch matches that are not available on terrestrial television in the home.[22] The hosting of this World Cup in Korea and Japan meant that in the UK, matches were shown between 6.00 a.m. in the morning and 12 noon – times that are not traditionally those when there is a lot of demand for visiting the pub, or for drinking alcohol. Furthermore, as the World Cup is a 'protected event' under the UK government's sports broadcasting policy, all of the matches were shown on free-to-air terrestrial television, and thus would be available to all homes that owned a television set. With matches being shown in the early mornings, and being available to all on terrestrial television, surely people would prefer to sit in their own homes with a cup of tea and watch the matches than to go to the pub?

In the run up to the World Cup it appeared that landlords, pub management companies and breweries were confident that, even in the early mornings, people would still want to come to the pub to watch football. However, there were some doubts about whether there would be much demand for alcohol, with Mark Hastings of the British Beer and Pub Association stating:

> People will still come to pubs because they want the atmosphere, the singing, the banter of watching a big-occasion game as a shared communal experience, but most will want eggs with their Beckham rather than beer. Instead of happy hours there will be full English breakfasts on offer at bargain prices.

However, pubs and bars still needed to apply for license extensions to open at this time of day. The precedent for such extensions dated from 1978 when the World Cup had been held in Argentina. This judgement allowed only limited flexibility and so, on 12 April 2002, a 'test case' hearing was held in the Queens Bench Divisional Court. Lord Chief Justice Woolf and Mr Justice Harrison heard the case, and in issuing a 'Special Licensing Judgement' concluded that:

> There is evidence to show that there will be participation in and celebration of the events, there will be demand for intoxicating liquor, and there is evidence of a change since the previous judgement in 1978. Televised sport has now become a major part of public and pub life and the World Cup is a major sporting event.

The final sentence here supports aspects of the discussions above which traced a growth in watching televised football in the pub, and this is reinforced further by the final part of the court judgement:

> the way such competitions are watched in public houses is now quite different. Customers go to the public house to take part in collective enjoyment of an event, just as attending a football match in person is a different experience from watching at home.

Therefore, in the run up to the World Cup in 2002, voices as disparate as the Lord Chief Justice and the British Beer and Pub Association were highlighting their perception that pubs provide 'atmosphere' for a 'big-occasion game as a shared communal experience', and that such occasions are a 'major part of public and pub life' that provide for the 'collective enjoyment of an event'.

Experiences during Euro 2000 (the European nations football championship) had shown that many of those intending to watch matches in the pub would 'prepare' for an evening match by drinking all day. However, as the latest kick-off times for the 2002 World Cup were around midday, such daytime drinking preparations were not possible. Nevertheless, preparatory drinking still took place, but was simply shifted to the night before, with only a few hours sleep being taken before the early morning matches started. For the first England match, which kicked of at 10.30 a.m., some fans were queuing outside the pub from 5.50 a.m. (the pub opened at 6.00 a.m.) in order to get a good seat in front of the big screen! The observations during the 2002 World Cup certainly showed that even when matches are shown on terrestrial television at times when pubs are not even usually open, the demand for pub sport spectating was still high. Furthermore, the comments before the tournament regarding the significance of 'collective enjoyment' and 'shared communal experience' were fully borne out during the matches, and are best highlighted by the most anticipated match of the tournament (for England fans) between England and Argentina.

The England v Argentina match had one of the latest start times of the tournament, and kicked-off at 12.30 p.m. UK time. As this match took place on a Friday, many people had either booked time off work months in advance, or feigned illness to allow them to watch the match in the pub. In a bar in Sheffield with a capacity of 750 (Weed, 2006), the pre-match atmosphere was boisterous and alcohol-fuelled, and many people went on to drink late into the evening after the match. Anti-Argentinean singing was widespread and often pervasive, with the IRA also featuring in the repertoire. In the usual course of events, the sound of around 700 drunken people inside a closed and confined space joining in unison in a rowdy and in some cases aggressive rendition of 'No Surrender to the IRA', would likely be cause for police intervention. Of course, in a bar, unlike at a ground, there is a plentiful supply of alcohol and no police or stewards to quell any racist or xenophobic chanting. The popularity of this nationalist chant is a somewhat strange feature of modern day England supporting, although it is unlikely that many of those joining in have any particular commitment to English Nationalism or to defeating the IRA, they simply want to enjoy communal singing and chanting. It is this communal desire to join in with the carnivalesque party atmosphere that appears to swell the numbers of 'hooligans' at international tournaments, and was a particular problem, as Weed has argued, at Euro 2000 in Holland and Belgium.[23] While this chanting may be uncomfortable, it is perhaps better that it takes place in a closed bar in England where there are no 'opponents' other than the virtual ones on the TV, than in the streets, bars and football grounds of another country. However, it is an indication of the 'out-of-the-ordinary-ness' of pub football spectating that such chanting is tolerated. On a Friday or Saturday evening it is highly likely that security staff would intervene to prevent such chanting or to eject from the bar those involved.

However, notwithstanding the above, the atmosphere in the Sheffield bar was very intense, and some of the comments of those in the bar highlight this:

> It feels so loud in here, I s'pose that must be cos there's a roof on, which you don't have at the stadium – this is all enclosed. We're all England fans as well, and that contributes … I think you pick up on and join in the singing started by other people easier.

> Well, here in this bit down here [a lower section for which tickets had not been sold in advance] its a bit like the old terraces, we're all packed in and you can feel you'self swaying with the chants and songs – there must be far more people per space than in a ground.

> Its got to be the beer hasn't it … eveyone's really tanked up cos they're not waiting til half time or whatever to get the next drink in – you can see the TVs everywhere. It's a good job we're all on the same side or there might be trouble.[24]

The Sheffield police had a significant presence in the city centre and had obviously realized that many people had been drinking heavily and were buoyed by the match result, in which England beat Argentina 1-0. The singing and chanting continued after the match and contributed to an atmosphere where the police decided to ask bars in the city centre to close for two hours in the early evening. While there had been no hint of any trouble, the police clearly felt this was a sensible preventative measure. Given the events of two years later, when there were a number of instances of disorder around UK following the screening of England matches from Euro 2004 in Portugal, this request seems to have been justified. Although there were no incidents during the 2002 World Cup, the potential for trouble surrounding 'big occasion' pub football spectating could certainly be anticipated from the observations during this tournament. What is a celebratory and 'electric' atmosphere if England win appears to be a clear recipe for trouble if England lose. The potential problems of 'virtual' football hooliganism will be briefly reconsidered in the concluding comments to the paper, but the discussion now turns to the nature of pub football spectating, and the implications this may have for the way in which the sport spectating experience is conceptualized.

The Nature of the Sport Spectating Experience

Sport Spectating would appear, by definition, to be about watching a match, game, race or event live and in person. As a spectator one can become a 'vicarious' participant in the live event. In fact, in a conference paper around ten years ago, Baines refers to travel to watch sports events as 'the leisure pursuit of being there'.[25] While part of the pleasure of 'being there' is obviously the immediate pleasure and excitement of witnessing live events, a further motivation for live presence is the retrospective recall of the event upon returning. This is a concept that has long been recognized in the more general travel and tourism literature. MacCannell, for example, highlights the importance of 'returning' as a significant part of the travel experience, explaining that 'returning home is an essential part of being a tourist – one goes only to return'.[26] MacCannell believes that tourists travel with the expectation that they will have some kind of experience of 'otherness' that will set them aside from their peers on their return. In the football context, the experience of otherness is having 'been there' at a major international fixture or for a significant result or achievement for the team one supports. For years to come, such an experience will allow the spectator to recount to friends stories of, for example, 'I was there when we beat Germany in Charleroi at Euro 2000'. Such stories can often be the source of considerable status in some groups, and as such reinforce the importance of 'being there' live and in person as a key part of the sport spectator experience. There is considerable resonance between the idea that 'being there' enhances the experience of the event upon return, and John Urry's description of the motivation to 'collect places'.[27] Here, travellers will direct their 'gaze' onto more exotic and unusual places that they can 'collect', and thus display to their friends upon return through photographs, souvenirs, and most importantly of all, the retelling of experiences. Travel to, for example, the 2002 World Cup in Korea and Japan, might be regarded as such a 'collected place', that through merchandise and story-telling can be displayed to others long after the actual trip itself has ended.

In relation to the excitement of witnessing live events, some writers have discussed the importance of physical presence. Boden and Molotch, for example, in their paper on 'The Compulsion of Proximity' describe the need to be in the company of others and to feel a physical proximity to the place (or in this case, the event) being visited.[28] This is reinforced by Urry who also discusses the significant role played by 'intermittent moments of *physical proximity*, to particular peoples, places or events, [which] in significant ways … is felt to be obligatory, appropriate or desirable'.[29]

It would appear, therefore, that the two key features of the sport spectating experience are, firstly, a desire to experience physical proximity to the live event, and secondly, a desire to have an experience that can be re-told to others after the event. Given these features, how does the experience of watching football in the pub measure up to such live football spectating?

The immediate response, of course, would be that watching football in the pub is a secondary experience to that of watching live at the event. Consequently, people only go to the pub to watch football when travel to the event itself (for whatever reason) is not possible and the match is not being shown on terrestrial television and so, for many, it is not available to watch at home. Certainly the discussions earlier in the paper indicate that the move of live televised Premier League football to the satellite broadcaster BSkyB in 1992 served as an initial stimulus for a growth in pub football spectating in the UK. This initial stimulus was largely due to the lack of penetration of satellite television into homes which thus 'forced' many fans to watch football in pubs and bars.[30] However, some have argued that there is another force at work related to the 'sanitisation' of football grounds in the wake of the Taylor report and the commodification and commercialization of football since the mid-1990s.[31] Williams describes pubs and bars as the 'new terraces' in which fans can celebrate their identity without the increasing restrictions of 'sanitised and allegedly atmosphere-free all-seater grounds'.[32] This perspective is further reinforced by some of John Bale's work on sports places and spaces.

Bale describes three views of the 1992 European Nations Cup Final in which Denmark beat Germany.[33] He refers to three spectating environments: the first was the stadium, the 'real' game; the second was the homes of millions of European television viewers. In both of these environments Bale identifies constraints – in the stadium there are constraints on both behaviour and movement, as fans are allocated a seat, one viewpoint from which to watch the game, with a range of stadium regulations to limit their 'consumption', both of the game and of alcohol. Similarly, at home viewers are 'confined in domestic space in which domestic constraints on behaviour are as rigid – if not more so – than those in the stadium at which the game is "actually" being played'.[34] The third environment identified by Bale was both conceptually and geographically somewhere between the stadium and home – a huge television screen erected in the open space of the Faelled (in Denmark). Here Bale notes that the fans watching in this space took part in:

> a form of carnival, with drunken fans celebrating their small nation's victory over the German 'machine'. Who is to say that the experience of the Faelled was anything but the optimal sporting experience for late modernity – thousands watching in open

spaces ... standing in opposition to the panopticised confinement which the modern stadium enforces.[35]

Bale's view of the stadium would seem to resonate with Williams' view of sanitised stadia.[36] Furthermore, it also seems to reinforce the view, discussed earlier in the paper, that the end of open terraces, which allowed some freedom of movement, has been detrimental to the atmosphere at live football.[37] Therefore, it may be that the 'optimal experience' of this third environment has much in common with the experience of pub football spectating, but what are the key elements of this experience?

The answer may lie in sentiments expressed by voices as diverse as the Lord Chief Justice, John Williams of the Sir Norman Chester Centre for Football Research, former football hooligan and now popular culture writer, Dougie Brimson, and Mark Hastings of the British Beer and Pub Association. Each refer in some way to the 'collective enjoyment' or 'shared communal experience' that is part of the pub spectating experience, with the Lord Chief Justice noting that the experience is closer to that of actually attending the match in person than it is to watching at home. It certainly appears to be the case that watching in the pub is qualitatively different to both watching at home and watching live at the stadium, the pub being a sort of 'third place',[38] akin to that referred to by Bale.[39]

The concept of a shared communal experience is at the crux of understanding the attraction of the pub as a sport spectator venue, and perhaps of understanding the nature of the sport spectating experience itself. Underpinning the desire for such shared experiences is 'the place-making quality of people as sports spectators'.[40] Bale describes how an open space can become a sporting place as a result of the addition of spectators, who create a cultural and historical 'fandom' associated with that place. This can happen temporally as over time certain spaces become enclosed sporting places (for example, Lords cricket ground or Old Trafford football ground). In fact, some sporting places become defined more by the culture associated with them than the space in which they exist, and it is this that allows some sports clubs to move their grounds to new spaces without losing the importance of the cultural place. However, spaces can also be transformed into sporting places temporarily as spectators (and, indeed, participants) bring the culture and history of a sport or sport event with them—consider, for example, the effect of the Monaco Grand Prix or the London Marathon on spaces that usually have nothing to do with sport. Here, the place-making quality of people has transformed an urban space into a sporting place. Similarly, the open space of the Faelled described by Bale, was transformed into a sporting place by the Danish spectators during the 1992 European Nations Cup final.[41]

It seems reasonable, therefore, to apply these ideas about the transformation from space to place to pubs and bars. Here a social space is transformed into a sporting place by the addition of football spectators. One of the most obvious signifiers of this is the different spatial and social configuration of pubs and bars when football matches are shown, particularly the weakening of conventions about 'personal social space', with people being much more prepared to be in really close proximity to people they have never met before.[42] However, while pubs are temporarily transformed into sporting places, some pubs and bars also experience a temporal transformation over a period of time as they increasingly become known as places in which to watch football, and ones to which fans will gravitate, thus reinforcing their credentials as sporting places.

However, discussions of transformations from social spaces to sporting places, and the comments about the restrictions imposed by modern stadia, still do not satisfactorily address the two key features of the sport spectating experience described earlier, namely: the need for a physical proximity to the event, and; the importance of the retelling of the experience of being there. In addressing the need for proximity, it is perhaps useful to begin with a consideration of Gammon's (2002) work on sports 'Halls of Fame'. Here, Gammon describes two journeys: the first, the physical journey made to the attraction itself, and the second, an imagined journey that takes place once there.[43] There certainly seems to be a process similar to this taking place in relation to pub spectating. Activities such as the singing and chanting that take place inside the pub are an attempt to make an imagined journey to the event itself. However, some authors would argue that the experience of such 'imagined journeys' will always be secondary to physical travel because of the 'powerful compulsion to proximity'. This is explained further by Boden and Molotch:

> Different social groups require or feel obligated to experience at least intermittent moments of proximity, and this makes corporeal travel necessary. This means that virtual or imagined travel will only 'replace' such mode of physical movement if they can in part simulate the pleasures and benefits of such physical proximity.[44]

The question, therefore, would seem to be: what are the pleasures and benefits of such physical proximity? In a 2002 paper entitled 'Mobility and Proximity', Urry elaborates three bases for physical proximity: 'face-to-face', 'face-the-place' and 'face-the-moment'.[45] Face-to-face proximity refers to the need for people to come together to be with others in moments of 'intense co-present fellow feeling'.[46] Szerszynski includes festivals, conferences, holidays, camps, seminars and sites of protest as among such moments, and it would seem reasonable to include major sports matches in this list.[47] Indeed, the 'intense co-present fellow feeling' Urry describes clearly resonates with the 'shared communal experience' identified earlier from a range of sources as being a key part of pub football spectating.

Urry describes how many places need to be directly experienced by physical presence, and it is this that he labels 'face-the-place' proximity.[48] In this respect, the earlier discussions of the place-making qualities of sports spectators are important. If, as discussed above, the distinctive features that make a space a sporting place are those that are brought by the people who occupy that space, and the culture and history they bring with them, then the place experience is related to the sporting nature of the place as created by sports spectators. Consequently, in respect of pub football spectating, the 'face-the-place' basis of physical proximity is provided by the transformation of the pub as a social space into a sporting place by such spectators. As such, 'shared communal experience' is as much a part of 'face-the-place' proximity as it is of 'face-to-face' proximity.

The final basis for proximity described by Urry is 'face-the-moment', in which timing is everything:

> This occurs where what is experienced is a 'live' event programmed to happen at a
> very specific moment. Co-presence involves 'facing-the-moment'. Examples include
> political, artistic, celebratory, academic and sporting occasions, the last being espe-
> cially 'live' since the outcome is unknown. Each of these generates intense moments
> of co-presence … [and they] cannot be missed.[49]

Given the centrality of 'shared communal experience' in the 'face-to-face' and 'face-
the-place' proximities described above in relation to pub football spectating, it would
seem that the pub would provide an excellent setting in which to 'face-the-moment' of
a live sporting event, albeit relayed through a technological medium. The tension as a
player steps up to take a penalty kick differs only by degree (that is, the numbers of
those co-present) in a crowded pub or bar from that at the ground itself. The moment
is being faced collectively by all present, and the joy or despondency at the outcome is
a shared and communal emotion.

The discussions above would appear to indicate that the need for proximity
described by Boden and Molotch and elaborated by Urry is not to the sport event itself,
but to other people sharing a communal experience in a space that has become a sporting place in which the 'moment' of the event can be collectively faced by all those co-
present.[50] Armstrong and Young describe this as, 'the creative self-expression of
spontaneous group association or partisan spectatorship. Such activities when manifested around football create a comradeship of fellow fans.'[51]

However, while the creation of such a 'comradeship of fellow fans' sharing a
communal experience in a pub or bar may satisfy the need for proximity, the second
element of the sport spectating experience, the importance of the re-telling of the experience of being there, has not yet been accounted for. Once again, however, this can
perhaps be addressed by a consideration of the nature of proximity. If the need for
proximity is not to the event itself, but to a sporting place where the moment of the
event can be faced with a 'comradeship of fellow fans', then the experience that is retold
after the event can be the 'shared communal experience' of the collective enjoyment of
the event in the pub. Such a phenomenon clearly existed among fans who watched the
England versus Argentina match during the 2002 World Cup in a pubs and bars in
Sheffield:

> The carnivalesque party atmosphere continued into the early hours, with many
> people who had never met before chatting to each other, not only about the football
> and the result, but also about their experiences of watching the match in the pub![52]

In fact, the importance of the retelling of the pub spectating experience is reinforced
and perpetuated by media coverage of major football and rugby tournaments in recent
years. During the 2002 World Cup, the 2003 Rugby World Cup and Euro 2004, the vast
majority of front page stories were focused on the places in which people watched the
matches. TV news coverage sent reporters to pubs to report on the atmosphere generated. There were many more reports from pubs and bars than from the stadia, particularly on regional news programmes that were looking for a local angle. Such coverage
legitimizes watching the match in the pub as a re-tellable experience, with stories about
how many people were there, how loud the pub was, and how it was as good as being
there at the stadium.

Perhaps, therefore, the nature of the sport spectating experience should be reconsidered. The discussions above, and the earlier descriptions of the ethnography of watching the 2002 World Cup in the pub, would seem to indicate that sports spectators need for proximity is not for proximity to the event, but to others sharing in the experience of watching the event.[53] It would appear that 'spontaneous group association' is a key part of the sport spectating experience, and that the primary element of sports spectatorship can be redefined: rather than being about seeing the game, it is centred on sharing the experience.[54] As such, all the elements needed for the experience are present in pubs as sports spectator venues. The need for proximity is to the experience rather than to the game.

Concluding Comments

As a second foray into the issues surrounding watching football in pubs and bars, the construction of this more conceptual paper has been an interesting exercise. The first paper I produced on this topic, as noted earlier, was an ethnography in which there was less space for theorizing about the nature of proximity, sporting spaces and the sports spectator experience.[55] As this paper has focussed more on the nature of sport spectating, it has allowed me to consider at greater length the implications of recasting sports spectatorship as a shared experience rather than a live presence. In doing so, two key areas for comment seem to emerge.

The first is a comment I also made in the first paper relating to the potential for 'virtual' football hooliganism or disorder.[56] It seems perfectly reasonable to extend the propositions that this paper makes about the nature of the pub supporting experience to provide some insights into 'virtual' football violence. If the 'experience' of pub spectating can approximate to that of the live event for the 'peaceful' supporter, then surely it can also provide the stimulus for disorder that live football provides for violent supporters. One of the comments provided earlier, made inside the Sheffield bar during the 2002 World Cup ethnography, was: 'It's a good job we're all on the same side or there might be trouble'. Well, two years later during the showing of matches from Euro 2004, the fans weren't always on the same side and there was trouble. Following England's defeat against France, over 100 people were arrested across the UK. When England went out of the tournament against Portugal, 200 English fans surrounded a pub in Thetford, Norfolk, which contained around 80 Portuguese fans, and tried to force their way in.[57] The celebratory atmosphere of England's win over Argentina in 2002 had turned sour as the team lost to France and Portugal in 2004. The match against France was played on a Sunday and many fans had 'prepared' for their pub spectating experience by drinking all day. The media 'feasted' on the trouble in the UK, with the next morning's newspapers describing 'fans on the rampage'. There are perhaps two issues here: firstly, the media, lacking any material for a story on rampaging English fans at the tournament itself had to look closer to home and, secondly, pubs and bars, in an effort to encourage 'atmosphere' and thus gain a reputation as a 'sporting place', overlook the more aggressive elements of behaviour that are a clear indicator of potential trouble. This begs the question as to whether the future will bring police patrols outside pubs and bars that are known to become 'sports places' during such major tournaments, similar to those that are routinely seen outside football grounds themselves.

The second area for comment is on the implications that thinking about sports spectating in the way proposed in this paper has for our understanding of sports fandom. As Bale's description of the Faelled in Denmark, and the big screens erected in city centres and other open spaces during the 2002 World Cup show, it is not just to the pub that sports spectators gravitate to share the experience of sport spectatorship.[58] The question remains, though, is this still a secondary experience to attending an event live and in person. Is it simply a way to provide a 'shared communal experience' for those who cannot attend the event. Despite the discussions above about the increasing legitimacy of the pub spectating experience as one that can be 'retold', such stories are never likely to rival the stories that can be told by those who were at the live event itself. As such, while pub sport spectating can perhaps provide an experience 'in-the-moment' to rival that of being present at the event itself, the longevity of such experiences, as measured by their retelling after the event, is likely to be much shorter than 'live' event spectating. It is this, more than any other part of the sport spectating experience, that is likely to ensure there is a continued demand for 'being there'.

Notes

[1]   Brimson, *The Geezers Guide to Football*, 166.
[2]   Weed, 'The Story of an Ethnography'.
[3]   Mintel, *Leisure Intelligence: Themed Pubs and Bars*.
[4]   Emery and Weed, 'Fighting for Survival?'.
[5]   Freeman, *Own Goal!*, 86.
[6]   Keynote, *Market Review: The UK Sports Market*, 17.
[7]   Mintel, *Leisure Intelligence: Themed Pubs and Bars*, 23.
[8]   Mintel, *Leisure Intelligence: Spectator Sports*, 5.
[9]   Mintel, *Leisure Intelligence: Satellite and Cable TV*; Keynote, *Market Report: Cable and Satellite TV*.
[10] Ibid.
[11] Mintel, *Leisure Intelligence: Spectator Sports*; Mintel, *Leisure Intelligence: Satellite and Cable TV*; Keynote, *Market Report: Cable and Satellite TV*.
[12] Weed, 'The Story of an Ethnography'.
[13] Boyle and Haynes, *Power Play*, 97.
[14] Quoted in *The Observer*, 25 February 2001.
[15] Former Minister of Sport, Kate Hoey, quoted in the *Guardian*, 25 February 2002.
[16] Quoted in the London *Evening Standard*, 3 March 2002.
[17] Armstrong and Young, 'Fanatical Football Chants'.
[18] Ibid., 176.
[19] Williams, 'The Changing Face of Football', 99.
[20] Brimson, *The Geezers Guide to Football*, 166.
[21] Keynote, *Market Report Plus: Public Houses*.
[22] See Weed, 'The Story of an Ethnography', for the detail of this work.
[23] Weed, 'Ing-ger-land at Euro 2000'.
[24] Reported by Weed, 'The Story of an Ethnography', 89.
[25] Baines, 'Sports Tourism'.

[26]   MacCannell, *Tourist or Traveller?*, 4.
[27]   Urry, *The Tourist Gaze.*
[28]   Boden and Molotch, 'The Compulsion of Proximity'.
[29]   Urry, 'Mobility and Proximity', 258.
[30]   Mintel, *Leisure Intelligence: Spectator Sports.*
[31]   For example, Williams, 'The Changing Face of Football'.
[32]   Ibid., 99.
[33]   Bale, 'Virtual Fandoms'.
[34]   Ibid., 275.
[35]   Ibid.
[36]   Williams, 'The Changing Face of Football'.
[37]   Boyle and Haynes, *Power Play.*
[38]   Lloyd and Jones, 'Where Everybody Knows your Name?'
[39]   Bale, 'Virtual Fandoms'.
[40]   Ibid., 272.
[41]   Ibid.
[42]   Weed, 'The Story of an Ethnography', 80.
[43]   Gammon, 'Fantasy, Nostalgia and the Pursuit of What Never Was', 65.
[44]   Boden and Molotch, 'The Compulsion of Proximity', 272.
[45]   Urry, 'Mobility and Proximity', 262.
[46]   Ibid., 261.
[47]   Szerszynski, 'The Varieties of Ecological Piety'.
[48]   Urry, 'Mobility and Proximity', 261.
[49]   Ibid.
[50]   Boden and Molotch, 'The Compulsion of Proximity'; Urry, 'Mobility and Proximity'.
[51]   Armstrong and Young, 'Fanatical Football Chants', 180.
[52]   Weed, 'The Story of an Ethnography', 90.
[53]   Ibid.
[54]   Armstrong and Young, 'Fanatical Football Chants', 180.
[55]   Weed, 'The Story of an Ethnography'.
[56]   Ibid.
[57]   BBC News, 25 June 2004.
[58]   Bale, 'Virtual fandoms'.

References

Armstrong, G. and M. Young. 'Fanatical Football Chants: Creating and Controlling the Carnival.' In *Football Culture: Local Contests, Global Visions* edited by G.P.T. Finn and R. Giulanotti. London: Frank Cass, 1999.

Baines, S. 'Sports Tourism: The Leisure Pursuit of Being There.' Paper to the *4th World Leisure and Recreation Association World Congress*, Cardiff, July 1996.

Bale, J. 'Virtual Fandoms: Futurescapes of Football. In *Fanatics: Power, Identity and Fandom in Football*, edited by A. Brown. London: Routledge, 1998.

Boden, D. and H. L. Molotch, 'The Compulsion of Proximity'. In *Now Here: Space, Time and Modernity*, edited by D. Boden and R. Friedland. Berkeley, CA: University of California Press, 1994.

Boyle, R. and R. Haynes. *Power Play: Sport, the Media and Popular Culture.* Harlow: Longman, 2000.

Brimson, D. *The Geezers Guide to Football: A Lifetime of Lads and Lager.* London: Mainstream Publishing, 1998.

Emery, R. and M.E. Weed. 'Fighting for Survival? The Financial Management of Football Clubs outside the "Top-Flight" in England.' *Managing Leisure 111*, no. 1 (2006): 1–21.

Freeman, S. *Own Goal! How Egotism and Greed are Destroying Football.* London: Orion, 2000.

Gammon, S. 'Fantasy, Nostalgia and the Pursuit of What Never Was.' In *Sport Tourism: Principles and Practice,* edited by S. Gammon and J. Kurtzman. Eastbourne: LSA, 2002.

Keynote. *Market Report: Cable and Satellite TV.* London: Keynote Market Information, 2003a.

Keynote. *Market Report Plus: Public Houses.* London: Keynote Market Information, 2003b.

Keynote. *Market Review: The UK Sports Market.* London: Keynote Market Research, 2004.

Lloyd, E. and I. Jones. 'Where Everybody Knows your Name? The Health Club as the new "third place".' Paper to the Leisure Studies Association Conference, *Journeys in Leisure: Current and Future Alliances,* Luton, July 2001.

MacCannell, D. *Tourist or Traveller?* London: BBC Education, 1996.

Mintel. *Leisure Intelligence: Themed Pubs and Bars.* London: Mintel, 2003a.

Mintel. *Leisure Intelligence: Spectator Sports.* London: Mintel, 2003b.

Mintel. *Leisure Intelligence: Satellite and Cable TV.* London: Mintel, 2003c.

Szerszynski, B. 'The Varieties of Ecological Piety.' *Worldviews: Environment, Culture, Religion 1,* no. 1 (1997): 37–55.

Urry, J. *The Tourist Gaze,* 2nd Edition. London: Sage, 2002a.

Urry, J. 'Mobility and Proximity.' *Sociology 36,* no. 2 (2002b): 255–74.

Weed, M.E. 'Ing-ger-land at Euro 2000: How Handbags at 20 Paces was Portrayed as a Full-scale Riot.' *International Review for the Sociology of Sport 36,* no. 4 (2001): 407–24.

Weed, M.E. 'The Story of an Ethnography: The Experience of Watching the 2002 World Cup in the Pub.' *Soccer in Society 7,* no. 1 (2006): 76–95.

Williams, J. 'The Changing Face of Football: A Case for National Regulation?' In *Football in the Digital Age: Whose Game is it Anyway?* Edited by S. Hamil, J. Michie, C. Oughton and S. Warby. London: Mainstream Publishing, 1998.

Epilogue: The Persistence of Fandom in the Face of (Unnecessary) Adversity

Sean Brown

Every year, a company known as Team Marketing collects data on the price to attend a baseball game in the US. The survey, known as the Fan Cost Index, tracks in each park the price for a family of four to attend a game. Included in the survey are game tickets, food and beverage items, programmes and parking. The first year of the survey was 1991, and the average cost to attend a baseball game was $79.41. Ten years later, in 2001, the average price for attendance was $140.63. In 2006, this average was $171.19. In just 14 years, the price had more than doubled.[1] Allowing for inflation, this still amounts to a 40 per cent increase in price. Yet Major League Baseball recorded record-breaking attendance in 2006. Clearly the tensions articulated in the pieces of this volume are being played out in other sporting realms.

Capitalism is not going anywhere. If anything, the shrinking of the geographical and financial worlds has strengthened capitalism beyond what could have been imagined even 20 years ago. Likewise, sport fans are likely to remain on the scene. Therefore, it is entirely unlikely that the tensions articulated and implied in this volume will disappear. Indeed, they are likely to increase if anything. If Mike Weed's study is indicative of a larger trend–that is, if fans view alternative sites of sporting consumption as legitimate facsimiles of 'being there', and that this view is fueled at–least partly by the profit-maximizing motives of team management and ownership and there is every reason to think that it is, then what can the response be?

What then is the role of modern sport for the modern fan? At the very least, this collection has shown that being a soccer fan is a source of tension. By extension and illustrated by the example above, simply being a sport fan is a source of tension. For some, the tension is economic. For American soccer fans, there is a certain tension and intensely felt frustration at the way the game is perceived in the US, and the way in which the US is perceived within the game. For others, such as the Dutch hooligans and the Italian and Spanish *ultras*, there exists the threat of actual physical harm as a result of being associated with one particular team rather than another team. Modern professional sport does not carry with it the weight of some of its preceding forms.

When the reader peruses Majumdar's opus on Indian cricket[2] or watches the film *Lagaan*, it is understood that that game at that time carried particular political meaning. In those situations, being a fan could certainly be worth the inevitable tension caused by the affinity for a particular side. In the post-colonial world, major sport is dominated by the professional, the mercenary. The class divisions that marked matches like Flamenco and Fluminense in Brazil are slowly disappearing.[3] In the United States, they never existed at the highest levels of competition.

So why are sports, and soccer in particular, thriving all over the world? Why does Major League Baseball set attendance records when the costs of attending are high? Why do billions of fans tune into the World Cup every four years when all of the tensions described above and within this volume are at their peak? Some fans and researchers point to fan identification as the source of social networks. Rick Grieve, a psychology professor at Western Kentucky University claims:

> Identification with a team gives you a kind of social support network that provides a buffer from things like anxiety, loneliness, and depression … There's also evidence that people who have established social support networks have some protection against physical illness. There are a whole host of benefits.[4]

While the professor is almost certainly correct (empirical research seems to bear him out), as usual the academic explanation leaves everyone a little cold when dealing with affairs of the heart, which sport fandom certainly is. In order to more adequately sum up why fans are willing to suffer, it is prudent to examine two examples, one American, one British; one baseball and one soccer. Together they more accurately answer the question of why the benefits of sport fandom outweigh the costs.

In his book *Now I Can Die in Peace*, Bill Simmons explains what it felt like to be a lifelong Red Sox fan after the team won the World Series (please excuse the malapropism) in 2004, after a championship drought that began in 1918:

> Now the 1918 jokes are done. Now TV networks can't ruin our playoff games anymore. Now we can watch Red Sox games without waiting for the Other Shoe. Now we don't have to deal with manipulative books and documentaries, or hear about Buckner, Zimmer, Grady, Pesky, Torrez, Stanley, and Schiraldi ever again. It's a clean slate. Eighty-six years wiped away, just like that. It was … destiny.[5]

In another book that both celebrates and laments sport fandom, Nick Hornby in *Fever Pitch* even further articulates what it means to have the ultimate sports payoff, having first dismissed comparisons to sex, promotions and childbirth:

> There is then, literally, nothing to describe it. I have exhausted all of the available options. I can recall nothing else that I have coveted for two decades (what else *is* there that can reasonably be coveted that long?), nor can I recall anything else that I have desired as both man and boy. So please, be tolerant of those who describe a sporting moment as their best ever. We do not lack imagination, nor have we had sad and barren lives; it is just that real life is paler, duller, and contains less potential for unexpected delirium.[6]

These descriptions are perhaps the most persuasive arguments for the 'sport as religion' analogy. The suffering, the waiting, the anticipation and heartache are all erased in the one moment of rapture. *That* is what it means to be a sport fan. It is imperative that one keep in mind the reasons that sports and fandom persist despite the varied tensions presented in this volume.

Omissions and Apologies

It is necessary, while celebrating the very diverse collection gathered in this volume, to acknowledge its shortcomings, both geographical and cultural. A volume on soccer fan culture cannot claim to be comprehensive without multiple contributions from Africa and Asia, two areas where not only is the game well rooted, but whose participants are becoming major players in international soccer. South Africa will be hosting the first Africa World Cup in 2010, as did Japan and Korea in 2002. The iron, as they say, is hot in these areas. It is with regret that this volume is presented without these areas represented, and it must therefore be considered incomplete and inherently flawed. It is hoped that this volume will spur additional study into those areas beyond what is already taking place, so that when this type of work is repeated, they will receive their proper due.

Additionally, it is regrettable that women were not specifically addressed in this volume, either as players with fans or as fans themselves. It can only be said that the subject certainly deserves its own volume. The 'soccer mom', for example is still a palatable political constituency in the United States, and soccer as a professional event is perhaps more family-oriented than any other professional sport in the US. The work currently being done on women in and around soccer is very scattered. A comprehensive volume on women as players or as fans is certainly needed.

Notes

[1]   http://www.teammarketing.com/fci.cfm?page=fci_mlb2006.cfm. Accessed 10 January 2007.
[2]   Majumdar, *Twenty-Two Yards to Freedom*.
[3]   See Lever, *Soccer Madness* for a description of this conflict.
[4]   Grieve, interviewed for Handwerk, 'Sports Riots'.
[5]   Simmons, *Now I Can Die in Peace*, 342.
[6]   Hornby, *Fever Pitch*, 231.

References

Handwerk, Brian. 'Sports Riots: The Psychology of Fan Mayhem.' In *National Geographic,* http://news.nationalgeographic.com/news/2005/06/0620_050620_sportsriots.html. 2005. Accessed 10 January 2007.
Hornby, Nick. *Fever Pitch.* New York: Riverhead Books, 1992.
Lever, Janet. *Soccer Madness.* Chicago: University of Chicago Press, 1983.
Majumdar, Boria. *Twenty-Two Yards to Freedom: A Social History of Indian Cricket.* New Delhi: Viking, 2004.
Simmons, Bill. *Now I Can Die in Peace: How ESPN's Sports Guy Found Salvation, with a Little Help from Nomar, Pedro, Shawshank and the 2004 Red Sox.* New York: ESPN Books, 2005.
Team Marketing Report. 'Fan Cost Index Survey.' In http://www.teammarketing.com/fci.cfm?page=fci_mlb2006.cfm. 2006. Accessed 10 January 2007.

Index